A FEAST OF WORDS

A
FEAST
OF WORDS

The Triumph of Edith Wharton

Cynthia Griffin Wolff

OXFORD UNIVERSITY PRESS
Oxford   London   New York

OXFORD UNIVERSITY PRESS
Oxford London Glasgow
New York Toronto Melbourne Wellington
Ibadan Nairobi Dar es Salaam Cape Town
Kuala Lumpur Singapore Jakarta Hong Kong Tokyo
Delhi Bombay Calcutta Madras Karachi

Library of Congress Cataloging in Publication Data

Wolff, Cynthia Griffin.
  A feast of words.

  "Published works of Edith Wharton": p.
  Includes index.
  1. Wharton, Edith Newbold Jones, 1862-1937—
Criticism and interpretation. I. Title.
PS3545.H16Z94 1978   813'.5'2   78-18905
ISBN 0-19-502434-6 pbk.

Printed in the United States of America

FOR BOB
AND THE BOYS IN THE FRONT ROOMS

Preface

I am fortunate in the friends I have the pleasure of thanking. My principal academic debt is to R. W. B. Lewis of Yale University. In the first instance his gift is one that I share with the rest of the educated world—that is, the bounty of his biography of Edith Wharton. I simply cannot estimate what my own book might have been without the information that Professor Lewis brought to light. However, mine is a special debt, for he was kind enough to allow me to read portions of his work in typescript so that I would not have to delay the beginning of my own writing. For many years one of the Trustees of the Edith Wharton Archives at the Beinecke Library, he gave me access to the manuscripts and letters. He also generously made documents available to me that were not in *any* archive. Thus it was through his kindness that I obtained copies of the Love Diary and the Line-a-Day pocket Diary for 1908. It was he who provided me with copies of Wharton's juvenile "reviews" of her novel "Fast and Loose." He even lent me his own transcriptions of the correspondence between Edith Wharton and Bernard Berenson because I was not in a position to travel to I Tatti and review the letters for myself. The reader will, I hope, see the results of this pervasive generosity throughout my work. However, in the last analysis, my debt to Professor Lewis cannot be calculated: it consists in his willingness to discuss our mutual subject, and it resides in a continuing friendship born of deep kindred interests.

Other colleagues have played a role in the preparation of this work. Professor Mary Sirridge of the Philosophy Department at the University of Wisconsin at Madison read the manuscript with careful attention to the aesthetic assumptions about the nature of fiction that underlie my argument. Professor Ellen Rose of the English Department at Dartmouth followed my evolving psychological analysis of Edith Wharton step by step. Professor Priscilla Hicks in my own department at the University of Massachusetts at Amherst offered invaluable suggestions concerning my exposition of the relationship between Wharton and Henry James.

All of the people who work behind the desk in the Beinecke were of immeasurable help to me. I must thank in particular Anne Whelpley, who many times searched for fugitive documents that I needed to explore one or another theory.

But most of all, I must thank my husband, Robert Paul Wolff. A distinguished philosopher and scholar, he took time from his own work to discuss mine—even to read several of Edith Wharton's novels so that I might discuss them with him. He is familiar with every word, every nuance of every word, in this book; and his enthusiasm and loving support can never be described adequately. Perhaps the quality of his "sacrifice" might best be measured by totaling the hours he has spent of a Saturday afternoon in the sticky darkness of a movie theater with Walt Disney and two boisterous little boys—so that I might write.

Northampton, Mass.   C.G.W.
October 1976

Acknowledgments

I should like to thank the following for permission to use manuscript material:

Amherst College, Amherst, Mass., for allowing me to quote from the correspondence between Edith Wharton and William Crary Brownell.

Beinecke Library of Yale University, for allowing me to quote material from the Edith Wharton Papers, Collection of American Literature, The Beinecke Rare Book and Manuscript Library, Yale University.

Cecil Anrep, for allowing me to quote from the correspondence between Edith Wharton and Bernard Berenson.

The Edith Wharton Estate, for granting me general permission to use unpublished Edith Wharton material.

Firestone Library of Princeton University and Charles Scribner's Sons, for allowing me to quote from the correspondence between Edith Wharton and Charles Scribner's Sons.

The Honorable William R. Tyler, for kindly allowing me to examine the Commonplace Book and to quote from it.

The photographs on pages 55, 186, and 337 are reprinted by courtesy of the Edith Wharton Estate; those on pages 56, 57, 58, 185, 187, 188, 335, 336, and 338 are courtesy of the Beinecke Library.

I am indebted to the National Endowment for the Humanities, which gave me a full-year grant so that I might write this book. I am also indebted to the University of Massachusetts at Amherst, which gave me a summer research grant, thereby facilitating my archival work.

I wish to thank the editors of *American Literature* and *The Southern Review* for permission to reprint the essays that appear here, in altered form, as II, 5 and III, 9.

Contents

Prologue

It is usually easier not to write than to write. A glance at the "public" events of Edith Wharton's life makes the puzzle of creativity particularly intriguing in her case.

Born on January 24, 1862, Edith Newbold Jones seemed blessed with a life that must be called easy by any objective standard. Her parents, especially her mother, belonged to the most aristocratic element in New York society, and the family lived so comfortably on inherited income that George Jones, Edith's father, was never obliged to work. It is true that during the period of inflation just after the Civil War, Edith and her parents went abroad for six years—genteel and elegant life being much less expensive there than in the United States; however, when they returned, a life divided between the spaciousness of a country home in Newport and the bustle of a New York brownstone awaited them. During her childhood, Edith spent much time in the care of a beloved nurse, Doyley; as she advanced toward young womanhood, a kind of governess-companion was added to the entourage (although Edith was clearly intellectual by inclination, she never attended school as her two older brothers had done—in aristocratic families of old New York, girls never did). In some sense her "real" life was reckoned to begin at seventeen when she "came out."

Edith Jones was more fortunate than many shy debutantes because the popularity of her older brother Harry soon encompassed her and she was taken up by an enjoyable set of fashionable young people. She led an active social life, was briefly engaged to the bachelor Harry Stevens, had a flirtation with another highly eligible man, Walter Berry (who was to become, in later years, her most beloved friend), and finally married an easygoing Bostonian named Edward ("Teddy") Wharton when she was twenty-three. Teddy Wharton's family, like Edith's, was comfortably fixed; and the couple managed to live very well on the income from their combined inheritances (like Edith's father, Teddy never had a regular occupation). The couple settled in a house at Newport near Edith's mother (her father had died some four years earlier) and spent considerable time traveling. They had no children.

Beginning in 1889, Edith Wharton suffered intermittent spells of fatigue and nausea; in 1898 she put herself under the care of Dr. S. Weir Mitchell for several months, and his treatment appears to have cured her illness. Meanwhile, other areas of her life were opening up. The Whartons acquired a substantial new home in Newport and a pair of brownstones in New York City. In 1902, after Edith had begun her writing career, they completed a stately home in Lenox, Massachusetts—The Mount.

Edith had been writing since childhood; when she was sixteen, her mother had had a small book of her verses printed privately. Yet during the years after her debut and during the first years of her marriage, she seems not to have written at all. When she began again, she began slowly—a few poems and scattered short stories. Her first major novel, *The Valley of Decision* (1902), was an immediate success, and when she published her next major novel, *The House of Mirth* in 1905, her reputation soared. From that time until her death, she produced fiction and travel books and books of poetry and translations with astonishing regularity. She wrote prolifically; she wrote well; and her work was a commercial success.

Edith and Teddy Wharton had always enjoyed traveling, and as Edith grew more successful in her writing, she longed to spend more and more time in the stimulating climate of Europe—especially Paris. During this period Edith came to know many of the most respected intellectual figures of the day: Henry James, for example, was one of her closest friends. Perhaps it is not surprising that as Edith was increasingly drawn into the cultural life of this cosmopolitan world, she would begin to have less in common with her husband. In any case, the couple drifted apart; in 1913 they were divorced; Edith sold The Mount and took up more or less permanent residence in France (retaining her American citizenship all her life).

She lived in Paris during World War I and contributed heroically to the war effort; and in April of 1916, she was made a Chevalier of the Legion of Honor. After the war, other honors came her way. In 1921 she won a Pulitzer Prize, and in 1923 she was awarded the honorary degree of Doctor of Letters by Yale University. Her trip back to the United States that year was the last time she set foot on American soil.

After World War I, Edith Wharton purchased two lovely, large homes in France—the Pavillon Colombe just outside of Paris and the restored abbey of Sainte Claire at Hyères on the French Riviera. During the last seventeen years of her life she divided her time between them. She died on August 11, 1937, at the Pavillon Colombe.

Such are the "facts" of Edith Wharton's life. And yet, they speak not at all to the puzzle with which we began. In such a world of inherited wealth and ease, living in a society that did not encourage men to work and that positively discouraged women from any occupation save having babies and being a good hostess, Edith Wharton became a novelist. One of the half-dozen greatest novelists that America has produced. How could she have written so well? Indeed, why did she write at all?

If the facts fail to answer such queries, we must turn to less easily verifiable elements in Wharton's life—to her memories and emotions as she has reported them—to the reality of her inner world. Edith Wharton was never a deliberate prevaricator; yet we are all fabricators when it comes to reconstructing our own histories. Many things that seem sharply etched memories are actually subtle distortions; occasionally, even those recollections that seem most authentic are no more than stories that have been concocted from partial truths in order to explain or justify some feeling or fantasy. If we were interested in achieving an absolutely accurate estimation of her life—in assessing the culpability of a mother or a husband or a lover, for instance—we would have to despair: given only Edith Wharton's side of the story, we could never attain certainty.

Fortunately, our concern is ultimately the fictions, not the life. Exploring the contours of an artist's mind *can* help us to understand the verbal artifacts that she left, can even, perhaps, allow us to know some of the forces that compelled her to creativity in the first place.

I

A Portrait of the Artist as a Young Woman

He recalled the old days of his poverty and obscurity in New York, when he had sat alone in his fireless boarding-house room pouring out prose and poetry till his brain reeled with hunger and fatigue; and he knew now that those hours had been the needful prelude to whatever he had accomplished since. "You have to go plumb down to the Mothers to fish up the real thing," he thought exultantly.

Vance Weston in *The Gods Arrive*

It is a strange fact that while many men begin their novel-writing careers with fictional accounts of their apprenticeship, until very recently most women who became novelists have never written fictional accounts of their apprenticeship at all. In *A Backward Glance* Edith Wharton gives a very limited chronicle of her own artistic growth, and the tone is stately—even when it is most candid—and measured and modulated. We catch only fitful glimpses of the child who was so perilously obsessed with "making up"; and the cultured voice of the novelist who seems always (and even primarily) to have thought of herself as a "lady" gives little hint of turmoil. It is tempting to conclude that she cared too little about the mysterious forces that shape the life of the artist to be bothered examining them; yet her fictions belie such a view, for the theme of artistic creativity darts through them like some quick, anxious creature of the air, now sweeping into view, now disappearing momentarily only to reappear in more distinct and focused relief. In truth, Wharton spent a lifetime writing about art and the life of the artist, but her own life seems always to have been kept at a discreet remove from these fictions. The artists of her fictions were usually men, and women appear as agreeable subjects for them or as more or less sufficient attendants to the muse. What profound ambivalence and fierce reticence this lifelong preoccupation suggests!

One thing was always clear to Wharton: good art must grow organically out of the deepest fathoms of the artist's own experience. She was fond of Goethe's invocation in *Faust* of the mysterious "Mothers" who move among the primal forms of life. The artist's courage lies in his ability to plunge into these recesses and to confront his most secret self. This is the lesson that the novelist-hero of her last two completed novels must learn—an awesome yielding up of that "irreducible core of selfness" to the artistic process. It was a lesson that Wharton as novelist had to learn herself. The reality of her life was far from stately: she was conversant with imperfect happiness and relinquished dreams. She grew to love life with the passion of a triumphant warrior, and she paid life the ultimate compliment of becoming a profoundly anti-Romantic realist. She could be a devastating social critic; the satirical vein is strong in the best of her work. Yet the deepest thing in all of her best work is, finally, her complex and compassionate understanding of human nature. She met the challenge of reaching into her own irreducible core of selfness and transmitting it into art. But she could not fictionalize that process as it related directly to herself—not because she cared too little, but because she cared far too much.

If we dare to try to re-create the artist, we must accept the voice of maturity and authority that speaks to us in *A Backward Glance*, for that polished woman is certainly Edith Wharton, the novelist. However, we must try to see not only this—which she allows to us—but also that shadowy realm from which she came. We cannot speak of "Edith Wharton: The Author," as if she were the unchanging God of Creation, ever the same. The elderly woman ("The Author" who gazes from the first photograph in *A Backward Glance*, serene in pearls and fur) was once a passionate lover, a lover for the first time unexpectedly, miraculously, in middle age; the middle-aged woman was once a young matron running excitedly up and down the stairs of her brownstone home (because there was nowhere else to run) and holding her first "real" letter of acceptance, on her way to becoming a "real" author; the young matron was once a timid debutante, awkwardly hesitant, refusing to dance out of sheer fright; the debutante had been a perplexing little girl—given to intense passions and paralyzing fears—assertive, impudent, ferociously intelligent, oddly sentimental, and preoccupied with death; and finally, the little girl had once been a small, desolate, lonely child, convinced of the world's implacable hostility and impenetrable caprice. All of these "selves" are suspended in the harmonious and precarious balance of the woman we call Edith Wharton. Growth entails not the supplanting one by one of successive selves but rather the addition, the slow accretion of one and yet one more. If we are to understand the complex assemblage of these into the character of the novelist, we must take more than a glance backward. We must follow the faint footprints beyond the matron, the debutante, the little girl—we must begin with the lonely child.

1

In May of 1924, when she was sixty-two, Edith Wharton began a diary. She had tried to write diaries in the past, but the confessional attitude was painful to her and she usually failed to manage more than a few sentences. Old age now, a last chance "to gather together the floating scraps of experience that have lurked for years in corners of my mind." What is most important—how to begin? "The lonesome time alone is what remains to me; what I recall is of a lone life, and what I have gone through has made me alone." [1] Here is the beginning, the oldest and most grievous injury—terrifying, empty isolation. "If I ever have a biographer, it is in these notes that he will find the gist of me . . . But let us begin with some stray thoughts—The sub-conscious, that Mrs. Harris of the psychologists. I am secretly afraid of animals—of *all* animals except dogs, and even of some dogs. I think it is because of the *us*ness in their eyes, with the underlying *not-us*ness which belies it, and is so tragic a reminder of the lost age when we human beings branched off and left them: left them to eternal inarticulateness and slavery. *Why?* their eyes seem to ask us." [2]

To be doomed to feel, possibly to suffer, and not to be able to command comfort; to be small and defenseless, and to be consigned forever to that primitive state, not-quite-human. If this was the last and deepest horror, it was also the first. "Dogs of all ages, sizes and characters swarmed through my early years—and how I loved them! The first—a furry Spitz puppy—was given to me before I was four years old, and from that moment I was never without one except during a brief interval in Europe, when a delicious brown rabbit named 'Bonaparte' ruled alone in my heart. I always had a deep, instinctive understanding of animals, a yearning to hold them in my arms, a fierce desire to protect them against pain and cruelty. This feeling seemed to have its source in a curious sense of being somehow, myself, an intermediate creature between human beings and animals, and nearer, on the whole, to the furry tribes than to homo sapiens. I felt that I *knew things about them*—their sensations, desires and sensibilities—that other bipeds could not guess; and this seemed to lay on me the obligation to defend them against their human oppressors. The feeling grew in intensity until it became a morbid preoccupation." [3] These are the earliest conscious memories; they retreat to that time of childhood when speech and some sense of autonomy begin, and yet they trail the glooming echoes of an earlier time, an infancy of total dependency and longings that cannot be articulated. Edith Wharton would always carry with her this strange sense of kinship with animals, a sense of herself (like "them") as intolerably isolated—uniting the "usness" and the "not-usness," feeling herself "an intermediate creature between human beings and animals." The passions of this infantile "self" persist—even into her adult personality—with appalling ferocity. The first experiences of her life, disconnectedly reflected in later memories, were the most influential experiences and the most painful: an aching, ineradicable sense of comfort not given, of coldness and hunger. When she grew old enough to discover some creature smaller and more helpless than herself, she showered upon it the attention that this earliest self had craved and not found. But nothing—not ever—would entirely compensate this sense of fundamental deprivation; and her modes of thinking, of formulating thoughts and problems, of perceiving the world—all these were essentially formed by Wharton's earliest sense of insufficiency.

The most immediate legacy was a sense of cosmic imperfection. Lucretia Jones, Edith's mother, was thirty-seven years old when her only daughter was born. The other two children were fifteen and thirteen years older than their little sister—a baby who was, almost certainly, an unplanned surprise to Lucretia. She may also have been a most unwelcome surprise to the mother who had long been unaccustomed to the inconveniences of baby-tending. There are no nursery records, and we have only Wharton's childhood memories to guide us; but she certainly perceived her mother as remote, disapproving, impatient, and unloving. The little world of Edith Wharton's infancy, with Lucretia as its prime mover, was an unpredictable and hostile place. When the notion of a being more powerful even than Lucretia entered the girl's youthful imagination, the image of a deity merged with that earlier image—the deity of the nursery—and both images reflected the despair of infant disappointments. "I was never free from the oppressive sense that I had two absolutely inscrutable beings to please—God and my mother—who, while ostensibly upholding the same principles of behavior, differed totally as to their application. And my mother was the most inscrutable of the two." [4] An early sense of moral bewilderment (which later experience would serve only to intensify) laid upon the little girl the necessity of creating her own order. As an adult, this quest for order became, perhaps, the most ardent passion of all ("Order the beauty even of Beauty is," she was to transcribe as the motto of her book *The Writing of Fiction*). It would lead her to organize her various homes and gardens with the most exquisite precision, to arrange and rearrange the books on her shelves—and above all, to create world upon world in her fictions where she, and not the untrustworthy Lucretia or God, would be the Demiurge.

But we are moving in advance of ourselves; this love of creating order was a hard-won adult joy, and it had its foundation in the desolation of childhood. Wharton ponders the importance of a youthful appreciation of Coleridge's poem "Friend": "Let no one ask me why!! I can only suppose it answered to some hidden need to order my thoughts, and get things into some kind of logical relation to each other: a need which developed in me almost as early as the desire to be kissed and thought pretty! It originated, perhaps, in the sense that weighed on my whole childhood—the sense of bewilderment, of the need of guidance, the longing to understand *what it was all about*. My little corner of the cosmos seemed like a dark trackless region 'where ignorant armies clash by night,' and I was oppressed by the sense that I was too small and ignorant and alone ever to find my way about in it." An inscrutable and capricious universe portends no comfort in life. One must accept God's existence, just as one had accepted Mother's, but one could learn at least never, never to trust either one of them. Wharton accepted this "truth" as "one of the dark fatalities that seemed to weigh on the lives of mortals; and I think it was at about this time that I wrote in one of my note-books the lugubrious phrase: 'If I ever have children I shall deprive them of *every pleasure*, in order to prepare them for the inevitable unhappiness of life!' " [5]

It is impossible to stress too strongly the pervasive effect of the failure of this basic sense of trust in Wharton's life. Those who met her as an adult felt a kind of frigid, impenetrable *hauteur* that absolutely dispelled any pretensions to intimacy. [6] Some few who knew her better were able to recognize this manner as the outward manifestation of a morbid form of timidity or shyness. Only a very few were allowed to see that at the heart of her social formalities was an unconquerable expectation of pain. "I can imagine no happiness in human intercourse," she wrote to Bernard Berenson, "except when a *very* few are gathered together." [7] To Sara Norton she confided at the end of a period of depression: "I am sleeping better, and am very glad I came away, for the change and movement carry me along, help to form an *outer surface*. But the mortal desolation is there, will always be there." [8] It was difficult for her to make friends, almost impossible for her to accept emotional intimacy; and this difficulty did not spring from indifference (though indifference was the social manner that she evolved to cover her embarrassment). Quite the contrary, her need for affection, for love, for genuine communication was too great to find ready expression; and she carried so deep a conviction that these needs could never be met, that the threat of disappointment dominated her imagination. One might truthfully say of her, as she said of one of her own characters, that her cold reluctance "concealed a passion so violent that it humiliated her, and so incomprehensible that she had never mastered its language." [9] Indeed, we might ask whether Wharton's deepest and most secret needs *had* a language—or whether they were, like the feelings of those mutely reproaching animals of which she was so frightened, too primitively powerful for socialized discourse.

If the primary and most persistent remnant of those early disappointments in Wharton's life was a failure of trust, a voracious need for human comfort that carried with it the cosmic conviction of inevitable disappointment, certainly an equally important legacy was a striving for communication. How can I *represent* my feelings, my needs, my dilemmas: this seems to be a question that echoes throughout all of Wharton's life. Inevitably, the failures of communication that date from primitive, inarticulate infancy were destined to be repeated in some measure again in the adult life. A newborn infant cannot dissociate his emotions from the sensations of his body; thus his passions and dilemmas must be represented by the simplest and most limited bodily images. An adult who has suffered early and traumatic disappointment will often quite unconsciously re-create this fusion of emotion and bodily sensation. In the adult, this conversion of emotions into physical symptoms serves several functions. In Wharton's case, two important ones were that it allowed her to retain feelings that seemed too "dangerous" to be given direct ventilation and that it provided a primitive form of communication—became a way of "talking" with the body. When Edith Wharton was very young, she sustained neglect at what Erik Erikson has called the "oral-respiratory-sensory stage." [10] When she was an adult, Wharton often converted her inner anguish into precisely those physical symptoms that related directly to this period of development: her illnesses had to do with ingestion (she suffered nausea and loss of appetite), breathing (she had repeated attacks of bronchitis and asthma), and acute reactions to heat and cold (she was, in the broadest sense, morbidly vulnerable to atmosphere).[11] This became one characteristic mode of expression.

Her use of language also reflects the persistence of these characteristic habits of representing emotions and problems. Rejection and emotional isolation are "cold" (Wharton renders her own adolescent awkwardness as a "cold agony of shyness"). Her mother's ungenerous emotional attitudes are variations on the theme of *froideur:* the first childish "novel," shown to Lucretia with great hesitation, is met with an "icy comment" of dismissal that adequately dampens the girl's enthusiasm; [12] later, inquiries into the secrets of reproduction are greeted with an even more frigid response as Lucretia's face "at once took on the look of icy disapproval which I most dreaded . . . [and] the coldness of expression deepened to disgust." This physical coldness, at once the representation of emotional deprivation and a physical embodiment of it, is often linked in Wharton's speech with the sensation of being stifled. When she appeals to Lucretia, she does so "with a heart beating to suffocation." [13] The world itself closes in upon her—"narrow houses so lacking in external dignity, so crammed with smug and suffocating upholstery." [14] And this vocabulary—this particular way of striving for representability—will be repeated over and over again in more subtle and sophisticated forms when Wharton finally turns her attention to serious writing.

However, important as these images of coldness and claustral isolation are, they are less significant than the persistent, insatiable language of starvation. The very last portrait Wharton was ever to write of "A Little Girl's New York" plunges back with frightening directness to that earliest and most painful loss: the quavering modulations of the author's voice (the author now seventy-five years of age) and the genteel discussion of opportunities for imaginative growth conceal hardly at all the strident cry of a child who was not fed upon love and understanding. It is the rehearsal of the oldest and least-forgotten deprivation. "I have often sighed, in looking back at my childhood, to think how pitiful a provision was made for the life of the imagination behind those uniform brownstone facades, and then have concluded that since, for reasons which escape us, the creative mind thrives best on a reduced diet, I probably had the fare best suited to me. But this is not to say that the average well-to-do New Yorker of my childhood was not starved for a sight of the high gods. Beauty, passions, and danger were automatically excluded from his life (for the men were almost as starved as the women); and the average human being deprived of air from the heights is likely to produce other lives equally starved." [15] Lucretia had not been able to feed the infant's craving for care and love; when the little girl's craving fell upon reading and writing for pleasure, the fare was scarcely better. "It was not thought necessary to feed my literary ambitions with foolscap, and for lack of paper I was driven to begging for the wrappings of the parcels delivered at the house. . . . I always kept a stack in my room . . . and I used to spread them on the floor and travel over them on my hands and knees, building up long parallel columns of blank verse." [16] It is hardest, perhaps, to forgive this sign of niggardliness in Lucretia's nature. As Wharton later reflected, "I was starving for mental nourishment. . . . There was no measure to my appetite"; [17] and she might continue to starve for all Lucretia cared! Subsequent chroniclers of Wharton's life have wondered at the constancy of her devotion to Walter Berry (Percy Lubbock is perhaps most obtuse in this regard). There is little doubt that the intellectual and emotional fare was Spartan with Berry, but compared to Lucretia's allotment, his attention was a veritable feast. "I cannot picture what the life of the spirit would have been to me without him," Wharton was to write in her autobiography. "He found me when my mind and soul were hungry and thirsty, and he fed them till our last hour together." [18]

It is strange, but undeniable (since her language so clearly reflects it), that throughout her life, Wharton carried within her the conviction that she was at base a small, hungry, helpless creature. Age did not diminish the vibrant and voracious life of that first "self"—though other selves of greater confidence and self-sufficiency grew up beside it. There must have been times—the unpublished and incompleted reminiscence "Life and I" suggests that there *were* times—when the primitive and uncompromising demands of the unsatisfied infantile self threatened almost to engulf the growing child. The emotions and reactions of that earliest stage of development are absolute and entirely consuming: the whole organism becomes a raging lust for food and comfort, and until those needs have been satisfied, the little person who is that organism is possessed by them entirely. In normally supportive environments, the inarticulate infant's needs are met with some regularity and predictability, and the infant eventually learns to temper the passion of his demands; he learns to wait, and he learns to feel his needs as part but not all of himself. He is not "eaten up" with his own hungers; and his primitive rage is gradually modulated into anger and then into impatient expectation. However, when these needs are not met, when the environment is not normally supportive, then his emotions retain their primitive and insatiable intensity. They are not felt in modulated and socially acceptable measure—but as absolute imperatives; simple desire or anger can become tantamount to demonic possession.

There is no doubt that the oral deprivation Wharton suffered left in her a residue of the terrifying tendency to absolute responsiveness: on the one hand her sense of loneliness and of the environment's indifference to her wants and needs moved quickly to an image of complete desolation; on the other hand her infant joys—responses to sound and to visual beauty, eventually the response to literature itself—were felt with equivalent exaggeration. She speaks often of these in terms of "ecstasy" or "rapture"; and in attempting to recapitulate this early period, she acknowledges the peculiar intensity of her shifts of mood. "The picture I have drawn of myself . . . is that of a morbid, self-scrutinizing and unhappy child. I *was* that—and yet I was also, at the same time, a creature of shouts and laughter, of ceaseless physical activity, of little wholesome vanities and glowing girlish enthusiasms. And I was also—and this most of all—the rapt creature who heard the choiring of the spheres, and trembled with a sensuous ecstasy at the sight of beautiful objects, or the sound of noble verse. I was all this in one, and at once, because I was like Egmont's Clarchen, 'now wildly exultant, now deeply downcast,' and always tossed on the waves of a passionate inner life. I never felt anything *calmly*—and I never have to this day!" [19]

In the genesis of the novelist, this emotional intensity is a source of strength; however, in the development of the child, such conflicting and consuming alternations of feeling must have been exhausting and frightening. Many children would have retreated from emotion entirely in the face of this dilemma. The fact that Wharton did not must be attributed in part, at least, to the more benign influences that presided over her nursery years. One of the most important of these was her nurse, Doyley. "How I pity all children who have not had a Doyley—a nurse who has always been there, who is as established as the sky and as warm as the sun, who understands everything, feels everything, can arrange everything, and combines all the powers of the Divinity with the compassion of a mortal heart like one's own! Doyley's presence was the warm cocoon in which my infancy lived safe and sheltered; the atmosphere without which I could not have breathed." [20] In short, Doyley was everything that Lucretia was not: warm, sustaining, understanding—the very life breath of the child. Like Lucretia, she is remembered as a Divinity, a compassionate God who is bountiful, merciful, comprehensible, and loving. Yet she must have been a lesser Divinity in Edith Wharton's childhood; for though she is mentioned lovingly—she is mentioned very little. She survives in Edith Wharton's capacity for passion, in the fact that the child chose to suffer the tormenting conflicts of her emotions rather than to snuff them out altogether. That portion of the child's rearing that was turned over to Doyley was spared shame, humiliation, and deprivation; and this factor must have made a decisive difference in Wharton's growth. In the end, however, Doyley was a servant and not a parent; thus her role in the development of Wharton's life was probably less significant than the role played by the other "warm" creature of her childhood, her father.

The very first event that Edith Wharton remembers from her childhood is a walk taken with this beloved father. It is recalled in the characteristic language of heat and cold: "It was on a bright day of midwinter. . . . She had been put into her warmest coat. . . . As the air was very cold a gossamer veil of the finest white Shetland wool was drawn about the bonnet and hung down over the wearer's round red cheeks like the white paper filigree over a Valentine; and her hands were encased in white woolen mittens. One of them lay in the large safe hollow of her father's bare hand; her tall handsome father, who was so warm-blooded that in the coldest weather he always went out without gloves, and whose head, with its ruddy complexion and intensely blue eyes, was so far aloft that when she walked beside him she was too near to see his face. It was always an event in the little girl's life to take a walk with her father." The passage is striking—not only because the genial demeanor of the father contrasts so markedly with the icy attitudes that seem habitual to Lucretia, but also (and more significantly) because the entire scene is invoked in such romantically fanciful terms. Indeed, perhaps the strangest thing of all is that a stylist such as Edith Wharton would lapse into language that is dominated by cliché: a tall, handsome man with a ruddy complexion and intensely blue eyes—he might be the hero of any popular novel. Certainly he is construed as the hero of this little domestic drama: and it may be difficult for the reader to remember that his heroine, who is so conscious of wearing her "new winter bonnet, which was so beautiful (and so becoming)," [21] with a gossamer veil drawn over her head, is in reality his three-year-old daughter. The scene is dubious as the reflection of an actual event: it is, however, exceedingly accurate, albeit naive and poignant, as a re-creation of the little girl's feelings.

Edith Wharton declined to read "children's literature"; her disdain is, perhaps, too pronounced: "Fairy-tales bored me, and as I have always had a sense of the 'au delà,' and of casements opening on the perilous foam of the seas of magic, I can account for the fact only by supposing that I had heard of fairies only through 'Children's' books, a form of literature which I despised, as any intelligent child does after a taste of 'real books.' " [22] In the light of these protests, it is even more remarkable that her remembrances of Lucretia and George Jones should be so strangely haunted by the shadow images of wicked stepmother and handsome prince. In actual fact, George Jones seems to have been as prosaic as his name; like most men of his class, he pursued no career and expended his limited talents by serving as "a director on the principal charitable boards of New York—the Blind Asylum and the Bloomingdale Insane Asylum among others." [23] For amusement he "read sermons, and narratives of Arctic exploration." [24] Yet his little girl contrived to pour all of her passionate imagination into some representation of him that satisfied the emotional storms within her. Thus George Jones, mild and benevolent, was tinged forever in his daughter's remembrance with the glow of mysterious realms beyond the brownstone world she knew.

> The new Tennysonian rhythms . . . moved my father greatly; and I imagine there was a time when his rather rudimentary love of verse might have been developed had he had any one with whom to share it. But my mother's matter-of-factness must have shrivelled up any such buds of fancy; and in later years I remember his reading only Macaulay, Prescott, Washington Irving, and every book of travel he could find. Arctic explorations especially absorbed him, and I have wondered since what stifled cravings had once germinated in him, and what manner of man he was really meant to be. That he was a lonely one, haunted by something always unexpressed and unattained, I am sure.

Wharton had a good deal of her father's company as a child: he often lunched at home with the family, and he walked with his daughter often of an afternoon. His warm presence, like the encompassing touch of his warm hand, must have been a powerful emotional magnet, drawing to it all the child's unsatisfied cravings. Wharton's memories of him are colored by a deep and possessive attachment, and his death was a blow to be matched in her life only by the death of Walter Berry forty years later. "He died . . . in the early spring, suddenly stricken by paralysis; and I am still haunted by the look in his dear blue eyes, which had followed me so tenderly for nineteen years, and now tried to convey the goodbye messages he could not speak. Twice in my life I have been at the death-bed of some one I dearly loved, who has vainly tried to say a last word to me; and I doubt if life holds a subtler anguish." [25]

Perhaps Edith Wharton was not so much "bored" by fairy-tales as she was made acutely uncomfortable by their primitive emotional directness. Could such a little girl, so predisposed by her own experiences and by the vitality of her own precocious capacity to envisage the world in highly charged emotional terms, be very much charmed by tales which emphasized and reemphasized the conflicts that threatened to consume her? What could Cinderella or Snow White or Sleeping Beauty have said to Edith Wharton that she was not already living (and living all too violently for comfort)? She gives some small answer to this question in a revealing account of one disastrous early encounter with "children's" books.

My aunt's house, called Rhinecliff, afterward became a vivid picture in the gallery of my little girlhood; but among those earliest impressions only one is connected with it; that of a night when, as I was ready to affirm, there was a Wolf under my bed. This business of the Wolf was the first of other similar terrifying experiences, and since most imaginative children know these hauntings by tribal animals, I mention it only because from the moment of that adventure it became necessary, whenever I "read" the story of Red Riding Hood (that is, looked at the pictures), to carry my little nursery stool from one room to another, in pursuit of Doyley or my mother, so that I should never again be exposed to meeting the family Totem when I sat down alone to my book. [26]

This childhood phobia must have occurred at almost exactly the same time as the stroll with her father that is celebrated in the opening pages of *A Backward Glance*. A little girl whose image of emotional satisfaction would forevermore carry with it the lingering fantasy of total incorporation (or total annihilation), a little girl whose yearnings have gradually turned to a generous and affectionate father—how frightened she must have been by the strength of the almost palpable fantasies that thronged in her imagination. Every little girl of four or five "falls in love" with her father; and for every little girl, this attachment is a crisis whose resolution is beset with difficulty. For Edith Wharton, however, the crisis of early affection for her father was made infinitely more difficult by the residue of that unresolved earlier crisis. "I love you so much that I could eat you up." This is a common phrase in families with small children, and the adults who voice it give harmless utterance to their children's fantasies. Yet at some level of Edith Wharton's emotional life at the age of four or five, such a turn of phrase would have signified a terrifying and literal truth—that her love would annihilate the beloved object. Or perhaps the suppressed thought was: "I love you so much that my feelings will consume me and destroy me." Or perhaps both of these confused fantasies floated through the child's mind. In any case, the little girl's notions of "love"—intense love for her father, eventually for any man—became insensibly colored by those earlier images of incorporation; thus "love" could be both very powerful and very dangerous. We all know what the big bad Wolf was going to do to Little Red Riding Hood: he was going to eat her up.[27]

That cryptic phrase, "I am secretly afraid of animals—of *all* animals except dogs, and even of some dogs," acquires another meaning now. Originally, Wharton's feelings about animals sprang from her perception of them as inarticulate, helpless, suffering creatures (as she was when she was very young). In this context they are fearsome because the intensity of need that they represent is fearsome. As this longing begins to have an explicitly sexual component, so does the fear of animals. Hence Wharton's early phobia concerning the Wolf. When the little girl fled the "Wolf" by seeking Doyley or her mother, she was seeking an older woman who might act as a restraint upon her own competitive sexuality. Yet, since what she fled was ultimately inside her, her efforts were in vain. Thus this initial phobia was but the first in a long series of fears that were to paralyze her childhood.

The earliest fear has directly to do with the little girl's consuming love for her father; later fears have to do with her anger at her mother as well.

When my parents settled down in Paris—I must have been six or seven at the time—I was sent to a small private dancing-class kept by a certain Mlle. Michelet, who had been a danseuse at the Grand Opera. Mlle. Michelet was a large good-humored swarthy person, who, while destitute of beauty, inspired in me no physical repugnance; but she had a small shrivelled bearded mother whom I could not look at without disgust. This disgust I confidentially revealed to the little boy I was in love with at the time (I was always in love with some little boy, and he was generally in love with another little girl). I described Mme. Michelet as looking like 'une vieille chèvre,' and the description was greeted with such approval that, if I had been a normal child, I should have been delighted with the success of my witticism. Instead of this, however, I was seized with immediate horror at my guilt; for I had said something *about* Mlle. Michelet's mother which I would not have said *to her*, and which it was consequently "naughty" to say, or even to think. Now the only possible interest connected with this anecdote lies in the curious fact that my compunction was entirely self-evolved. . . . I had never been subjected to any severe moral discipline, or even to the religious instruction which develops self-scrutiny in many children. . . . I had never, as far as I know, been told that it was "naughty" to lie. . . . I had, nevertheless, worked out of my inner mind a rigid rule of absolute, unmitigated truth-telling, the least imperceptible deviation from which would inevitably be punished by the dark Power I knew as "God." Not content with this, I had further evolved the principle that it was "naughty" to say, or to think, anything about anyone that one could not, without offense, avow to the person in question; with the grim deduction that this very act of avowal would in such cases, be the only adequate expiation of one's offense. I therefore nerved myself—with what anguish, I still recall!—to the act of publicly confessing to Mlle. Michelet, before the assembled dancing-class, that I had called her mother an old goat; and I perfectly remember (such are the sophistries of the infant heart) a distinct sense of disappointment when, instead of recognizing and commending the heroism of my conduct, she gave me a furious scolding for my impertinence.[28]

It is not difficult to creep into the bosom of this small, fierce girl and listen to the voice that she was trying, with such desperate measures, to keep still. The attack that she dares not mount is, of course, against a "mother"—here, Mlle. Michelet's mother is a convenient substitute. "Old goat" is the least of the accusations the hot-tempered, red-headed Edith Wharton might have flung at Lucretia. We must understand that in her relations with her mother, too, there is a residue of infantile emotion; and a large portion of that residue is the undispelled, unmitigated rage of the hungry and unsatisfied infant. Now, as the girl's emotional life becomes complicated by a powerful affection for her father, this rage acquires the additional component of explicit jealousy. (The goat is both an ugly and a lascivious animal.) Generations of mothers can testify to the fact that many little girls give quite precise ventilation to their feelings of rivalry when they pass through this period; Edith Wharton, however, could not. Her anger at Lucretia was so strong and of such long standing that she could *not* speak of it; indeed, so the concocted prohibition ran, she could not even *think* it!

Nor was this episode in dancing school an isolated one. "Nothing I have suffered since has equalled the darkness of horror that weighed on my childhood in respect to this vexed problem of truth-telling, and the impossibility of reconciling 'God's' standard of truthfulness with the conventional obligation to be 'polite' and not hurt anyone's feelings [this was *Mother's* injunction]. Between these conflicting rules of conduct I suffered an untold anguish of perplexity, and suffered alone, as imaginative children generally do, without daring to tell anyone of my trouble, because I vaguely felt that I *ought* to know what was right, and that it was probably 'naughty' not to." [29]

Wharton was pursued by this demon of guilt and rage until another came to take its place when she was nine years old and fell so ill with typhoid fever that her case was considered hopeless. When she recovered, her moral scruples concerning "truth-telling" had vanished, but they had vanished only to be replaced by another set of unreasoning fears.

This illness formed the dividing line between my little-childhood, and the next stage. It obliterated—as far as I can recall—the torturing moral scruples which had darkened my life hitherto, but left me the prey to an intense and unreasoning physical timidity. During my convalescence, my one prayer was to be allowed to read, and among the books given me was one of the detestable "children's books" which poison the youthful mind when they do not hopelessly weaken it. . . . The volume in question was lent by two little playmates, a brother and sister, who were very "nicely" brought up. . . . To an unimaginative child the tale would no doubt have been harmless; but it was a "robber-story," and with my intense Celtic sense of the supernatural, tales of robbers and ghosts were perilous reading. This one brought on a serious relapse, and again my life was in danger; and when I came to myself, it was to enter a world haunted by formless horrors. I had been naturally a fearless child; now I lived in a state of chronic fear. Fear of *what?* I cannot say—and even at the time, I was never able to formulate my terror. It was like some dark undefinable menace, forever dogging my steps, lurking, and threatening; I was conscious of it wherever I went by day, and at night it made sleep impossible, unless a light and a nurse-maid were in the room. But whatever it was, it was most formidable and pressing when I was returning from my daily walk (which I always took with a maid or governess, or with my father). During the last few yards, and while I waited on the door-step for the door to be opened, I could feel it behind me, upon me; and if there was any delay in the opening of the door I was seized by a choking agony of terror. It did not matter who was with me, for no one could protect me; but, oh, the rapture of relief if my companion had a latch-key, and we could get in at once, before It caught me! [30]

Did the child suppose that the mysterious combination of God-and-Mother which had been conceived in the earliest years was able to peer into her mind and divine even the thoughts that were not allowed to be there? A "robber story" is a powerful threat to a little girl who construes her father as a handsome hero and herself as a would-be heroine. Sickness might portend an ominous warning of more deadly retaliation to follow future misdemeanors. In any case, Wharton is pursued by an animal once again—but now a formless, nameless, panting specter, always on her heels and haunting her steps. We can follow a gradual pattern of retreat in these terrifying episodes: Doyley's presence or Mother's presence is sufficient to banish the Wolf, and that fantasy eventually seems to have melted away; a price has been paid, however, for even such relative peace, the price of what Wharton terms "moral scruples," a constant monitoring of speech and thought to protect herself from uttering or even thinking the forbidden thing; finally, at just that stage of development when the child might have begun to attain some sense of independence, she is beset by anxiety and guilt—dreadful products of her rage and longings—and these cannot be banished even with constant monitoring of word and thought.

Thus we have traced aspects of the child's development to the very edge of adolescence. The unresolved crises of this period have left a residue—a language that instinctively turns to evocations of heat and cold or starvation and suffocation, and a view of the world that focuses excessively upon the dangers of emotion and the threat of isolation. We might say that we have discovered a characteristic style of representation that will inevitably be reflected throughout Edith Wharton's life and, since the fictions are a part of that life, throughout the fictions as well. Yet our principal focus so far has been the child rather than the potential artist. Before we carry our examination of the life further, we must turn backward once more—to discover the particular ways in which the girl's earliest adaptions foretold the eventual emergence of the artist.

2

As an adult, Edith Wharton was obsessed by the need to be able to talk to sympathetic and understanding friends. "I have no one to *talk* to" is the lament that characterizes her most despondent moments.[31] This imperative to communicate is a very ancient one in her life, and an account of her reading habits as a child gives some clue to its origin and to its remarkable duration. "I never cared much in my little-childhood for fairy tales, or any appeals to my fancy through the fabulous or legendary. My imagination lay there, coiled and sleeping, a mute hibernating creature, and at the least touch of common things—flowers, animals, words, especially the sound of words, apart from their meaning—it already stirred in its sleep, and then sank back into its own rich dream, which needed so little feeding from the outside that it instinctively rejected whatever another imagination had already adorned and completed. There was, however, one fairy tale at which I always thrilled—the story of the boy who could talk with the birds and hear what the grasses said. Very early, earlier than my conscious memory can reach, I must have felt myself to be of kin to that happy child." [32]

The image that Wharton evokes of her imagination here, at a time "very early, earlier than . . . conscious memory can reach," is that of a rosy baby or small animal curled in sleep and roused only to "feed" upon a chance intrusion from the outside world. The sense of deprivation is here, even in this charming and restrained picture, but the deprivation is perceived as tolerable because, so Wharton protests, her imagination "needed so little feeding from the outside." It is the selfsame protest that we have heard in "A Little Girl's New York" where men and women are portrayed as "starved" for beauty and passion, and the little girl who was to become Edith Wharton survived because (again, the protest) "the creative mind thrives best on a reduced diet." But then, these are the protective excuses of a woman who *has*, with whatever pain, gotten by; and these denials are betrayed most effectively by the persistence of that fantasy which must have captured the yearnings of the helpless, "mute hibernating creature" that was her most infantile self. To feel a happy oneness, a warm mutuality—if not with Mother, then with "birds" and "grasses." The longing to be kin to that fairy-child carries a pathetic echo of the little girl who felt "nearer, on the whole, to the furry tribes than to homo sapiens." There is a reiteration of the old unsatisfied need for warmth and affection; and at a very early age this longing has become inextricably bound in Wharton's mind with the ability to communicate. Nothing is worse than to be "mute." To be "mute"—either as animal or as small and helpless baby—is to be vulnerable to pain; and words, even "the sound of words, apart from their meaning," can offer the promise of an escape from loneliness and helplessness. The will to survive, to take what Mother would not give, becomes in very little girlhood identical with the compulsion to manipulate language. Language is the link to other human beings, human beings more responsive than Mother; language allows for the articulation of demands and thus for a mastery over the inarticulate passivity of earliest childhood. The child who cannot rely on Mother's world turns all her trust to words, and unlike Mother, words never disappoint her.

In a direct and almost primitive way, the child contrives to use orality—words—to compensate an oral deprivation; and she substitutes the act of communication for the more gratifying comforts of passive receptivity.

However, words have additional significance at this earliest period. In normal infancy, a sense of comfort, security, and trust is "taken in"; as we have seen, all of the child's emotional energy at this period has to do with the process—satisfactory or not satisfactory—of incorporation. In a general way, the baby is attuned to all of the different ways by which he may "take in" that which is pleasurable.[33] Many different organs become involved in this complicated initial acquaintance with the world. "The eyes, first part of a relatively passive system of accepting impressions as they come along, have now learned to focus, to isolate, to 'grasp' objects from the vaguer background, and to follow them. The organs of hearing have similarly learned to discern significant sounds, to localize them, and to guide an appropriate change in position (lifting and turning the head, lifting and turning the upper body)."[34] The initial failure to receive a more or less constant sense of security and love can never fully be compensated; however, the child who feels a sense of deprivation at this early stage may find partial compensation by developing—even to the point of exquisite acuteness—other forms of "taking in": extraordinary talents of hearing and of seeing, for example. Wharton's own account of her early life suggests that she did this, and that her initial responsiveness to words had some foundation in their capacity to be "taken in" and to give pleasure.

> . . . I was enthralled by *words*. It mattered very little whether I understood them or not: the sound was the essential thing. Wherever I went, they sang to me like the birds in an enchanted forest. [Here the child seems almost to have willed her favorite fairy-tale to come true for her.] And they

had *looks* as well as sound: each one had its own gestures and physiognomy. What were dolls to a child who had such marvellous toys, and who knew that as fast as one wearied of the familiar ones, there were others, more wonderful still, to take their place? . . . [Nothing] compared to the sensuous rapture produced by the sound and sight of . . . words. I never for a moment ceased to be conscious of them. They were visible, almost tangible presences, with faces as distinct as those of the persons among whom I lived. And, like the Erlküng's daughters, they sang to me so bewitchingly that they almost lured me from the wholesome noonday air of childhood into some strange supernatural region.[35]

We cannot measure the multitude of intangible components that lead to the creation of an aesthetic capacity. Yet surely by a fateful and ironic stroke, the very intensity of the small child's desolate need becomes converted into the keenness of the artist's sensibility. Wharton's lifelong love of words sprang from her early emotional impoverishment, and words were a rich bounty that she could absorb with hungering appreciation.

But the feast of words was no more a delight than the feast of visual beauty. This, too, Wharton "took in" with an almost indiscriminate voracity. Perhaps nothing is so characteristic of her style as an adult author than the sureness of her eye for detail; but this talent for minutiae went hand in hand with a painful vulnerability to the atmosphere of her surroundings. Sometimes in childhood, her tender receptivity brought happiness—a "secret sensitiveness to the landscape—something in me quite incommunicable to others, that was tremblingly and inarticulately awake to every detail of wind-warped fern and wide-eyed briar rose." Sometimes, because she was so little able to monitor the influx of those elements about her that were devoured by her eyes, the perception of something that disgusted her became a palpable threat. "My visual sensibility must always have been too keen for middling pleasures; my photographic memory of rooms and houses—even those seen but briefly, or at long intervals—was from my earliest years a source of inarticulate misery, for I was always vaguely frightened by ugliness." Eventually the treasures stored up by this splendid receptivity were to enrich the pages of her fiction; and what had been the replenishing pleasure of childhood became the informing memories of adult creativity. Thus Wharton says of the writing of *The Valley of Decision:* "The truth is that I have always found it hard to explain that gradual absorption into my pores of a myriad details—details of landscape, architecture, old furniture and eighteenth century portraits. . . . My years of intimacy with the Italian eighteenth century gradually and imperceptibly fashioned the tale and compelled me to write it; and whatever its faults—and they are many—it is saturated with the atmosphere I had so long lived in." [36] She was to make a very similar statement when *The Age of Innocence* came to be dramatized: "I am very anxious about the staging and dressing. I could do every stick of furniture and every rag of clothing myself, for every detail of that far-off scene was indelibly stamped on my infant brain." [37]

What we have, then, is a beginning. In the small child's earliest life, a failure of trust and emotional satisfaction; the residue of this initial crisis persists, shaping the various modalities by which the developing girl and the grown woman will fashion her world. The child's trust, betrayed by Lucretia, has been transferred to language as the means by which she may free herself from loneliness and desolation; the unsatisfied hunger for affection and reassurance has been converted into an insatiable, but infinitely rewarding, hunger for visual and aural beauty. The child is a nascent artist. As she grew older, these initial rather primitve defensive maneuvers were to be refined and expanded, and the next stage of the novelist's development has to do with the peculiar occupation that Wharton called "making up."

The sources of Wharton's impulse to create fictions reach far back into her childhood: "I cannot remember the time when I did not want to 'make up' stories," she says in *A Backward Glance*. [38] One early event must have strengthened her conviction of the value of this enterprise.

When I was not more than five or six, a friend of my father's who came to dine every Sunday used to take me on his knee after dinner . . . and 'tell me mythology.' I looked forward to this event during the whole week, for it came next to 'making up' in the order of my emotional experiences. It stands out, moreover, as the only glimpse my childhood ever had of the imaginative faculty in others. My parents and my teachers *read* me stories, but were the mere mouth-pieces of what they read; no one else ever *told* me a story, or gave a personal interpretation to the narrative; and our Sunday evening guest was the only person who ever showed signs of knowing anything about the secret story-world in which I lived. No doubt my complete isolation intensified all my sensations, and perhaps it now leads me to regard as singular many experiences that may be common to all fanciful children. [39]

What reassuring confirmation this must have been that words could be trusted to break through loneliness! Did this kindly old gentleman, with the curly gray hair and the long moustache, realize what comfort he gave by creating stories for the little girl—and more important, by giving "a personal touch" to the creations?

Indeed, that "personal touch" may have played a significant part in shaping the future novelist. Edith Wharton's childhood was haunted by the image of herself as "too small and ignorant and alone ever to find my way about in it." Now an old gentleman enters that world armed with "the domestic dramas of the Olympians." We might do well to recall those colossal, capricious creatures—the gods and goddesses of ancient Greece. How they must have resembled the grown-ups whose unpredictable moods shaped the world of the little girl who became Edith Wharton. What fun, what reassuring delight, to see such creatures subjected to the ordering of a narrator's will. Little wonder that Edith Wharton (who didn't like fairy stories) "felt more at home with the gods and goddesses of Olympus, who behaved so much like the ladies and gentlemen who came to dine, whom I saw riding and driving in the Bois de Boulogne, and about whom I was forever weaving stories of my own." Edith Wharton's stories were, from the very beginning, "about grown-up people, 'real people,' I called them." [40] The genesis of the narrative impulse is exactly coincidental with the impulse to re-create the adult world in some form that the small child could control and order, the desire to make intelligible what had been merely mysterious and alien. The mythology that she had heard—and that she construed as the "domestic drama of the Olympians"—gave reassurance and encouragement to the budding artist, and her creative spells were to acquire certain remarkable characteristics.

Oddly enough, I had no desire to write my stories down (even had I known how to write, and I couldn't yet form a letter); but from the first I had to have a book in my hand to "make up" with, and from the first it had to be a certain sort of book. The pages had to be closely printed, with rather heavy black type, and not much margin. Certain densely printed novels in the early Tauchnitz editions . . . would have been my richest sources of inspiration had I not hit one day on something even better: Washington Irving's "Alhambra." . . . Well—the "Alhambra" once in hand, making up was ecstasy. At any moment the impulse might seize me; and then, if the book was in reach, I had only to walk the floor, turning the pages as I walked, to be swept off full sail on the sea of dreams. The fact that I could not read added to the completeness of the illusion, for from those mysterious blank pages I could evoke whatever my fancy chose. Parents and nurses, peeping at me through the cracks of doors (I always had to be alone to "make up"), noticed that I often held the book upside down, but that I never failed to turn the pages, and that I turned them at about the right pace for a person reading aloud. . . . There was something almost ritualistic in the performance. The call came regularly and imperiously; and though, when it caught me at inconvenient moments, I would struggle against it conscientiously—for I was beginning to be a very conscientious little girl—the struggle was always a losing one. I had to obey the furious Muse. . . . Learning to read, instead of distracting me from this passion . . . only fed it; and during that Florentine winter it became a frenzy. . . . I still feel the rapture (greater than any I have ever known in writing) of pouring forth undisturbed the tireless torrent of my stories. . . . The speed at which I travelled was so great that my mother tried in vain to take down my "stories," and posterity will never know what it has lost! All I remember is that my tales were about what I still thought of as "real people" (that is, grown-up people, resembling in appearance and habits my family and their friends, and caught in the same daily coil of "things that might have happened").[41]

The future writer has already found her mode (realism) and her genre (fiction); how precisely they served her needs, even then.

We cannot pass over this period of "making up" without remarking what a clever (almost diabolical) device it was for asserting the small child's importance and independence. Thus far in the silent struggle that had been waged between the little girl and her mother, Mother had emerged victorious while the child suffered agonies of confusion and rejection. Now confusion begins to yield to control as the adult world is submitted to a reorganization in these precocious fictions; and rejection begins to yield to a certain satisfying domination of the mother by the child.

The urgency with which these spells came upon the little girl must have caused her some degree of discomfort; but that discomfort was undoubtedly more than compensated by the fact that no adult in her household was willing to punish her (in the grips of "the furious Muse") for her eccentric behavior. She becomes, by her own account, a veritable talking hurricane of activity—pacing up and down, demanding to be left alone, creating curious stories that fall pell-mell from her lips at a rate too rapid to be recorded. It is surely a dramatic account; it must have been a dramatic performance. And it is a performance that quite successfully relegated Lucretia to the wings with the rest of the crowd ("parents and nurses, peeping at me through the cracks of doors"). The child's rudimentary intellectualizing has a distinctively flamboyant quality; it commands attention (Mother, trying "in vain" to take down the stories) and marks the child as a special, "different" sort of being. "I think my parents by this time were beginning to regard me with fear, like some pale predestined child who disappears at night to dance with 'the little people,' " Edith Wharton is to record much later.[42] But how satisfying to be the object of such concern, especially when one's Mother, the more usual center of attraction, is a handsome woman with a generous gift for self-adornment.

Indeed, "making up" allowed the little girl to turn the tables on her mother in more respects than one. Intimacy had always been difficult for her because she had so little ability to trust herself to a relationship with others. Little boys (with whom, as she tells us, she regularly fell in love) were easier, resembling to some degree her handsome father. Little girls were another thing, much more difficult. Well, why not let Mother handle them? "There are deplorable tales," Edith Wharton recalls confidentially, "of my abandoning the 'nice' playmates who had been invited to 'spend the day,' and rushing to my mother with the desperate cry: 'Mamma, you must go and entertain that little girl for me. *I've got to make up.*' "[43]

In general the little girl employed her growing affinity for literature to relieve her multiple difficulties with Mother. It drew her closer to Father, who "by dint of patience, managed to drum the alphabet into me." When she returned to New York at the age of ten, she was allowed to roam at will through the room that she invariably refers to as "my father's library." But "for the leave to range in my father's library," she is to write later, "my mind would have starved at the age when the mental muscles are most in need of feeding." Even so late as the time of *A Backward Glance*, Edith Wharton recalls her father (however incorrect the remembrance may be) as a man whose rudimentary sensitivity to poetry and to literature in general was "shrivelled" by Lucretia's matter-of-factness; and Lucretia is remembered as a vulgar prig, surrounded by "the stacks of novels which she, my aunts and my grandmother annually devoured."[44]

The quiet struggle between mother and daughter in this matter of literature took several turns. Lucretia, "perplexed by the discovery that she had produced an omnivorous reader, and not knowing how to direct my reading, had perhaps expected the governess to do it for her. Being an indolent woman, she finally turned the difficulty by reviving a rule of her own schoolroom days, and decreeing that I should never read a novel without asking her permission. I was a painfully conscientious child and, conforming literally to this decree, I submitted to her every work of fiction which attracted my fancy. In order to save further trouble she almost always refused to let me read it—a fact hardly to be wondered at, since her own mother had forbidden her to read any of Scott's novels, except 'Waverley,' till after she was married!" [45] Lucretia seems to have spent her married life compensating for this early denial; characteristically, she imposed the same denial on her own daughter. The little girl was, as Wharton acknowledges, painfully scrupulous, and she submitted every novel she read for her mother's inspection—up to the very day of her own wedding! But Edith Wharton had the last victory after all; she spent most of her adult life writing novel after novel.

It is easy, too easy in fact, to fall into the formula of nasty mother and clever daughter. The relationship was more complicated than such a formula can suggest: the little girl loathed her mother, but she loved her too and yearned desperately for her approval; because she admired Lucretia, in many respects she longed to emulate her. Thus while there is a wistful suggestion throughout Wharton's various reminiscences that she shared a deep bond of communication with her father, a bond that included their literary affinities, the fact that the mother "devoured" fiction and that the daughter eventually wrote so much of it suggests an even more complex set of affinities. When she was a little girl, Edith Wharton used reading and writing to modulate and control her relationship with Lucretia; when she entered adolescence, however, the situation was to become a great deal more complicated. On the one hand, her devotion to literature grew into a tentative vocational commitment; on the other, her development as a woman (and her deep and ambivalent identification with Lucretia) presented a number of explicit obstacles to that commitment.

3

Lucretia was a handsome woman; and although she was already thirty-seven when her daughter was born, she must have still been handsome when the child was old enough to notice such things. The surviving photographs suggest that she was, but Wharton's remembrances suggest it even more strongly in the continuing evocation of a Mother "who wore such beautiful flounced dresses, and had painted and carved fans in sandalwood boxes, and ermine scarves, and perfumed yellowish laces pinned up in blue paper, and kept in a marquetry chiffonier, and all the other dim impersonal attributes of a Mother." Aunt Mary Newbold once asked the little girl what she would like to be when she grew up. " 'The best-dressed woman in New York,' " the child responded. "She uttered the horrified cry: 'Oh, don't say that, darling!' " to which the little girl could only rejoin in wonder: " 'But Auntie, you know Mamma *is*.' " [46] The child wanted to be very much her mother's daughter; the mature writer looking back upon her youth realized that she inevitably *had been* her mother's daughter.

A Backward Glance is curiously revealing in this respect. For example, it is Mother's (and not Father's) ancestral line that is traced at the beginning of the book with such elaborate care; and it is the lingering resentment of Mother's childhood of genteel poverty that captures Wharton's attention. Like many people who write autobiographies, Wharton tells us a good deal about those in her family who preceded her into the world; but she does not manage to re-create the texture of any of their feelings—except when she is describing her own mother's girlhood. In that case there is something that could only be called empathy for that other girl "who wore a home-made gown [when she 'came out'] . . . and her mother's old white satin slippers; and her feet being of a different shape from grandmamma's, she suffered martyrdom, and never ceased to resent the indignity inflicted on her, and the impediment to her dancing, and more so as her younger sisters, who were prettier and probably more indulged, were given new slippers when their turn came." There is a poignant longing in the narration that describes Mother when *she* was a girl—a Mother that Edith Wharton never knew—and a desire to get closer, somehow, and to understand. "The humiliation of . . . the maternal slippers led to a good many extravagances. . . . [Mother] had a beautiful carriage, and her sloping shoulders and slim waist were becomingly set off by the wonderful gowns brought home from that first visit to the capital of fashion. All this happened years before I was born; but the tradition of elegance was never abandoned, and when we finally returned to live in New York (in 1872) I shared the excitement caused by the annual arrival of the 'trunk from Paris,' and the enchantment of seeing one resplendent dress after another shaken out of its tissue-paper." [47]

Father and Doyley are benevolent presences in Edith Wharton's various memories; however, they are only silent visitors in the little girl's world. Never once, in any of her memoirs of childhood, does Wharton quote her father directly; never once do we hear his voice. Her portrait of him is, by consequence, blurred and indistinct. Mother's voice, on the other hand, penetrates throughout. We hear her first discussing a renegade uncle: " 'But, Mamma, *what did he do?*' 'Some woman'—my mother muttered." Mother's voice; the voice of the world that took little primitive creatures and made them into "nice" girls. "Fastidiousness of speech came chiefly from my mother's side," so Wharton the novelist is forced to acknowledge. "My father probably acquired it under her influence." "Nice" little girls learned to speak correctly: "I still wince under my mother's ironic smile when I said that some visitor had stayed 'quite a while,' and her dry: 'Where did you pick *that* up?' " [48] And Mother's supervision of the young girl's reading—what can we say? That Lucretia was so ignorant and so narrow in her education is, perhaps, only to be expected from a woman of that time and place. However, that the daughter should so totally comply with the prohibitions—and that she should do so until her own marriage at the age of twenty-three—this behavior is certainly remarkable!

There is every reason to suspect that Lucretia was at once too much and too little to her daughter, that she had a possessive need to intrude, to influence, perhaps to dominate. Every incident that we have seen thus far in Edith Wharton's life has involved her mother to some degree: Lucretia is the deity of the nursery; the little girl walking with Father, seeming some small morsel of a Valentine, is (now that we have a more complete picture) a self-conscious imitation of the beautiful Lucretia, who was the true consort of the handsome hero; Lucretia is behind the door as the child "makes up"; Lucretia is the model of verbal grace for the home. Lucretia is everywhere and everything, and she gave her daughter very little opportunity to become someone independent of her. [49] The little girl hated and resented Mother's cruelty, but she admired Mother's strength, beauty, and will—and she sought desperately to please Mother. Edith Wharton was acutely conscious of her own femininity; and as she grew from girlhood to womanhood, the difficulties that had always been a part of her life—the sense of inner desolation and loneliness, the fearful power of untamed passions—became an integral part of the difficulties attending that growth. The problem of becoming a novelist was inextricable from the problems involved in becoming a woman. For many years, Edith Wharton's sense of her own feminine identity was in thrall to Lucretia, and for all these years, the artist was imprisoned too.

There were several things that "nice" girls were not supposed to do: one of them was to have feelings.

The little girl who had returned from Europe at ten greeted the country life at Pencraig, the family's Newport home, with a shout of happiness. For a while, the beauties of the European past were wholly supplanted by the rapture of sheer animal pleasure. If there were invisible fears that pursued her, there were games and new friends to console her. "There was much to interest me in our new life, and I was always passionately interested in things! . . . I found everything to delight the heart of a happy, healthy child—cows, a kitchen-garden full of pears and quinces and strawberries, a beautiful rose-garden, a stable full of horses (with a dear little poney of my own), a boat, a bath-house, a beautiful sheltered cove to swim in, and best of all, two glorious little boys to swim with! . . . The younger of the two boys, Winthrop Rutherford, was just my age, the elder, Lewis, three or four years older. They were two of the most beautiful young creatures it is possible to imagine, the younger espiègle, gay and audacious, the elder grave, tender-hearted and shy. Need I say that I fell in love with the former, that the latter fell in love with me? With these delightful companions all my days were spent. . . . I was developing a happy healthy young body, learning to row, to swim and to ride, and taking long walks over the rolling rocky wilderness that extended between our place and the Atlantic." [50] This little girl, just perched on the edge of adolescence, is that same little girl of six who was "always in love with some little boy." But now her body is beginning to change and to complicate her emotional life with new and unexplained feelings.

All at once she was growing. In the library of the New York house, her mind was opening to new discoveries. "My love of poetry and letters was fed by all these studies, and I plunged with rapture into the great ocean of Goethe. At fifteen I had read every word of his plays and poems. . . . Faust was one of the 'epoch-making' encounters for me—another was Keats. A third was—a little volume called 'Coppée's Elements of Logic.' . . . It was certainly providential that, in the same shelf with Coppee, and almost at the same moment, I found an abridged edition of Sir William Hamilton's History of Philosophy! Oh, thrice-blest discovery! How I was going to know all about life! How I should never be that helpless blundering thing, a mere 'little girl,' again." She never would be a little girl again, but her growth to womanhood followed a strangely uneven path. She dined on the most sophisticated intellectual fare, for so long as she did not read any "novels," she could range as widely as the holdings of her father's collection would permit. She was not allowed to read the works of the Brontës, but she "longed for *more* of Ford and Marlowe and Webster! . . . read and re-read the great scenes of the Duchess of Malfy and The Broken Heart and Faustus and Edward II." [51] What on earth did she make of these remarkable works? In what respect was Faust an "epoch-making" encounter for her? She was, in the most fundamental sense, sublimely ignorant, and her only acquaintance with life came from what she had read in books.

She was still a passionate creature; her splendid young body strained toward some nameless delight—and yet the girl was like a befuddled wild animal stumbling through the dark. She knew nothing; she was not suppposed to know anything; "nice" girls didn't. "Life, real Life, was singing in my ears, humming in my blood, flushing my cheeks and waving in my hair—sending me messages and signals from every beautiful face and musical voice, and running over me in vague tremors when I rode my poney, or swam through the short bright ripples of the bay, or raced and danced and tumbled with 'the boys.' And I didn't know—and if, by any chance, I came across the shadow of a reality, and asked my mother 'What does it mean?' I was always told 'You're too little to understand,' or else 'It's not nice to ask about such things.' " [52]

The code of "niceness" was proclaimed throughout the land. Young ladies were kept "pure" for their husbands—and purity entailed a kind of systematic assumption of their total ignorance. Society assumed that they need be told nothing before they became wives and mothers, and so they generally were told nothing. Everyone believed in the myth that adolescent girls lived in a state of suspended animation—like some lovely troop of sleeping beauties—until their wait was ended by the magical kiss that would initiate them (instantly and painlessly) into the mysteries of marriage. There were many things that one simply never *said* in front of an unmarried lady—no matter what her age (we might recall that

Newland Archer's sister Janey grows discreetly older in gray dresses with pearls while the married folk in her vicinity speak softly of "indelicate" subjects just out of her hearing). There seems to have been complete cooperation in the maintaining of this myth of virginal purity; and Lucretia's enigmatic reply to her daughter's exasperated question about that renegade uncle reflected the norm, and not merely some malicious personal cruelty. A girl emerging into adolescence received no acknowledgment of the changes taking place in her body, no recognition of the surge in her passional life, no help at all in dealing with the confusions, the fears, the complexities of becoming a woman. Society had decreed that "nice" young women didn't really *have* feelings to be explained; if you did have feelings—well then, obviously you weren't "nice." Ladylike behavior demanded the total suppression of instinct.

All girls in this period of American Victorianism suffered in an environment that utterly discouraged the healthy development of their emotional lives. However, at least some enterprising girls with a full measure of curiosity were less ignorant—perhaps less virginal—than the popular mythology supposed. Even May Welland in *The Age of Innocence* says to Newland Archer: " 'You mustn't think that a girl knows as little as her parents imagine. One hears and one notices—one has one's feelings and ideas.' " Edith Wharton's own mother was courted in a manner that strongly suggests she did not live by her own voiced precepts of "niceness." George Frederic Jones's parents disapproved of his affection for the eldest of the poor Rhinelander girls. "But George Frederic was the owner of a rowing-boat. His stern papa, perhaps on account of the proximity of the beloved, refused to give him a sailing-craft. . . . But George was not to be thwarted. He contrived to turn an oar into a mast; he stole down before dawn, his bed-quilt under his arm, rigged it to the oar in guise of a sail, and flying over the waters of the Sound hurried to his lady's feet across the lawn." [53] We need not harbor dark suspicions about Lucretia and George (whose courtship seems to have inspired the first and last romantic act of his life). They were most probably perfectly usual young people—that is to say, it was probably perfectly usual for young people to find some way of mitigating the hostility of the emotional climate in old New York. It is not in the least surprising that the adolescent Edith Wharton suffered painfully under the cruel, repressive attitudes that society took toward young girls of her time; however, it is surprising that she offered so little in the way of rebellion or resistance (as her mother evidently had, for instance) and that instead, she responded by becoming such a perfect paragon of what would have been called "niceness."

To understand this strange compliance, we must recall the persistent intensity with which her emotions were felt: every new stage of emotional development reawakened the slumbering desires of earliest childhood. The primitive character of these feelings had persisted in the girl and had attached itself to each new set of emotional problems that confronted her. Thus every new surge of powerful feelings threatened to devour her (or at least so it seemed). By the definition of her own experience, strong emotions of any kind were innately dangerous.

Now a girl with this set of problems would have difficulty confronting the emotional storms of adolescence even if the society in which she lived were a genial one that tolerated her difficulties and assisted her to overcome them. However, if she obtains no help from society, if instead that society contrives to suggest that emotions *are* dangerous—or wrong—or "not-nice"—then even the most resilient adolescent will be inclined to run away from the emerging passions that signify sexual maturity. Edith Wharton's earliest responses to her fear of strong emotions had all involved some symbolic attempt to run away or to repress: she had artfully eluded the big bad Wolf, and later she had suppressed not only her spoken hostility to Mother but her unspoken hostility as well. With this residue of unresolved crises and with the atmosphere of this particularly malignant form of social coercion, the young Edith Wharton must have felt she had no other alternative than to become the "nice" girl that her Mother seemed to expect her to be. Indeed, the very scrupulosity of her conscience (so well developed a few years earlier) caused her to fulfill Mother's expectations in the most explicit and punctilious way. She did not look for ways to mitigate the hostility of the emotional climate in which she found herself; she did not let herself merely "seem" to be "nice" while in fact thinking (and doing) things that were not quite nice. In her later life she was to recognize that being such a model daughter had constituted a form of emotional suicide; however at the time (given her long accumulation of fears), such behavior must have seemed the only safe thing to do.[54]

Thus adolescence became a long and arduous period of retreat for the girl. Instead of attending to the flowering of her womanly feelings, she devoted herself to hiding them; instead of making herself independent of Mother and becoming a woman in her own right, she reverted to a kind of dependency upon Mother as a way of keeping the totem animals at bay. Her description of that last long episode of phobic fear is immensely suggestive: the most intense moment of agony, as she describes it, always occurred "while I waited on the door-step for the door to be opened." This last nameless beast pursued her for quite a while: "and I was a 'young lady' with long skirts and my hair up before my heart ceased to beat with fear if I had to stand for half a minute on a door-step!" [55] The house was Mother's realm; all the world outside was freedom and independence. This agony—poised as she was at the juncture of these two worlds—captures the fretful dilemma in which the girl was caught: being away from Mother offered the chance to feel freely and to grow self-sufficient; nevertheless, being away from Mother's control opened her to the risk of some terrible danger—being thrown to the Wolf or to some fate even worse. Many years later, Edith Wharton was finally to find the strength to rebel against the strictures of Mother's house (and, significantly, one important skirmish in that rebellion was the publication of a book entitled *On the Decoration of Houses*—a book that excoriates the standards of Mother's taste). However, this rebellion was not to take place until she had been married many years. The adolescent Edith Wharton could find no other way to manage her conflicts than by taking them to Mother.

Two anecdotes will suggest the pitiful hopelessness of her plight. "Once when I was seven or eight, an older cousin had told me that babies were not found in flowers but in people. This information had been given unsought, but as I had been told by Mamma that it was 'not nice' to enquire into such matters, I had a vague sense of contamination, and went immediately to confess my involuntary offense. I received a severe scolding, and was left with a penetrating sense of 'not-niceness' which effectually kept me from pursuing my investigations farther; and this was literally all I knew of the processes of generation till I had been married for several weeks—the explanation which I had meanwhile worked out for myself being that married people 'had children' because God saw the clergyman marrying them through the roof of the church!" [56] It is difficult to evaluate this frightful little tale. The "severe scolding" sums up society's official attitude toward the sexual enlightenment of little girls and calls to our minds most vividly the peculiarly vicious treatment that their perfectly natural inquiries were subjected to. The offending child is violently affected; she ceases all further investigations—not because an adult is supervising her so closely but because she has such a "penetrating sense of 'not-niceness.' " Now the scolding must bear some significant responsibility for the depth of her guilt—and yet, this is a child who has already been hounded by scrupulosity, who is, therefore, inclined to hear and accept the most vehemently punitive judgment of anything connected with her feelings. That other child had found out, somehow, that babies did not come from flowers; but Edith Wharton—who as an adolescent had an epoch-making encounter with Goethe's *Faust* and who read and reread the significant scenes of *The Duchess of Malfi*—Edith Wharton did not find out where babies came from until several weeks after her marriage. A fearful combination was at work to shut up spontaneous emotions: Lucretia, the standards of "niceness" for fashionable young ladies, and Edith Wharton's own habit of repressing primitive instincts.

Fifteen years later, this combination was still at work. "A few days before my marriage," Wharton recalls, "I was seized with such a dread of the whole dark mystery that I summoned up courage to appeal to my mother, and begged her, with a heart beating to suffocation, to tell me 'what being married was like.' Her handsome face at once took on the look of icy disapproval which I most dreaded. 'I never heard such a ridiculous question!' she said impatiently; and I felt at once how vulgar she thought me. But in the extremity of my need I persisted. 'I'm afraid, Mamma—I want to know what will happen to me!' The coldness of her expression deepened to disgust. She was silent for a dreadful moment; then she said with an effort: 'You've seen enough pictures and statues in your life. Haven't you noticed that men are—made differently from women?' 'Yes,' I faltered blankly. 'Well, then—?' I was silent, from sheer inability to follow, and she brought out sharply: 'Then for heaven's sake don't ask me any more silly questions. You can't be as stupid as you pretend!' The dreadful moment was over, and the only result was that I had been convicted of stupidity for not knowing what I had been expressly forbidden to ask about, or even to think of!" [57]

Thus the first lesson that Edith Wharton learned about becoming a woman was that society made no provisions for her feelings; and her unhealthy subservience to the letter of Lucretia's law (though not, ironically, to the model of Lucretia's behavior) was for years to cripple her as a woman and as an artist.

There were other lessons to be learned about becoming a woman. "There was an almost pagan worship of physical beauty, and the first question asked about any youthful newcomer on the social scene was invariably: 'Is she pretty?' or: 'Is he handsome?' " The lovely young ladies who waited for betrothal and marriage to inspire "appropriate" feelings in them were expected to present themselves as exquisitely beautiful vessels. Was it mere accident that the principal component of feminine beauty was "a complexion" and that the preservation of "complexion" required young ladies to wrap themselves in layer upon layer of protective veiling—veiling "as thick as curtains (some actually of woollen barège) . . . [veiling that] must have been very uncomfortable for the wearers, who could hardly see or breathe." [58] What can we say of this picturesque scene? This is no normal, healthy pride in appearance. This is a perverse displacement of passion into mere reductive preoccupation with the superficies of self. What could such people know of each other, save the veneer of beauty that was cultivated for popular approval? And for girls especially, what image of "self" could this social custom encourage other than the sense that one's "self" inhered entirely in the capacity to evoke admiration?

The little girl had spent years watching in rapt wonder as Mother's annual box of dresses from Paris was opened. She had a hunger for beauty in all its forms and must have been unnaturally susceptible to an image of the woman as a beautiful work of art. Her feelings were terrifyingly powerful. Thus a social code that expected women to be lovely creatures without feelings must have exerted no little force upon her; and her impulse to create art was compromised by the particular demands that becoming a woman in that society made upon her.

In the published autobiography *A Backward Glance*, Wharton ironically sums up that first childhood memory of her walk with father as indicating an awakening "to conscious life [of] the two tremendous forces of love and vanity." [59] In the more confessional pages of "Life and I" she gives a fuller and less guarded interpretation of the episode: "Thus I may truly say that my first conscious sensations were produced by the two deepest-seated instincts of my nature—the desire to love and to look pretty. I say 'to look pretty' instead of 'to be admired,' because I really believe it has always been an aesthetic desire, rather than a form of vanity. I always saw the visible world as a series of pictures, more or less harmoniously composed; and the wish *to make the picture prettier* was, as

nearly as I can define it, the form my feminine instinct of pleasing took."
To "make" beauty or to "be" beautiful? These alternatives vied in Wharton's mind for years; and on the whole, the option of "being" beautiful
seemed the only one consonant with society's definition of the feminine
nature. The problem did not become acute, of course, until adolescence
brought the explicit demands of womanhood directly to her. What palpable and subtle confusion the seventeen-year-old mind betrays! She returns to Europe with her family, ready "to see pictures and beautiful
things again. . . . I had spent rapturous hours in the National Gallery,
on our way through London. . . . But, vividly as I remember my first
moments there, they come back to me with less intensity than that first
rush of sensation before the Giorgione, the Titian and the Mona Lisa. I
felt as if all the great waves of the sea of Beauty were breaking over me at
once—and at the same time I remember being conscious of the notice of
the persons about me, and wondering whether I should be 'thought
pretty in Paris.' " [60]

Throughout the many years of adolescence and young womanhood,
Edith Wharton's impulse "to do" was engulfed by the imperative "to
be." We have few explicit recollections of this time, but the ones that
remain give poignant testimony to the hesitation which held this talented
and intelligent woman in check. It is her time of "long inner solitude," [61]
and no stories are quite so telling as the first two pathetic encounters
with Henry James. Old friends asked her to dine with them and to meet
the author whose works she had so long admired. "I could hardly believe
that such a privilege could befall me, and I could think of only one way
of deserving it—to put on my newest Doucet dress, and try to look my
prettiest! I was probably not more than twenty-five, those were the principles in which I had been brought up, and it would never have occurred
to me that I had anything but my youth, and my pretty frock, to commend me to the man whose shoe-strings I thought myself unworthy to
unloose. I can see the dress still—and it *was* pretty; a tea-rose pink,
embroidered with iridescent beads. But alas, it neither gave me the
courage to speak, nor attracted the attention of the great man. The evening was a failure. . . . A year or two later . . . the same opportunity
came my way. . . . Once more I thought: How can I make myself
pretty enough for him to notice me? Well—this time I had a new hat; *a
beautiful new hat!* I was almost sure it was becoming, and I felt that if he
would only tell me so I might at last pluck up courage to blurt out my

admiration for 'Daisy Miller' and 'The Portrait of a Lady.' But he noticed neither the hat nor its wearer—and the second of our meetings fell as flat as the first." [62] In these scenes, Edith Wharton is perhaps most clearly her mother's child; the impulse to be like Mother has been translated into a conviction that only the shimmering surface of her femininity could be of interest—that she had nothing but her youth and her pretty frock to commend her. It was a pernicious and debilitating belief.

However, by far the most destructive element in Edith Wharton's adolescence was the systematic manner in which her literary talents were discouraged. The problem would have been difficult enough even for a boy of Wharton's time and class. Her parents and their group, "though they held literature in great esteem, stood in nervous dread of those who produced it. Washington Irving, Fitz-Greene Halleck and William Dana were the only representatives of the disquieting art who were deemed uncontaminated by it; though Longfellow, they admitted, if a popular poet, was nevertheless a gentleman. As for Herman Melville, a cousin of the Van Rensselaers, and qualified by birth to figure in the best society, he was doubtless excluded from it by his deplorable Bohemianism, for I never heard his name mentioned, or saw one of his books. . . . But worse still perhaps in my parents' eyes was the case of such unhappy persons as Joseph Drake, author of 'The Culprit Fay,' balanced between 'fame and infamy' as not quite of the best society, and writing not quite the best poetry. I cannot hope to render the tone in which my mother pronounced the names of such unfortunates, or, on the other hand, that of Mrs. Beecher Stowe, who was so 'common' yet so successful. On the whole, my mother doubtless thought it would be simpler if people one might be exposed to meeting would refrain from meddling with literature." [63]

The polite disapproval that attended the occupation of writing was reinforced in Edith Wharton's life by the general view that a girl had no business training her intelligence. The happy time spent in "Father's library" was a secret retreat from the rest of her young-girlhood; and she was conscious of its being a life apart. No strain of Wharton's memories of this period is more painfully articulated than the themes of isolation and of loneliness. Her problem consisted not merely in neglect, but in an increasing discouragement of the talent that had, in earlier childhood, offered such a saving means for mastering her numerous difficulties.

We might contemplate the significance of the phrase "Father's library." There is no record that the girl had any library of her own—save birthday gifts of nicely bound copies of suitable books that she had already read elsewhere. She has spoken of the significance of her discovery of "Coppee's Elements of Logic"; the story, as she tells it, is revealing. "Faust was one of the 'epoch-making' encounters for me—another was Keats. A third was—a little volume called 'Coppee's Elements of Logic,' which I discovered among the books my brother Harry had brought back from Trinity Hall; and of the three, *at the time*, it was Coppee who made the greatest difference to me!" [64] Father's library and Harry's books. The girl is like some undernourished scavenger, rummaging through the family's literary leftovers.

A boy's literary inclinations would scarcely have been encouraged; but a boy would have had a tutor, and eventually boys went away to school. The little girl had not even such consolation as this. She could have her friends to romp with, but of the serious strain in her nature, "they never had so much as a guess! I often wonder," the mature author reflects, "if any other child possessed of the 'other side' was ever so alone in it as I. Certainly none in my experience. All the people I have known who have cared for 'les choses de l'esprit' have found some degree of sympathy and companionship either in their families or among their youthful friends. But I never exchanged a word with a really intelligent human being until I was over twenty—and then, alas, I had only a short glimpse of what such communion might be!" To be only a girl—what a terrible burden that could be. "It never occurred to my parents to give me anything beyond the ordinary teaching . . . or to have these acquirements made interesting by first-rate teachers. If I had only had a tutor—some one with whom I could talk of what I read, and who would have roused my ambition to study! My good governess was cultivated and conscientious, but she never struck a spark from me, she never threw a new light on any subject,—or made me see the relation of things to each other. My childhood and growth were an intellectual desert." [65] Much later in her life, Edith Wharton would comment upon the reverence with which other women writers had been treated by their families. In these remarks we have, perhaps, the truest measure of her own smoldering adolescent resentment. "The first time I lunched at Mrs. Meynell's I was struck by the solemnity with which this tall thin sweet-voiced woman, with melancholy eyes and a rather catafalque-like garb, was treated by her husband and children. . . . I, who had been accustomed at home to dissemble my literary pursuits (as though, to borrow Dr. Johnson's phrase about portrait painting, they were 'indelicate in a female'), was astonished at the prestige surrounding Mrs. Meynell in her own family." [66]

The family's attitude toward the adolescent girl was precisely calculated to diminish her self-esteem. Under the excuse conventionally used with girls of this age that they did not wish to "spoil" the child, Mother and brothers engaged in a campaign to "ridicule" her "supposed defects and affectations. I was laughed at by my brothers for my red hair, and for the supposed abnormal size of my hands and feet; and as I was much the least good-looking of the family, the consciousness of my physical short-comings was heightened by the beauty of the persons about me. My parents—or at least my mother—laughed at me for using 'long words,' and for caring for dress (in which heaven knows she set me the example!); and under this perpetual cross-fire of criticism I became a painfully shy self-conscious child." [67] She was accused of having less "heart" than her brothers (who did not have to endure this particular rite of initiation), and she did not have the courage to suggest that occasional praise might have brought her softer feelings to the surface.

Instead, she handled this unhappiness as she had handled earlier difficulties; and "making up" took the new form of writing down: "I found a new refuge from these outward miseries—I had begun to write!" [68]

Wharton's juvenilia are all very earnest and, like much adolescent writing, rather morbid. The only surviving piece of fiction, a short novel entitled "Fast and Loose," is remarkable chiefly for its pervasive insistence that all love relationships will inevitably conclude in unhappiness. Ironically, the only hint that this is the work of a talented author comes in several "reviews" of the novel that the girl wrote for her own amusement. She manages to capture in them precisely that air of condescension that so many reviewers strive for, but she captures, too, the often viciously destructive tone of the mockery she has heard. "In short, in such a case, it is false to reader and writer to mince matters—the English of it is that every character is a failure, the plot a vacuum, the style a fiasco. Is not—the disgusted reader is forced to ask—is not Mr. Olivieri [Wharton's pseudonym] very, very like a sick—sentimental school-girl who has begun her work with a fierce and bloody resolve to make it as bad as Wilhelm Meister, Consuelo, and 'Goodbye Sweetheart' together, and has ended with a blush, and a general erasure of all the naughty words which her modest vocabulary could furnish?" [69] How pathetically the bravado of this humor smacks of Lucretia; probably it was at least consoling to the girl to be in control of the most scathing criticism that could be leveled.

The early poems do not bear close scrutiny; one of them was published in *The World* when the author was seventeen, and like so much of the adolescent work, it took a melancholy subject—a little boy who had been put into jail and who had hanged himself. The poems that survive echo three themes: anticipation (poems about Spring or about growing into some indefinable maturity), loneliness, and death.

It is difficult to capture the malicious inconsistency with which these literary efforts were treated. On the one hand, the entire tone of the home made it clear to the girl that professional authors were not gentlepeople, that it was not "nice," therefore, to write. It was during this period that the girl was forced to collect brown wrapping paper to write on because foolscap was thought too expensive an extravagance to waste upon her scribblings. And it was throughout this long agony of puerile writing (much of which she knew to be very bad) that she was subjected to the most captiously cruel criticism from her family, and especially, of course, from Mother. On the other hand, now as before, the girl's literary efforts gave her something of an advantage over Mother; writing down was not so dramatic as "making up," but it set her apart and made her special. Neverthless, even here Lucretia's instinct was to intrude (when she was not criticizing) and to dominate (when she was not rejecting out of hand). "My mother took an odd inarticulate interest in these youthful productions," Wharton recalls, "and kept a blank book in which she copied many of them." [70] The same Mother who had belittled her daughter's "vanity" while thrusting upon her a model of self-adornment that absolutely demanded imitation assumed an equally unpredictable mood toward that daughter's intellectual precocity.

Standing apart from the bitter scene, what we can discern is a consistent policy of random reinforcement. Clearly Lucretia took more than occasional interest in her daughter's strange talent; clearly she sometimes took it into her head to reward the girl's efforts with notice, even praise. Yet one could never count upon Mother's goodwill, for Lucretia was often moved by whims of cruelty, too. What brought warm attention one day might bring freezing disdain the next; and the girl could never know in advance which mood would prevail. Yet she was a creature given to striving. Thus the vagaries of Mother's disposition had the perverse effect of encouraging the child to try even harder for that occasional moment of benevolence. Eventually the daughter developed into a woman with an iron determination to pursue the occupation of writing that brought increasingly reliable rewards.

As Wharton's adolescence progressed, however, Lucretia's judgment on the subject grew unmistakably negative. she was not pleased by the girl's public trial of her talent (in a *newspaper*); but having denied money even for paper to write on, she took it into her head to order an edition of the youthful poems—privately printed. How discreet! What a definitive and decorous conclusion to this adolescent hobby! And with what mortification does the daughter remember this premature exposure of her infant productions: Mother "perpetrated the folly of having a 'selection' privately printed when I was sixteen; and from a recent perusal of these two volumes I am reluctantly obliged to conclude that . . . nothing in my oeuvre de jeunesse showed the slightest spark of originality or talent." [71] Perhaps Mother thought definitively to domesticate her daughter's gifts. Certainly she succeeded, at least, in swooping into her daughter's private retreat, possessing herself of what was intimate and personal, and in an act of perverse "generosity" making every fault of youth available to the tolerant eyes of family and friends.

In Edith Wharton's memory, her one youthful literary triumph had been the acceptance of that poem by *The World:* that had demonstrated the genuine merit of her work; that had been a beginning—who knew of what. But her hopes were not sustained. "I continued to cover vast expanses of wrapping paper with prose and verse, but the dream of a literary career, momentarily shadowed forth by one miraculous adventure, soon faded into unreality. How could I ever have supposed I could be an author? I had never even seen one in the flesh!" [72]

Lucretia's appropriations of her daughter's poems into that lamentable private edition signaled the successful termination of the budding author's career. When Mother acted, she acted decisively: "Literary activity was checked by a much more important event: I 'came out.' Conventionally speaking—and everything in our family life was ordered according to convention—this important experience should have been postponed till I was eighteen; but (as I learned afterward) my parents were alarmed at my growing shyness, at my passion for study, and my indifference to the companionship of young people my own age, and it was therefore decided that, contrary to all precedent, I should be taken into the world at seventeen." [73]

The girl was now a woman in the official eyes of old New York. Having become a woman, she was obliged to foreswear her hopes of a literary career. Being a conscientious woman, she did. Edith Wharton was to write nothing more of significance (at least nothing that survives her) for eleven long years.

4

If we try to paint some portrait of the young woman at this point in her life, it is hard to bring her into focus. At seventeen, she should have been well into that age of "finding oneself" that necessarily precedes adulthood; yet far from finding herself, she seems more and more to have lost herself. Growing into womanhood had severely compromised her: she had relinquished first one significant element in her life and then another—passions subdued (hidden, like those beautiful Victorian complexions, under layer upon layer of protective covering); making up and writing down, both put aside; and the timid forays of rebellion against Lucretia, all quashed. By what significant characteristics might this frightened and thoroughly broken young creature identify herself as "somebody"—somebody different from all the rest? The terrible answer is that there were no particularities that had not been humiliatingly compromised. Photographs of this girl all show a timid thing who seems to offer herself apologetically to the camera's stare, her body leaning slightly away from the viewer. In her eyes there is a great sadness. Edith Wharton would not manage to become a genuinely coherent person until much later in her life; and now, she was living in the deceptive calm of a momentary truce among the various unresolved "selves" that were gathered together within her.

She had been a debutante for less than a year when the family returned to Europe to support Father's dwindling health; he seemed to rally during an autumn and winter spent abroad, and by the next summer he was well enough to do a little sightseeing with his daughter. This was a happy time. The following "autumn we went to Venice and Florence, and it must have been then that he gave me 'Stones of Venice' and 'Walks in Florence,' and gently lent himself to my whim of following step by step Ruskin's arbitrary itineraries." [74] That winter Father died, and Mother and daughter returned to New York. Shortly afterward, the girl was to have her first unfortunate encounter with love.

The young woman had three serious romantic attachments: her engagement to Harry Stevens which was broken off; her dalliance with Walter Berry which fell short of a declaration; and finally her marriage to Edward Wharton. All three men shared certain traits: they were punctiliously polite and emotionally reticent; above all, they were in no way sexually assertive. They would not intrude upon the delicate balance of the girl's privacy; they would not demand emotional intimacy from her; and it is altogether reasonable to suppose that she sought them for precisely these reasons. The case of Harry Stevens is instructive.

The most significant thing about Harry Stevens was that he had a mother, a most formidable and undaunted mother. Pictures show her as a large woman, holding her body proudly erect; Louis Auchincloss characterizes her as a "rich and forceful woman." [75] Anyone who married Harry Stevens would most surely be marrying his mother as well; and we must marvel at the perversity of human nature in a girl who had been so thoroughly reduced by Lucretia's tyranny and who managed to find a young man trailing a future mother-in-law even more dreadful than Mother. One simple explanation—a very plausible one—is that the girl's life had been so completely colored by her relationship with Mother that she unconsciously sought a similar "Mother" in marriage. Then too, Harry Stevens seems to have been a generous and kind young man—and a weak one. His wife would have had to bear with an intrusive mother-in-law, but she would not have had to contend with a demanding husband. All these things, unattractive as they might seem to an impartial observer, must have come together to make this proposal one that the girl could safely manage. In any case, the couple became engaged—and, in the face of Mrs. Paran Stevens's unrelenting opposition, became almost immediately disengaged. There are no lines in Wharton's memorabilia suggesting that she had loved Harry Stevens deeply or that she was profoundly affected by the termination of their engagement. Young Stevens's health had never been strong; and when he died two years later, in 1885, there is no sign that the girl was in the least grieved.

Against Mrs. Paran Stevens, however, there was a grudge of lifelong tenacity: she was held in contempt for fifty years. The first signal of retaliation came in the portrait of Mrs. Struthers in *The Age of Innocence*, for that flamboyant, vulgar woman with a disreputable past makes her way into New York society by giving interesting parties on Sunday evenings—just as the equally questionable Mrs. Stevens had done. But this thrust was not sufficient. In about 1928, when she was making the first notes for her last (and unfinished) novel, *The Buccaneers*, Edith Wharton would write: "Conquest of England by American adventurous (and adventuress) families in the seventies. Type: Jeromes, Stevens, etc." And then, just so there might be no mistake, the word "Paran" is inserted next to "Stevens." [76] Here is some measure of the tenacity of the girl's shame. And her lingering, malignant rage was directed at the mother who had opposed her and not at the son who had failed her. The truth is that the twenty-year-old Edith Wharton had not yet reached the point at which she could engage her passions with a man; she was still too thoroughly dominated by Mother.

The next romantic encounter was with Walter Berry in the summer of 1883. Walter Berry did not have a domineering mother to stand between himself and a future wife, but he was a man who "maintained a careful lack of final seriousness in his relations with women." [77] The flirtation was brief and (for Berry) characteristically inconclusive. As a young man, he was fastidious to a fault in his emotional postures.

During that same summer, Edith met Edward Robbins Wharton, the man she was eventually to marry. Teddy, as he was universally called, was of the same breed as the first two suitors—though on the whole, a much more benign variant of the species. At thirty-three, "Teddy was living on Beacon Street in Boston, in a household presided over by his capable mother. . . . His wants were also catered to by his younger sister Nancy, a somewhat rattlebrained spinster, inclined to stoutness. . . . He had no vocation, nor any intention of seeking one. He was popular and gregarious, and something of a gourmet and connoisseur of good wines." [78] Two years later the couple were married. Like the other men with whom she had been involved, Teddy was not assertive. He had accommodated himself to the easy routine of his mother's house before marriage; he was perfectly willing to fit himself into the pattern of his wife's life afterward. For the first three years of their marriage the couple lived at Pencraig Cottage, directly across the street from Lucretia's home in Newport. In all, Teddy's virtues seem to have rendered him a rather indulgent parent to his young bride: he "was willing—at least in the early years—to let his wife take the lead. He followed in her wake to all the shrines of France and Italy, meticulous about timetables and accommodations, and always keeping a thousand-dollar bill in his wallet 'in case Pussy wanted something.' " [79] Such a companion must, for a while at least, have seemed an agreeable alternative to the parent who had found writing paper too great an extravagance for a scribbling daughter. Nevertheless, this marriage eventually brought disaster; any marriage would have.

Throughout her young womanhood Edith Wharton had evaded a confrontation with her emotional problems by attaching herself only to reticent and distant young men. However, marriage, even marriage with the amiable Teddy, was the genuine article.

The years between the marriage and Edith Wharton's emergence as a public figure in the literary world filter through to us in mere disorganized scraps of misery. The marriage was not consummated for three weeks, and always thereafter the physical relationship between the pair (such as it was, and R. W. B. Lewis speculates that it soon became nonexistent) was agonized. Edith Wharton had never resolved the crises of her earlier life; she had merely tried to put aside the residue. Now marriage demanded intimacy from her. Erik Erikson has described Intimacy as the crisis central to early adulthood; and in meeting it, an individual must necessarily draw upon the strengths that have grown out of the resolution of earlier crises. A woman in Edith Wharton's position had no such legacy of early strengths to draw upon; and thus the crisis of sexual intimacy must merely have resurrected the bogies of childhood. Edith Wharton could not be a wife without feeling a flood of unsatisfied, unreckoned emotional demands from all those earlier selves; and the anguish of her adulthood turned to the modalities of her childhood as ways of finding representation for the dilemma.

Whenever she was forced to share a bedroom with Teddy, she suffered attacks of asthma; she could not articulate the message inherent in the symptoms—that the merest unspoken implication of his presence was suffocating to her—and so she talked with her body, and she found that she could not breathe. One plausible explanation for the couple's frenetic traveling during this period is that in traveling Edith did not have to share a bedroom with her husband. Not surprisingly, the asthmatic condition vanished when they took up residence at The Mount, their home in Lenox, Massachusetts, where they had separate bedrooms. In a 1908 diary entry, Edith Wharton is to comment bitterly on her time with Teddy: "I heard the key turn in my prison-lock. That is the answer to everything worthwhile! Oh, Gods of derisions! And you've given me over twenty years of it. Je n'en peux plus . . ." [80]

If she was stifled by the intensity of her own conflicted feelings, she was also stifled by her husband's insensitivity to her intellectual interests. Throughout the years of their marriage, she made efforts to palliate this problem, and she sought congenial friends whose interests more closely paralleled her own. One was Egerton Winthrop, whose "house was the first in New York in which an educated taste had replaced stuffy upholstery and rubbishy 'ornaments' with objects of real beauty." [81] Winthrop's friendship, like his house, must have given Wharton a little room to breathe. Eventually the list of such confidants became a long one, including such notables as Henry James. However, intellectual friendships could not solve the essential problem.

Affection was not the same thing as passion; satisfying literary comradeship with a variety of men who were all, each in his own way, "safe" could not speak to the underlying disorder. The unresolved conflicts that marriage had revived persisted, despite the sensible substitutions Wharton tried to offer herself. Two letters of a later period will recall the malignancy of her feelings at the time. There were few friends to whom Wharton confided the secrets of her emotional life; one was Sara Norton. On April 12, 1908, Wharton was writing to Sara Norton about the despondency of a mutual friend. "Tell Lily, if it's any comfort, that for *twelve years* I seldom knew what it was to be, for more than an hour or two of the twenty-four, without an intense feeling of nausea, and such unutterable fatigue that when I got up I was always more tired than when I lay down. This form of neurasthenia consumed the best years of my youth, and left, in some sort, an irreparable shade on my life. Mais quoi! I worked through it, and came out on the other side, and so will she." [82] Four years later, writing to Bernard Berenson and sympathetic with his own miseries, she confided: "Some occult and un-get-at-able nausea was my constant companion for twelve years! My 'seasickness' defied all cures . . . and then disappeared suddenly when we moved from the seashore to the hills." [83] Edith Wharton first visited Lenox in 1899, staying at the unoccupied summer home of Teddy's mother and sister; shortly afterwards, she determined to build there herself. By 1902 The Mount was finished. Those twelve years must, therefore, have ended sometime between 1899 and 1902; and it follows that they must have begun shortly after her marriage. Another example of talking with her body, and a much more telling one.

The nausea is one more translation of her "hunger" for love. The symptom itself explains a good deal. If a woman's desires are rendered in terms of this most infantile modality of incorporation, then one difficulty revealed in the very nature of the symptom is the primitive and un-modulated force of her feelings (the residue of that infantile need). It is not surprising that Wharton felt this problem; it was a logical conse-quence of her unresolved fear of the Wolf who was going to eat her up. That totem animal of childhood, this debilitating nausea in woman-hood—both carry the same implication. I want too much; I will an-nihilate everyone I care about; I will be consumed by my own appetites; I will be alone and starving. Wharton's reactions to such fears had always been consistent: she fled from the Wolf, seeking the safer refuge of Mother or Doyley—behaving like a baby who needs constant atten-tion and thus finding protection from such animals as Wolves. It is a way of saying, "Make those terrifying feelings go away." Later, the girl's anger toward Mother had inspired her not with active rebellion but with its opposite, excruciatingly strict rules to govern what it was allow-able to say and even to think. Still later the minor "rebelliousness" of ab-sence from Mother's house was enough to bring some unnameable fear upon her. Always the same impulse: deny the feelings, repress the thoughts. Now the adult responses repeat those of childhood, merely varying the form. A person with asthma is unable to breathe in the very air he longs for; a person with nausea is prohibited from eating the nourishment his body craves; a person who is fatigued and who must lie abed for most of the day is someone who must be treated like a baby. All of these symptoms serve to deny her feelings—even to deny her grown-up womanhood; and in this massive effort she is inevitably extinguishing self as well. It is difficult to see how the woman could be more thoroughly diminished than she has now become.

Such responses were not productive, and in the end they were to collapse. However, in our account we have not (she had not) reckoned with all the warring selves within: there were the starving baby and the child possessed by fears, but there was also that clever infant who could turn an injured sense of trust to the unfailing pleasures of language; there was the child who devised "making up" as a way of demanding Mother's attention when attention was not otherwise given; and there was the little girl who moved along to writing down as a way of ordering the complexities of her relationship with the adult world. These selves had not evaded the truth; these selves had sought to preserve feelings and to master problems. These selves would not permit the continuance of such treacherous disintegration. These selves demanded action and not submission.

And so, with what effort we can only guess, Edith Wharton returned to her most reliable strength; she broke her long silence and began to write.

Having begun, she did not stop, and in the midst of all this pain, an author was born. The path to health was discontinuous, but always the saving strength lay in her talent for creating. She summoned up worlds of fiction that articulated the feelings and conflicts that had been so unprofitably pushed aside; and as she worked with those fictional worlds—shaping them, giving them order, making decisions about them—she slowly learned to master her problems.

The first step seems to have taken up just where the seventeen-year-old had left off. Edith Wharton decided to send three poems to three of the leading magazines of the day. However, the "nice" young lady made one addition: the verses were accompanied not by a timid letter, but by a calling card. "A week or two elapsed, and then I received the three answers, telling me that all three poems had been accepted. We had a little house in Madison Avenue that winter (it was our first trial of New York), and as long as I live I shall never forget my sensations when I opened the first of the three letters, and learned that I was to appear in print. I can still see the narrow hall, the letter-box out of which I fished the letters, and the flight of stairs up and down which I ran, senselessly and incessantly, in the attempt to give my excitement some muscular outlet!" [84]

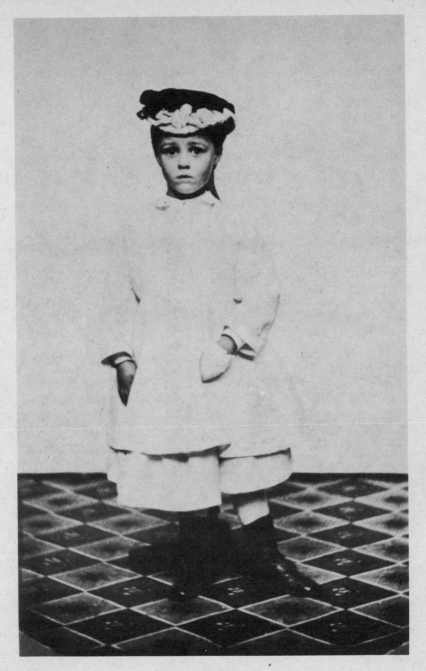

Edith Newbold Jones, 1867

Edith Jones, 1876

Edith Jones, 1880

Edith Jones Wharton, 1889

II

Landscapes of Desolation
The Fiction, 1889-1911

"Was hat man dir, du armes Kind, gethan?" (What's this, poor child, they've done to thee?)

From Mignon's Song: Wilhelm Meister
Headnote to Book I of "Disintegration"

It is the winter of 1889, and the author who is bounding about the house like a schoolgirl is, in reality, a matron of twenty-seven. Compared to her male contemporaries, she is somewhat advanced in years to be just beginning a career in literature. What is more, this initial success is to yield the publication of only a few poems, and she will be even older—twenty-nine, in fact—before seeing a single piece of her own fiction in print. We must not be misled by the joy, the exuberance of that scene as she is to remember it some forty-five years later in *A Backward Glance*. Certainly there *was* joy, a passion finally to be embarked on this great adventure; however, it was balanced for a very long time (perhaps overbalanced) by a pervasive and debilitating depressive lassitude. Genuine joy, deep unhappiness: these were to measure her emotional life for the next many years.

Wharton's career as a writer of fiction had a peculiarly mixed beginning, not unlike the motley of moods that ranged through her emotional life. On the one hand she can never be said to have struggled against a hostile publisher or an indifferent public. Indeed, she seems to have moved along a charmed pathway to success. The first three poems she sent out were all accepted for publication; the first story, "Mrs. Manstey's View," was also received with encouragement, even though her editors at Scribner's, William Brownell and Edward Burlingame, were accustomed to rejecting the likes of Hamlin Garland at the same time that they were accepting these first attempts of Edith Wharton. Almost all of her early stories were published without substantial criticism from her editors, and in 1893, after she had had only some four pieces of fiction accepted for publication, Burlingame suggested the possibility of bringing out a volume of her short stories. When that volume finally saw print in 1899, it was instantly acclaimed by the critics. Her first full-length novel, *The Valley of Decision* (1902), a two-volume affair running to more than six hundred pages, was praised on both sides of the Atlantic by such distinguished men of letters as Charles Eliot Norton and Henry James (who took the occasion to initiate a friendship by writing her an admiring letter). Her next major work, *The House of Mirth* (1905), was not only a brilliant fictional triumph, but a runaway popular success—selling 30,000 copies in the first three weeks! If we look for the swollen stack of rejection slips, the pile of manuscripts that have been turned away, we will not find them. Wharton's vocation as a writer appears to have flowered with inexorable majesty, and our account seems to return us to

"Edith Wharton: The Author," the composed and aloof personage of the publicity photos.

An examination of the dates, however, is revealing. The poems were accepted in 1889; two years passed before the first piece of fiction; a surprising six years elapsed before the publication of a slim volume of short stories that had been solicited by one of the most distinguished houses then publishing. Her work was not often rejected, that is true; but Edith Wharton appears to have had an uncommonly difficult time gathering her literary forces together so that she could make a genuine beginning. She started late, and she had a very long apprenticeship.

By her own account, she did not really become a novelist in full command of her material until well after the publication of even *The House of Mirth*, although the production of that novel marked a crucial moment in her work. "It was good to be turned from a drifting amateur into a professional; but that was nothing compared to the effect on my imagination of systematic daily effort. . . . When the book was done I remember saying to myself: 'I don't yet know how to write a novel; *but I know how to find out how to.*' I went on steadily trying to 'find out how to'; but I wrote two or three novels without feeling that I had made much progress. It was not until I wrote 'Ethan Frome' that I suddenly felt the artisan's full control of his implements." [1] *Ethan Frome* was published in 1911, twenty-two years after that joyous morning when the first poems were accepted for publication. This beginning had been almost intolerably protracted—not by the artist's own ineptitude nor even by the publisher's recalcitrance—but by the impeding irresolution of those personal conflicts that had dominated the woman's growth from childhood.

1

It is sometimes very difficult to date the exact time during which Wharton was working on a given piece of fiction. The peculiarities of her usual writing habits were such that she might well be working on several different things during the same period. A 1900 letter to Brownell concerning her progress on *The Valley of Decision* is typical: "The last two or three weeks have brought about what seems an inevitably recurring thing with me—the necessity of dropping one kind of work and taking up another. After doing over 40,000 words of 'The Valley' without a break I suddenly found the tank empty. I turned back to my short stories, and the change of air at once renewed my activity." [2] Now Edith Wharton seems almost always to have worked in this way; sometimes the delay was short, a matter of months, and sometimes it was very long, a matter of years. It threw her publishers into fits of exasperation, for she would propose one novel, find "the tank empty" for a while, and turn her attention to something quite different. *The Custom of the Country* was completed only after notorious delays that severely strained the amiable relationship between Wharton and her editors at Scribner's; and the misunderstandings that attended the dalliance over another projected novel, "Literature," that was in fact never completed, eventually caused Scribner's to lose two first-rate works, *Summer* and *The Age of Innocence* (the latter of which won the Pulitzer Prize). Sometimes we can date the periods during which works were being composed by noting entries in datebooks and Donnée books; sometimes we cannot. It is, of course, useful and informative to be able to discover when a work was begun. However, it is even more important to know when it was completed (a date more easily ascertained), for the delays that interrupted the progress of so many novels were most usually the result of Wharton's inability to resolve one or another problem inherent in the fiction. When she found herself blocked in this way, she wisely put the work aside and began to work on something else. When she was at last able to resolve the problem that had baffled her, she usually returned to the work and completed it. The completion of the work more or less coincided, then, with the solution of the difficulty that had preoccupied her—and will occupy us.[3]

The first three pieces of fiction that she offered for publication were probably the first three that she wrote: two short stories, "Mrs. Manstey's View" and "The Fullness of Life," and a novella, "Bunner Sisters." None of these is among her best work; all were perilously close to the problems that beset her at this period, and they are less genuine fictions than efforts at finding a mode of representation. The problem has haunted her from earliest childhood: how can I articulate my feelings. Even Wharton was very soon to recognize the literary limitations of these pieces, and she refused adamantly to include them in her first collection of short fictions, *The Greater Inclination*. "As to the old stories of which you speak so kindly," she wrote to Burlingame, "I regard them as the excesses of youth. They were all written 'at the top of my voice,' and The Fullness of Life is one long shriek.—I may not write any better, but at least I hope that I write in a lower key, and I fear the voice of those early tales will drown all the others. It is for that reason that I prefer not to publish them." [4] The narrative voice was Wharton's own, and she was wise enough to recognize it. Not only was there public embarrassment in this unself-conscious, uncensored directness; there was literary clumsiness, which might have seemed even worse to the developing writer. Certainly there was *not* the "artisan's full control of his implements" that she finally gained in *Ethan Frome*. The failures in these early efforts say much about the achievement of what is to come.

Like most novelists, Edith Wharton began by writing about herself, although she was so successful at hiding herself that the portraits are extremely oblique. The plot of her first story, "Mrs. Manstey's View," is very slender: an elderly woman living on the top floor of a boarding house has but one pleasure remaining to her, watching the little piece of life that passes beneath her window; she learns that an extension is to be built on the house next door, an extension which will block her view; she attempts to persuade the owner of the house to give up the planned addition, and when she fails in this effort, she slips out at night and sets fire to the partially erected wing; her exertions leave her exhausted and sick, and she dies. The problems of Mrs. Manstey's penurious life *seem* at a far remove from those of Mrs. Edward Wharton (fashionable East Side resident). R. W. B. Lewis remarks that "like several others of Edith Wharton's very earliest stories, this one has no obvious bearing at all on the life she was actually leading; it was, rather, an imaginative escape from that life." [5] This is the most widely accepted critical reading of the story, and it is not difficult to sympathize with it. Nevertheless, if we examine the plot in conjunction with other elements in the tale, we can find its author revealed with almost painful directness.

There is, for example, the way in which the character is located or placed. The thematic use of enclosed space—a house, a garden, a room, even a valley—can be found throughout Wharton's mature work in the most subtle and suggestive variations; it was a novelistic art that she shared with James and one which has caused them relentlessly to be compared. In "The Fullness of Life" the principal character enunciates a view that must have been close to Wharton's own. " 'I have sometimes thought that a woman's nature is like a great house full of rooms: there is the hall, through which everyone passes in going in and out; the drawing room, where one receives formal visits; the sitting room, where the members of the family come and go as they list; but beyond that, far beyond, are other rooms, the handles of whose doors perhaps are never turned; no one knows the way to them, no one knows whither they lead; and in the innermost room, the holy of holies, the soul sits alone.' " [6] If we accept this metaphor of self, we can return to Mrs. Manstey with renewed interest.

Mrs. Manstey is revealed to us in a series of reductions. She is widowed; she has been separated from her only daughter by the breadth of the entire country, a distance that accurately measures the indifference of their emotional tie; she has become so physically infirm that by now she can write only with difficulty; even her emotions have atrophied— "for many years she had cherished a desire to live in the country, to have a henhouse and a garden; but this longing had faded with age, leaving only in the breast of the uncommunicative old woman a vague tenderness for plants and animals." She has nothing left to distinguish her, and she has retreated at last to "the back room on the third floor of a New York boardinghouse." [7]

It is a "given" of this little tale that Mrs. Manstey has relinquished all desires but one: the daily habit of peering out at the world from the unpromising, narrow vantage of the single, small room to which she has retired. The view has little or nothing to recommend it—a disorderly back alley, yards strewn with the debris of life, slatternly windows—and yet Mrs. Manstey contrives to make a world out of it. She measures time by the slow passage of the seasons, waits patiently from one long year to the next for the blooming magnolia of the neighboring yard, and reaps the slender benefits of asking so little. "Perhaps at heart Mrs. Manstey was an artist; at all events she was sensible of many changes of color unnoticed by the average eye and, dear to her as the green of early spring was, the black lattice of branches against a cold sulphur sky at the close of a snowy day." [8] It is a reduced diet; but it may be true (as Wharton declared elsewhere) that "the creative mind thrives best on a reduced diet." It is not a difficult leap to move from this portrait of diminished existence to the life of the woman who had begun to write after so long a silence. Almost of necessity Wharton reveals her own situation, using this early story as a primitive representation of self (never mind that the "circumstances" are so different from her own—who in Wharton's position would not engage in clever disguise?). And it is a notable measure of her lack of skill at this point that having summoned up this inner world of loneliness and desolation, she does not know how to make a real fiction out of it.

For example, this first use of "place"—that utterly isolated, far-away-as-you-can-get room that is Mrs. Manstey's world—is not developed as an emblem of complex character. It is fitting, to be sure, but it is just there, part of the material of the story. Why Mrs. Manstey has retreated, why she has retreated *here*, what she has retreated from (what lies beyond), all these dimensions of the fiction remain unexplored and unhinted at. The reader must simply accept this setting. He must accept, too, the inevitability of Mrs. Manstey's remaining here. When the dreadful threat of a foreclosed view is offered, Mrs. Manstey does not seriously contemplate leaving. " 'Of course I might move,' said Mrs. Manstey aloud, and turning from the window she looked about her room. She might move, of course; so might she be flayed alive; but she was not likely to survive either operation. The room, though far less important to her happiness than the view, was as much a part of her existence. . . . She knew every stain on the wallpaper, every rent in the carpet. . . . 'We are all too old to move,' she said." [9] A careful reader must wonder at the violence of the narrator's association—that moving would resemble being flayed alive—but the horrible suggestion hangs unfinished and undeveloped. He might wonder too at the fundamental inertia that suffuses the entire tale (even the rash attempt at arson does not dispel the feeling); and this mood of complete, passive, fatalistic acceptance is, again, given but not explained. The crisis, when it comes, is thrust in obtrusively from without—a neighbor's whimsy, nothing more, would remove that last little touch with the outer world and close up all of this impoverished life into itself. But for that accident, there would be no plot and thus no reason to relate the story: Mrs. Manstey's life bears no intrinsic relation to that accident, only the relationship devised by an author who chooses to juxtapose them.

Were it not for Wharton's subsequent achievements, the story would be forgotten. Yet it is a tantalizing failure. There is a striking sense of mood, the illusion of some powerful emotional state (and the author does not manage to tell us just what the state is) at the center of the narrative. A reader who is familiar with Wharton's emotional history might give a more precise name to that state. The dwindling of Mrs. Manstey's life (along with the shrinking space in which she houses herself) suggests a gradual loss of self, a relinquishment of significant identity. The tone of the story reflects Wharton's anger and terror at the diminishments that have occurred in her own life. It is a strength of Wharton's writing, even at this point, that she can reach into the recesses of her longings to fix on a problem of such immense and complex importance; it is her weakness now that having found this subject, she can neither control it nor resolve it.

"Mrs. Manstey's View" was accepted for publication in May 1890; it appeared more than a year later (July 1891) in *Scribner's Magazine*. In the summer of 1891 Wharton was working on her second short story, "The Fullness of Life"; and in 1892 she attempted a more ambitious piece, a novella entitled "Bunner Sisters." "Bunner Sisters" seems a genuine effort to pick up and develop the loose ends of emotion that had marred "Mrs. Manstey's View." It is a thoroughly depressing tale, and its tone combined with its length to make Burlingame reluctant to publish it when it was submitted to him in the winter of 1892. In fact, it did not see print until 1916. The story was rewritten in minor ways to prepare it for publication then; however, most was left as it originally stood, and thus this tale must be seen as belonging to the early period of literary groping.

"Bunner Sisters" is the first fiction in which Wharton uses a double heroine. Many of her works will revolve about the fate of a *pair* of women: Bessy Westmore and Justine Brent, Matty and Zeena, May Welland and Ellen Olenska—the list could go on, for it is a long one. There is no simple formula that explains this habit; her ladies are not the fair and dark heroines of earlier American fiction, and their differences are always varied and complex when the women appear in the major works. Their relationships to the hero (who is often poised between them) describe different life choices, different solutions to the problems that inform the novel. However, before she could create this highly varied group of women, Wharton herself had to achieve a flexible understanding of the range of emotional options they offered. Very early in her career, when she was writing this first story of two women, she did not yet have an easy acquaintance with life, for her own experience had been sorely straitened. She may have wished to venture out (the fact that she had begun to write again and the themes of the early fictions suggest that she did), but she had not been able to swing the door wide. Thus in this first piece of its kind, the women have very little to distinguish between them.

Ann Eliza and Evelina are the joint proprietors of a little notions shop where handwork may be done to order. "It was a very small shop, in a shabby basement, in a side-street already doomed to decline; and from the miscellaneous display behind the window-pane, and the brevity of the sign surmounting it (merely 'Bunner Sisters' in blotchy gold on a black ground) it would have been difficult for the uninitiated to guess the precise nature of the business carried on within." A perceptive reader will recognize again the language of reduction—lives that have been constricted (here the "place" extends to a showroom and a bedroom, both in the basement) and an environment that is already "doomed" by the second paragraph. There is, initially at least, a certain pluckiness in the face of this narrow life: "The Bunner sisters were proud of the neatness of their shop and content with its humble prosperity. It was not what they had once imagined it would be, but though it presented but a shrunken image of their earlier ambitions it enabled them to pay their rent and keep themselves alive and out of debt; and it was long since their hopes had soared higher." [10] But their spirit has been bought at the price of renunciation. The women are linked indistinguishably in their sign; they share their simple meals and sleep together in the same big bed in which they were born: two pinched lives that might extend together unchanged into eternity.

The story opens on Evelina's birthday. Her older sister has made an unusual excursion of several blocks in order to purchase a little clock for the occasion, and she tenders her gift with "the awkwardness of habitually repressed emotion." [11] Habit and the repression it entails lie at the center of the narrative. The Bunner sisters seem content to expect no more from life than the ability to pay their rent and keep themselves alive; and the usual parameters of their movement—the grocery store around the corner, the church up the block, the dressmaker's apartment just above them—describe a meager but safe arc of activity. They have almost resigned themselves to a kind of life that never moves beyond the coldness of their physical surroundings and the somber grays and blacks in which they clothe themselves. However, the hope that life may offer more has not yet been entirely extinguished.

Ann Eliza is reluctant to seek happiness in her own right, but she is not averse to finding a vicarious happiness in her sister's fate. "In her scant jacket and skirt of black cashmere [Evelina] looked singularly nipped and faded; but it seemed possible that under happier conditions she might still warm into relative youth." Yet even this tentative thought is unsettling: there are unknown dangers in the world beyond. We see them, through Ann Eliza's heightened sensibilities, as strangely pleasing and terrifyingly ominous. "The mere act of going out from the monastic quiet of the shop into the tumult of the streets filled her with a subdued excitement which grew too intense for pleasure as she was swallowed by the engulfing roar of Broadway and Third Avenue, and began to do timid battle with their incessant cross-currents of humanity." [12] To remain in the familiar track is to grow safely but steadily more withered; to break through the habitual routine is to venture into the fathoms of that unknown world for what may prove only the phantom of youth and warmth. In the end, this beckoning phantom is too enticing to resist.

The birthday gift is, of course, the little clock; but a gift of greater importance is the story of the expedition on which it was purchased. Ann Eliza has met an immigrant German shopkeeper, Herman Ramy, a sick and lonely man who becomes fixed in the women's imagination as someone whose narrow existence might be fitted together with their own. Ann Eliza dreams of meeting him on one of her errands, and Evelina takes the even bolder measure of venturing to walk over to his shop to have the clock repaired. These minute variations from routine are frightening to Ann Eliza, who recognizes them as the beginnings of discontent. " 'I always think if we ask for more what we have may be taken from us,' " she falters. [13] Yet the die has been cast. Mr. Ramy begins to visit the women on a regular basis, and they grow inevitably dissatisfied with the things that have proven safe.

Herman Ramy is a strange presence in the story. He speaks almost not at all, spending his evenings with the sisters in meditative silence, pulling at his pipe. He is an alien—both to America and to the enclosed world of the Bunner sisters—and the faint odor of something indefinably dangerous lingers about his person. Occasionally he takes the women on short jaunts, and the descriptions of the perfectly mundane places that they visit are thrust into the calm tenor of the narrative with surrealistic, feverish intensity. "The kaleidoscope whirl of the crowd" in Central Park is "unspeakably bewildering to Ann Eliza." A journey to Hoboken, New Jersey, is rendered with a disjointed jumbling of imagery that converts it almost into a descent to hell.

They got into a street-car, and were jolted from one mean street to another, till at length Mr. Ramy pulled the conductor's sleeve and they got out again; then they stood in the blazing sun, near the door of a crowded beer-saloon, waiting for another car to come; and that carried them out to a thinly settled district, past vacant lots and narrow brick houses standing in unsupported solitude, till they finally reached an almost rural region of scattered cottages and low wooden buildings that looked like village "stores." Here the car finally stopped of its own accord, and they walked along a rutty road, past a stone-cutter's yard with a high fence tapestried with theatrical advertisements, to a little red house with green blinds and a garden paling.[14]

Ramy has determined to carry one of the sisters off in marriage; and while he is curiously indifferent as to a choice between them, the women have silently agreed that Ann Eliza will embrace "the chill joy of renunciation" [15] while Evelina awaits a romantic awakening. Their behavior grows arch and artificial as they play out the coy roles that will reinforce this distinction, and the older sister is startled and chagrined when Ramy unaccountably fails to fall in with the game and proposes first to her instead of to Evelina. She rejects his offer, and after a suitable interval Ramy turns his suit to the younger sister. They marry and move away from New York.

Ann Eliza is left alone. She tries to take pleasure from visions of her sister's new life, but "even the thought of Evelina's happiness refused her its consolatory ray; or its light, if she saw it, was too remote to warm her. The thirst for a personal and inalienable tie, for pangs and problems of her own, was parching Ann Eliza's soul." She has tasted the bitter seeds of hope, and she can never recover the comfort of the safe, diminished world she had once enjoyed. This is a harsh fate, and it becomes even harsher when she discovers that her little world has been sacrificed entirely in vain. Evelina returns after several years—sick and broken. Ramy is an incurable drug-taker; Evelina has had a baby who died; the couple has been reduced to penury and brutality. " 'I've been in hell all that time,' " Evelina flares at her sister. " 'I must say it. . . . You don't know what life's like—you don't know anything about it—setting here safe all the while in this peaceful place.' " Everything has been lost, even the hope in some benevolent God. "If he was not good he was not God, and there was only a black abyss above the roof of Bunner Sisters." [16]

The story ends with cosmic desolation: Evelina dies, Ann Eliza dismantles the shop and sells its few remaining goods, and then she wanders out into the unknown, unfriendly world—seeking some means to keep herself alive.

This longer piece demonstrates many of the strengths that had been hinted in "Mrs. Manstey's View." The atmosphere of the Bunner sisters' world becomes morbidly vivid to the reader, and its haunting sense of isolation foreshadows such works as *Ethan Frome*. If there is occasional mawkishness (the rather too regular and pathetic appearance of a gift of jonquils in the spring to reinforce our understanding of the eternal winter in the sisters' lives), there are also descriptive passages in which the language is managed with mastery. Nevertheless, the faults are still more revealing than the successes.

Wharton cannot yet effectively conjure the illusion of a coherent larger fictional world in which her story may be presumed to take place. We are never entirely sure why things happen: the tale moves from a sense of diminishment to a sense of universal gloom without our knowing either the reasons for the initial wretchedness or the cause of the disintegration that follows. We might be tempted to slide the tale into the "Naturalistic" pigeon-hole, but that would be a mistake: there is no thoroughgoing sense of a malevolent God or an indifferent cosmic mover (the Bunner sisters do not share Jude Fawley's world); nor is there any systematic suggestion that dark animal forces will inevitably work their way (the Bunner sisters do not live in Carrie Meeber's world either). The management of personal motivation is almost entirely unsatisfactory. In creating her two heroines, Edith Wharton proceeded with crippling economy. I will make two women instead of one, she seems to have said, but I will make them only different enough to tell apart: one shall go into the world and one shall choose to stay at home. Why they have fixed upon their original life, why they should expand it in such a pernicious direction, why they are so entirely blind to Ramy's nature—all such questions are left open. Wharton has posed the tantalizing problem of the habit of repression, but she has not come close to resolving it.

Although there is much in the story for which we cannot give literary explanations, we can remark the extent to which this fiction reveals its author's own personal predicaments. At the beginning of the tale, the sisters are united in their agreement to live an entirely secluded life, a life of "habitually repressed emotion." This life is the one that Wharton has consistently chosen for herself, and the language that renders it comes directly out of the reports of her childhood—coldness, suffocation, hunger, thirst. Why does the author pose as ultimately "safe" this terrible picture of slow death? Perhaps because the glimpses we get of the alternatives are so terrifying. When Ann Eliza ventures even so far as Broadway or Third Avenue, she is besieged by a "tumult" that both fills her with "subdued excitement" and threatens to "engulf" her. Now the portraits of the city are not very realistic or convincing, especially as they are given in such small doses throughout the story. But the narrator's language is suggestive. It may remind us of the strange violence that Mrs. Manstey was said to have risked: moving would have been like being "flayed alive." In short, while this vocabulary is inappropriate to the fictional setting, it probably *is* appropriate to the terrible fantasies that had haunted Wharton's childhood and adolescence, to the renewed terrors that had been awakened by marriage—to the accumulation of fears that are tapped now by the process of writing fiction.

These early works are, supposedly, stories about an adult world that stands independently of the author's personal life. They are flawed because they cannot be wrenched away from that life, and thus they carry the cumbersome freight of Wharton's unresolved emotional difficulties. The desire to create a work of art has been undermined by the more primitive need to find a way of representing intolerable conflict. The control needed for literary excellence is not there; and it will continue to be absent until Edith Wharton has sufficiently resolved her problems so that her fictions may be distinguished from them.

The last of Wharton's three first efforts, "The Fullness of Life," trails an intriguing story. Like the other two, it is a direct reflection of her emotional conflicts; unlike the other two, it tells a little tale that might be related with embarrassing directness to the author's own married life.

The woman about whom the story is told is presented at the beginning of it floating resistlessly in a sea of semiconsciousness. "Like a tepid tide" it rises around her, "gliding ever higher and higher, folding in its velvety embrace her relaxed and tired body." The woman is dying; shortly, she is dead. Her first reaction is pleased astonishment, for she finds herself in a genial country landscape and concludes that "death is not the end after all." Far from being the end, death seems merely a delightful beginning, for the wandering lady is soon confronted by a benevolent presence who is identified as the Spirit of Life. " 'Have you never really known what it is to live?' " the shade inquires. " 'I have never known . . . that fullness of life which we all feel ourselves capable

of knowing; though my life has not been without scattered hints of it.' "
The woman was married, in life, to a kindly man with creaking boots
and insensitive, inartistic inclinations. The many rooms in the mansion
of her nature have been waiting for some sympathetic visitor who might
softly penetrate into even the most hidden recesses. But alas, in this
woman's life, "in the innermost room, the holy of holies, the soul sits
alone and waits for a footstep that never comes." The husband never
manages to get beyond the family sitting room. It is a plaintive song of
loneliness and partially glimpsed happiness that can never be reached.
Will the after-life be thus as well? The Spirit reassures her: " 'There is a
compensation in store for such needs as you have expressed. . . . It is
ordained . . . that every soul which seeks in vain on earth for a kindred
soul to whom it can lay bare its inmost being shall find that soul here
and be united to it for eternity.' " [17] And at the Spirit's word, her
soul's mate appears, the perfect companion to accompany her.

For a few moments of happy dialogue with the new but intimately familiar mate, the woman rests happy. But then she recollects her husband. What of him? When he dies, will he find a soul's mate too? The
Spirit of Life shakes his head solemnly. " 'No . . . for your husband
imagined that he had found his soul's mate on earth in you. . . . Some
field of activity and happiness he will doubtless find, in due measure to
his capacity for being active and happy.' " The woman contradicts him;
her husband never *will* be happy without her. He may not be able to
become her true companion, but he loves her in his own way. " 'Besides,
no one else would know how to look after him, he is so helpless. His ink-
stand would never be filled, and he would always be out of stamps and
visiting cards. . . . Why, he wouldn't even know what novels to read. I
always had to choose the kind he liked.' " What will she do, the Spirit of
Life inquires. " 'Why I mean to wait for my husband, of course. If he
had come here first *he* would have waited for me for years and years.' "
She rejects the offer that the Spirit of Life has made and settles herself to
wait for her husband. When the story ends, she is waiting for him still.
"Seated alone on the threshold, she listens for the creaking of his
boots." [18]

It is not difficult to identify the sensitive woman in the story with
Edith Wharton and the good-natured but callous husband as Teddy. As
Millicent Bell has observed, the woman's decision to bear with her hus-
band was a solution that Edith Wharton had certainly made in 1891.

"Life with the gallant and generous if unintellectual 'Teddy' was still supportable, even if it was perfectly true that he read only railway novels and sporting advertisements." [19] Nevertheless, this revelation of the deficiencies of the marriage (rather baldly opened to the public in this story) may have caused friction between the couple and almost certainly embarrassed its author. She never allowed the story to be reprinted in her lifetime.

Yet there is more in this tale that reveals the tenor of its author's life than merely the plot. Mrs. Manstey has died at the end of her story; Evelina Bunner dies (after rashly leaving her secure niche to seek happiness with a man). Now in "The Fullness of Life" we are given a seductive and sensually beckoning portrait of death—of letting go, ceasing to struggle, allowing oneself to be swallowed up by the "velvet embrace" of total passivity. Almost certainly these images of death do not relate to any specific suicidal inclination, but rather to the almost irresistible lassitude that was possessing itself of Edith Wharton at this time. Eventually, this attitude led perilously close to virtual stasis. In the conflict between adult activity (with its attendant insecurity and pain) and the engulfment of childlike passivity, how appealing the passivity must have seemed, sometimes. This story again affirms inaction and the futility and possible danger of struggling against it.

But perhaps the most revealing thing in this piece, when we think of it in connection with the later work, is Wharton's almost complete inability to represent a convincingly adult relationship between the sexes. For example, the woman's "soul mate" is really nothing more than a replica of herself, and their brief conversations sound distressingly like a parody of "Little Sir Echo." " 'Did you never feel at sunset—' 'Ah, yes; but I never heard anyone else say so. Did you?' 'Do you remember that line in the third canto of the *Inferno?*' 'Ah, that line—my favorite always. Is it possible—' 'You know the stooping "Victory" in the frieze of the "Nike Apteros" ?' 'You mean the one who is tying her sandal. Then you have noticed, too.' " [20] This is not a relationship; it is an image of total oneness, fusion, a complete (and infantile) identification. It conjures no image of passion, only a chasm of uninterrupted boredom. The relationship with the husband gives no hint of passion either, and the wife chooses to wait for him solely because he needs her to take care of him. If we were to venture an assessment of the author's own emotional growth as revealed through this tale. we would have to conclude that she was still imprisoned in the modalities of childhood dependency and that she was not yet able to trace the map of mature experience and desire.

When Edith Wharton sent "The Fullness of Life" to Burlingame in 1891, he liked it and wished to publish it; however, he wanted her to make a very few emendations, and so he returned the manuscript to her and waited. He was to wait for a long time. Wharton found herself utterly unable to work on the piece. Months passed. Burlingame jogged her from time to time, gently because he knew the fragility of writers, but persistently. Finally on August 26, 1893, she responded to one of his letters by sending the piece back virtually unchanged. "I have been ill for three or four weeks," she said, "or I should have written before to acknowledge your kind note asking me to send you 'The Fullness of Life.' I send it now, with sincere regret that it is not better suited to your purposes. I have run my pencil through one sentence on page 7 which seemed to me over-done, but I leave it entirely to your discretion." She concluded with a postscript: "Our new address is *Land's End*." [21]

The last sentence is a red flag. Great changes were taking place in Wharton's personal life, and they were often coupled with a total inability to write.

2

The years 1889–93, during which this early work was done, constituted a period of upheaval in the hitherto accepted routines of Wharton's existence. They probably marked the initial stage of that black period, twelve years at least, as Wharton was later to affirm, of lassitude, nausea, and anxiety. The crisis, which intensified into a breakdown in 1898, extended at least until 1902, when *The Valley of Decision* was published, and remnants of it were to linger for almost a decade after that. The many components of the crisis were related in complicated ways; however, the central fact was that Edith Wharton had decided to halt her retreat from life. The history before 1889 traces an accumulation of unresolved problems; yet this pattern of withdrawal was ultimately unproductive. To deny feeling, deny hope, deny even fear will leave nothing but a lingering empty shell of self; this is a pernicious means of defense, and Wharton must have determined that she was unwilling to suffer such radical reduction. Thus the impetus to withdraw began to yield to a stronger and stronger yearning to venture into life again. (The terrible ambivalence of the conflict is captured in those first three fictions.) No simple formulation will capture the complexity of the struggle: there were too many different threads. Certainly one of them traces the path by which Edith Wharton finally came to terms with Mother's domination.

Marriage in 1885 had not really liberated the daughter from her mother. Edith Wharton tells a Newport tale which nicely captures Lucretia's tenacious hold on familial *froideur*. In those days before the automobile, it was decreed that a less important person would not permit his carriage to pass that of his social superior; the custom had evolved because the carriage behind had to "take the dust" of its predecessor. "Once, several years after my marriage," Wharton recalls, "a new coachman, who did not know my mother's carriage by sight, accidentally drove me past it on the fashionable Ocean Drive at Newport. . . . I had to hasten the next morning to apologize to my mother, whose only comment was, when I explained that the coachman could not have known the offence he was committing: 'You might have told him.' " [22] Edith Wharton was almost thirty at the time, and Lucretia's manner was becoming less and less tolerable. A process of distancing began.

In 1891 Edith and Teddy purchased a new home in town; its address was 884 Park Avenue, and as R. W. B. Lewis remarks, "it was nearly as far removed from Lucretia's home on West 25th as social decency permitted." [23] It must have been the address above all that recommended the new house, for it was remarkably uncomfortable. (It was only fifteen feet across—and the Whartons had to wait to occupy it until they could acquire the house next door for their servants!) That postscript to Burlingame indicating the new address signified another gesture toward independence. Land's End, the summer home to which the Whartons retreated in 1893, was the geographically furthest point in Newport from Lucretia's home, Pencraig, whose cottage the couple had occupied before. Again, the location must have been the primary attraction, for the house itself was—as Wharton herself admits—"incurably ugly." [24] Edith Wharton was willing to pay for her gestures; Land's End cost $80,000, a veritable fortune in those days.

Relations between Lucretia and her daughter continued to cool. "At some time after the fall of 1893 (the date of Edith's last reference to her mother as being in Newport), Lucretia, now around seventy years old, had removed herself to Paris, where she was living in close proximity with both her sons." [25] The Whartons went abroad every year for several months. At first, Edith paid the obligatory visit to Mother; gradually this amenity fell into desuetude.

The most jubilant thrust of Lucretia came in Wharton's first real book, *The Decoration of Houses* (1897). Here all the suffocating implications of Mother's house are held up to the light of reason and taste, and then thrown out the widely opened window. The entire work is an appeal to simplicity, openness, and warmth—extolling a treatment of rooms that will enhance the use for which they were designed rather than one that merely shrouds them in layers of fussy ornamentation. If this description sounds like a complaint against the way young ladies were reared in Wharton's girlhood, then that is exactly as it should be. There is even a rather nasty suggestion that Father had been as unhappy with life at home as his daughter.

It is no exaggeration to say that many houses are deserted by the men of the family for lack of those simple comforts which they find at their clubs: windows unobscured by layers of muslin, a fireplace surrounded by easy-chairs and protected from draughts, well-appointed writing-tables and files of papers and magazines. Who cannot call to mind the dreary drawing-room, in small town houses the only possible point of reunion for the family, but too often, in consequence of its exquisite discomfort, of no more use as a meeting-place than the vestibule or the cellar? The windows in this kind of room are invariably supplied with two sets of muslin curtains, one hanging against the panes, the other fulfilling the supererogatory duty of hanging against the former; then come the heavy stuff curtains, so draped as to cut off the upper light of the windows by day, while it is impossible to drop them at night: curtains that have thus ceased to serve the purpose for which they exist. [26]

This graduated estrangement between Edith Wharton and her mother was a necessary step in the campaign to create a separate self; however, we must not suppose that it was an easy renunciation. Mother was undoubtedly offended (she offended easily, as the incident of the carriage suggests), and she betook herself to her sons abroad, whom she had always preferred to her daughter anyway, as soon as the first hints of Edith's new independence began to emerge. *The Decoration of Houses* seems a confident response to Lucretia's removal, but Wharton's true agitation revealed itself, as it often did at the beginning of her career, in a flurry of concern over the production of the book.

The work had been completed in a fever of activity: some manuscript and photographs had been left with Scribner's in the summer of 1897; Wharton signed a contract in July, and the book was delivered in more or less completed form in September. Writing the text was not enough for Wharton, however. "She began showering Brownell with suggestions about its manufacture. She regularly apologized for interfering, hoped she was not being a bore, begged to be forgiven for her inexperience and ignorance; and proceeded to some new and insistent proposal. She argued about the binding and the lettering on the front cover, the design and the exact style of print for the title page, the number and size of the illustrations." [27] Sometimes she wrote and posted several letters a day. She complained that Scribner's had failed to send her this or that photograph, and then she found that she had mislaid it herself. The correspondence between the author and her publishers at this period is a veritable pyramid of anxiety. The book came out in December 1897, and Wharton wrote Burlingame from Land's End that she had received three copies of it. She agreed to do some translating for Scribner's. Then silence.

On February 23, 1898, she wrote to Burlingame: "I have been really ill and my matière grise is so soft and sloppy that I can't do much work, but I can surely manage the two de Annicis things by March. As to the third story—shall I do it if I have time, or must I decide at once?—If the latter, I had better return it, as I am so new at translating that I don't know how long a time I shall have to allow." [28] To anyone who has read those querulous, insistent letters of the July–December 1897 period, this note seems almost to have been written by a different person. Perhaps the work had been too intense, perhaps the various conflicts too wrenching; in any case, in the wake of this attack on Mother, Edith Wharton had subsided into one of the nervous collapses that characterized this stage of her life. She is still "taking the dust"—even though Mother has long since moved to Paris.

Later in 1898, Lucretia would be indirectly involved in another protracted engagement over a book, this time *The Greater Inclination*. For years Wharton had been trying to pull together a collection of short stories. In the spring of 1898 she completed an excellent short story,

"The Pelican," and by July she was finally on the way to completing the work for the book. Suddenly there was trouble with Scribner's: she and her editors discovered that they disagreed as to when the book should appear. Wharton was eager to have it out as soon as possible; Burlingame and Brownell wanted to wait until at least two more of the stories in it had appeared in *Scribner's Magazine*. The journal's need to cover the Spanish-American War, which had erupted that summer, delayed the publication of the stories, and hence of the book. By autumn Wharton had grown frantic. The tone of the correspondence was almost a repeat performance of the frenzy that had preceded *The Decoration of Houses*. Wharton wrote to both men, sometimes to both on the same day, urging that her book come out immediately. In September she explained to Burlingame: "My reason for pressing the publication of the book is that my mother, who lives in Paris, has been ill lately, and that there is a strong probability of my having to go abroad in December or January for an indefinite length of time.—I do want to see the book through before going." [29] In October of 1898, a major collapse. "Since I last wrote to you I have been seriously ill," she explained from Land's End, "and we have been obliged to give up our plan of going abroad." [30]

There are many reasons for the nervous crisis of this period, and we shall draw in more threads as we go along. However, the guilt Wharton felt in fighting free of Lucretia, the bad feelings on both sides, cannot easily be dismissed. It was a large sweep of the pendulum to go from the role of excessively pious daughter, who had lived the letter of Mother's law, to the responsibilities of an even relatively self-sufficient adult woman. And Lucretia did not take her daughter's declarations of independence with any sort of good will.

On June 28, 1901, Lucretia died. But she would have one last, long battle with her daughter. Her will divided her money as, perhaps, her affections had been divided: "Freddy received outright the sum of $95,000. . . . Harry was left $50,000. The rest of the estate was divided into three equal shares. One of these was bequeathed outright to Freddy and another to Harry. The third share was left . . . [in trust] for Edith Wharton." [31] The trust was arranged so sloppily that there was no guarantee of regular payments, and Edith Wharton had to go abroad that summer to rearrange things on a more businesslike basis. Characteristically, she got violently sick to her stomach on the boat trip over and was convinced that she had contracted ptomaine poisoning from the food. "I am so easily unhinged by anything of the kind that I am only just beginning to regain my strength," she wrote to Sara Norton in August.[32]

The bitterness of this breach would have upset anyone. Lucretia had never been above personal cruelty, and she was apparently not above the most niggardly retaliation either. Merely the objective problem of placing herself at a physical remove from Mother must have caused no end of anxiety for Wharton. Yet much of Lucretia's influence could not be disposed of by a distance of any miles. Even with Mother safely in Paris, even with Mother eventually dead, Edith Wharton had to contend with the part of herself that carried Mother's imprint. This conflict was intensely acute in the matter of becoming a writer.

Wharton could not have ventured into life again without finding some adult role that drew upon the genuine accumulation of strengths in her personality. The role of writer did, and it pulled these strengths together in a way that gave shape to her earlier life and substance to her adulthood: it utilized her talent for absorbing the world with cameralike precision and grew upon the foundation of her trust in words. It was the natural extension of making up and writing down. Wharton's scrutiny of herself was as relentless and as penetrating as her examination of the world around her, and many years later she was to acknowledge the connection between her choosing a vocation and the coalescing of her sense of self. "I had as yet no real personality of my own [in the early 1890's], and was not to acquire one till my first volume of short stories, [*The Greater Inclination*], was published—and that was not until 1899. . . . *I* had written short stories that were thought worthy of preservation! Was it the same insignificant *I* that I had always known? Anyone walking along the streets might go into any bookshop, and say: 'Please give me Edith Wharton's book,' and the clerk, without bursting into incredulous laughter, would produce it, and be paid for it, and the purchaser would walk home with it and read it, and talk of it, and pass it on to other people to read! The whole business seemed too unreal to be anything but a practical joke played on me by some occult humourist; and my friends could not have been more astonished and incredulous than I was. I opened the first notices of the book with trembling hands and a suffocated heart. What I had done was actually thought important enough to be not only printed but reviewed! With a sense of mingled guilt and self-satisfaction I glanced at one article after another." [33] The "mingled guilt and self-satisfaction" of 1899 represented the last remains of a disabling conflict over her writing career; and this conflict was yet another thread in the complex struggle of Wharton's twelve-year ordeal. We can see the beginning of her anguish in this regard if we retreat to the period of the first three fictions.

"Mrs. Manstey's View" had been accepted for publication in 1890; "Bunner Sisters" was written (but not published) in 1892; even before that time, Burlingame had returned "The Fullness of Life" for minor revisions and had not received them—did not receive them in any form until August of 1893, when Wharton confessed to having been "ill for three or four weeks." Her nervous illness and her great delay in addressing the minor problems of revision both suggest how deeply ambivalent Wharton was about the whole business of writing.

In the fall of 1893, the French novelist Paul Bourget came with his wife to Newport, and the couple became acquainted with Edith Wharton—an acquaintance that was to ripen into one of Wharton's deepest and longest friendships. This contact with the world of literature must have encouraged Wharton to continue her own writing. She had two more stories for Burlingame by late autumn 1893: "That Good May Come" and "The Lamp of Psyche." Both were related to certain of her past and present concerns, but they stand at a significantly more distinct remove than those first three tales; within a limited context, she was beginning to exercise real control over the fictive process.

Indeed, "The Lamp of Psyche" remains one of Wharton's better short stories, and though Burlingame was cautious in his praise of it, he must have felt the surge in her literary power. At any rate, on November 24, 1893, when he accepted "The Lamp of Psyche" for publication, he made the suggestion that Wharton do a collection of short stories for Scribner's. For more than five years, the project (ultimately completed in 1899 as *The Greater Inclination*) hung unfinished. Wharton wanted very much to become a professional writer; Bourget's visit had undoubtedly fueled that desire, but she could not accept the role. Thus, although she wrote Burlingame that she was gratified by his offer, she did not bring the project to an immediate conclusion.

In early 1894, Edith Wharton sent Burlingame a very slender tale which he rejected rather vigorously. She was humiliated, thrown into a state of dreadful uncertainty about herself. On March 26, she wrote a pathetic letter: "I should like to bring out the book without adding many more stories, for I seem to have fallen into a period of groping, and perhaps, after publishing the volume, I might see better what direction I ought to take and acquire more assurance (the quality I feel I most lack). You were kind enough to give me so much encouragement when I saw you, and I feel myself so much complimented by the Messers Scribner's request that I should publish a volume of stories, that I am very ambitious to do better, and perhaps I could get a better view of what I have done and ought to do after the stories have been published. I have lost confidence in myself at present." [34] This new self was very tender; criticism from any source sent great waves of sympathetic vibration shattering through Wharton's memory, and the new self retreated. In July 1894 Wharton wrote again to assure Burlingame that she wanted to do the collection; she even suggested that she could have it ready in six months. Thereafter, she lapsed into complete silence. The silence continued for more than sixteen months.

When she returned to the correspondence again, on December 14, 1895, Wharton began with the usual apology: "Since I last wrote you over a year ago I have been very ill, and I am not yet allowed to do any real work." [35] Another nervous collapse—and a long one. The apologetic letter accompanied a strange story entitled "The Valley of Childish Things, and Other Emblems"; it is the most bizarre piece that Wharton ever published, and its disjointed ramblings give stunning insight into some of the concerns that were producing her deep disturbance. The tale is a collection of short parables (only one is longer than a page); they swirl about the various problems that beset Wharton's adult life and haunted her from childhood, and several of them echo themes that we have encountered before in her fiction. The sixth parable, for instance (in its entirety): "A soul once cowered in gray waste, and a mighty shape came by. Then the soul cried out for help, saying, 'Shall I be left to perish alone in this desert of Unsatisfied Desires?' 'But you are mistaken,' the shape replied; 'this is the land of Gratified Longings. And, moreover, you are not alone, for the country is full of people; but whoever tarries here grows blind.' " [36] The first of these parables—by far the longest and the one that gives the collection its name—is most revealing of the particular crisis Wharton was trying to master.

The tale begins: "Once upon a time a number of children lived together in the Valley of Childish Things, playing all manner of delightful games, and studying the same lesson books. But one day a little girl, one of their number, decided that it was time to see something of the world about which the lesson books had taught her; and as none of the other children cared to leave their games, she set out alone to climb the pass which led out of the valley. It was a hard climb, but at length she reached a cold, bleak tableland beyond the mountains. Here she saw cities and men, and learned many useful arts, and in so doing grew to be a woman. But the tableland was bleak and cold, and when she had served her apprenticeship she decided to return to her old companions in the Valley of Childish Things." On the long and difficult way back the little girl, who has grown into womanhood, encounters a man, one of her former playmates who, like herself, has chosen to explore the world outside. He had been a rather dull little boy, "but as she listened to his plans for building bridges and draining swamps, and cutting roads through the jungle, she thought to herself, 'Since he has grown into such a fine fellow, what splendid men and women my other playmates must have become!' But what was her surprise to find, on reaching the valley, that her former companions, instead of growing into men and women, had all remained little children." They are all playing at the same games that had occupied them when she left. At first they seem glad to have her back, but soon she sees that her presence interferes with their games. She turns to her fellow traveler, who is the only other grown-up in the valley, but he is busily playing with a little girl, building bridges for her in the sand. The story concludes with a numbing encounter. "When she who had grown to be a woman laid her hand on the man's shoulder, and asked him if he did not want to work again with her building bridges, draining swamps, and cutting roads through the jungle, he replied that at that particular moment he was too busy. And as she turned away, he added in the kindest possible way, 'Really, my dear, you ought to have taken better care of your complexion.' " [37]

The story is rich in implication, and we can glance only at the central suggestion. A man has many options. If he chooses to leave the Valley (and consciously at least, Wharton intended the Valley to stand for the superficial society of monied New York), he may pursue any number of useful skills, building bridges and roads, for instance. A woman has different alternatives and, as the principal character's struggle suggests, more difficult ones. If she manages to follow the hard pathway out of the Valley of Childish Things, the world is liable to judge her harshly, assuming that she should have remained forever in infantile safety rather than trying to seek the opportunities that are available in the outside world to men. Take care of your complexion, the fellow suggests; for Wharton these words were an injunction to smother her emerging identity in veiling layers of protective gauze.

Burlingame rejected "The Valley of Childish Things"; he admitted rather frankly that he couldn't understand it. Another rejection. Wharton received few enough, but her dreadful insecurity about the validity of this new role and her readiness always to hear simple criticism as a scornful derision of her efforts (for what else had adolescence taught her?) combined to render her mute. She did not write Burlingame for another ten months, and we must presume that these were ten months more of "illness." They were not, however, months of total inactivity. On December 29, 1896, Wharton wrote anxiously to know whether Burlingame had received her most recent story, "The Twilight of the God," which he had not acknowledged. He had indeed received it, but he didn't much like it. In fact, it had to be thoroughly reworked before it eventually saw publication in *The Greater Inclination*. Yet another rejection. Wharton was trying resolutely to move forward, despite the internal resistance, but this cluster of rejections made her pause definitively. There were no more fictions for a while. She published a few poems in the first half of 1897, but by July she was completely occupied in working on a project of quite a different sort, *The Decoration of Houses*.

This book served several purposes. It was, as we have seen, a nicely calculated slap at Mother; it was also an appropriately "feminine" book, dealing as it did with domestic arrangements, and as such it was probably an easier book for this author, who still carried strong traces of the "nice" young matron, to accept as a valid expression of self. Certainly it was a pivotal point in Edith Wharton's progress, a real book and a significant rejection of Lucretia: two major problems in her adult life converged and were dealt with together—but not without consequences. As we have seen, the production of the volume was attended by a deluge of anxious letters, and its publication was followed by another of those periods of "illness."

Nevertheless, *The Decoration of Houses* was very well received, astoundingly so for a book with such a limited subject. If Wharton found negative comment devastating, she always found praise exhilarating: she consumed it in great, triumphant draughts and gleefully called her favorable reviews to the attention of her editors. This major success gave sustenance to the developing author, and in the spring of 1898 Wharton rallied from the latest spell of debilitation to write several additional short stories: "The Muse's Tragedy," "Souls Belated," "The Coward," "The House of the Dead Hand," and "A Cup of Cold Water." Although she is at the top of her form only in the second of these—which is one of her best short stories—the flurry of activity suggested that the long-awaited volume of stories might follow quickly upon the heels of *The Decoration of Houses.* However, as Lewis observes in the biography, "this first genuinely creative period . . . soon unsettled her." As the emerging self asserted itself with new strength, the "illness" grew more acute. In his comments on the early stages of her illness, Lewis ventures: "One can only employ the sometimes casually misused phrase 'severe identity crisis' to describe the terrible and long drawnout period Edith Wharton was passing through: a period of paralysing melancholy, extreme exhaustion, constant fits of nausea, and no capacity whatever to make choices and decisions. Those more knowing in these matters tell us that such a condition may itself be a decision of sorts—a deliberate, if unconscious, putting off of commitment." [38] Our own tracing of the gradual development of "Edith Wharton: The Author" suggests how valid Lewis's speculations are. Part of Edith Wharton was eager to write and ready for commitment to this new, vigorous, healthy self; part of her was still morbidly afraid. Lucretia was ill at the time, and the mother's illness (coming in conjunction with the daughter's long-delayed rebellion against her) must have contributed to the conflict. The dilemma hung unresolved, and Wharton lapsed into psychological paralysis. By default, the truculent part of herself had temporarily gained ascendency.

In August 1898 (during the protracted argument with Scribner's), she began a severe spell of "illness"; this time she got worse and worse, and by October it had become clear that she was suffering a major breakdown. S. Weir Mitchell, a prominent Philadelphia neurologist, had gained considerable reputation for his successful treatment of women who had the psychological symptoms that Wharton displayed. Therefore, in the depths of this crisis, it was decided that she should take the unusual step of journeying to Philadelphia to put herself under his care. In mid-October she did so. It was not thought necessary to hospitalize her, and so she stayed at the Stanton Hotel throughout her treatment and was supervised by one of Weir Mitchell's associates, a Dr. McClellan. The prescribed therapy demanded that patients be completely separated from all elements of their usual lives. Thus, although Wharton saw doctors and nurses who were accustomed to providing psychological support, she was not allowed to have one single visitor from October 1898 through January 1899 (she was allowed letters—and both Teddy and Walter Berry wrote almost daily).

But why *now* had she suddenly grown so much worse? If anything, we might have expected her first period of successful writing to have lifted her up—not cast her down. To answer this question, we must follow yet another twisted thread of the struggle—this one pursuing Wharton's desperate attempts to deal with a flooding into consciousness of hitherto-repressed infantile feelings.

Clinging to Lucretia had served several purposes: one, perhaps the major one, was keeping the beasts away. So long as the girl retained an inappropriately dependent relationship with Mother, the feelings that she could not manage and the conflicts that she could not handle were kept out of mind. When her excessive filial reverence ceased, the beasts returned, and Edith Wharton had to deal with the residue of her unresolved crises: that ravenous totality of longing for comfort and gratification, eventually for sexual gratification; the unutterable rage and sense of cosmic destruction that accompanied her accumulation of disillusionments; and finally, an intolerable fear for her own safety in the face of possible retaliation for all her uncivilized impulses. Writing and her vocation as author were to prove indispensable in the movement away from this stalemate of childhood and adolescence. However, the initial efforts at writing only made things worse: writing, too, summoned the beasts to consciousness.

In allowing her imagination to relax and wander freely in search of a "subject," Edith Wharton necessarily lessened the vigilance of her severely monitoring conscious mind. Her choices of subject very often reflected her sense of herself and her own problems (certainly this is not unusual in any writer of fiction); however, she had so little control over the passions that were attached to these problems that the first fictions did not even stand clearly separated from them. We have seen the intrusions. Violent imagery that is inappropriate to the story and plots that may be adequately explained only by a reversion to the author's personal history. We have alluded to all of these failures as primitive efforts at a representation of self, and so they were. But they were *revelations* of self as well—expressions, in however muted and indirect a way, of those hitherto-repressed emotions and conflicts. Insofar as writing gave Wharton access to these elements in her personality, it forced them to her conscious attention. All of the lapses into severe lassitude and nausea were successful methods of rendering herself unable to write; and when she was unable to write, she could elude the unwelcome contact with her hidden self that writing so often provided.

Thus the vocation of writing carried more than one implication for Edith Wharton. It was a career that had been forbidden in her adolescence, and this fact made commitment to it difficult. In terms of her emotional history, it had even more serious consequences. Becoming a writer would entail a relinquishing of the habit of denial and retreat. It demanded some permanent capacity to confront her inner self. If we understand this fact, we can understand why her symptoms became more and more severe only after she had begun to write—and why they became most acute at the point when a commitment to the vocation of writing seemed just at hand. Writing offered undeniable dangers.

The irony was, of course, that writing offered great strengths as well. The adult identity of author provided continuity and coherence for Wharton's life. However, the greatest potential strength of writing lay close to its greatest danger. The very fact that writing gave Wharton access to hidden elements in her nature meant that she would be able to use the process of writing as a means of coming to terms with these parts of her character.

The psychiatrist and critic Ernst Kris has commented upon this constructive component in the process of artistic creativity: he calls it "regression in the service of ego." Kris notes that artists must have an ability to summon up emotions from the repressed past life in order genuinely to create, and he argues that the artist's regression serves a valuable function in his life. "The regression in the case of aesthetic creation—in contrast to . . . other cases—is purposive and controlled. The inspired creativity of the artist is as far from automatic writing under hypnosis as from the machines recently marketed for 'composing' popular songs. The process involves a continual interplay between creation and criticism, manifested in the painter's alternation of working on the canvas and stepping back to observe the effect. We may speak here of a shift in psychic level, consisting in the fluctuation of functional regression and control. When regression goes too far, the symbols become private, perhaps unintelligible even to the reflective self." [39] At the beginning of her writing career, Wharton's regression went too far; it outstripped her control. Kris might say that this was evidence of her incipient illness; we would say that it was a sign that she had not yet achieved mastery over her fiction. Both views would be correct.

The notion of "purposive" regression (as Kris uses it) can refer to two purposes that operate together. On one hand there is the artistic intention to create a work of aesthetic unity; on the other hand there is the artist's personal desire to deal with the emotions that have been raised from the unconscious and, if possible, to resolve the problems inherent in them. Both of these purposes might be identified with any given artistic endeavor; they do not exclude each other. The principal *psychological* strength inherent in the process of writing, however, derives from its capacity to be employed by the artist as a mechanism for resolving emotional conflict. "Aesthetic creation," Kris maintains, "may be looked on as a type of problem-solving behavior." [40]

If Wharton could tolerate the regressive impulse of the creative act, if she could control this movement and manipulate the components of her dilemmas within the artistic frame, then she might gain a method for coming to terms with at least some of them.

Kris is careful to define his notion of "problem-solving" very precisely. If we compare Kris's statements with Wharton's own mature statements about her creative activity, they bear an astonishing resemblance. Kris says:

Schematically speaking we may view the process of artistic creation as composed of two phases which may be sharply demarcated from each other, may merge into each other, may follow each other in rapid or slow succession, or may be interwoven with each other in various ways. In designating them as inspiration and elaboration, we refer to extreme conditions: One type is characterized by the feeling of being driven, the experience of rapture, and the conviction that an outside agent acts through the creator; in the other type, the experience of purposeful organization, and the intent to solve a problem predominate. The first has many features in common with regressive processes: Impulses and drives, otherwise hidden, emerge. The subjective experience is that of a flow of thought and images driving toward expression. The second has many features in common with what characterizes "work"—dedication and concentration. We are aware of the fact that not all artistic creation derives from inspiration—neither all kinds nor one kind wholly. [41]

Wharton says:

> The analysis of the story-telling process may be divided into two parts: that
> which concerns the technique of fiction (in the widest sense), and that which
> tries to look into what, for want of a simpler term, one must call by the old
> bardic name of inspiration. . . . I do not think I can get any nearer than this
> to the sources of my story-telling; I can only say that the process, though it
> takes place in some secret region on the sheer edge of consciousness, is
> always illuminated by the full light of my critical attention.[42]

Both see that artistic creation entails two steps—inspiration (or regression) and work (manipulating the "given" and resolving the artistic and
psychological problems inherent in it). If Wharton was to embrace the
vocation of writer, she had to find a way of accepting both components
of the process.

Several forces were at work during her period of confinement that
made acceptance easier. One was Weir Mitchell's method of treatment.
Broadly defined, it consisted in supportive encouragement to regress
within a controlled atmosphere that was completely distinguished from
the patient's everyday life. Thus total bed rest was required (although
the patient was in no way treated like an invalid), and muscle tone was
maintained through skillful and liberal massage. Weir Mitchell termed it
"exercise without exertion." At the same time, Wharton was encouraged
to eat nourishing and appetizing food, and she gained back most of the
weight she had lost. Throughout this period she encountered cheerful,
accepting, understanding people. In short, she was encouraged to act like
a baby, and even more important, everything in her environment assured her that it was *safe and acceptable to do so*. The intensity of her infantile longing could never be dispelled, but treatment such as this did a
good deal to remove its fearsomeness. The message that inhered in this
therapy—and that must have remained with Edith Wharton for the rest
of her days—was that controlled regression would not harm her.

As she began to improve, she was allowed to begin writing again. At
this point Walter Berry's support proved invaluable. He was the first real
judge of her work—and always thereafter the most important and reliable critic. Edith Wharton respected his intelligence and was willing to
trust not only his suggestions for improvement but his admiration as
well. That admiration—a continuing and unstinting assurance that she
was a good novelist, that all good writers (even George Eliot, whom they

both vastly admired) had suffered spells of great difficulty—gave necessary support now to the part of her that yearned to begin a genuine career.

Slowly, this combination of forces prevailed, and Edith Wharton returned from the darkest spell of "illness" that she was ever to suffer. By December 1898, she was writing to Burlingame about the book again, and in February she was even well enough to complain about a lack of advertising.

It is difficult to capture the extremes of her moods throughout this year of anguish. Perhaps Wharton's own notations give us the best insight. Several years earlier she had begun to keep a Commonplace Book, and she copied into it quotations from her reading that seemed particularly moving. One day in 1898 she inscribed the following lines from Whitman's "Song of Myself":

> I think I could turn and live with animals, they are so placid
>   and self-contained,
> I stand and look at them long and long.
>
> They do not sweat and whine about their condition,
> They do not lie awake in the dark and weep for their sins,
> They do not make me sick discussing their duty to God,
> Not one is dissatisfied, not one is demented with the mania
>   of owning things,
> Not one kneels to another, not to his kind that lived
>   thousands of years ago,
> Not one is respectable or unhappy over the whole earth.

Later in the same year, she returned to the Commonplace Book in a different frame of mind and entered Whitman's "Life" in its entirety:

> Ever the undiscouraged, resolute, struggling soul of man;
> (Have former armies failed? then we send fresh armies
>   —and fresh again);
> Ever the grappled mystery of all earth's ages old or new;
> Ever the eager eyes, hurrahs, the welcome-clapping hands,
>   the loud applause;
> Ever the soul dissatisfied, curious, unconvinced at last;
> Struggling today the same—battling the same.[43]

The first quotation captures her need to retreat, and in this mood she withdrew for a while from all the conflicts of present life and past experience. Yet, on the whole, the second quotation is more in keeping with the resolution of will that characterized her. She completed this long year finally prepared for the difficulties that would follow. She armed herself well, determined to confront life and come to terms with it. Her tools would be words—fictions. She had begun her apprenticeship as a writer in earnest.

3

Wharton emerged from her illness with a quality of energy that was to remain her best ally against a serious return of the malady. *The Greater Inclination* appeared in March 1899, and almost immediately began to receive notices that were enthusiastic enough to satisfy even the most uncertain author. Several praised the special "feminine delicacy" of the author's mind, and some even compared Wharton's work with that of Henry James (a comparison that was flattering at first but which became intolerably vexing to her after a few years). In the summer of 1899, Edith and Teddy Wharton met the Bourgets in Italy, and Edith Wharton began to collect background information for an historical novel dealing with the Italian eighteenth century.

She was not yet free from setbacks: her periods of work tended to be interrupted by lapses into nervous exhaustion; these were often aggravated by any especially long period of time that she had to spend with Teddy. Her work on the Italian novel was broken by several long spells during which she had to turn her attention to some other work of lesser dimensions. Thus, although we can see the clear beginnings of *The Valley of Decision* in that summer trip of 1899, Wharton did not manage to finish it until early in 1902. In the meanwhile she published two other rather slender works: a novella, *The Touchstone* (spring 1900), and a second book of short stories, *Crucial Instances* (spring 1901). Both received favorable notices (although the second book of short stories was generally conceded to be inferior to the first), and these good reviews helped Wharton finally to overcome the uncertainty that had hampered her determination to embark upon a major work. Different as it is in many ways from the rest of her fiction, we must consider *The Valley of Decision* as her first important novel.

Like the earliest short stories, this first long work seems at an irreconcilable distance from Edith Wharton. Yet the differentiating marks serve principally to obscure.[44] Wharton has not divested her work of the personal component (if Kris is to be believed, no good artist can); however, she has found a way to refashion the personal so that it can stand entirely separate from her. The problems that inform *The Valley of Decision* exhibit a direct relationship to Wharton's life, and the language here as elsewhere bears her characteristic stamp. Nevertheless, the work has independent life: it is a true fiction.

Wharton achieves this differentiation by assuming a creative attitude that might be termed responsive or "antiphonal." In the later work, her antiphonal cadence was put to vigorous, flexible usage (perhaps *The Age of Innocence* best displays the dazzling possibilities of such a method). However, now, at the beginning, antiphony serves principally as a mechanism for placing her fictional world in a suitable, larger context— definitively distinct from self.

Wharton has been harried, and dismissed, by critics determined to see her as a lesser "imitator" of James (here, Percy Lubbock surely takes the lead).[45] In fact, Wharton never intended to perpetuate the Jamesian sensibility: she openly disavowed a debt to "le maître" and found herself genuinely hard put to admire much that James wrote after 1889. Nevertheless, Wharton *was* acutely conscious of her work as part of a literary tradition. She rarely thought of her novels as standing alone, and the isolated cry of creativity was alien to her nature. Hence, she wrote novels that answered other novels, or she designed novels that exposed one or another literary practice, or she selected a specific tradition (the *bildungsroman* or the chronicle novel) and reworked its conventions so that her own work became a comment on it. She rarely imitated: she often responded and corrected; and this habit of response begins with special significance in her initial novel.

At the back of the Commonplace Book, Wharton made three lists of her favorite books—one in 1898, one in 1902, and one in 1909. The lists are by no means dominated by novels, but four novels appear on each list: *Harry Richmond*, *The Egoist*, *Madame Bovary*, and *The Charterhouse of Parma*. It was the last of these toward which she chose to direct her own first novel. We might wonder at the selection: *Madame Bovary* seems relevant to Wharton's concerns, while Stendhal's work is at a discernible remove from everything that was familiar to her adult life—so much that she was obliged, literally, to do extensive research on the historical period in which it takes place.[46]

But the paths of creativity are devious: actually, Wharton satisfied several different needs in this choice of subject. First and most pressing, she decisively wrenched the fictional world outside of self—not merely by selecting subject matter that was foreign to her own life ("Mrs. Manstey's View" had done as much), but by responding to an already existing fictional construct. Wharton does not *imitate* Stendhal, does not adopt his vocabulary, his method of plot construction, the particularities of his narrative interest; rather she addresses herself to the problems of his fictional world as he has posed them. Thus she establishes the distance and control that are necessary for the manufacture of a genuine verbal artifact.

However, merely the assurance of a distinction between self and fictional world is insufficient for novel writing. Although good fiction must be more than a primitive representation of self, it must, paradoxically, treat the deepest articulations of self. As Wharton herself attested, her subject matter would always have to come from "some secret region on the sheer edge of consciousness": the very first creative step would always necessarily entail controlled regression, a plunging into self. The world Stendhal had made in *The Charterhouse of Parma* served Wharton adequately only because it spoke to this second need as well. The crucial point of contact lay in Stendhal's preoccupation with the problems of repression and self-assertion, for these were dilemmas that worried Wharton exceedingly in 1902.

The two novels pivot upon the Napoleonic era. For Stendhal, the years of empire measure France's moment of greatness; and "the cult of Napoleon, above all, is the touchstone whereby we can tell his heroes and heroines from the ordinary people." [47] Stendhal's work celebrates the wonder of man's capacities and excoriates those institutions that would limit his freedom. *The Valley of Decision* is designed to expose the terrible dangers of such a view.

The differences between the two novelists may be seen at once in their notions of characterizing the hero. The hero of *The Charterhouse of Parma* is a public man whose heritage is bound to the historical moment; the accident of Fabrizio's parentage is at one with the pulsing influence that Napoleonic France exerted intermittently over its Italian neighbor (for all the novel tells us, Stendhal's hero might have had no childhood, for we never hear of it). Wharton, too, saw the individual experience as necessarily tied to communal interests; she always would. It is, perhaps, the most consistent assertion of her fictions. Nevertheless, when she seeks to explore man's fate—for Odo, the future Duke of Pianura, is a kind of Everyman, and this novel is fundamentally preoccupied with the existential dilemma—she focuses on the *origins* of adulthood.

A scant three years after the most critical phase of her illness, just embarking on that long recovery from the laceration of her past, Edith Wharton began this first major fiction—at the significant beginning, with a lonely child, conscious of nothing so much as of pain. "It was very still in the small neglected chapel. . . . A ray of sunshine . . . brought out the vision of a pale haloed head floating aginst the dusky background. . . . The face was that of the saint of Assisi—a sunken ravaged countenance, lit with an ecstacy of suffering that seemed not so much to reflect the anguish of the Christ at whose feet the saint knelt as the mute pain of all poor downtrodden folk on earth." [48] What does the boy Odo know? He knows that he has "suffered in a dumb animal way" (I, 7), that he is "cold and hungry and half afraid" (I, 8); and his commitment to the cause of ameliorating man's lot is affirmed here in Wharton's initial placement of him.

This very long and opulent historical novel appears at first to accord with the vision of history that Stendhal had championed. The feudalism of pre-Napoleonic Italy intrudes upon the boy as a system of organized brutality "which had long outlived its purpose" (I, 56); the Church, instead of being the healer of men's wounds, seems a merciless, inexorable tyrant. Balanced against these is the force of enlightenment, rationality. Endow men with the freedom to express their natures; that way lies temporal salvation—such is Odo's creed when at last he ascends the throne of Pianura to begin his reign. Tragically, he learns that his subjects do not want to be free, that they cannot comprehend freedom when it is thrust upon them, that they will use their liberty to rise up and depose this man who would force them to be free. Thus does Odo's individual adventure fail.

Odo's experience is to be reaffirmed on a gargantuan scale in the French experiment; there, in the name of "freedom," restraints and "tyrannies" have been wrenched asunder. And again, the consequences of freedom are woeful. "All the repressed passions which civilization had sought, however imperfectly, to curb, stalked abroad destructive as flood and fire" (II, 299). The age of revolution yields in the terrible course of time to the age of Napoleon. Wharton's novel concludes with it (as *The Charterhouse of Parma* had begun with it), and the rash hopes of her hero are finally tossed upon the balance of this great undertaking—only to fall into miserable disillusion. "France was become a very Babel of tongues. The old malady had swept over the world like a pestilence. . . . The new year rose in blood and mounted to a bloodier noon. All the old defences were falling. Religion, monarchy, law, were sucked down into the whirlpool of liberated passions. Across that sanguinary scene passed, like a mocking ghost, the philosopher's vision of the perfectibility of man. Man was free at last—freer than his would-be liberators had ever dreamed of making him—and he used his freedom like a beast" (II, 300, 303).

Several critics have drawn a comparison between elements in this first novel and the circumstances of Edith Wharton's life. Blake Nevius observes that the social tensions of eighteenth-century Italy were not unlike those of late-nineteenth-century New York. "To one for whom the past was so much a part of the present, the resemblances between [the two societies] would have been inescapable. . . . The reader who finds a double significance in the background events of what otherwise might pass as an innocent, if unusually solemn historical novel may be teased by another question. Was it simply by accident that during the heyday of progressivism in this country Mrs. Wharton chose to write a novel so contrary in spirit to that vast movement of philanthropy and reform . . . a novel so devoid of optimism and so skeptical of panaceas?" [49] Nevius's remarks are, perhaps, insufficient as a commentary upon Wharton's "personal" involvement with her historical subject; however, they hit upon an important truth.

The earliest fictions had failed insofar as they were no more than rather simple articulations of "self": they gave expression to passions that had not been dealt with in the author's conscious life, and they groped toward an attempt to "place" the author's emotional dilemma. Their true subject was Edith Wharton; they were "about" the author's conflicts. Now *The Valley of Decision* may reflect the dilemmas of its creator (the impetus to write may have begun in some outcropping of unacknowledged feeling), but it is in no way *about* its author. The true "subject" of this novel is the conflict between progressivism and traditionalism as it is mirrored in both the larger movement of history and the smaller world of an individual life. Aided, undoubtedly, by her referential relationship to the grid of Stendhal's work, Wharton has moved from mere "inspiration" to well-articulated fiction.

That is not to say, of course, that her quandary is absent from this novel. In some sense, she has begun her career as a writer at the uttermost depths of her own character—with a neglected, hungry, shivering child. Who cannot hear the echoes of her infancy in Odo's loneliness, in his passionate, intuitive sympathy for animals? Animals: indeed, they prowl throughout the novel. The human element about which Wharton wished to write—that sentient, longing, raging, irrational, inarticulate core of humanity—is consistently represented by a series of allusions to animals that give thematic and emotional unity to the fiction. Odo's primary misery is endured in a "a dumb animal way"; his ideal of rational government is founded on the hope that "the people will not always be deaf and dumb. . . . Some day they will speak" (II, 262). The failure of his hopes comes from the inescapable fact (as Wharton sees it now) that mankind's deepest and most primitive needs cannot be uttered, can never be entirely subjected to the discipline of rational moderation. Ultimately, this certainty is figured forth in the explosion of the Napoleonic era when man uses his freedoms "like a beast."

We have seen that the irrational component of man's nature—the element that he shares with all other animals—was the last and first fear of Wharton's own life. Now her concern over man's ability to articulate his needs and to satisfy them becomes a central problem of the first major fiction. It was a logical, perhaps a necessary, place to begin.

Triumphantly, this problem (so individual in its origins) takes palpably public shape in the fiction. In the almost-fiction of "Mrs. Manstey's View" we catch glimpses of an author worrying over the dangers of venturing beyond the drastic reductions of her own constricted life; in this genuine, fully formed novel, we are enjoined to consider the general question of man's nature. The language of the novel may reiterate the themes of Edith Wharton's life in images of hunger and isolation and cold and suffocation; nevertheless, we can accept such language here as an appropriate vocabulary to describe the forces at work within a coherent, consistently motivated fictional world. *The Valley of Decision* may not rise to the level of Stendhal's work, but it was the product of a significantly accomplished artist. Charles Eliot Norton read it and liked it, and so did Vernon Lee. Henry James, who had but slight acquaintance with

Wharton in early 1902, wrote an ornately eulogistic letter: "In the presence of a book so accomplished, pondered, saturated, so exquisitely studied, and so brilliant and interesting from a literary point of view, I feel that just now heartily to congratulate you covers plenty of ground." [50]

Wharton has finally succeeded, as a novelist must, in creating independent fictional worlds and presiding over them as demiurge. Yet even in this (appropriate) relationship, the aspirations and limitations of the creator inform the artifact. A critic who was thoroughly familiar with Wharton's development as an artist could identify *The Valley of Decision* as an early work—not because it betrays clumsiness or inexperience (as the first short stories did), but because its problems are resolved so forcibly in the direction of submission and such solutions were characteristic of Wharton's initial fictions.

By 1902 the self that had posited the rule that it was forbidden even to *think* things that could not be said aloud without offense—the self that had imposed first the scruples of "truth-telling" and finally a profundity of silence—was beginning to lose ascendency. After all, Edith Wharton had begun to write in earnest. Nonetheless, the powerful influence of that self could still be felt; passions still loomed as dangerous, even potentially annihilating. Thus when Wharton employs the medium of her first novel to examine the implications of the freedom to express passion, this personal conviction inevitably assumes cosmic dimensions. Odo's world *is* a world where mankind's irrational self (so much stronger than his rational capacity for temperance and control) takes the shape of ravening bestiality. Even as *novelist*, at this point in her life Edith Wharton can think of no way to manage passion save to decree that all strong feeling must submit to the stifling forces of oppression. The fictional possibilities available to her are stifled by the insufficiencies of her personal development.*

Throughout the novels and stories of this first period, the years of ap-

---

* There were other possibilities in those repressed feelings than merely violence, of course, but these gave Wharton little hope. Take this possibility. Suppose an individual allows his deepest feelings to be felt; suppose that these emerge as longings and hungerings for affection. Can one, then, be satisfied? Chillingly, the answer comes (Wharton's own answer, again, at the beginning of her career): if an individual dared to recognize the depth of his sentient needs, he would discover that they are, *by nature,* insatiable. He would have exposed himself in vain and would be left not only starving and unsatisfied, but now miserably conscious of his hopeless state. Any number of the early short stories treat this dilemma—most notably the brilliant piece "Souls Belated." These, too, are variations on the theme of despair.

prenticeship that culminated in the publication of *Ethan Frome*, there is a pervasive mood of lassitude, of joyless, profitless submission, a sense of inevitable disappointment and emotional emptiness. Not one of these fictions manages to portray any genuinely strong feeling save despair. Sexual passion is scarcely touched. Truly, these are landscapes of desolation.

Yet the persistent specter of human unhappiness did not remain altogether unchallenged. The increasing boldness and surety of Wharton's commitment to the vocation of writing gave sustenance to other, stronger selves. Gradually, she began to develop hope for happiness, even if it was happiness of a limited sort; gradually she began to be able to look back upon her own work, to see the desolation at the core of it, and to reject that ultimate pessimism. *Ethan Frome* is at once the existential statement of the dominant tone of this early period and the definitive rejection of it. Yet Edith Wharton had a long road to travel between *The Valley of Decision* and *Ethan Frome*.

4

The publication of *The Valley of Decision* affirmed Wharton's sense of professionalism. One of the clearest signs of her commitment to career is the diversity of writing that she poured out during this very productive period: she did translations (*The Joy of Living* by Sudermann in 1902 was the most substantial); she wrote reviews, including an important review of Leslie Stephen's biography of George Eliot in the May 1902 *Bookman*; she wrote more poetry; and in response to the encouragement of Burlingame, who had a good eye for the popular market, she wrote two books of essays on Italy—*Italian Villas and Their Gardens* (1904) and *Italian Backgrounds* (1905). She wrote another novella, *Sanctuary*, which came out in 1903,[51] and another volume of short stories, *The Descent of Man, and Other Stories* (1904). She liked to write; she enjoyed the sense of self-respect that the vocation of writing gave her; and like every professional author, she enjoyed making money. It gave her a feeling of self-sufficiency and independence: it enabled her to buy motor cars and to keep up the great house at Lenox; but most of all, it reassured her of the genuine value of her work. Good reviews and good returns on the writing—these did more than anything to continue her progress away from the dark cavern of depression.

However, despite her remarkable productivity, Wharton did not complete a second full-length novel until 1905, though she had evidently intended to write another immediately after *The Valley of Decision*. "I am slowly getting to work on a new novel, which I planned before I began the Valley," she wrote to Sara Norton on May 18, 1902, "but I don't expect to do much till we get to Lenox." [52] The new novel was to be called "Disintegration," and it was to be set in contemporary New York. (We can see that Wharton had anticipated the advice Henry James was to give her some months later, when he urged her to *"Do New York!"* [53]) Wharton had difficulty organizing the plot of "Disintegration": she worked on the book until late August of 1902, amassing somewhat more than seventy typed pages of manuscript, and then she broke off. Oddly, although Wharton could not finish "Disintegration," she could not forget it either, and she seems to have been absolutely hounded by the imperative to master the several different problems that inhered in it. The ghosts of "Disintegration" were not finally exorcised until 1925, when Wharton wrote the story in its final form as *The Mother's Recompense;* and some evidence of the novel in one or another of its many reworkings appears in every single Donnée Book between 1900 and 1925.

There are four central characters in the novel: Mr. and Mrs. Clephane, their daughter Valeria, and a family friend, George Severance. The unfinished fragment suggests two possible foci of interest, and Wharton's inability to choose between them—to select one coherent set of problems and to resolve them—may have been the ultimate cause of her suspending work on the novel. On the one hand, there is the little girl. *The Valley of Decision* had begun with a neglected little boy; "Disintegration" begins with a neglected little girl. "Was hat man dir, du armes Kind, gethan?"—the headnote to Book I. We encounter her as she is walking up Fifth Avenue with her beloved nurse Noony (the mother has abandoned the family, divorced the father, and married another man). There is a great deal to suggest that the principal emotional center of "Disintegration" is to be Val's loneliness, Val's sense of deprivation, Val's anger; and a comparison of this fragment with the accounts that remain of Wharton's childhood confirm that the author was drawing upon memories of her own early experience (Noony's name is so close to Doyley's that the connection must have been conscious).* And yet, per-

---

* A passage from this fragment (the entire seventy-four-page typescript of "Disintegration" can be found in the Wharton Archives at the Beinecke Library) will demonstrate just how close this child's situation was to Wharton's own. Noony, for example, is "the ocean

haps because the desolation of childhood had been so thoroughly worked through in *The Valley of Decision*, the tracing of Val's disintegration is not a theme of sufficient force to hold Wharton's attention now. In fact, it does not even successfully dominate the unfinished work, for another theme erupts with contrapuntal insistence, introducing another possible set of problems and another locus of interest. This is the plight of the mother—the former Mrs. Clephane, now Mrs. Tillotson Wing—a woman threatened with slow annihilation in a lifeless marriage, yet a woman conscious of social mores and the genuine obligations that they represent. We see a great deal of Val in this unfinished work and very little of her mother; but the woman's plight has an hypnotic fascination. "Disintegration" seems to be mainly about the little girl; *The Mother's Recompense* is about the conflicted woman.

In 1902 Wharton's novelistic attention was drifting away from the explicit problems of childhood, even though the legacies of childhood remained to be dealt with. The dual interest of "Disintegration" reflects her own emotional state: she had made the decision to reverse her long retreat from life, had rejected the crippling dependency on Mother, and had embraced the task of assembling a viable adult identity. Much of that task had to do with the problems attached to femininity—both as they sprang from Wharton's unique personal experiences and as they were introduced by the social customs of her time. The "woman problem" was to be the subject of her next (some would say her greatest) novel, and during the years preceding 1905, she gathered her forces together to deal with that problem.

Recall the girl of seventeen, standing in the National Gallery, feeling "the great waves of the sea of Beauty" breaking all about her, and wondering at the same time whether she would be "thought pretty in Paris." The seventeen-year-old had been poised between the impulse to *make* beauty and the imperative to *be* beautiful; and as we have seen, for many years she had accepted the latter state as the only appropriate one for a nice young lady. Commitment to a career in writing finally pulled her away from this malignant passivity, and now the problem of the nature

---

bounding [the little girl's] world." She has many gifts, among them "her power of sustained attention while pages of 'story-book' were poured into her ear in the monotonous shout of infancy: her familiarity with the wants and habits of puppies, rabbits, squirrels, and other small mammals; her tolerance of messy live things in basins, and her unfailing readiness to 'tidy up' the nursery after those holiday afternoons which, to most children, are dimmed by the impending obligation of having to put things away" (2–3).

of femininity is taken up by Edith Wharton, the maker of beauty. Yet the tension between these two poles—doing and being—remains very strong in her nature. What is more, there is still an underlying sense of pessimism, the legacy of the failed sense of trust in childhood; and this pessimism leads her to explore the plight of the unhappy woman. The problem is superbly rendered in *The House of Mirth;* but the study of Lily Bart is anticipated in any number of preliminary sketches.

As early as *The Greater Inclination* there are two stories that hover about the fringes of the subject; they balance each other nicely, treating the two poles of "doing" and "being." "The Pelican" tells the tale of a pretty young widow. Nature had not really "meant her to be 'intellectual'; but what can a poor thing do, whose husband has died of drink when her baby is hardly six months old, and who finds her coral necklace and her grandfather's edition of the British Dramatists inadequate to the demands of the creditors?" [54] The poor thing "gets up" a series of light lectures, imposes on people's sympathetic admiration, and manages to make a living out of the arrangement. Years go by; the subjects of the lectures change in response to changing audiences—and alas, the deficiencies of the lecturer become more and more painfully evident to those who still go to hear her out of sympathy. One evening, an acquaintance of many years chances to stop in and hear her speak; he ponders the long course of her career and begins to wonder whether the "baby" whom she has been supporting has not grown rather old by now, whether in fact he is not of an age to be many years out of college. The acquaintance voices his doubts to a man in the audience only to find that the man is the woman's grown son. The son had not known of the excuses that had been given for his mother's career; he had thought her a genuinely successful lecturer, and now he is mortified. He confronts his mother with the truth, and then he storms out, leaving her in bewildered tears. No one, it seems, had ever understood the fierceness of her need to *do something;* society had given her nothing to do unless it could be done in the name of maternal sacrifice. And so the poor lady had prolonged the fiction of that child who needed support—prolonged it because without the excuse it offered, she would have had nothing. At the end of the story, the excuse has been torn from her, and she does have nothing.

"The Muse's Tragedy" treats the other side of the dilemma: it is the story of Mrs. Anerton, "the Silvia of Vincent Rendle's immortal sonnet cycle, the Mrs. A. of the *Life and Letters.* Her name was enshrined in some of the noblest English verse of the nineteenth century." Mrs. Anerton has tasted the joys of being celebrated by the foremost poet of the day: she has "been" in the most glorious way, by having served as his inspiration. We discover her after Rendle's death, " 'a young woman still—what many people would call young,' " as she is approached with devotional respect by Lewis Danyers, a man who wishes to write a definitive study of the work of Vincent Rendle and who seeks out the woman who had been that artist's ideal. The two become friendly; they agree to collaborate on a book, and then they slip imperceptibly into an affair. The story concludes with a letter written to Danyers by Mrs. Anerton, who has just broken off and gone away.

You thought it was because Vincent Rendle had loved me that there was so little hope for you. I had had what I wanted to the full. . . . It is because Vincent Rendle *didn't love me* that there is no hope for you. . . .

Let me begin at the beginning. When I first met Vincent Rendle I was not twenty-five. That was twenty years ago. . . . He fell into the way of spending more and more of his time with me. He liked our house; our ways suited him. . . . When we were apart he wrote to me continually—he liked to have me share in all he was doing or thinking. . . . The pity of it was that I wanted to be something more. I was a young woman and I was in love with him. . . .

People began to talk, of course—I was Vincent Rendle's Mrs. Anerton; when the *Sonnets to Silvia* appeared, it was whispered that I was Silvia. . . . But what are they? A cosmic philosophy, not a love poem; addressed to Woman, not to a woman! . . .

After his death—this is curious—there came to me a kind of mirage of love. All the books and articles written about him, all the reviews of the *Life*, were full of discreet allusions to Silvia. . . . And I knew that, to all these people, I was the woman Vincent Rendle had loved.

After a while that fire went out too and I was left alone with my past. Alone—quite alone; for he had never really been with me. . . .

Then there set in a kind of Arctic winter. I crawled into myself as into a snow hut. . . .

My poor friend, do you begin to see? I had to find out what some other man thought of me. . . .

. . . I was drawn to you (you must have seen that)—I wanted you to like me; it was not a mere psychological experiment. And yet in a sense it was that, too—I must be honest. I had to have an answer to that question.[55]

Mrs. Anerton had been the perfect, passive incarnation of femininity; she had inspired great art; and she had been reduced, in the process, to the status of a friend, at best, and a convenient object, at worst. She has become Silvia, the perfect ideal of "Woman," and in so becoming, she has lost the last shred of sentient emotional satisfaction.

Wharton's work continues to show an interest in both extremes of the feminine possibility; but for a while, she seems to have been more interested in the difficulties and dangers of daring to act. There was no doubt that while her literary successes were making her life easier in many ways, they were also introducing new problems. Edith and Teddy had never had a great deal in common; the most reliable bond had been Teddy's kindness and Edith's dependency during the long years of sickness. Edith's growing independence as a manifestation of new health upset the emotional balance. Yet the dominant mode of their relationship would continue to be dependency. If Edith persisted in getting well and taking care of herself, Teddy retaliated by becoming sick. Thus with an almost mathematical perversity, as Edith gave up the need for protection, Teddy asserted it. In 1902, when the good reviews of *The Valley of Decision* began to roll in, Teddy suffered one of the first attacks of what came to be called a grave case of "neurasthenia" (we would call it manic-depression today, most likely). At just that point in her life when Wharton felt herself able to tolerate a more adult and satisfying relationship, Teddy's response to her success made it clear that she would not be allowed to do so. And, of course, as she developed that side of her that was least congenial to Teddy's nature, the intellectual side, she moved further and further away from him. The theme of the unhappy marriage in her early fiction is almost too obvious to need mentioning.

She was beginning to be acutely aware of her loneliness. The first Donnée Book contains a number of short inscriptions under the title "Miscellaneous"; many of them bear a sad resemblance. "A dim woman cloistered in ill-health. (Myself! E. W.)" [56] Whose ill-health at this point, we might wonder, hers or Teddy's? And the image of being cloistered does suggest a sexual abstinence that has become unwelcome. "That middle joy that is rooted in young despair"; the phrase is copied twice in widely different sections of the book. [57] "I foresee the day when I shall be as lonely as an Etruscan museum." [58] This last phrase finds its way into a story about a successful woman novelist; the woman is Mrs. Dale and she appears in a story entitled "The Copy," which was part of the collection *Crucial Instances* in 1901.

Many of the reviews of Wharton's books spoke self-consciously of her as a "woman novelist." The only review that she kept of *Crucial Instances* is one from the *New York Times;* and it begins, "Mrs. Wharton is another writer of a distinctly feminine talent. . . . It is only with the finest of fine shades that she will dally, with the most delicate perceptions of humour." [59] What on earth did it mean to have a "feminine talent"? Did women writers always have to play with the "finest of fine shades" (could not one plunge in with dark and violent passion)? What exclusions in the practice of art did that delicate compliment imply—and what personal exclusions? This question troubled Wharton for any number of years, and one of the most tantalizing women in her early fiction is a successful woman novelist, Mrs. Aubyn in *The Touchstone.*

Mrs. Aubyn has died before her story begins, and we never see her directly. We see her genius reflected in the shimmering admiration of all who have read her work; but most of all we find her in the memory of the man whom she loved, but who had never loved her. Glennard had met Margaret Aubyn while they both lived in the remote New England academic community of Hillbridge, where, having just published her first novel, she was something of a celebrity. The two drifted together. "It would be unjust, however, to represent his interest in Mrs. Aubyn as a matter of calculation. It was as instinctive as love, and it missed being love by just such a hair-breadth deflection from the line of beauty as had determined the curve of Mrs. Aubyn's lips." [60] She had fallen desperately, passionately in love with him, and he had merely grown more acutely embarrassed by his inability to return her feelings. Eventually, she moved away, far away to England, principally to permit him to hide his failure to respond to her. They had corresponded for several years, and then Margaret Aubyn died. We encounter Glennard as the story opens, trying to recall her as she had looked at their first meeting, "the poor woman of genius with her long pale face and short-sighted eyes, softened a little by the grace of youth and inexperience, but so incapable even then of any hold upon the pulses. . . . Now that the remembrance of her face had faded, and only her voice and words remained with him, he chafed at his own inadequacy, his stupid inability to rise to the height of her passion. . . . It was not that she bored him; she did what was infinitely worse—she made him feel his inferiority." [61] Glennard is down on his luck. The public is clamoring for memoirs of Margaret Aubyn, and Glennard has a large treasure horde in the correspondence that passed between them after she went to live abroad. He hesitates to publish the letters, but he feels that he cannot afford to let the opportunity slip by. And so, with the utmost secrecy (and of course not using his own name), he does.

For a while all goes well. Glennard marries, and he and his new wife live in comfort. But then his fortunes take a curious twist. Margaret Aubyn's reputation remains intact, if anything enhanced by the authenticity of feeling that her correspondence reveals. But her beloved is less fortunate: as a friend remarks to Glennard with unwitting cruelty, " 'It's the woman's soul, absolutely torn up by the roots—her whole self laid bare; and to a man who evidently didn't care; who couldn't have cared. . . . They're unloved letters.' " Glennard is horrified, embarrassed, unable for a long time to confront the image of himself that is captured in the letters. Little by little, he forces himself to contemplate the part he has played, and as he does so, he reanimates the image of Margaret Aubyn. Suddenly, she grows nearer to him than she ever had been in life. "All that was feminine in her, the quality he had always missed, stole toward him from her unreproachful gaze . . . and the joy of recovery was embittered to Glennard by the perception of all that he had missed." [62]

This portrait must have touched upon one of Wharton's deepest fears at the beginning of her career. Certainly she was very brilliant, she was talented (and beginning to be celebrated for being so), and she was desolately lonely. Margaret Aubyn's failure, like the failure of the other women in the early stories who yearn to do something with their lives, suggests Wharton's concern about her own future. She longed for a passional life, and she was terrified that the very burst of creative activity that had lifted her out of depression might also have put her beyond the reach of emotional fulfillment. "The Pelican," "The Copy," and *The Touchstone* each gives different voice to the suspicion that a final commitment to the life of making and doing might lead to irretrievable isolation.

Yet insofar as Wharton had a faith, that faith had been reposed in words. There is no doubt that her new career made her fearful, but there is also no doubt that her faith in the power of the word was ultimately greater than these fears. *The Touchstone* wears the air of depression that characterizes all the work of the early period; but it carries an aspect of sly triumph, too, in Margaret Aubyn's belated victory. There is nothing intrinsically unlovable about an active, creative woman; there are only people who are inadequate to appreciate her. Wharton's interest in the history of other women writers quickened during these years: the example of George Sand was reassuring (if flamboyant); and the example of George Eliot was even more so, being more susceptible of imitation. In her review of Leslie Stephen's biography of George Eliot, she defended Eliot against the charge that it was somehow indelicate for a novelist to have read nonfictional works: "The principal charge against her seems to be that she was too 'scientific,' that she sterilised her imagination and deformed her style by the study of biology and metaphysics." We can hear, surely Wharton could hear, the echoes of Lucretia dismissing Mrs. Stowe and all such intellectual women to the never-never land of "not nice." Several years of reviewers who had praised Wharton's "feminine talent" had undoubtedly quickened her sensibility in this direction. Thus she points out that while Eliot is condemned for her interest in science, other authors—Milton, Goethe, Tennyson, for example—are not. "Is it," she asks with uncharacteristic asperity, "because these were men, while George Eliot was a woman, that she is reproved for venturing on ground they did not fear to tread? Dr. Johnson is known to have pronounced portrait-painting 'indelicate in a female'; and indications are not wanting that the woman who ventures on scientific studies still does so at the risk of such an epithet." [63]

Of more timely interest than these intellectual speculations, however, was the fact that (as Wharton repeatedly acknowledges in the essay) Eliot's relationship with George Lewes flowered along with her literary growth, that Lewes both helped her and loved her, supported her and appreciated her. Clearly writing was no real impediment to an emotional life, even with so apparently unpromising a romantic figure as George Eliot. Indeed, as Wharton observes with remarkable acuity, writing was clearly an emotional asset to Eliot, for it allowed her to work through many of her feelings of deep ambivalence. "She may have been satisfied that [the course of her own life] was defensible; but, to all appearances, it was an open contradiction of her teachings, and the seeming inconsistency must have tortured her as social disapproval would have tortured an inferior nature. Pride, and the inability to justify herself to the world, drove her into seclusion, and, unconsciously, perhaps, she began to use her books as a vehicle of rehabilitation, a means, not of defending her own course, but of proclaiming, with increasing urgency and emphasis, her allegiance to the law she appeared to have violated." [64] At the most superficial level, this conflict between traditional mores and a rebellion against them seems an identical tracing of one level of conflict in Wharton's own life; surely there were similarities. But the deeper insight, that the process of writing might be a rehabilitating one, was a final validation of the lodging of Wharton's trust.

In this early period of puzzlement over "the woman problem," Wharton was growing increasingly confident that "doing" was a source of strength while "being" merely diminished individual resources. Yes, there were objective problems that confronted the woman who chose to create beauty; but on balance, writing offered no intrinsic obstacle to emotional intimacy (as the example of George Eliot proved), and it offered strengths that could be found nowhere else. The conflicts of the woman who has embarked upon an active life are internal to her nature only insofar as she has accepted the narrow prejudices of an unenlightened society and made them a part of her. If she genuinely rejects these prejudices, the conflicts can become increasingly external (though never, perhaps, entirely so). They are painful, but little by little they can be managed. The problems inherent in the injunction "to be," however, are of quite a different order. The woman who elects to form her nature as a pleasing accommodation to the demands of those around her can do so only by a systematic mutilation of her own identity. Becoming a beautiful object, acquiring a perfect state of compliant passivity, achieving an equanimity that betrays no hint of self-assertion—all of these erode the very heart of character. The woman who manages to satisfy society's appetite for "feminine" delicacy may find that she has retained no more than a hollow, empty shell of self. [65] If she discovers her mistake, she may find that she has entirely spent whatever resources she may once have had; she can realize the utter emptiness of her life, but she has no fundamental identity, no real core of self upon which to build a new life. Thus the woman who elects to "be" may be confronted with the ironic tragedy that she can never really *be* anybody!

We have seen Wharton tentatively playing with this problem in "The Muse's Tragedy," where the famous Mrs. Anerton must turn in desperation to a contrived affair merely to reassure herself that someone can respond to her as a real person. Wharton takes the theme up again in a ghoulish tale entitled "The Other Two" (1904). The woman in question is a Mrs. Waythorn; we are introduced to her as she is seen through the admiring eyes of her third husband (the first had been a youthful mistake, the second a man who gave her grievances that "were of a nature to bear the inspection of the New York courts"). Really, her husband reflects, one might almost see her as having come to him in a state of blushing widowhood. He is charmed by her elasticity, her pliancy; it is as if she had been born only to resonate in sympathetic harmony to his moods and wishes, and he fancies himself as blissful as a youth with his first love. Waythorn is acquainted with his wife's second husband, a man named Varick, but he has never met the partner of her girlish affection. Yet she has a daughter by that first marriage, and the girl's sickness brings her father to see her. Waythorn is struck with the man. He is not entirely certain why—perhaps because his wife had led him, in a series of implications of an indescribably shaded nature, to fancy the first husband as something of a brute. Waythorn finds him to be nothing of the sort, merely an inoffensive man who is concerned for the welfare of the child. The chance encounter starts Waythorn's mind working: his foremost thought is of the way in which his wife has sloughed off every shred of that part of her that had been implicated in the first marriage. "It was as if her whole aspect, every gesture, every inflection, every allusion, were a studied negation of that period of her life." [66]

Waythorn chances to encounter Varick in a business exchange; and when he returns home, he recognizes in his wife the faintest traces of having been to her second husband the very epitome of adaptability and pliancy that she is, now, to him. She is, perhaps, like some subtle sachet of flowers, combining the delicate hints of many blossoms, but the definite odor of none. Imperceptibly Waythorn's affection for her begins to sicken. "Had she really no will of her own," he wonders, "no theory about her relation to these men? . . . With sudden vividness Waythorn saw how the instinct had developed. She was 'as easy as an old shoe'—a shoe that too many feet had worn. Her elasticity was the result of tension in too many different directions." He cannot even enjoy her perfect receptivity to his moods, her ability immediately to adopt an easy air when he abjures her to put her cares to one side, her brightening at his hint that she is looking peaked, her subsiding at the merest expectation of an objection. He wonders *who* she is, really, wonders indeed, whether she is anybody at all in particular. He marvels at the art of her personality, "for it *was* an art, and made up, like all others, of concessions, eliminations and embellishments; of lights judiciously thrown and shadows skillfully softened." [67]

The story ends on just such a note of irresolution. We still see Alice Waythorn through the unrelenting eyes of her third husband. But now she has become a grotesque, some specialized form of monster, endlessly mutating—willing to please, not malicious, but not—not quite—human.

So long as we are allowed the luxury of the masculine point of view (as we are throughout this story), we can permit ourselves to rest in relative comfort with the notion of the amiable Mrs. Waythorn as a unique perversion of the human condition. But if we link Mrs. Waythorn's fate with that of Mrs. Anerton (whose apologetic manner suggested that she, too, was almost willing to accept herself as something less than human), we can begin to see these poor ladies as unwilling or unwitting victims of some general social injunction concerning the behavior of women. After all, the life of each might be construed as a logical extension of Edith Wharton's own adolescent preoccupation: "Shall I be thought pretty in Paris?" More axiomatically we might say: Who am I? I am the sum of the impressions I have made upon other people; I am only what others think of me; I am valuable only insofar as I can please others. This is femininity as the art of "being"; and it is this pernicious form of femininity that Wharton chooses as the subject of her next novel, *The House of Mirth*.

Many critics have noted the satirical components in *The House of Mirth*, and most have linked Wharton's satire with her aversion to the monied class of commercial New York. [68] Wharton's own judgment was more specific: "In what aspect could a society of irresponsible pleasure-seekers be said to have, on the "old woe of the world,' any deeper bearing than the people composing such a society could guess? The answer was that a frivolous society can acquire dramatic significance only through what its frivolity destroys. Its tragic implication lies in its power of debasing people and ideals. The answer, in short, was my heroine Lily Bart." [69]

In the first Donnée Book, *The House of Mirth* went by the title "A Moment's Ornament." This title captures the decorative imperative of that aspect of femininity that Lily embodies and the ultimate fragility of a self that has grown out of that imperative. In the typescript copy, the title was changed to "The Year of the Rose." Wharton still has in mind the pervasive influence of the art of femininity—her invocation of the rose probably has directly to do with the conventions of Art Nouveau, and her choice of the flower name suggests a deliberate attempt to make the reader aware of Lily's familial relationship to Daisy Miller (there was a sly, private meaning, too, in this naming process, for Edith Wharton had carried the nickname of Lily when she was a girl). Her final title, drawn appropriately from Ecclesiastes, broadens the attack to all those vanities of a society whose moral failures are captured in its devastating impact upon the lives of such women as Lily Bart.

Here as never before, Wharton focuses the full fury of her satirical voice. One reason for the brilliant success of *The House of Mirth* is that it pulls together so many threads of her own experience—deals concurrently with several susperimposed problems in her own life—and so allows her to speak with an undiluted intensity of expression that is rare in any novel. The first object of her attack is, of course, that shallow society whose narrow notions of propriety are so crippling and so perverse, a society that exercises cruelty without any semblance of underlying moral coherence. More specifically, Wharton intends to ridicule the notions of femininity purveyed in such a world, notions that would restrict women to a limited repertoire of pleasing attitudes: the governing injunction of such a world has already been articulated in an early story—take care of your complexion, my dear—and as we have seen, such injunctions toward women are ultimately infantilizing; they restrict the women who obey them to the Valley of Childish Things. Any woman who wished to come to terms with her position as an adult would have to recognize that the world expected her to continue playing the role of child. For Wharton, whose childhood memories plunged her into such a well of hopelessness and rage, this recognition resurrected very powerful feelings. *The House of Mirth* is about the disintegration of Lily Bart, about the psychological disfigurement of any woman who chooses to accept society's definition of her as a beautiful object and nothing more; and (because this is an infantilizing attitude to take toward women) the novel justifiably bores down into that core of Wharton's own childhood rage. But it does so without being *about* childhood and without being *about* the feelings of its author.

There is a final twist to the subject of this fiction. Wharton was always acutely aware of her art as art. She forced herself to be bluntly honest; there were no contrived happy endings in her work, and there was no illusion that suffering within a novel should be satisfying to the reader. Wharton had faced too much suffering and too many unhappy endings in her own life to rest comfortable with such artistic contrivances, however exquisite they might be; the brutal directness of Odo's disillusionment will suggest how strongly she felt the realistic impulse. Yet Wharton was well aware of the history of the sentimental American heroine, the woman whose death (or dishonor) wrings a sympathetic but self-caressing tear from the eye of the admiring reader. This tradition, Wharton would say, is the literary analogue to that pernicious real-life injunction to "be": it does not present suffering as suffering; it offers suffering as an artistic spectacle, the woman who feels the pain being little more than the central figure in a beautifully concocted arrangement that stimulates the reader's tender sensibilities. Wharton continues her habit of antiphony in *The House of Mirth;* but she is responding now not so much to a particular book as to an artistic tradition. She offers us a tantalizing display of seemingly stock figures—the beautiful, suffering heroine and the analytical, judgmental masculine observer. But she turns them askew. Instead of merely observing the woman, we discover her genuine feelings, and we learn what it *really* means to have become no more than a beautiful object; instead of identifying with the man and accepting his evaluations as the moral center of the novel, we learn that he is nothing more than the unthinking, self-satisfied mouthpiece for the worst of society's prejudices. Selden is, as Wharton declared to Sara Norton, "a negative hero." [70] The novel has, then, two subjects: the real-world perversions of the woman's role and the artistic distortions of women that often pass for "realism."

Many people are inclined to think of *The House of Mirth* as Wharton's first novel; certainly it is her first great novel. Perhaps it emanates this air of initiation because it takes art and the artist for its subject, as early novels so often do. Yet, as all these preliminary stories and short fictions suggest, the "great tradition" had evolved no conventions designed to render a woman as the maker of beauty, no language of feminine growth and mastery. Thus Wharton was constrained to couch her first *kunstlerroman* in a satiric vein: if she could not conveniently chronicle her own coming of age as an artist, she could turn her fury upon a world which had enjoined women to spend their artistic inclinations entirely upon a display of self. Not the woman as productive artist, but the woman as self-creating artistic object—that is the significance of the brilliant and complex characterization of Lily Bart.

Within the world of the novel, Lily is perceived confusedly: she is an uncertain blend of art and nature with a "streak of sylvan freedom in her
nature that lent such savour to her artificiality." [71] Often neither she nor
her closest observers can distinguish between the merely spontaneous
and the studiedly affecting (the careless lack of definition in her "suicide"
is of a piece with the rest of her behavior). Indeed, it is not too much to
say that this consistent confusion between the ideal and real as it is
manifested by all the characters in the novel—and the resultant depersonalization of the chrysalid character that is Lily's only inheritance—leads directly to the heart of her tragedy.

The distortions that flow from Lily's attempts at self-definition grow
inexorably from her sense that she is obliged to "be" whatever her audience demands. "New" New York was a society of collectors, and Wharton had this world of rapacious dilletantism specifically in mind when
she framed the terms of Lily's downfall. *The House of Mirth* is built upon
a series of explicit allusions to the art of the day. These would have been
immediately clear to a reader in 1905; however, a modern reader may
profit from having them rehearsed.

The aesthetic self-images of the newly rich were smugly reflected in
the indigenous art of the later nineteenth century. Such work was designed to capture the spirit of America (the ideal Republic); and for
reasons that have deep roots in this country, "America Victorious" most
usually took the palpable shape of "Perfect Womanhood."

One of the most generally visible art forms developed during this
period was the mural. The tone of such murals is remarkably consistent:
they represent in all their manifestations the virtues of a democratic, industrial society; and they embody this panoply of virtues in the figures
of chaste women and girls, "an extraordinary number of sexless females,
draped in white or the national colors or some other appropriate tinted
garments and variously labeled 'Justice,' 'America,' 'The Law,' 'Alma
Mater,' 'The Future,' 'The Triumph of Manhattan,' or 'The Ballet.' " [72]
The deliberate idealizing of the colossal women who adorned the walls of
public buildings could hardly be mistaken for realistic representation;
these are women used as symbols, mere visual embodiments of virtue.
Yet the possible inference is not without significance: "Our women are
pure"—so the public lesson could be read—"indeed, they are effortless

monuments of purity." Whatever exigencies the men of America had found necessary in preserving the order of things (and in amassing corporate and national wealth), their women are portrayed symbolically as rising above aberration, relentlessly and uncomplicatedly pure.

The clear use of woman as *symbol* of virtue becomes somewhat ambiguous when we examine the portrait art of the period. Here, too, it is the woman (not her successful husband) who is the artist's most frequent subject; and portraiture offers more beguilingly realistic representation of the virtues that had been splashed across the walls of public buildings. Occasionally the same artists worked in both media; John Singer Sargent, the premier portrait painter of the day, was widely applauded for his murals as well. In the area of portraiture, the artist's attitude toward his subject is difficult to define: the technique suggests a quest for genuine representation; Sargent's work was even widely praised for its "psychological" incisiveness.[73]

Yet Edith Wharton, who knew a great deal about art, was not impressed by this virtuosity of surfaces. "Sargent is the only artist I can think of," she wrote, "who has the technique of genius without its temperament." [74] Wharton recognized the difference between superficial rendering and a genuine understanding of psychological complexities, and she gives a skeptical view of the society portraitist in *The Custom of the Country:* "All [new society] asked of a portrait was that the costume should be sufficiently 'life-like,' and the face not too much so; and a long experience in idealizing flesh and realizing dress-fabrics had enabled Mr. Popple to meet both demands. 'Hang it,' Peter Van Degen pronounced, standing before the easel in an attitude of inspired interpretation, 'the great thing in a man's portrait is to catch the likeness—we all know that; but with a woman's it's different—a woman's picture has got to be pleasing. Who wants it about if it isn't?' " [75]

This is a damning indictment of both artist and patron. What the society of monied New York wanted was deception; and it was apparently a deception that the artist was willing (consciously or not) to provide—the pleasing illusion that the *idealized* renderings of the women he painted were in fact *realistic* representations.

The idealizing, "neoclassical" portraiture and mural work fostered a public delusion about the nature of women—an untruth at once so palatable and so generally insisted upon that its lofty expectations concerning the feminine nature could not easily be dismissed, either by women themselves or by the men who "worshipped" them. What is more, this confusion between the real and the ideal, reiterated throughout American neoclassical art, found substantial reinforcement in the Art Nouveau movement of the same period. Here as in portraiture and murals "it is the woman who is featured, almost to the total exclusion of the male." However, the emphasis is different: now, the woman's capacity to be decorative is her chief attraction. "In spite of, or perhaps because of, woman's increasing public role, she was even more zealously patronized as a fragile, helpless object, used in a decorative and literal sense to adorn the household: a man's wealth and position were judged by the style in which he kept his wife." [76]

These two schools of art, flourishing at the same historical period though apparently widely different, share a number of attitudes toward women. The rarefied virtue of the neoclassical woman is greatly diminished in the woman of Art Nouveau; but it does find expression in flowing, sentimentalized visual renderings. Here her purity is identified with the repeated floral motif: and of these masses of flowers, none were more consistently used than the lilies adapted from Japanese art themes— Easter lilies, tiger lilies, water lilies, liquescent calla lilies, fluttering clusters of lily-of-the-valley—they droop and spring from page after page, painting after painting. The Junoesque impressiveness of mural art is absent from Art Nouveau, which depicts its women as tall but willowy— attenuated forms surmounted by a halo of bright, abundant hair. Visual renderings of the woman as source of inspiration portray her as though she had grown naturally in her floral surroundings, a being literally incorporated into a world of nature which is, ironically and perversely, flat and unnatural. The confusion between art and nature is sustained,*

But the spiritual may descend to the sensational: there is a latent sexuality in the Art Nouveau woman. Her layers of clinging drapery and the fullness of her hair often offer a promise, if not more, of concealed pas-

---

* Sargent's famous painting of the Wyndham sisters demonstrates the extent to which these two schools of art interacted. Sargent's portrait was painted in 1899 at the height of the Art Nouveau movement. The figures are elongated, with the central figure extended and languid in the most fashionable manner. The ruffling of the dress fabric is suggestive almost of sea foam, and the attenuated fingers of the central figure trail off the right side of the canvas, framed by what appear to be massive groups of flowers, only the edges of which are seen in the picture. The whole, while clearly idealizing in the manner of Reynolds or Gainsborough, captures the slender, decorative quality of the Art Nouveau woman as well.

sion. Loïe Fuller, an internationally famous dancer of the period, made extensive use of transparent veiling and colored lights in her performances, and she named her dances after the prevalent Art Nouveau imagery: the Butterfly Dance, the Fire Dance, and the Lily Dance.[77]

One could scarcely enter a significant public building without discovering militant visions of feminine virtue on the walls; however, Art Nouveau penetrated not only public art, but the more private recesses of American culture. Book decoration, pictures and end papers, decorative lettering, chapter headings, all tended to bow to the influence of Art Nouveau. Architectural fittings, the appointments throughout a home, clothing in its multiple mysteries of fabric and underpinning and shoes and hats and accessories—these were all affected by the sinuous line of the New Art. Everywhere, Art Nouveau might be cited as synonymous with decorative elegance; and everywhere this influence was felt, there was an implicit image of the woman as ultimate exquisite.

The two manners of expression—widely different but often overlapping—agreed in one respect: both viewed woman as an essentially "artistic" creation, worthy of representation and innately disposed to "appropriate" behavior. The effect on actual women was direct; it was revealed in their clothing, in the manner in which they wore their hair, in the numerous accouterments of private life. The varied nuances of this particular notion of femininity would have been familiar to all of Wharton's audience; its atmosphere pervades the world of *The House of Mirth*, creating the distinctive climate in which Lily Bart spends the lingering summer of her youth. For many real women, perhaps for most, the effect of this artistic definition of the feminine might have been superficial. Any woman who was subject to strong alternative influences and any woman who had significant real-life roles to play might reflect the aesthetic attitude toward women and women's virtue in little more than a fashionable attitude. But other women, women like Lily who had nothing more to offer than a superb capacity to render themselves agreeably, might be lured by the seductive confusion between representation and reality and come to view themselves not as persons but as objects—to be admired, to be sustained in their beauty. The men around them would have significance principally as connoisseurs or collectors. It is this exquisite, empty image of self that has contaminated Lily's life; it is, ultimately, this confusion between the ideal and the real that leads to her tragedy.

It is not altogether easy to trace the origins of Lily's failure. Lily's past is conjured in memories of a mother who had "died of a deep distrust. She hated dinginess, and it was her fate to be dingy" (55). The agonies felt by Lily's mother when she is called upon to confront poverty spring from a relatively vulgar desire for display. "Mrs. Bart was famous for the unlimited effect she produced on limited means; and to the lady and her acquaintances there was something heroic in living as though one were much richer than one's bankbook denoted" (46). Thus Lily's mother cares for artistry principally as an indication of the family's monetary status. She is entirely familiar with the rate of exchange in the world in which she lives, and she nurtures and indulges Lily's beauty—first as the visible sign of the family's station (Lily had, typically, a "dazzling debut") and finally as its one remaining asset. Lily is trained to become a decorative object.

Lily's own ability to assess the various forms of currency in her society is a good deal less fully developed. Her mother had been "a wonderful manager" (46), a woman with the cold-blooded capacity to limit her private delicacies in pursuit of public display. Lily, on the other hand, has been pampered and spoiled: she is childishly, sublimely insensitive to the facts that inform her mother's management and "she knew very little of the value of money" (49). She sees money almost as a natural resource that is supplied by a "neutral tinted" father who "filled an intermediate space between the butler and the man who came to wind the clocks" (45). She has been encouraged in the expansive development of her taste at the expense of practical knowledge. The family's concerted effort in the production and sustaining of Lily's aesthetic nature has endowed her with a limitless responsiveness to beauty—in herself and elsewhere; but her rarefied sensitivity has left her absolutely dependent upon finding an environment that will support such refinement. She is not merely self-indulgent. She is still a child emotionally. She genuinely needs the quick succession of fashionable clothes, the "dressing-case of the most complicated elegance" (178), the "few frivolous touches, in the shape of a lace-decked toilet table and a little painted desk surmounted by photographs" (176); these examples of the New Art are the necessary accessories to her personality. "No; she was not made for mean and shabby surroundings, for the squalid compromises of poverty. Her whole being dilated in an atmosphere of luxury; it was the background she required, the only climate she could breathe in" (39–40). Lily's mother wanted artistic effects because they suggested wealth, success.

Lily needs wealth because it is the only atmosphere in which her exquisite femininity can thrive. As she finally realizes, "she had been brought
up to be ornamental, [and] she could hardly blame herself for failing to
serve any practical purpose" (480).

Lily could not have become the finished masterpiece she is without a
good deal of innate talent: thus in the creation of the *tableaux vivants* "her
vivid plastic sense, hitherto nurtured on no higher food than dress-mak-
ing and upholstery, found eager expression in the disposal of draperies,
the study of attitudes, the shifting of lights and shadow" (211). Here the
Art Nouveau insistence upon woman as the ultimate artistic elegance is
made clear (though, for reasons we shall discuss later, Lily chooses the
"classical" work of Reynolds to emulate). The contemporary reader
might well have been reminded of Loïe Fuller's somewhat more sensational public displays (Ned Van Alstyne obviously reacts to Lily's nudity and the purely physical suggestiveness of her pose). This fascination
with sweeping, clinging drapery, the addiction to personal accessories of
every sort, the pitiful longing to "re-do" Aunt Penniston's house are all
assertions of Lily's beautiful, limited "self."

One of Lily's genuine virtues is that she never fully loses her naiveté,
never completely corrupts the artistic finish of her nature. Yet she is,
from the very beginning of the novel, portrayed as conscious of the distortions created by a society that offers such flattering limitations of the
woman's role (but not of the man's). " 'A girl must [marry to get out of
dingy routine], a man may if he chooses.' She surveyed [Selden] critically. 'Your coat's a little shabby—but who cares? It doesn't keep people from asking you to dine. If I were shabby no one would have me: a
woman is asked out as much for her clothes as for herself. The clothes
are the background, the frame, if you like: they don't make success, but
they are a part of it. Who wants a dingy woman? We are expected to be
pretty and well-dressed till we drop—and if we can't keep it up alone,
we have to go into partnership' " (17–18). Her beauty—even more, her
general aesthetic aura—is not only her fortune in this newly capitalistic
society; it is the only thing about her that makes her interesting or valuable to others. The man who marries her will select her as the final prize
in his collection; Lily knows this fact, and her "skill in enhancing [her
beauty], the care she took of it, the use she made of it, seemed to give it a
kind of permanence. . . . She knew that Mr. Gryce was of the small
chary type most inaccessible to impulses and emotions. . . . But Lily

had known the species before: she was aware that such a guarded nature must find one huge outlet of egoism, and she determined to be to him what his Americana had hitherto been: the one possession in which he took sufficient pride to spend money on it. She knew that this generosity to self is one of the forms of meanness, and she resolved so to identify herself with her husband's vanity that to gratify her wishes would be to him the most exquisite form of self-indulgence" (78).

Lily never does learn her mother's capacity for management, and in the transactional portions of her life she suffers a failure of will, a revulsion, perhaps, from the final human compromise. The everyday habit of self-adornment indicates that Lily has internalized the New Art's notion of woman; but the merely decorative is in the end not entirely sufficient for her. Even when she was very young, "there was in Lily a vein of sentiment . . . which gave an idealizing touch to her most prosaic purposes. She liked to think of her beauty as a power for good, as giving her the opportunity to attain a position where she should make her influence felt in the vague diffusion of refinement and good taste" (54). But this pining after moral significance brings with it no capacity to make choices, draw difficult distinctions, or bear hardship; it is, like much else in her nature, diffuse and indolent and undeveloped. She is genuinely puzzled by the difficulties (when they come to her attention, as they rarely do) of the moral life conscientiously lived. "She could not breathe long on the heights; there had been nothing in her training to develop any continuity of moral strength: what she craved, and really felt herself entitled to, was a situation in which the noblest attitude should also be the easiest" (422). She would be like the Wood Nymph of the Art Nouveau, her evocative purity casually, "naturally" placed in a bower of flowers—or like the unwaveringly chaste women of the neoclassical school, poised to preside majestically over significant public events. In other words, virtue and nobility should be effortless companions to her artistically rendered self.

Most often, Lily handles her moral queasiness by choosing not to know the full implications of her plight. She permits the pleasing aesthetic *appearance* that she can give to a situation to substitute for its reality. "She was always scrupulous about keeping up appearances to herself. Her personal fastidiousness had a moral equivalent, and when she made a tour of inspection in her own mind there were certain closed doors she did not open" (131). When an acceptable interpretation cannot be found, Lily characteristically removes herself to a different, more spiritually consoling atmosphere. After all, "moral complications existed for her only in the environment that had produced them; she did not mean to slight or ignore them, but they lost their reality when they changed their background" (314). This need to avoid serious moral reflection is, of course, a principal cause of her social downfall. She must accept Gus Trenor's stock market "tip" as a fraternal gesture; she is not prepared to sort out the moral and financial problems that would be revealed by a frank appraisal. She must perceive Bertha Dorset's invitation to join in her vacation as springing first from mere friendship and then from deep wells of human need; the option of recognizing Bertha's malicious and immoral use of her raises problems that she has not the stamina to resolve. She must linger lazily in her secretary/companion role to Mrs. Hatch until all the world believes in her actual duplicity and moral compromise; she has not the discipline to refuse (nor, ironically, the sustained habit of calculation to partake in that lady's social rise). In the end when Lily tries to review her relationship to Bertha and Selden dispassionately, she cannot overcome the deficiencies of a life devoted to evasion: "What debt did she owe to a social order which had condemned and banished her without trial? She had never been heard in her own defense; she was innocent of the charge on which she had been found guilty; and the irregularity of her conviction might seem to justify the use of methods as irregular in recovering her lost rights" (485–86). But she cannot think her way through these complexities (the possibility of going directly to Selden does not occur as an option, for reasons that we shall discuss later); she has not been bred to offer anything more than the appearance of moral righteousness. "Was it her fault that the purely decorative mission is less easily and harmoniously fulfilled among social beings than in the world of nature? That it is apt to be hampered by materialistic necessities or complicated by moral scruples?" (487).

When Lily's habits of moral evasion fail her as she meets one reversal after another, she does not put her aesthetic-moral talents to a real examination of the problem; instead she reverts to a more energetic summoning of the Grand Manner, an infusion of her being with the appearance of spiritual command which in no way corresponds to to the fact of increasing inner desolation. When Bertha dismisses her and Selden offers support of sorts, Lily rises and stands "before him in a kind of clouded majesty, like some deposed princess moving tranquilly to exile" (353). When Gerty Farish makes similar gestures of sympathy and help, "she drew herself up to the full height of her slender majesty, towering like some dark angel of defiance above the troubled Gerty" (362). This behavior represents a literal translation of the confusion in Lily's early training that had led her to believe that "the noblest attitude should also be the easiest." If one supposes attitude to signify not a habit of mind but merely an artistic pose, a semblance, then Lily can continue for a while to satisfy the "moral" demands of her deeply aesthetic nature.

It is a nature that needs, in all its manifestations, the reassurance of a perceptive audience. In the passages cited just above, Lily gains some measure of deceptive confidence by convincing the onlookers of the consonance between appearance and reality. This manner of relating to others is relatively consistent throughout the novel. Indeed, it is an indispensable clue to understanding the role that Selden plays.

Selden's artistic training has been as thorough as Lily's, though it has a strong neoclassical bias: "In a different way, he was, as much as Lily, the victim of his environment" (245). His tastes incline him to appreciate instructive art; and while he is susceptible to the decorative (as both his initial reactions to Lily and the history of his affair with Bertha Dorset suggest), the full depth of his aesthetic passion has a moralistic character. "It had been Selden's fate to have a charming mother: her graceful portrait, all smiles and Cashmere, still emitted a faded scent of the undefinable quality. . . . His views of womankind in especial were tinged by the remembrance of the one woman who had given him his sense of 'values' " (245–46). Selden has learned, from the example of his parents' elegant poverty, a moral finickiness that is every bit as divorced from reality as Lily's. Selden's parents have both refused to compromise the pursuit of absolute quality in their material lives, but they adopt a pious, self-congratulatory attitude toward what they perceive as their habit of "restraint." They are self-deceived; they suffer from the sin of pride. "Neither one of the couple cared for money, but their disdain of it took the form of always spending a little more than was prudent. . . . Selden senior had an eye for a picture, his wife an understanding of old lace; and both were so conscious of restraint and discrimination in buying that they never quite knew how it was that the bills mounted up" (245).

The son grows up believing that life fully led must necessarily satisfy both his own moral habit of self-righteous otherworldliness and the indulgence of his keenest sensitivities; and the fact that these two appetites might be mutually contradictory is a problem that Selden has no capacity to confront. Given the attitudes of the society of which he is a part, it is not surprising that Selden chooses instead to project these ambivalences into his notions of femininity. "Life shorn of either feeling appeared to him a diminished thing; and no where was the blending of the two ingredients so essential as in the character of a pretty woman" (246).

He has been trained as a connoisseur, well equipped to appreciate the nuances of Lily's display; but he necessarily carries his own artistic-moral complications into their relationship. Lily must be beautiful, but her beauty must have an uplifting quality; she must be beautiful, all the while appearing to be above material concerns. (Even inherited wealth would not solve Lily's predicament thus defined, for Lily could seem *genuinely* above material concerns only if she ignored or rejected whatever wealth she might have—and ignoring the uses of money, as even Lily knows, would diminish her capacity for the very decorative display that Selden so admires.) Until his entanglement with Lily Bart, Selden had handled this essential contradiction in his own nature and in his expectations about the nature of women by a series of "voluntary exclusions" (244). Quite wisely, "he had meant to keep free from permanent ties. . . . There had been a germ of truth in his declaration to Gerty Farish that he had never wanted to marry a 'nice' girl: the adjective connoting, in his cousin's vocabulary, certain utilitarian qualities which are apt to preclude the luxury of charm" (244–45). Selden would have Miss Bart be a Lily of the Field in very truth, enacting her parable of beauty effortlessly. Little wonder that in judging her "he had always made use of the 'argument from design' " (6). And yet this "streak of sylvan freedom" is not central; it only lends interest, for Selden, to her "artificiality." The Lily unadorned would, after all, fail to sustain his interest.

The novel opens with a meeting between Selden and Lily, establishing the terms of their relationship and alerting the reader to Wharton's structuring of the process of Lily's decline.[78] The narrator begins in Selden's mind, presents Lily only as *he* sees her, and shows him to have the lingering, appraising, inventorial mind of the experienced collector: he is fascinated with her surface appearance, misses no detail of her exquisite finish. He remarks the chiaroscuro effect of "her vivid head, relieved against the dull tints of the crowd," takes in the details of her clothing and "the purity of tint, that she was beginning to lose after eleven years of late hours and indefatigable dancing" (4). As they walk up Madison

Avenue, the inspection continues, with Selden "taking a luxurious plea-sure in her nearness: in the modelling of her little ear, the crisp upward wave of her hair . . . and the thick planting of her straight black lashes" (6–7).

Selden's reactions to this surfeit of decorative art reveal, even here, his inbred moral-aesthetic ambiguities. There is first the self-indulgence of his appreciation of her, then the startled, guilty awareness of the mone-tary implications of even such indulgence as this, then disapproval—but not of his own indulgence, rather disapproval projected onto Lily—and finally the longing to see such beauty allied in some indefinable way with the lofty virtue that his nature craves:

> Everything about her was at once vigorous and exquisite, at once strong and fine. He had a confused sense that she must have cost a great deal to make, that a great many dull and ugly people must, in some mysterious way, have been sacrificed to produce her. He was aware that the qualities distin-guishing her from the herd of her sex were chiefly external: as though a fine glaze of beauty and fastidiousness had been applied to vulgar clay. Yet the analogy left him unsatisfied, for a coarse texture will not take a high finish; and was it not possible that the material was fine, but that circumstance had fashioned it into a futile shape? (7)

Selden's musings might almost pass for social criticism were it not for the fact that the "futile shape" he seems to deplore is a shape he ob-viously and extensively admires and that his admiration is part of the continuing "circumstance" that fashions it. There is satire, of course; but it inheres in the narrator's use of irony—an irony which places Selden as part of the *uninformed* audience.

His assessment of Lily is gradually revealed to deal almost entirely with externals: he is willing at every point to accept the appearance for reality. Thus, while people have indeed "been sacrificed" to "produce" Lily, the reader learns (though Selden never fully does) that the principal sacrifice has been Lily herself. While he imputes "far-reaching inten-tions" to her "simplest acts" (3), we discover that Lily is capable only of short-term schemes, one of which—the learning-up of Americana for Percy Gryce—is hatched here under Selden's unsuspecting eye. When Lily does essay direct frankness, attempting to move beyond the superfi-cialities of their emotional relationship, Selden responds with a nervous evasion into inconsequential flirtation, though "he felt a slight shiver down his spine as he ventured this" (12)—even this pseudointimacy.

Their "frankness" leads to nothing more than an inventory of Lily's chances for marriage and a continuation of Selden's "appreciation" of Lily, now that he has settled her at a safe emotional distance. Selden is thoroughly encapsulated in his own preoccupations, needs, and prejudices. The ambiguities that grow out of his early experiences make him reluctant to permit serious emotional ties; his stance as connoisseur gives a socially acceptable definition to this reluctance, and the pervasive judgmental quality of his manner generally precludes sympathetic response. She is for him here merely an object for appraising examination. Lily, by contrast, is all too able to see the world (herself in particular) through *his* eyes—to identify with his values and his artistic standards. She is, as even this first exchange suggests, willing to try to meet him on some common emotional ground. Yet if she is to meet him at all, it must be entirely on his terms, for his values are settled.

Selden's thorough capacity for sensuous aesthetic enjoyment is revealed in this first scene; the other half of his oddly assorted nature, the moralistically righteous side, is revealed at Bellomont in their second intimate encounter. He draws her on to talk about her schemes, her failure to find "success"; and then he turns on her "worldliness" to outline his own image of success. " 'My idea of success,' he said, 'is personal freedom. . . . [Freedom] from everything—from money, from poverty, from ease and anxiety, from all the material accidents. To keep a kind of republic of the spirit—that's what I call success' " (108). Lily is attracted to this utopian vision; her moral fastidiousness is offended by the necessity of maintaining herself as a "collectable." Yet she cannot help questioning the genuine workability of Selden's system. " 'The only way not to think about money is to have a great deal of it,' " she sensibly replies (110). Selden, flushed with the purity of his vision, discounts real-world problems. " 'You might as well say that the only way not to think about air is to have enough to breathe. That is true enough in a sense; but your lungs are thinking about the air, if you are not. And so it is with your rich people—they may not be thinking of money, but they're breathing it all the while; take them into another element and see how they squirm and gasp!' " (110–11). Lily's wry observation that he seems to spend a lot of time " 'in the element you disapprove of' " (111) elicits only the evasion that he is an "amphibious" creature.

Wharton offers clear satire here—not in Selden's remarks, but in the illogical self-deception of his narrowly virtuous position. Like Gryce,

Selden will accept Lily only if she can identify herself with his "vanity."
Gryce's vanity is of a simple order: he collects Americana; he would add
her to that collection. Selden's is more complex—and more seductive.
He luxuriates in her studied decorative quality: he would have her retain
that quality (not become "nice," to use Gerty Farish's term), but he
would have her absolutely reject the material world that sustains it.
What is more, as his subsequent behavior reveals, he would have her do
this without sympathetic support from him. He is to remain aloof, judgmental.

His attitude of sustained condemnation wears away at Lily's confidence. " 'You despise my ambitions—you think them unworthy of me!'
. . . 'Well, isn't that a tribute? I think them quite worthy of most of the
people who live by them.' . . . 'Why do you do this to me? . . . Why
do you make the things I have chosen seem hateful to me if you have
nothing to give me instead?' " (113–14). Lily's words move Selden to a
declaration, and her answering tears almost, but not entirely, break his
stance of ironic detachment.

At this point the lovers seem united in some higher sphere. "The soft
isolation of the falling day enveloped them: they seemed lifted into a
finer air. All the exquisite influences of the hour trembled in their veins"
(116–17). However, Wharton is quick to alert us to the fact that it is only
in this other world that they can be united. In order to be morally
worthy of Selden's collection, Lily must not waver in her disdain for the
things of this world: as little as a fleeting hesitation will betray sufficient
flaw. And that hesitation comes almost immediately when the sound of a
motor car intrudes the real world upon them. Lily falters, remembering
the maneuvers by which she has managed to extricate herself from a
Sunday outing with the other guests, remembering particularly her evasions with Percy Gryce; this recollection is sufficient to return Selden's
somewhat softened manner to an attitude of contempt.

> "I had no idea it was so late. We shall not be back till after dark," she
> said, almost impatiently.
> Selden was looking at her with surprise: it took him a moment to regain
> his usual view of her; then he said, with an uncontrollable note of dryness:
> "That was not one of our party; the motor was going the other way."
> (117–18)

Lily's weakness is everywhere evident: in the crudest terms, she wants to
copper her bets. However, given the flimsiness of Selden's lofty moral

system and—even more significant—given his incapacity to cast off his own cold disdain and guide her through her moments of uncertainty, Lily's hesitation is at least understandable. Later (see 517–18), Lily is to review this moment and place the blame for its failure heavily on herself; but the reader, who can view the entire House of Mirth more clearly and critically than Lily, sees the contributing effect of Selden's attitude.

There are other kinds of men—men who can love sympathetically, who can tolerate weakness in the beloved—but these men exist outside the House of Mirth. For all his vulgar preoccupation with money, Mr. Rosedale is revealed as having traces of compassion, elements of sympathy which are being systematically eradicated by his "successful" social climbing. Nettie, disgraced and reclaimed, who gives Lily "her first glimpse of the continuity of life" (516), suggests an alternative, too, in ths husband who has "faith," who can "know" the deepest failures of his wife and not recoil. But within the House of Mirth there is no alternative; and both Lily and Selden are too thoroughly acclimated to live elsewhere.

Wharton's satire is structured on a series of such intimate confrontations between Selden and Lily. Ironically, given Selden's self-consciously moral definition of his own role, he is changed very little by his contact with Lily's tragedy. He is always the connoisseur, always willing to evade complicity; and at the very end of the novel as at the beginning, we return to view Lily through his judging and imperceptive eyes. He still regards her as a moral-aesthetic object—the episode with her has proved uplifting, "he could even draw from it courage not to accuse himself for having failed to reach the height of his opportunity" (532)—and he still has no knowledge of or sympathy with her pain. By contrast, Lily does gain insight, though not the capacity to free herself. She recognizes that "the very quality of [Selden's] love had made it the more impossible to recall to life" (517). Yet Lily has been formed to accept a definition of femininity of which men like Selden are the supreme evaluators. The first two confrontations outline the conflicting demands she must satisfy, and the scenes with Selden that follow detail her desperate and finally fatal efforts to satisfy them. Lily comes closest to Selden's expectations for her in the third encounter, the evening of the *tableaux vivants*.

Her choice of costume reveals her increased understanding of Selden's visionary demands of her; and though she toys with a presentation that would emphasize the purely decorative, she settles finally on a perfect union of the sensual and the morally significant: she presents herself in the classical guise of Reynolds's *Mrs. Lloyd.*

> Her pale draperies, and the background of foliage against which she stood, served only to relieve the long dryad-like curves that swept upward from her poised foot to her lifted arm. The noble buoyancy of her attitude, its sugges-tion of soaring grace, revealed the touch of poetry in her beauty that Selden always felt in her presence. (217)

Wharton means the reader to understand this as an illusionary image of Lily; it touches, is intended to touch, "the vision-building faculty in Sel-den" (216). It is doubly an artifice, being a recreation of a portrait which is, itself, an idealized and exalted rendering of reality. It reveals nothing of Lily's suffering—nothing, even, of the artistic effort that has been ex-pended in producing the image. It is the instantiation of ideal beauty as employed by the artist to elevate the life of the beholder; only such a creature as this could inhabit Selden's "republic of the spirit." And in it Selden fancies that he sees before him for the first time "the real Lily Bart" (217). Selden has made an error that captures the essence of his so-ciety's demands for the "best" women: he has mistaken the ideal for the real.

Lily savors her success, prolonging the illusion in her interview after the display (an interview which is held, appropriately enough, in the false summer of a conservatory). "The magic place was deserted. . . . Selden and Lily stood still, accepting the unreality of the scene as a part of their own dream-like sensations" (221). Yet the attempt to move from this level to more mundane reality fails: Selden can "love" Lily, on his own terms; but he cannot "help" her surmount the inconstancies of her nature (see 222).

Selden's inability to have a loving faith in Lily's capacity for redemp-tion is underlined by his reaction to seeing her emerge from Gus Trenor's house the next evening. As in the second confrontation, the moment of "perfect union" is destroyed by a hint (not a confirmation) of weakness. Selden moves from a totality of adoration to a totality of dis-dain; and though Lily is, ironically, not guilty of the transgression he im-putes to her, his capacity for understanding and his tolerance for imper-fection are so slight that he is rendered incapable of knowing her true situation. (The same mistake almost occurs at the end of the novel when Selden, going through Lily's papers, finds the note to Trenor. Only the accident of its being open saves Lily's reputation, for even in this final moment Selden is willing to condemn her.) Hereafter, the relationship between Selden and Lily is but a chronicle of her destruction. She saves face in Italy by an adoption of "the Grand Manner"; and Selden characteristically accepts this fiction. She rises to her one act of genuine heroism in the destruction of his letters, but by this time "her presence was becoming an embarrassment to him" (496); and when he confronts her lifeless body, he has lost forever the opportunity to discover that she has sacrificed herself to preserve his reputation and his memory of her. Wharton measures the insufficiency of Selden's understanding of Lily by constructing her novel so that he *never does* know that Lily possessed Bertha's letters to him, never does know that she destroyed them when she might have saved herself by using them: the very nature of this fictional world defines the mawkishness of his sorrow at her death.

Wharton herself saw the tragedy of the novel as centering in the character of Lily, and a modern reader can trace rather explicitly the ways in which Lily has been destroyed. Lily has adopted her society's images of women narrowly and literally. She has long practiced the art of making herself an exquisite decorative object, and under Selden's eye she comes to think of herself as a moral object as well. Yet the crucial term here is "object." She learns to evoke approval and appreciation in others by a subtle and ingenious series of graceful postures. It is an art she has practiced so well and for so long that she can no longer conceive of herself as anything but those postures; she can formulate no other desire than the desire to be seen to advantage. "There were moments when she longed blindly for anything different, anything strange, remote and untried; but the utmost reach of her imagination did not go beyond picturing her usual life in a new setting. She could not figure herself as anywhere but in a drawing-room, diffusing elegance as a flower sheds perfume" (160–61). Like Mrs. Waythorn, she has developed a self that is nothing more than a series of "lights judiciously thrown and shadows skillfully softened."

Repeatedly Wharton gives evidence that Lily's special skill in the representation of herself lies in an uncanny ability to experience herself as others must see her (and thus to anticipate their reactions and control them). On the train, looking ahead to the possible meeting with Gryce, Lily "arranged herself in her corner with the instinctive feeling for effect which never forsook her" (26). The ceremony of the tea she shares with him is a model of manipulation. Her every mood, motion, public attitude (except for those few impulses for which she pays so dearly) is a deliberate piece of acting. She knows, always, when she is being observed; and she automatically plays to her audience. She has learned so thoroughly to experience herself as an object that is being observed by others—not directly as an integrated human being—that her sense of "self" is confirmed only when she elicits reactions from others; and when she is alone (and she increasingly fears loneliness), her inner emptiness becomes terrifying, unbearable. The symptoms of this depersonalization are found throughout the novel.

For example, Lily's capacity to feel emotion has almost entirely atrophied. Does she love Selden? It is a question she raises almost academically, for she "had no definite experience by which to test the quality of her feelings" (102–3). Certainly she wants to be loved *by* him, for that would confirm her own sense of worth, of lovability. She has no real capacity for generosity; "the other-regarding sentiments had not been cultivated in Lily" (179). She derives pleasure in giving money to Gerty Farish's charities; but her pleasure is in Gerty's admiration of her act, her "surprise and gratitude. . . . And Lily parted from her with a sense of self-esteem which she naturally mistook for the fruits of altruism" (180). Selden observes, rather cruelly, "that even her weeping was an art" (115); but his evaluation of her in this respect is probably correct. She can see herself only as a reflection—in others' judgments of her or literally in the series of mirror images that stalk her through the novel. Whenever she wants to know how she feels, she looks into a mirror to find out. When the mirror returns a reassuring message, life seems good to Lily. "Mrs. Bry's admiration was a mirror in which Lily's self-complacency recovered its lost outline. . . . The sense of being of importance among the insignificant was enough to restore to Miss Bart the gratifying consciousness of power" (181). But when her reverses are not put right by an appreciative audience, her sense of deformity (and unbearable self-loathing) finds expression in descriptions of the mirrored "self" that come almost self-consciously from the school of Dorian Gray. Thus after her encounter with Trenor, she tries to explain her sense of shame to Gerty Farish: "Can you imagine looking into your glass some morning and seeing a disfigurement—some hideous change that has come to you while you slept? Well, I seem to myself like that—I can't bear to see myself in my own thoughts—I hate ugliness, you know"

(265). And when Selden reacts to her lapse with Trenor by leaving to go abroad, her response is characteristic and immediate. "She rose, and walking across the floor stood gazing at herself for a long time in the brightly-lit mirror above the mantelpiece. The lines in her face came out terribly—she looked old; and when a girl looks old to herself, how does she look to other people?" (289).

Given the entirely dependent nature of Lily's sense of self, we can understand Selden's importance to her: his critical stance adds a moral dimension to her life; for although she has repeatedly succeeded in confirming her effect as a merely decorative object, she has found this success insufficient. Thus intimacy between Lily and Selden involves her adopting his point of view, submitting to his judgments. And his judgment is generally harsh. "That was the secret of his way of readjusting her vision. Lily, turning her eyes from him, found herself scanning her little world through his retina: it was as though the pink lamps had been shut off and the dusty daylight let in" (87). Yet, as we have seen, his own moral-aesthetic code is deeply flawed. It is a code that even he can follow only by a series of suppressed hypocrisies: he is as much a parasite on the society of the House of Mirth as Lily is—she timidly points this fact out, but has not the internal stamina and coherence to pursue her point (109–15); his affair with Bertha Dorset scarcely justifies the chaste horror he manifests at the possibility that Lily's conduct has been less that absolutely perfect. In submerging her ethical view into his, Lily has accepted impossible standards.

There is, however, an even more seriously destructive element in Selden's system as applied to Lily: it continues the process by which society has dehumanized her. Selden is willing to judge her worthy if and only if she can become a flawless, absolutely constant embodiment of virtue. When Lily accepts his unattainable ideals as her "realities," she is merely perpetuating on a somewhat loftier plane the lifelong habit of seeing herself as an object to be judged by others. In her relationship to Selden "she longed to be to him something more than a piece of sentient prettiness, a passing diversion to his eye and brain" (152), but she evokes from him little more than ironic, detached disapproval. And since she has accepted the notion that his reactions are the only "mirror" in which her "real" self can be reflected, she perceives that self as increasingly disgusting and loathsome. Each episode of gentle admonition on his part is a blow. "She looked at him helplessly, like a hurt or frightened child:

this real self of hers, which he had the faculty of drawing out of the depths, was so little accustomed to go alone" (152). Little wonder that she does not think of loving him; that act would require an independent identity. Instead her needs are expressed in terms that plead for his reassuring response: "It seemed to her that it was for him only she cared to be beautiful" (220).

The artificial quality of Lily's one great success—her impersonation of Reynolds's portrait—indicates the impossibility of sustaining Selden's idealized image on any but an otherworldly level. Thus afterwards she sighs, " 'Ah, love me, love me—but don't tell me so!' " (222).

Lily's acceptance of Selden's demands on her renders her even less able than before to return to the moral lassitude of an easier environment. "The renewed habit of luxury—the daily waking to an assured absence of care and presence of material ease—gradually blunted her appreciation of these values, and left her more conscious of the void they could not fill" (381). When Selden visits her at Mrs. Hatch's apartment, Lily is conscious of her emotional need for an expression of feeling on his part (449); but when he proffers only cold, cruel judgment, she is incapable of resisting her revulsion from the "real self" that his criticism seems once more to have uncovered. The narrator repeatedly suggests that "the situation between them was one which could have been cleared up only by a sudden explosion of feeling" (449). But the habits of a lifetime cannot be dismissed. Selden has been formed as connoisseur, Lily as collectable; "their whole training and habit of mind were against the chances of such an explosion" (449). Lily must persist to the end with the only roles she understands, and her final preoccupation becomes the reclamation of "self" in Selden's eyes—at no matter what cost.* The significance of her death becomes clearer when we define her dilemma in this way. We can

---

* The introduction of Nettie with her baby has several implications. As inhabitants of the House of Mourning they give a moral focus to the satire; Lily's powerful identification with the baby gives silent testimony to the infantilizing force of the mutilating image of women that society fosters. Finally, this scene gives poignant evidence of Lily's inability to conceive of herself in any other way than as the object of aesthetic attention; even her apparently genuine and spontaneous response to the little rosy creature who seems so obviously an emblem of herself is contaminated by this habit, for at the most intimate moment in her brief fondling of the child she reverts to type. "At first the burden in her arms seemed as light as a pink cloud or a heap of down, but as she continued to hold it the weight increased, sinking deeper, and penetrating her with a strange sense of weakness, as though the child entered into her and became a part of herself. *She looked up, and saw Nettie's eyes resting on her with tenderness and exultation*" (510, emphasis mine).

never know whether it was a conscious act; so many of her finer gestures seem acts of carelessness, of thoughtless inattention. Yet the effect of her death is redemptive: it recaptures and fixes forever Selden's esteem for her; it apotheosizes her triumphant *tableau vivant*.

It is not insignificant, then, that her first act upon returning to her room for the last time is the resurrection of the Reynolds dress, nor that she should end her life by a final surrender to her fate as aesthetic object. "All her interest and activities had been taught to centre around it. She was like some rare flower grown for exhibition, a flower from which every bud had been nipped except the crowning blossom of her beauty. . . . There had never been a time when she had any real relation to life. . . . There was no centre of early pieties, of grave endearing traditions, to which her heart could revert and from which it could draw strength for itself and tenderness for others" (512–13, 516). She has destroyed Selden's letters; she has paid her debt to Trenor. But these impulsive gestures are not integrated into a sustaining moral vision of herself. Given the limitations of Lily's nature, only Selden's continued faith in her could support such a vision; "the uplifting memory of his faith" (517–18) cannot. "She felt an intense longing to prolong, to perpetuate, the momentary exaltation of her spirit. If only life could end now" (519).

There is a sensuous fulfillment in yielding, finally, to the imperative to be nothing more than beautiful; and there is relief in the relinquishment of all those difficult pretenses to adulthood—relief in a retreat to the velvet embrace of infancy, the identity that lives at the core of this notion of the feminine nature. Lily is returning wearily to the Valley of Childish Things: "She stirred once, and turned on her side, and as she did so, she suddenly understood why she did not feel herself alone. It was odd—but Nettie Struther's child was lying on her arm: she felt the pressure of its little head against her shoulder. She did not know how it had come there, but she felt no great surprise at the fact, only a gentle penetrating thrill of warmth and pleasure. She settled herself into an easier position, hollowing her arm to pillow the round downy head, and holding her breath lest a sound should disturb the sleeping child" (522).

When Selden confronts her lifeless body, Lily has been irretrievably transformed into an object; her "self" has finally been transfixed, rendered suitably free from weakness and flaw. It is ironic that confronted with this extreme he should feel "that the real Lily was still there, close to him" (526–27); the "real" Lily—the *only* Lily he can tolerate—is the beautiful idealized memory he carries of her, the most superb piece in his collection.

Selden is satisfied with this resolution to the problem of Lily Bart. He reassures himself that "at least he *had* loved her" (532). However, the structure of the novel demands more discrimination from the reader: Nettie and the husband "whose faith in her had made her renewal possible" (517) live in the House of Mourning,[79] a place where the moral-aesthetic "vanities" of men like Selden have been relinquished for the saving acceptance of suffering and human limitation. Far from being Wharton's spokesman, Selden is the final object of her sweeping social satire.

Once we reject Selden, reject the lapses into bathetic sentimentality that so aptly render his final moments with Lily, we must revaluate the peculiarly American literary tradition of which this last episode is a part. For whatever reason, this situation—the death of a beautiful woman as seen through the eyes of her lover—had become a set piece in American literature. For example, in a novel like *Daisy Miller* the death of a realistically rendered (and possibly deeply troubled) young woman is described principally in terms of the aesthetic-moral effect it has upon a highly sensitized, loverlike man. She becomes, primarily, the object of his idealistic artistic sensibilities. Until Wharton wrote *The House of Mirth*, no one had troubled to detail what it would be like to be the women thus exalted and objectified. Blake Nevius makes the obvious comparison between the two novels: "Like Winterbourne in *Daisy Miller*, [Selden] is betrayed by his aloofness, his hesitations, his careful discriminations. He is the least attractive ambassador of his 'republic of the spirit,' and Mrs. Wharton knows this as well as her readers." [80] Selden surely does share Winterbourne's inadequacies; but Wharton surpasses James specifically in her ability to reveal the psychological distortions, the self-alienation, that a woman suffers when she accepts the status of idealized object. We see the inner desolation to which Lily is reduced; we know very little of a reliable sort about Daisy, for Daisy's martyrdom (or her canonization) has precipitately robbed her of complexity, perhaps of her full share of humanity.

If (as we must) we condemn Selden for savoring the resonances of Lily's death, we might want to reconsider the moral status of any narrator or any reader who would reduce human suffering to an artistically satisfying (albeit morally uplifting) experience. We have seen the extent to which Wharton weaves the confusions of contemporary visual art into her portrait of that "frivolous society" she would have us scorn; the last scene of the novel, Lily's own Beautiful Death, forces us to look for distortions in the art of fiction as well. Henry James said admiringly of Sargent's work that he "handles [the delicate feminine elements] with a special feeling for them, and they borrow a kind of noble intensity from his brush." [81] Wharton's own portrait of a lady must lead us to wonder how well any real or realistically conceived woman could tolerate the compliment of being thus ennobled.

6

The *House of Mirth* more than confirmed Wharton's trust in words. Building upon the solid successes of her first novel and the early volumes of short stories, it sent her reputation soaring. And it was a resounding best seller as well: 30,000 copies were sold in the first three weeks; by the end of a month 60,000 copies had been ordered from Scribner's; ten days later the number reached 80,000; and in another ten days it climbed to 100,000. Edith Wharton was a celebrity. The notations in her appointment books for 1905 and 1906 make it clear that she took an active interest in her increasing fame, for she kept careful and gleeful accounts of the sales and favorable reviews. A sense of strength and self-assurance was coursing through her now, and she wrote confidently to Charles Scribner in November of 1905 about the royalties on her projected next novel: the hero, by contrast with Selden, was "going to be a *very* strong man; so strong that I believe he will break all records. Perhaps in consideration of his strength you will think it not unreasonable to start with a 20% royalty? If you were to refuse, he is so violent that I don't know whether I can answer for the consequences!" [82] We must measure her strides by comparing this playful letter with the pathetic cry for help and patience that she had written to Burlingame just ten years earlier when she had confessed herself to have "lost all confidence." In 1895 Edith Wharton could not have joked about violence, could not have suggested that the characters in her fiction might break *anything at all*—for then, even the most tentative journey beyond a narrowly prescribed arc of controlled and regulated behavior had conjured images too savage for comfort.

Many things in the routine of her life had changed. As early as 1902 she had established herself in the mansion at Lenox, regularly spending a considerable portion of each year visiting abroad, where she participated more and more fully in the intellectual life of London and Paris. When he visited America in 1904, Henry James spent several weeks with the Whartons, and the acquaintance between the two authors blossomed into deep friendship, each finding in the other a mind quick enough and subtle enough for genuine companionship. They disagreed about each other's novels. Wharton did not like the later fictions of Henry James: "For all their profound moral beauty, [they] seemed to me more and more lacking in atmosphere, more and more severed from that thick nourishing human air in which we all live and move. 'The Wings of the Dove' and 'The Golden Bowl' seem isolated in a Crookes tube for our inspection." [83] But in the years following 1904, the two novelists evolved an understanding according to which they refrained from commenting upon each other's work (for James had reservations about Wharton's novels, too). After all, they were separate artists. He could do things that she couldn't—his management of structure was unsurpassed; she had insights into "that thick nourishing human air in which we all live and move" that were increasingly excluded from his work. Though the chroniclers of their friendship often assume a different relationship, in actuality they moved in each other's company as equals. [84] This was a coming of age for Wharton that increased her self-confidence.

Yet above all these external things, nothing was so bracing as the very act of writing that momentous novel, *The House of Mirth*. Wharton's significant fictions had always drawn upon the deep well of feeling whose accumulated intensity had precipitated the breakdown in 1898: in the earliest works, these feelings had literally intruded into the work without Wharton's conscious knowledge or artistic control, and her first reaction had been an involuntary cessation of writing, an evasion by repression. Yet on the whole, Wharton did not want to stop writing, and she did not really want to continue to deny the force of these feelings; and so, gradually, the residue of the past crept more and more directly into the fictions. *The Valley of Decision* acknowledges the potential fury of man's irrational self explicitly and consciously, and the central problems of the novel turn upon political and historical dilemmas that involve this self. Yet, having raised the irrational element, Wharton's first novel recoils from it, postulating that it must be suppressed, not even that it must be mitigated or accommodated (for solutions such as these were to emerge only in the later works), but that regardless of the sacrifice, mankind can survive only by submitting to a rigid, often punitive, often cruel authority that will save him from his own impulses. We can see advancement in this initial novel—Wharton no longer denies powerful feelings altogether—but it is a very small gain. She acknowledges instinct only to conclude that it is best to keep instinct tightly in check. The artist's regressive movement is carefully monitored by the imperative to control that is preached in the novel. In *The House of Mirth*, however, Wharton takes a giant stride forward. For the first time, she gains full access to one part of her reservoir of deepest feeling and manages to fuse that feeling with an artistically appropriate problem. Wharton treats the case of the woman-made-object, and the sure cutting edge of her satire carries the deadly fury of her own childhood rage, rage that is finally articulated, rage that has found a suitable, finite focus. In *The House of Mirth* Wharton not only acknowledges the existence of deep feeling; she draws upon the energy of that feeling. She uses feeling to her own psychological and artistic advantage, and in ventilating some portion of her smoldering anger, she manages to make great fiction of it! What a triumph!

There is no doubt that the controlling form of the fiction reassured Wharton and played a large role in encouraging the expression of these hitherto confined emotions. *The Valley of Decision* is the first major work of a relatively inexperienced writer, and her anxieties concerning control are articulated explicitly within the thematic development of the fictional world in the admonition for submission to external restraint. However, as Wharton became more mature in the exercise of her craft, she recognized that control is inherent in the formal nature of a novel; and having recognized this fact (whether consciously or not) she could relax her own resistance to regression somewhat. Psychoanalytic critics like Simon Lesser have long recognized that the form of a fiction may play this role.[85] Yet I would argue that in addition to permitting a controlled fictional articulation of feelings that seem otherwise dangerous, the writing of *The House of Mirth* served two other important functions in Wharton's development.

First, she not only resurrected feelings and articulated unresolved conflicts, but in so doing she also made decisions about them. These decisions, made in the context of a novel, might then affect the subsequent pattern of decisions in her real life (often they seem clearly to have done so). No one knew better than Wharton herself the odd hybrid quality of fictional worlds; and no one had a keener appreciation of the absolute need to control them, shape the fate of the characters who dwell within them, and resolve the emotional problems that these characters had postulated. "In this world," Wharton wrote, "are begotten and born the creatures of [the author's] imagination, more living to him than his own flesh-and-blood, but whom he never thinks of as living, in the reader's simplifying sense. Unless he keeps his hold on this dual character of their being, visionary to him, and to the reader real, he will be the slave of his characters and not their master. When I say their master, I do not mean that they are his marionettes and dangle from his strings. Once projected by his fancy they are living beings who live their own lives; but their world is the one consciously imposed on them by their creator. Only by means of this objectivity of the artist can his characters live in art." [86]

Let us take the case of Lily Bart as an instance. Lily Bart is *not* Edith Wharton; *The House of Mirth* is anything but an unself-aware outpouring of Wharton's unconscious. Yet much about Lily, many of Lily's problems, reflect a *part* of Wharton—the infantile part, the part that felt helpless and alone and unable to relate with emotional closeness to other human beings (and even as we say this we must remember that another aspect of Wharton's nature is fixed in the person of the writer who manipulates Lily's fate). Everything that we have learned about Wharton suggests that she was obliged to come to terms with that infantile part of herself in order to continue to function as an adult. The very fact that she had committed herself to a career in writing indicates that she had already begun this process; the actual decisions that were made in the context of creating *The House of Mirth* extended and confirmed it. Lily Bart is not a viable adult. The book concludes with her death (by her own hand—an ambiguous suicide). Wharton as the demiurge of that fictional world *chose* to have Lily die—decided against shaping a world in which a lovely, dependent creature such as Lily Bart might survive. It was Wharton's novel; within broad limits she could have chosen any fate for her heroine, and she chose to kill her. That choice implies a judgment upon the elements of femininity that Lily embodies: they are not viable, not worth preserving.

If we look ahead to Wharton's next major novel, *The Fruit of the Tree*, we can see that the decisions implicit in Lily's fate are extended in it. In this novel there is a strong woman, Justine Brent, a nurse, someone who is capable of taking care of herself, even of taking care of others. Wharton had not abandoned the modalities of dependency, but she had left behind a primary focus on the weaker half of that relationship. Justine Brent is given the job of ministering to a hopelessly ill woman; the woman who is sick, Bessy Westmore, bears a generic resemblance to Lily Bart. She begs to be relieved of her pain and of her life, and Justine engages in a mercy killing, one that is unequivocally justified in the mind of the author and narrator. This is a further step in mastery over the emotional difficulties that had been reflected in *The House of Mirth*. Not only does Wharton recognize (again) the nonviability of a weak and infantile character who so aptly reflects that part of her own nature which is growing less and less dominant; but she introduces a new kind of woman who has self-esteem, competence, and the determination to be strong and independent. And the strong woman literally eliminates the weaker one.

The second consequence of writing *The House of Mirth* was a flowing back into her real life of the results of her self-expression and of her increased mastery over emotional conflict. The relationship between her life and work was dynamic, not static. There was a constant tension between the two. Wharton tapped those deep wells of infantile rage to strengthen the satirical thrust of *The House of Mirth*, with consequences for her life as well as for her fiction. In giving voice to anger through her art, Wharton also permitted herself to yield to the affect of that anger. She always acknowledged this kind of relationship between her life and work. "What happens [in my fictional worlds] is as real and as tangible as my encounters with my friends and neighbours, often more so, though on an entirely different plane. It produces in me a great emotional excitement, quite unrelated to the joy or sorrow caused by real happenings, but as intense, and with as great an appearance of reality." [87] If the hitherto unutterable rage of childhood finds utterance and if that utterance takes place without harm, without the annihilation that had been feared for so long, then—the conclusion follows quietly, even unconsciously—perhaps one *may* express some of the other strong emotions that have been covered over and laid to sleep beneath the snows of many years. Perhaps one might even allow them to grow and to bloom.

Wharton's inner life had changed since 1895; the changes enabled her to write a novel like *The House of Mirth*, for the sick and frightened woman of the earlier period certainly could not have done so. In turn, the process of writing *The House of Mirth* changed the inner life. Experiencing emotions within the comfortable constraints of a fiction was a way-station to experiencing them in the real world. Thus it is perhaps not too bold to suppose that writing a novel like *The House of Mirth* prepared the way for the affair with Morton Fullerton. However, we are moving too quickly ahead. Before we look at the events of 1907–8 and the years that followed, we must look at the intervening fictions.

The period between 1905 and 1908 continued the tremendous productivity that Wharton had already demonstrated herself capable of. There is a novella, *Madame de Treymes* (1907), another full-length novel, *The Fruit of the Tree* (1907), another travel book, *A Motor-Flight Through France* (1908), and another book of short stories, *The Hermit and the Wild Woman and Other Stories* (1908). Yet in all of these there is a falling-off, a failure to reach or even to approach the high pitch of achievement that had distinguished *The House of Mirth*. For one thing, Wharton had not yet established her own fictional voice with surety. If we look over the entire range of her fictions, we find a great diversity; yet there are consistent elements in her best works. We hear her characteristic voice quite clearly in *The House of Mirth*, but we hear only muffled catches of it in the works that immediately followed. *Madame de Treymes* is an interesting piece with a scintillating surface and little depth. It recounts the bewilderment of an American who confronts the convolutions of French family customs and social restrictions for the first time (these mannered complexities being captured in the perverse and elusive nature of the lady whose name gives the story its title). It was written in the interstices of the period during which Wharton worked on *The Fruit of the Tree*, and it doubtless reflects the author's own astonishments at the tortured patterns of the ancient civilization that she was coming to know better and better during her protracted visits to France. No book more convincingly supports the claims of those who would view Wharton as a disciple of James than *Madame de Treymes*, and no book more clearly demonstrates her genuine inferiority to him when she chose, as she almost never did, to be imitative of him.

The short stories are no better. There is not a single tale in *The Hermit and the Wild Woman and Other Stories* that rises to the level of "Souls Belated," "The Pelican," "The Copy," or "The Other Two." The artistic strength of *The House of Mirth* and the psychological growth that emanated from it propelled Wharton into an entirely different level of fictional possibility. This was unfamiliar territory, and she was still groping her way. *The Fruit of the Tree* displays some of her problems pretty clearly.

The Fruit of the Tree has enough raw material for three or four different novels. R. W. B. Lewis notes, "There are too many 'subjects' in the book." [88] That brief judgment really sums up its deficiencies, and an attempt to summarize the plot will support the evaluation. The novel focuses on three people: John Amherst, an intelligent and idealistic man who has gone into the business of supervising a cotton mill; Bessy Westmore, a beautiful young widow who owns the mills; and Justine Brent, an old school friend of Bessy's, now a nurse. Bessy and John encounter each other when she comes to inspect the factory; improbably, they fall in love and marry. Bessy's taste for luxurious living and indolence quickly comes into conflict with Amherst's idealistic desire to reform the mills, and the marriage sours. Bessy takes a severe fall from a horse one evening, suffers a paralyzing blow to the head, and lingers in crippled pain with no genuine hope of recovery. Justine nurses her throughout the illness and, responding to Bessy's pleading, one day administers a lethal overdose of morphine that mercifully releases the patient. Justine and Amherst subsequently fall in love, marry, and collaborate in bettering the conditions of their workers. They seem ideally happy. However, Amherst eventually learns that Justine has killed Bessy, and this bitter knowledge takes their happiness away forever. They continue as partners in running the mill, but their love has been marred beyond repair. What is the "problem" of the novel? Euthanasia, the need for industrial reform, the old problem of idealized expectations coming up against the harsh realities of real-world existence, marriage, the role of women, the devastating results of failures in communication between the sexes, men's unrealistic expectations of women, the insufficiency of women's education and of the roles they are given to enact—the list could go on and on. [89]

Lewis is quite correct when he concludes that "if Edith Wharton had . . . written a tightly packed novella devoted to [Justine Brent's] moral and psychological crisis, she might have composed one of her strongest shorter works of fiction." [90] Unfortunately, she didn't. Perhaps she couldn't. Justine Brent is an entirely new kind of creation for Edith Wharton: she is unlike any other major woman in the fiction thus far. At this point in her career, Edith Wharton was capable of summoning the character of Justine Brent, but she was not able to decide what to do with her. The surfeit of subject in *The Fruit of the Tree* can plausibly be taken as an attempt to camouflage precisely this problem.

Wharton was in no doubt about the focus of her book when she began it. *The House of Mirth* had been finished on March 22, 1905, and published in book form several months later; quickly upon its heels, Wharton launched into another major fiction. "Saturday, November 4, 1905," she notes in her diary. "Began *Justine Brent*." At first work went quickly. "Saturday, November 25, 1905. Written about 20,000 words of *Justine Brent*." [91] Then there was a long pause. Wharton made her annual pilgrimage abroad (though that was no reason not to write, for she seemed always to be able to put in a steady morning's work wherever she found herself, *provided* that she was embarked upon a good subject. What happened in this case was that she ceased working on the novel and wrote *Madame de Treymes* instead). Further delays ensued when she undertook to collaborate with Clyde Fitch in a dramatization of *The House of Mirth* which proved highly unsuccessful. Meanwhile, *Justine Brent* lay unattended. The first 20,000 words had been written in less than a month; it took nine months to write the next 19,000 words. The novel came, but it came slowly. In early November 1906, Wharton had completed about 100,000 words, and by this time she was calling the novel *The Fruit of the Tree*. The book had been put aside, and when it was taken up again, it soon assumed a different guise. If we look at the heroine closely, we can understand some of the reasons for Wharton's difficulty.

Justine's nature is articulated by contrast to Bessy's, a deliberate chiaroscuro effect in the limning of heroines that Wharton had already used several times before. [92] Bessy is beautiful and dependent, the product of society's false expectations for women: as one of her friends remarks, " 'Isn't she one of the most harrowing victims of the plan of bringing up our girls in the double bondage of expediency and unreality, corrupting their bodies with luxury and their brains with sentiment, and leaving them to reconcile the two as best they can, or lose their souls in the attempt?' " [93] We are not meant to condemn Bessy, but there is little to make us love her either, for her soft nature can rise to no stronger desire than the need to be noticed and attended to.

By contrast, Justine is fiercely independent and deeply concerned that she should never be thought otherwise. She is willing to visit her old school friend; however, she insists upon defining their relationship clearly. "She was not in the least ashamed of her position in the household, but she chose that every one else should be aware of it, that she should not for an instant be taken for one of the nomadic damsels who form the camp-followers of the great army of pleasure" (220). We might reasonably wonder (remembering how closely this heroine follows in the wake of Lily Bart) whether the concern that is imputed to Justine is not also a concern of her creator, a need to demonstrate how different this woman is from the women in her earlier fictions. In any case, if Bessy (like Lily) is a helpless child at the core, Justine is a competent caretaker. Her vocation as a nurse merely gives quotidian substance to her general inclination to feel "pity for all forms of weakness" (315).

At the very center of her being is an unfailing confidence in her own stability and power of regeneration. "She was more concerned with Bessy's fate than with her own—her poor friend seemed to have so much more at stake, and so much less strength to bring to the defence of her happiness. Justine was always saved from any excess of self-compassion by the sense, within herself, of abounding forces of growth and self-renewal, as though from every lopped aspiration a fresh shoot of energy must spring; but she felt that Bessy had no such sources of renovation, and that every disappointment left an arid spot in her soul" (318). The image drawn from nature here is not, as it was in the development of Lily's character, an indication of the decorative component; it is an affirmation of the capacity for endless renewal, a surging of power that is as unfailing as the passage of the seasons.

There is, too, a tentative introduction of animal imagery to describe the supple grace of the woman. Bessy's normal environment is a drawing room or a fussy boudoir; Justine's is the forest. She moves through it with agile quickness, guiding others "across the treacherous surface as fearlessly as a king-fisher, lighting instinctively on every grass-tussock and submerged tree-stump of the uncertain path . . . so free and flexible in all her motions that she seemed akin to the swaying reeds and curving brambles which caught at her as she passed" (300). As her name suggests, she has a burnished beauty, a flamelike intensity of spirit that flares intermittently in flashes of passionate longing. We know that in the language of Wharton's life and fictions, animals are connected with instinctual impulses. All the motions of Justine's body, all of the yearnings of her being suggest the natural depth of her capacity for feeling.

Her strength has led her initially to care for those less competent than herself, and she will always feel a welling sympathy for such beings. Yet in the blossoming of her mature desires, she wants to move beyond the restricting terms of dependency; she wants to spend her energies in some pattern other than the one of caring for and being taken care of—though she does not know how to make this transformation. "She no longer felt herself predestined to nurse the sick for the rest of her life, and in her inexperience she reproached herself with this instability. Youth and womanhood were in fact crying out in her for their individual satisfaction. . . . She wanted happiness, and a life of her own, as passionately as young flesh-and-blood had ever wanted them; but they must come bathed in the light of imagination and penetrated by the sense of larger affinities" (223).

If Justine does not know how to disengage the straightforward hungers of her womanhood from the alluring phantoms of her imagination, the dreams of a world made better by the infusion of her sense of high purpose, then it is equally true that Wharton did not yet know how to create a fictional world in which these two motives might be separated. In *The Fruit of the Tree* it is difficult to disentangle Justine's confusions from those of her creator; and it is the demands of Justine's frank animal nature that Wharton finally cannot manage.

There *is* a unifying problem at the core of this novel, the problem of Justine's need to find fulfillment as a woman. An inescapably sexual problem. Wharton can formulate the initial phase of this dilemma well enough; she has at last admitted longing, apparently even sexual longing, into her vocabulary of fictional experience. However, Wharton herself had not progressed beyond dissatisfaction. She did not yet know what it would mean to say that longings like Justine's *had* been satisfied. In fact, she did not even know how to render their ultimate frustration in well-articulated and explicit terms.

At this point, the dynamic relationship between life and art is working very much to her disadvantage, and she is limited in the range of available fictional worlds by the insufficiency of her experience in the actual world. Thus, confronted with the difficulty that should have been central to the novel, she lapses into a series of evasions: she introduces other "subjects"—many, many other subjects.

The problem of Justine's longing is never resolved (even the language in which it is postulated has an awkward, effusive quality that is unlike

Wharton's usually deft control). We follow her attempts to establish a relationship with Amherst (whose insensitivity to the feelings of others would make him unfit to be the companion of anyone in any context); and we follow the novel to its dreary conclusion—the long, gray years of indifferent marriage that stretch before her with no hope, now, that her fierce yearning will ever be satisfied. We must accept this conclusion; the fictional world of the novel offers no other. It is another landscape of desolation—like *The Valley of Decision*, like *The House of Mirth*—a lesson of submission to suffering, with no release save the release of death.

Yet we have the right to be impatient with this end and with the novel as a whole. In the two earlier works we could understand the emptiness of the ending; we might not agree that Wharton's fictions offered an adequate representation of the totality of real-world options, but they had the virtue of internal consistency. *The Fruit of the Tree* does not. Little wonder that Wharton suspended the novel so long in mid-composition. Perhaps she, too, felt the vacillation in her own progress.

It is certainly no accident that the period following the publication of *The Fruit of the Tree* continues to reveal Wharton's particular deficiencies at this point in her creative life. The next novel for which she contracted was *The Custom of the Country:* just as she had progressed from Lily Bart to Justine Brent, so she intended to progress from Justine to Undine Spragg. Here again, however, the tank ran dry. Wharton simply could not get started on her new novel. We do not have to look far for the reason. If she could not get a clear hold on Justine's dilemmas, how much less able would she be to comprehend Undine? She had ruined *The Fruit of the Tree* by completing it too soon. She did not make the same mistake with *The Custom of the Country*. She put that novel aside—for many years. By the time she returned to it, the emotional terrain through which she merely groped in 1906 had become familiar at last.

In 1907 when *The Fruit of the Tree* was published, Edith Wharton exhibited many signs that she was moving toward some major change in her life. If, as she claimed, she felt the emotions of the creatures she created, then Justine's dissatisfactions not only reflected Wharton's own feelings but reinforced them: that is, the participation (within the safety of "not real" fiction) was a way-station for Wharton along the path that led to acknowledging the full force of sexual longing in real life. Five years earlier Wharton had written about George Eliot as a way of reassuring herself that it was all right for a woman to become a professional novelist. Now, her interest in other women writers began to acquire an inescapably more sensual focus, although Wharton was clearly not yet comfortable with this new disposition. On November 6, 1907, she wrote to Brownell in an almost unrecognizably skittish mood

> I have been very much emballée lately about the poems of Mme. de Noailles [Anna de Noailles, a French woman whom Wharton had recently met]—the first time such a thing has happened to me about the poems of *any* lady in *any* language—my own (poems) included. In her last volume, especially, she seems to me to have reached that point of white heat, of perfect fusion, which even Ella Wheeler Wilcox does not attain—but lest this last flippancy, suggested by the words 'white heat,' should make you think I have been joking all along, I hasten to say that I do seriously think Mme. de Noailles a poet, and the only one of her sex I know—Sappho in the original being inaccessible to me!—Well, my point is that in reading her—more particularly in reading Les Éblouissements—I have been struck by a curious, deep-down, utterly un-French resemblance to Whitman's feeling about nature; and from there it was but a step (a rush-in-where-angels-fear kind of step) to think what *fun* it would be to tell French people so! [94]

Wharton had written the piece on George Eliot, but she never did write the projected essay on Mme. de Noailles. This time her literary rehearsals had already sufficiently prepared her for a real-life adventure.

7

Edith Wharton was forty-five in 1907. Like many women in their forties, Wharton worried intermittently about advancing middle age. "I excessively hate to be forty," she had written Sara Norton five years earlier. "Not that I think it a bad thing to be—only I'm not ready yet!" [95] At forty-five, Wharton was still not ready—not ready to accept the many emotional frustrations and lost opportunities that her life had seemed to force upon her. She was still an extremely attractive woman, slender (she had a lovely figure of which she was very vain), with auburn hair and deep-set, wistful eyes; and she had begun to exude a subtle glow of slumbering sensuality. This was the period during which Henry James began to coin those many epithets for her—"The Princess Lointaine, the whirling princess, the great and glorious pendulum, the gyrator, the devil-dancer, the golden eagle, the Fire Bird, the Shining One, the angel of desolation or of devastation, the historic ravager." [96] These are not names that James would give to a mousy, frightened woman; and in the ten years since the breakdown of 1898, Edith Wharton had grown into splendid, radiant vitality. If 1898 marked the time of most radical regression, then 1907 and 1908 marked the most definitive rejection of that crippling defense. At forty-five Wharton was "not ready" for placid middle age; however, she was ready, at long last, for sexual intimacy. She had firmly established her adult identity by having embraced the career in which she had become so successful; and the role confusion whose most acute stage had been marked by the terrible time of mental illness was now put behind. At forty-five, Wharton was prepared to face the rigors of adolescence.

Readiness often begets opportunity. In the next few years more than one man would fall in love with Edith Wharton; [97] but the one who mattered was Morton Fullerton.

Fullerton was a protégé of Henry James and a friend of the Nortons'. He had had a brilliant college career, during which he studied under Charles Eliot Norton, the distinguished Harvard professor, but his adult life had not fulfilled the promise of his youth. Three years younger than Wharton, Fullerton had pursued a moderately successful career in journalism. He worked as a Paris representative for the *London Times* and had been married, very briefly, to a French actress. This marriage, however, had in no way inhibited his extraordinary amatory adventures.[98] Fullerton had had numerous affairs before he met Edith Wharton; many, of course, were casual encounters, but several were of relatively long duration. When Morton Fullerton did engage in a serious liaison, he seemed always to follow the same pattern: his wooing and love-making was invariably given a lofty tone by his lavish literary inclination, and he wrote sensitive letters to the woman with whom he was involved (these letters occasionally got him into trouble later); his affairs, even when they were most sincerely passionate, seldom lasted longer than three years (Fullerton never made the mistake of confusing a love affair with the preliminaries to marriage, and an eventual termination was implicit in the inception); finally, miracle of miracles, he almost always remained on exceptionally good terms with his former mistresses. Insofar as women can divine the nature of men by intuition, these were the characteristics that Wharton would have sensed (or learned from friends). Many of them highly recommended Fullerton as someone with whom it would be safe to have a first affair.

Although Edith Wharton had met Morton Fullerton at social gatherings in the spring of 1907, they had their first opportunity to be alone together in late October of that year when he turned up in Lenox with introductions from James and the Nortons. Winter was early that year. There was already snow on the ground when he arrived, and he and Edith alternated talking literature and driving through the ghostly countryside. On one of their outings the chauffeur had to stop the car to put on chains, for the roads had become slippery; while he did, Edith and Morton strolled through the neighboring woods and sat down briefly upon a damp, cold hill to smoke a cigarette together and talk. They talked intently. Neither broke the mood of the moment by making explicit the current of emotion that was passing between them. As they rose to go, each picked a sprig of witch hazel from a bush growing nearby. After Fullerton had left, he enclosed a sprig of witch hazel in his courtesy note. Three days later, Edith Wharton began the Love Diary.

The Life Apart. (L'âme close.)

The Mount. Oct. 29th 1907.

If you had not enclosed that sprig of wych-hazel in your note I should not have opened this long-abandoned book; for the note in itself might have meant nothing—would have meant nothing to me—beyond the inference that you had a more "personal" accent than week-end visitors usually put into their leave-takings. But you sent the wych-hazel—and sent it without a word—thus telling me (as I choose to think!) that you knew what was in my mind when I found it blooming on that wet bank in the woods, where we sat together and smoked a cigarette while the chains were put on the wheels of the motor.

And so it happens that, finding myself—after so long!—with some one to talk to, I take up this empty volume, in which, long ago, I made one or two spasmodic attempts to keep a diary. For I had no one but myself to talk to, and it is absurd to write down what one says to one's self; but now I shall have the illusion that I am talking to you, and that—as when I picked the wych-hazel—something of what I say will somehow reach you . . .

Your evening here the other day was marked by curious symbols; for the day before you arrived we had our first autumn snow-storm (we have October snow in these hills); and on the bank where you and I sat we found the first sprig of the "old woman's flower"—the flower that blooms in the autumn!

Nov. 27th. Your letter from Paris . . .[99]

The Love Diary is a curious document. It spans the brief period between October 29, 1907, and June 12, 1908; the entries in it are widely scattered (it is by no means a daily record). It was, perhaps, a special kind of travel book for Edith Wharton, who had written so many others, a memoir in which she recorded the essential moments of her passion so that she might keep them forever with her, look back upon them and remember: there is a sense of inevitable ending even in the beginning of such a book. R. W. B. Lewis observes that "it was also a long love letter; and speaking to Sara Norton a little later about the quality of love letters as one read them in reports of divorce proceedings, [Edith] said that they might have been written by a child of ten. 'Yet the emotional inspiration,' she argued, 'ought to help expression in love as in architecture!' In her own case, it led to a form of expression that was at times uncharacteristically adolescent (not surprisingly, perhaps, since urges stifled since adolescence were among those being brought into play); and it did not always escape the clichés upon which strong emotion tends to fall back. To speak in chillingly aesthetic terms, the journal cannot be ranked among Edith Wharton's best efforts." [100] The awkwardness is to be expected.

We can speak in psychological terms of Edith Wharton at forty-five finally confronting a conflict that rightly belongs to the period of adolescence, and we can say that resolving the conflict will allow her to grow into greater maturity. All of this is true. Yet it is equally true that a forty-five-year-old woman has largely solidified the lines along which her personality may develop; options that are genuinely available to a person of seventeen are not available to someone thirty years older. Delayed adolescence can never be true adolescence: the highly sophisticated author, Edith Wharton, retained an ironic self-awareness throughout this period. Undoubtedly she *knew* that the Love Diary was bad literature, and she allowed it to be so. In the dynamic relationship between fiction and life, the period of 1907–10 was a time for living. Any attempt to make the Love Diary into a great work of art would have falsified that time by intruding the self-conscious adult even more directly into the affair than was already necessary. Edith Wharton decided to live for the moment. Later, the accumulated effects of that living would be thoroughly assimilated, and only then would they find their way back into the fiction.

Edith moved up the date of her annual voyage to Europe from January to early December, and the Whartons were in Paris well before Christmas that year. She wrote rapturous descriptions of the city back to Sara Norton: "I am sunk in the usual demoralizing happiness which this atmosphere produces in me. Dieu, que c'est beau after six months of eye-starving! The tranquil majesty of the architectural lines, the wonderful blurred winter lights, the long lines of lamps garlanding the avenues and the quays—je l'ai dans mon sang!" [101] Fullerton had been there, waiting for her. The tension between them was maintained for more than two months: they met at parties, they went to the theatre and to concerts, they dined together—and there was no definite change in their relationship. Edith was in a state of palpable excitation. Finally, some time in early spring, they became lovers. They remained lovers for three years, and then they drifted apart, remaining on very good terms for the rest of their lives. Not one of their friends except Henry James knew of the affair (although Edith's lifelong, faithful servants must have known— and conspired silently with her to keep it a secret). The emotional importance of the relationship can best be judged by looking at the Love Diary, that intimate record of the first few months of happiness.

Wharton's choice of title, "The Life Apart," comes from a love poem by the sixteenth-century French poet Ronsard: "Une tristesse dans l'âme close/Me nourrit, et non autre chose." The voracious child who had lived at the heart of Wharton's nature for more than forty years was at last to be fed! Typically, Wharton construes this nourishment in terms of words, communication: Fullerton has understood her thoughts, her needs—understood even without her having to tell him. Until now, she has had no one but herself to talk to; with Fullerton, the long soul-silence could finally be broken. The talisman of the witch hazel meant they both understood that it was not too late for an "old woman's" love. After November 27, the next entry is February 21, 1908. On that day in February, Morton finally pressed his suit, and Edith was both relieved and frightened. "I thought after all I had been mistaken; and my poor 'âme close' barred its shutters and bolted its doors again, and the dust gathered and the cobwebs thickened in the empty rooms, where for a moment I had heard an echo . . . Then we went to Herblay. . . . In the church it was still and dim, and in the shadowy corner where I sat while you talked with the Curé, a veiled figure stole up and looked at me a moment. Was its name Happiness? I dared not lift the veil . . . When you came to dine, two nights afterward, you said things that distressed me. At first it was exquisite. . . . Why did you spoil it? . . . You hurt me—you disillusionized me—and when you left me I was more deeply yours . . . Ah, the confused processes within us!" [102] The terrible poise is caught here: Edith yearned to be released from the bondage of being mute, isolated, and lonely; but implicit in that release was the necessity of expressing passion and of having the courage to trust herself to emotional intimacy. Her scruples against finally yielding to this man are couched in a variety of terms (is it right? will I be violating some genuine moral imperative? shall I do violence to the social fabric?). Yet the most powerful resistance to the relationship was far deeper: it grew from a lifelong habit of denial and repression. She had always been afraid of passion. She had no real doubt, now, as to the direction she would finally take, but the fear was there—inevitably there.

As the Diary proceeds, an interesting theme emerges: the theme of systematic self-examination, a fundamental questioning of identity. It is developed through the introduction of a shadow image, an alter ego of "some other woman." This joy cannot be truly mine—these feelings cannot live in my soul—so Edith seems to argue, for loving openness does not rightly belong in the world of Edith Wharton. "I said to myself all the week: 'I have never in my life known what it was to be happy (as a woman understands happiness) even for a single hour—now at last I shall be happy for a whole day talking à coeur, saying for once what I feel, and all that I feel as other women do.' " Her fantasies all conjure the picture of some creature who seems born of her own most wishful imagination—a happy woman, the woman she had always dreamed of being and felt she could never become. Over and over again the image is summoned. "March 3d. The other night at the theatre, when you come into the box—that little, dim baignoire (no. 13, I shall always remember!) I felt for the first time that indescribable current of communication flowing between myself and some one else—felt it, I mean, uninterruptedly, securely, so that it penetrated every sense and every thought . . . and said to myself: 'This must be what happy women feel . . .' " Sometime in early April Edith and Morton became lovers, and the momentous event is chronicled in the same terms. "I haven't written for six weeks or more. I have been afraid to write . . . Since then I have had my 'day'—two 'days' . . . one at Mountfort, one at Rovins. I have known 'what happy women feel' . . . with the pang, all through, every moment of what heart-broken women feel! Ah, comme j'avais raison de vous écrire: 'I didn't know what it would be like.' " [103]

Having committed herself completely, Edith soon begins to dread the inevitable separation: "There are . . . days, tormented days—this is one of them—when that sense of mystic nearness fails me, when in your absence I long, I ache for you, I feel that what I want is to be in your arms, to be held fast there—'like other women!' And then comes the terrible realization of the fugitiveness of it all, the weariness of the struggle, the à quoi bon? the failing courage, the mortal weakness—the blind cry: 'I want you! I want you!' that bears down everything else." [104]

And in this furnace of passion, the shadow self finally slips into her being. Who am I, Edith Wharton wonders. Can I be that "happy woman"—I, whose life has been so cold and so empty? Slowly and painfully, she recognizes that the identity she has always accepted has been fundamentally changed. "Malgré moi, I am a little humbled, a little ashamed, to find how poor a thing I am, how the personality I had moulded into such strong firm lines has crumbled to a pinch of ashes in this flame! For the first time in my life *I can't read* . . . I hold the book in my hand, and see your name all over the page! I always thought I should know how to bear suffering better than happiness, and so it is. . . . 'Je vais me ressaisir'—mais saisir quoi? This pinch of ashes that slips through my fingers? Oh, my free, proud, secure soul, where are you? What were you, to escape me like this?" From the ashes is born a new self. On May 7, 1908, she marks its coming. "Let us not lose one of the few remaining chances to 'be happy together' . . . Strange words!—that I never spoke, or heard spoken to me, before . . . I appear to myself like a new creature opening dazzled eyes on a new world. C'est l'aube!" [105]

All of the modalities that we have come to associate with Edith Wharton have been transposed in this monumental transaction: hunger has been converted into satisfaction: muteness into communication: isolation into communion. Edith Wharton would never have a basic sense of trust or of optimism; but in daring to mingle her life with that of Morton Fullerton, she found enough nourishment to give her hope and allow her to grow. "My two months, my incredible two months, are almost over!" she wrote on May 21. "I have drunk of the wine of life at last, I have known the thing best worth knowing, I have been warmed through and through never to grow quite cold again till the end . . ." [106]

Edith returned to The Mount on May 30, 1908, when she made the penultimate entry in the Love Diary. "At sea I could bear it," she wrote. "Ici j'étouffe . . ." [107] Stifle. Indeed she did. Her old, familiar life was now silhouetted against the intimacy of her springtime in Paris, and what had been acceptable before seemed an appalling desert of loneliness, a mortal solitude of terrible aspect. Fullerton was not there to confide in, and so she lapsed back into talking with her body: she developed a severe attack of hay fever and asthma that left her literally gasping for breath until mid-July.

Wharton's marriage had worsened. It would have worsened even if she had not encountered Morton Fullerton, for Teddy's own health had decayed frighteningly. He was more and more an invalid (his emotional distress also tended to be converted into physical symptoms of a widely various sort—all of them disabling), and he became pettish and demanding of attention when he was not well. From 1907 until 1913 when the couple was finally divorced, Edith Wharton's emotional energies were parceled among her work, her affair with Fullerton (which concluded amiably in 1910 or so), and her efforts to minister to Teddy. Several short stories—"The Pretext," "The Verdict," "The Potboiler," and "The Best Man"—all of which were published in *The Hermit and the Wild Woman and Other Stories* (1908), turn upon the problem of making moral choices; and since some of these were written before the liaison with Fullerton had been consummated, we must infer that Wharton had already felt herself compelled to settle upon a more harmonious set of alternatives for her life even before she met him. That the affair more clearly defined the options, however, is indisputable.

8

On the boat trip home in May of 1908, Edith Wharton wrote a story that continued the theme of these recent short fictions, but introduced into that theme the new element of Fullerton's presence. The tale is entitled "The Choice," and it was not published until 1916. If we reflect upon the delicacy of Wharton's situation, we can understand the delay. It is a story about a woman who is having an affair. One dark night, she and her lover meet in her husband's elegant boat house. The husband strolls down to the water's edge, and before he catches sight of the couple, he falls off the dock into the deep water of the lake. The lover dives in to save him, and both men struggle blindly in the dark. The woman is poised above—unable to see clearly. She puts out an oar, and someone, she cannot tell who, grabs on. Straining and pulling with all her force, the woman succeeds in rescuing the man. It turns out to be her husband. The lover has drowned, and the choice has been made for her. "The Choice" is not one of Wharton's better efforts. Clearly her energies are still too divided, her experience still too new in her mind, for her to return to the writing of fiction with mastery.

She had written several longish poems before the Fullerton affair; after the first months of their intimacy, she turned to writing poetry again, and in 1909 she published *Artemis to Actaeon and Other Verse.* She had been solicited to do several translations from the French, and, weary with reformulating other people's words, she wrote her own original French story, "Les Metteurs en Scene," which appeared in *Revue des Deux Mondes* in October 1908. But all of this writing was just a form of drifting, drifting as her life was drifting. Finally, she began to take stock—*se ressaisir.*

The entries in the Commonplace Book during 1908 suggest that Wharton was giving sustenance to that new identity who had emerged in the early part of the year and had gradually begun to be absorbed into her sense of self. She read, enjoyed, and transcribed the profane poetry of John Donne with a sense of wonderment and newness. "I wonder by my troth, what thou and I/Did till we loved?" echoes her own thought so poignantly—"I appear to myself like a new creature opening dazzled eyes on a new world. C'est l'aube." The perfect union of lovers that Donne figures in "The Ecstasy"—a spiritual joining that must descend to physical union "Which sense may reach and apprehend,/Else a great Prince in prison lies" (these two lines heavily underlined in her transcription of the poem)—seems again an almost perfect rendering of her own grateful release into ecstasy. On May 19th, she had written these lines in the Love Diary: "I knew then, dearest dear, all that I had never known before—the interfusion of spirit and sense, the double nearness, the mingled communion of touch and thought . . . One such hour ought to irradiate a whole life." [108] During the first lonely summer without Fullerton, Wharton plunged into the writings of Nietzsche, and transcriptions from his works, too, find their way into the Commonplace Book. On July 7, she wrote to Sara Norton about his philosophy: "I think it salutary now and then, to be made to realize what he calls die Un-werthung aller Werthe [the valuelessness of all values] and really get back to a wholesome basis of naked instinct. There are times when I *hate* what Christianity has left in our blood—or rather, one might say, taken out of it—by its cursed assumption of the split between body and soul." [109] In the light of her own reactions to the new self that had breathed life when Wharton fell in love, she must have been particularly fascinated by Nietzsche's constant ironic juxtapositions: "true Christian values," which are false and degrading; "false consciousness" which drives us mad; the "Saint," who exemplifies what is weakest and worst in man; and the "Beast," who embodies man's strengths. Nietzsche's veneration of the raw brute force in man's nature—his recurrence to the figure of the ani-mal self, with the usual connotations inverted—must have exerted a magnetic appeal upon Wharton, whose own earliest life had been con-jured in images such as these. At last the sensual element, the self-preserving instinct, the will to live and to grow, all these were gaining force in her nature. "I should like to get up on the house tops," she wrote to Sara Norton, "and cry to all who come after us: 'Take your own life, every one of you!' " [110] A more vehement reiteration: *se ressaisir!*

By mid-1909, the changes in her life were finally beginning to find their way back into the fiction. She was at work on a collection of stories entitled *Tales of Men and Ghosts*, which would be published in 1910. The most striking thing about these tales is the recurrent preoccupation with the theme of the double—the alter ego, the shadow self.

In several of the stories the theme is developed in very muted tones. "His Father's Son," for instance, tells the wry tale of Mason Grew, a successful businessman whose genuine sensitivity and poetic nature have been submerged in a life of dreary routine. Providence has rewarded Mr. Grew, after all, with a talented son, whose prerogative it will be to live the life that has been denied to his father. Whenever Mr. Grew watched his son bending over the fair hair of the girl he was to marry, the sight conjured a silent shade from the past. "He recalled the vision now; and with it came, as usual, its ghostly double: the vision of his young self bending above such a shoulder and such shining hair. Needless to say that the real Mason Grew had never found himself in so enviable a situa-tion. . . . Now at last his dream was coming true! His boy would taste of the joys that had mocked his thwarted youth and his dull middle-age. And it was fitting that they should be realised in Ronald's destiny. Ronald was made to take happiness boldly by the hand and lead it home like a bride. He had the carriage, the confidence, the high faith in his fortune, that compel the wilful stars." [111] There are two pairs of doubles here: the son and the vision of Mr. Grew as a young man; and, more poignant, Mr. Grew as he appears to the world—a dull and unimaginative man—and Mr. Grew as he really is. At the beginning of the story we are preoccupied with the first pair; however, the story turns upon an ironic discovery of the second.

After his mother's death, Ronald Grew came upon a collection of letters that had passed between her and a famous concert pianist. The letters are poetic, lyrical; and they suggest, irresistibly, that the two had been engaged in an affair. The boy, so apparently unlike his putative father, drew the inescapable conclusion: he is the illegitimate son of the pianist. Torn by scruples, at last he confides his discovery to his father, and to his amazement, Mr. Grew is merely amused. " 'You're your father's son, every inch of you! . . . Your father's son, and no mistake. . . . You're the son of as big a fool as yourself. And here he sits, Ronald Grew! . . . Here he sits, with all your young nonsense still alive in him. Don't you begin to see the likeness? If you don't I'll tell you the story of those letters.' " [112]

Many years ago, Mr. Grew had gone to a concert with his wife. Not a usually responsive woman, Mrs. Grew was moved deeply that evening. When the couple returned home, she wanted to write the pianist and tell him of her enjoyment; but she was inarticulate, unable to write, and her husband wrote for her. A correspondence grew up, at once intensely personal and profoundly innocent: the letters were copied out by Mrs. Grew, but they had all been written by her husband. " 'But how could you go on with such a correspondence? It's incredible!' " the boy exclaims. "Mr. Grew looked at his son thoughtfully. 'I suppose it is, to you. You've only had to put out your hand and get the things I was starving for—music, and good talk, and ideas. Those letters gave me all that. You've read them, and you know Dolbrowski was not only a great musician but a great man. There was nothing beautiful he didn't see, nothing fine he didn't feel. For six months I breathed his air, and I've lived on it ever since. . . . Look at here, Ronald Grew,' " the father grows tender and humorous as he senses his son's disappointment, " 'do you want me to tell you how you're feeling at this minute? Just a mite let down, after all, at the idea that you ain't the romantic figure you'd got to think yourself. . . . I'll tell you what it proves. It proves you're my son right enough, if any more proof was needed. For it's just the kind of fool nonsense I used to feel at your age—.' " [113]

"His Father's Son" is a gentle story in which many variations of real and shadow self are blended together with the reassuring harmony of a resonant chord.[114] Other tales in the collection deal with the theme in a harsher manner.

"The Legend" is about the double life of the famous author, John Pellerin. In his young manhood, Pellerin had poured himself into the creation of books that were ignored. He disappeared; people presumed that he had died. And some years after his death, his work was "discovered." Scholars and dillettantes stepped forward to explain the intricacies of "Pellerinism", clubs were founded to study his work; his name was given to a school of imitators; the world raised its voice in chorus to his legend.

One cold winter day, an old man is found in a New York park, the victim of robbers. He is a literate, cultivated man, obviously a gentleman, and he is "taken up" by a wealthy Long Island family. His name is Mr. Winterman. He lives quietly and unobtrusively in the guest cottage of the estate, and only gradually does he confide in one, just one, of his benefactors that he is, indeed, the vanished John Pellerin. " 'I went away in a rage of disappointment, of wounded pride—no, vanity! . . . Nobody wanted what I had to give. I was like a poor devil of a tramp looking for shelter on a bitter night, in a town with every door bolted and all the windows dark. And suddenly I felt that the easiest thing would be to lie down and go to sleep in the snow.' " [115] And so John Pellerin became Mr. Winterman. Neglect was thus easily attained. Recognition comes with greater difficulty. Winterman is reluctant to reveal his secret; he swears his confidant to silence, but he does agree to begin writing once more. When his new work appears, it receives a respectful but diffident reception; after all, it is just a minor example of "Pellerinism"—highly imitative and not really having the essential elements of the master, anyway. Kind-hearted members of the cult undertake to explain the gist of "Pellerinism" to the author, to reform his style. Not surprisingly, at the end of this story Mr. Winterman disappears again, back into the snows of oblivion.

There are several other tales in his collection that skirt the theme of the double, but by far the most powerful (and the most indicative of the direction that Wharton's creative imagination would next take) is a horror story entitled "The Eyes." As Nevius quite correctly observes, this story is a systematic flaying of the kind of man that Selden had represented, a man who is aloof and judgmental and who—without even allowing himself to be aware of his own behavior—uses people, and in using them, destroys them. "Nowhere else in her fiction are the silent traits of a Selden or a George Darrow (*The Reef*) subjected to so merciless an interpretation, as if for the first time Edith Wharton felt impelled to carry her observations to their logical conclusion and to speak more plainly than her usual ironical strategy permitted. The protagonist, an elderly bachelor named Andrew Culwin . . . is 'essentially a spectator, a humorous detached observer of the immense muddled variety show of life.' . . . His plentiful leisure has been devoted 'to the cultivation of a fine intelligence and a few judiciously chosen habits; and none of the disturbances common to human experience seemed to have crossed his sky.' . . . We first encounter him in his library, 'with its oak walls and dark old bindings,' on the evening he is to open a revealing chapter of his autobiography to a group of friends who have been matching ghost stories. He does not think highly of the queer, inconclusive tale he is about to relate; he leaves it to his guests, among whom is a young man he has recently adopted as a protégé, to determine its significance." [116]

Most commentators have labeled this tale "Hawthornesque" (as it certainly is); and although as Nevius suggests, some of its themes are more clearly related to *The House of Mirth* than to *Ethan Frome*, it is in many ways a rehearsal in miniature for the methods that are to be deployed in the subsequent novel. *Ethan Frome* is the only long Hawthornesque piece of fiction Wharton ever wrote.

One notable thing about the story is Wharton's choice of point of view. Sometimes in the short stories she allowed a tale to be told by one of its participants; however, this was not her usual narrative vantage. Usually, she employed an omniscient narrator or a narrator of limited omniscience: such an approach, like James's or Austen's, allowed her talent for irony full play. None of the novels is told in the first person— none, that is, save *Ethan Frome*. A second feature of the tale that is uncommon in Wharton's work is the use of a fiction within a fiction (here,

Culwin's "ghost story") as a vehicle for self-discovery. The horror of that self-discovery is the ultimate subject of this tale.

Culwin begins his anecdote. He is diffident and at the same time intensely uneasy. Oh yes, he has a ghost—in fact, he has two of them. " 'I could probably have exorcised them both by asking my doctor for a prescription, or my oculist for a pair of spectacles.' " You couldn't call them real ghosts. They weren't, in fact, even *whole* ghosts—only parts of a ghost—two pairs of eyes. The first pair appeared to him many years ago when he was living with an aunt and cousin and idly dallying over the writing of a book. Culwin had relieved his boredom by flirting with the cousin, a girl who was neither beautiful nor intelligent and who intrigued Culwin (as he ingenuously confesses) only because " 'it interested me to see any woman content to be so uninteresting, and I wanted to find out the secret of her content.' " Culwin drew out the girl's affection; but when he belatedly recognized the unmistakable signs of her entanglement with him, he decided to leave. He announced that he was going to Europe immediately; the girl broke down, and Culwin was so flattered by her devotion that he impulsively proposed to her. That night when he went to bed, he was visited by the eyes.

> The room was pitch black, and at first I saw nothing; but gradually a vague glimmer at the foot of the bed turned into two eyes staring back at me. I couldn't distinguish the features attached to them, but as I looked the eyes grew more and more distinct: they gave out a light of their own.
> . . . They were the very worst eyes I've ever seen: a man's eyes—but what a man! My first thought was that he must be frightfully old. The orbits were sunk, and the thick red-lined lids hung over the eyeballs like blinds of which the cords are broken. One lid drooped a little lower than the other, with the effect of a crooked leer; and between these folds of flesh, with their scant bristles of lashes, the eyes themselves, small glassy disks with an agate-like rim, looked like sea-pebbles in the grip of a starfish.[117]

They kept appearing thus, night after night; and panic-stricken, Culwin fled to Europe. Subsequently, the eyes no longer haunt him.

After two years of living desultorily in Rome, pottering about randomly on another book, Culwin was presented with a companion. A beautiful young man (there is no other way to capture him) came bearing letters of introduction. The young man, so charming, so entirely engaging, wrote poetry and fiction—very bad poetry and fiction. However, he was utterly obliging, and Culwin found himself so entirely dependent on the young man's company that he could not bear to tell him that his writing was totally without promise. And so he dangled the young man along, luxuriating in the richness of his companionship. Suddenly the eyes returned.

It was three years since I'd seen them, but I'd thought of them so often that I fancied they could never take me unawares again. Now, with their red sneer on me, I knew that I had never really believed they would come back, and that I was as defenceless as ever against them. . . .

It's not enough to say they were as bad as before: they were worse. Worse by just so much as I'd learned of life in the interval; by all the damnable implications by wider experience read into them. I saw now what I hadn't seen before: that they were eyes which had grown hideous gradually, which had built up their baseness coral-wise, bit by bit, out of a series of small turpitudes slowly accumulated through the industrious years. Yes—it came to me that what made them so bad was that they'd grown bad so slowly. . . .

There came over me a sense of their tacit complicity, of a deep hidden understanding between us that was worse than the first shock of their strangeness.

It occurred to Culwin that he could get rid of the apparition if he was willing to give up his charming companion; but it was painful to contemplate relinquishing his conveniences. Eventually, the young man took care of the matter himself. He ran out of money and time, and he asked Culwin's advice. Culwin suggested he take a 'job' as the secretary to a wealthy widow. There was " 'a salary of five thousand dollars. There may be a lot more in it than that.' " [118] The young man left angrily, and the eyes gave up their ghostly vigil once more.

Culwin pauses now in his story and glances across the room at the young man who has become his protégé and his most recent companion. The young man has sunk back into his chair and covered his face. " 'Phil—what the deuce?' " Culwin starts in astonishment. " 'Why, have the eyes scared *you?* My dear boy—my dear fellow—I never had such a tribute to my literary ability, never!' " Culwin chuckles engagingly, but his banter fails. He moves across the room and lays his hand upon the young man's shoulder. When the young man fails to respond, Culwin draws back, affronted. As he does so, the light upon the table throws his face into full relief in a mirror just opposite him. He looks up and catches sight of himself, really catches sight of himself for the first time.

"He paused, his face level with the mirror, as if scarcely recognizing the countenance in it as his own. But as he looked his expression gradually changed, and for an appreciable space of time he and the image in the glass confronted each other with a glare of slowly gathering hate." [119]

"The Eyes" is one of Wharton's most brilliant short stories. It is a talisman of the literary strength she has regained and a fitting prelude to the masterpiece of *Ethan Frome*.

9

Ethan Frome was an important book to Edith Wharton. In 1936 when Owen and Donald Davis did a dramatization of the novel, Wharton took the unusual step of writing a short preface. "My poor little group of hungry, lonely New England villagers will live again for a while on their stony hill-side before finally joining their forebears under the village headstones," she says. "I should like to think that this good fortune may be theirs, for I lived among them in fact and in imagination, ten years [her ten years of residence at Lenox], and their strained starved faces are still near to me." [120] Wharton was seventy-four when she wrote these words (just a little less than a year before her death), and there is a sense of insistent presence attached to the people of Starkfield that does not emerge when she refers to any other of her fictional creations.

There are other things that signal this novel for special attention. When Scribner's brought out a Modern Student's Library edition of *Ethan Frome* in 1922, Wharton wrote an introduction to it (something she had hitherto refused to do for any of her novels). Some years later Scribner's began to contemplate another edition with a different introduction. Wharton was notified, and she immediately voiced her distress to Mr. Scribner:

> I have a letter from the firm referring to the inclusion of "Ethan Frome" in the Modern Student's Library.
> I should be very glad to have it appear in this series, and the royalty suggested is perfectly satisfactory in the circumstances; but I should like, without appearing indiscreet, to ask about the proposed author of the introduction.
> I am rather fond of "Ethan Frome," and I should not care to have it spoken of by any one who does not understand what I was trying to do.

Would you mind telling me a little about Professor Eskine's capacity for writing of the technique of fiction? How I wish that Mr. Brownell would do this preface for me! Is it quite impossible to persuade him to? [121]

In the end, the novel was issued with her introduction. This is a kind of concern she showed for no other of her works. In *A Backward Glance*, as we have already observed, she points to *Ethan Frome* as the work that marked an end to her long period of apprenticeship. "It was not until I wrote 'Ethan Frome' that I suddenly felt the artisan's full control of his implements. When 'Ethan Frome' first appeared I was severely criticized by the reviewers for what was considered the clumsy structure of the tale. I had pondered long on this structure, had felt its peculiar difficulties, and possible awkwardness, but could think of no alternative which would serve as well in the given case; and though I am far from thinking 'Ethan Frome' my best novel, and am bored and even exasperated when I am told that it is, I am still sure that its structure is not its weak point." [122]

Wharton's sensitive comment on her own novel points directly to the heart of it: the structure of *Ethan Frome*—different from any other of her major fictions—is in an ultimate sense the true subject of the tale.

We must acknowledge the importance of this novel to its author if we are fully to understand it. The perseverance of those images of starvation and loneliness is, perhaps, easiest to understand: Starkfield and its inhabitants must be taken as a map of one portion of her mind, a systematic tracing of the contours of the child's desolation and the young woman's depression. Yet if this fiction *is* an existential statement of the part of Edith Wharton that carried the immutable traces of that early trauma, it is a *controlled* statement, the kind of statement that could be made only by one who was no longer enmeshed in the toils of such a life. The novel was written towards the conclusion of the affair with Fullerton, and as she herself avowed, Wharton had been significantly altered by the experience. "I have drunk of the wine of life at last," she wrote. "I have known the thing best worth knowing, I have been warmed through and through never to grow quite cold again till the end . . ." Never to grow quite cold is not an optimistic prediction; it is not the same thing as remaining forever warmed by the embers of love. But Wharton was in all things a realist, and she was able to accept the limitations even of this liberating experience. A person who will never grow quite cold again is, unavoidably, someone who will always be fearful of the cold, but someone who can discern quite clearly, nevertheless, the differences between her own life and the lives of those who *are* quite cold.

In terms of her personal development, Wharton had begun to explore her passional self, her sexual self. The intimacy of the affair gave her access to these. Eventually her discoveries would be returned to the fictions in novels that dealt primarily with passion—novels like *The Custom of the Country, Summer*, and *The Age of Innocence*. The initial fictional response, however, was not the beginning of a new set of subjects but the conclusion of the ones she had been working with. *Ethan Frome* is the last novel of desolation: it proclaims a triumphant command over both the emotions that shape it and the nature of fiction itself.

The novel has a fascinating provenance. Wharton begins the story for us. "I have a clearer recollection of its beginnings than of those of my other tales, through the singular accident that its first pages were written—in French! I had determined, when we came to live in Paris, to polish and enlarge my French vocabulary. . . . To bring my idioms up to date I asked Charles Du Bos to find, among his friends, a young professor who would come and talk with me two or three times a week. An amiable young man was found; but, being too amiable ever to correct my spoken mistakes, he finally hit on the expedient of asking me to prepare an 'exercise' before each visit. The easiest thing for me was to write a story; and thus the French version of 'Ethan Frome' was begun and carried on for a few weeks. Then the lessons were given up." [123] We cannot date this exercise precisely, but the most likely time is 1906 or 1907; a later date is highly implausible, and an earlier one impossible. [124] This little story in French has survived in its original black notebook and may be found in the Beinecke Library of Yale University. [125]

The French story is short, only eight printed pages, and it is skeletal by contrast with the finished novel. There are but three characters: Hart, his wife Anna, and her cousin Mattie. When the tale opens, Hart and Mattie are conversing intently as they walk through the woods; we soon discover that they are lovers and that Mattie has been asked to leave Hart's home. The story begins with Hart's voice: " 'Tu as raison . . . je ne puis rien pour toi . . . mais ne me quitte pas, chère petite. Je serai raisonnable, tu verras . . .' balbutia-t-il, comprenant que, pour la retenir et pour effacer le souvenir des paroles échangées, le seul moyen était de reprendre courageusement son rôle de frère ainé." [126] The tale is told by an omniscient narrator; there is no frame story and no first-person narration. The events central to the final novel are scarcely anticipated, and only one or two short passages (which we shall remark later) find their way into the longer fiction. Hart and Mattie continue their walk home, arriving to discover that Anna, who is sickly and complaining, plans a trip to the doctor in a neighboring town. The next day she makes the trip, and Hart, who is embarrassed and timid, stays at a local tavern until late in the evening when he returns rather tipsy. The next day Anna comes home announcing that she has found a job for Mattie in a city some distance away. Hart protests mildly, but in the end he submits. The tale concludes as he is putting Mattie on the train. Now the tone of the French version is flat, the sense of longing and of frustration muted; the desolation of the sledding accident and of the resultant eternal, infernal triangle is simply not there. What we have in the Black Book *Ethan* is only the germ of an idea—a lengthy donnée that has not yet been explored and shaped and wrought into a focused fiction. That would come only three or four years later.

In her introduction to the Modern Student's Library edition of the novel, Wharton reiterates her interest in the novel's structure. "I make no claim for originality in following a method of which 'La Grande Breteche' and 'The Ring and the Book' had set me the magnificent example." (Despite the pellucidity of its prose and its apparent simplicity, *Ethan Frome* is a tantalizingly literary work; certainly Wharton's careful planning of it followed a complex tradition, of which the works by Balzac and Browning are only two examples.) In both "La Grande Breteche" and *The Ring and the Book*, it is not the "facts" themselves which are of primary importance in the end, but the collection of facts and—perhaps above all—the impact of these facts upon the mind of the observer. In *Ethan Frome*, Wharton reminds us, "only the narrator of the tale has scope enough to see it all, to resolve it back into simplicity, and to put it in its rightful place among his larger categories." [127] It is the *relation* of the tale to the narrator's larger categories that must be our primary interest, the focus of the story as Wharton has defined it. Other writers, the venerable regionalists of New England, had already given us the surface view that Wharton scorned: a prettified spectacle of billboard art, a pastoral land seen through awestruck eyes. Wharton would look through the surface to discover what was timeless in the human mind, just as Browning had done before her.

We can follow the subtle associations of her creative intelligence. Browning had had a "source"—a kernel of subject in the Yellow Book which contained the historical account of Guido's trial; Wharton had an analogue at hand, the Black Book *Ethan*. But this source alone was now seen to be an insufficient subject. Browning's narrator impresses the importance of his method upon us in Book I of *The Ring and the Book:* "From the book, yes; thence bit by bit I dug/The lingot truth, that memorable day/Assayed and knew my piecemeal gain was gold,—/Yes; but from something else surpassing that,/Something of mine which, mixed up with the mass,/Made it bear Hammer and be firm to file." Not situation alone, not narrator alone, but each illuminating the other; the situation filtered *through* the larger categories of a narrator's consciousness (the author outside the work, controlling that delicate relation)—this is to be the subject of the work. In the end, such a method focuses our attention more clearly and precisely on the narrator than on anything else. Refracted thus, a particular event may gain significance beyond the limitations of its time and place, may finally tell us about human consciousness itself. That is the function of Art. ("Why take the artistic way to prove so much?/Because, it is the glory and good of Art,/That Art remains the one way possible/Of speaking truth. . . .")

It helps our understanding of *Ethan Frome* to have this literary kinship dangled before us (perhaps that was Wharton's reason for agreeing to write a preface to the work). But it is not necessary. There are literary affinities inherent in the work itself that force themselves upon us. Outside of *Ethan Frome*, for example, the most notorious Zenobia in American literature is Hawthorne's heroine in *The Blithedale Romance;* one of the changes that Wharton made from the Black Book *Ethan* was the change of Anna's name to Zeena (Zenobia), though Mattie's name was left unaltered. Hart's name was changed to Ethan. If we wonder why, we might plausibly connect this change with Hawthorne as well, for the only other notable Ethan in American literature is Ethan Brand of Mount Graylock (a geographical neighbor of Wharton's Lenox and psychological kin of the villagers in Starkfield—amongst whom Wharton lived in imagination for ten years). Ethan Brand had found the Unpardonable Sin in a willed isolation from the brotherhood of humanity. Wharton was not interested in sin, but she was interested in the effect of isolation upon the workings of man's emotional life: thus Ethan Frome is related to Ethan Brand; but his deadening isolation is in the cold world of unloved and unloving inner emptiness—a world of depression, loneliness, and slow starvation. Why, in the end, would Wharton be interested in so deliberately suggesting an affinity between her work and the tales of Hawthorne? Again, we must look to the structure of the novel and the role of the narrator for our answer. In much of Hawthorne (and in that most "Hawthornian" of Edith Wharton's stories—"The Eyes"), we follow the tale principally as a revelation of the teller. *The Blithedale Romance* is, ultimately, about Coverdale. Just so, *Ethan Frome* is about its narrator.

The novel begins with him, begins insistently and obtrusively.

> I had the story, bit by bit, from various people, and, as generally happens in such cases, each time it was a different story.
>
> If you know Starkfield, Massachusetts, you know the post-office. If you know the post-office you must have seen Ethan Frome drive up to it, drop the reins on his hollow-backed bay and drag himself across the brick pavement to the white colonnade; and you must have asked who he was.
>
> It was there that, several years ago, I saw him for the first time; and the sight pulled me up sharp.[128]

We must ask why Wharton would begin thus, assaulting us with the narrator's presence in the very first word. It is a decidedly unusual way to open a fiction. Only two like it come readily to mind: *Wuthering Heights* and "Bartleby the Scrivener." Wharton has informed us that she was consciously indebted to Brontë's work when she wrote *Ethan Frome;*[129] and her preoccupation at the time with the techniques of Hawthorne suggests that she may have had Melville's tale in mind as well. What does all of this suggest? First of all, an extraordinarily literary self-consciousness. Second, a focus on the narrator (for however intricate Brontë's story is, however compelling Melville's vision, it is the *narrator's reaction* that must be deemed the ultimate "subject" in both fictions).

Bearing this fact in mind, let us rush momentarily ahead—to that point in the novel where the "real subject" is generally assumed to begin. An astounding discovery awaits us: the man whom we come to know as the young Ethan Frome is *no more than a figment of the narrator's imagination.* Wharton's method of exposition leaves no doubt. We are not permitted to believe that the narrator is recounting a history of something that actually happened; we are not given leave to speculate that he is passing along a confidence obtained in the dark intimacy of a cold winter's night. No: the "story" of Ethan Frome is introduced in unmistakable terms. "It was that night that I found the clue to Ethan Frome, and began *to put together this vision* of his story . . ." (27, emphasis mine). Our narrator is a teller of terrible tales, a seer into the realms of dementia. The "story" of Ethan Frome is nothing more than a dream vision, a brief glimpse into the most appalling recesses of the narrator's mind. The overriding question becomes then—not who is Ethan Frome, but who in the world is this ghastly guide to whom we must submit as we read the tale.

The structure demands that we take him into account. Certainly *he* demands it. It is *his* story, ultimately his "vision" of Ethan Frome, that we will get. His vision is as good as any other (so he glibly assures us at the beginning—for "each time it was a different story"), and therefore his story has as much claim to truth as any other. And yet, he is a nervous fellow. The speech pattern is totally unlike Wharton's own narrative style—short sentences, jagged prose rhythms, absolutely no sense of ironic control over the language, no distance from it. Yes, the fellow is nervous. He seems anxious about our reaction and excessively eager to reassure us that had *we* been situated as *he* was, catching a first horrified glimpse of Ethan Frome, we "must have asked who he was." Anyone would. Frome is no mere bit of local color. He is, for reasons that we do not yet understand, a force that compels examination; "the sight pulled me up sharp." (It would pull all of you up sharp, and all of you would have done as I did.)

Certain elements in Wharton's story are to be taken as "real" within the fictional context: Ethan Frome is badly crippled; he sustained his injuries in a sledding accident some twenty-four years ago; he has been in Starkfield for most of his life, excepting a short visit to Florida, living first with his parents and then with his querulous, sickly wife Zeena; there is a third member of the household, his wife's cousin, Miss Mattie Silver; she too was badly crippled in the same sledding accident that felled Ethan. To these facts the various members of the town will all attest—and to *nothing more*. Everything that the reader can accept as reliably true can be found in the narrative frame; everything else bears the imprint of the narrator's own interpretation—as indeed even the selection of events chronicled in the frame does—and while that interpretation *might* be as true as any other, we dare not accept it as having the same validity as the bare outline presented above. Even at the end of the narrator's vision, in the concluding scene with Mrs. Hale, Wharton is scrupulously careful not to credit the vision by giving it independent confirmation.[130]

At this point the narrator himself is still probing. He has now spent a long winter's night in the Frome household, where no one outside the family has set foot for many years, and he is an object of some interest. He responds to that interest by attempting to use it to gain information. "Beneath their wondering exclamations I felt a secret curiosity to know what impressions I had received from my night in the Frome household, and divined that the best way of breaking down their reserve was to let them try to penetrate mine. I therefore confined myself to saying, in a matter-of-fact tone, that I had been received with great kindness, and that Frome had made a bed for me in a room on the ground-floor which seemed in happier days to have been fitted up as a kind of writing-room or study" (190). Despite this tactic, the narrator elicits nothing that he has not already known. Mrs. Hale agrees that " 'it was just awful from the beginning. . . . It's a pity . . . that they're all shut up there'n that one kitchen' " (192, 194). And these fervent platitudes fall so far short of assuring the narrator that he has touched upon the truth that even as they come tumbling inconsequently from her lips, he withdraws into himself. "Mrs. Hale paused a moment, and I remained silent, plunged in the vision of what her words evoked" (194). Her words, vague generalities—driving the narrator back into his own "vision."

If we return now to the opening of the story, we must remind ourselves that the status of the narrator is doubly significant: we are surely meant to credit the information that is given to us in the frame as "true" (and the contrast between the validity of the contents of the frame and the unreliability of the contents of the internal story is clearly signaled by the recurrence of that key word, vision); however, since it, too, is reported by the narrator who has thrust himself before us in the first word of the first sentence, we must recognize that it is biased information and that evaluations and judgments have been built even into the language and choice of incident which make it up. Wharton does not do what Conrad often did, open with a reliable omniscient narrator only to introduce her talkative character when the "facts" have already been established. Instead she forces us to traffic only with the narrator from the beginning; if we are to do that effectively, we must weigh his introduction as carefully as we measure his vision, for only by doing so can we understand, finally, why the vision is so important.

The obsessive anxiety of the narrator's opening statements reveals his need to assure us that we would have reacted just as he did. He wants to elicit our confidence; perhaps he also wants to reassure himself that he is part of our company.

Many of his preliminary remarks about Ethan have a double thrust, carrying the strong implication that he is (or seems) one way, but that he might be (or might at one time have had the option of being) quite dramatically different. It is, indeed, striking how often the narrator's conjuration of Ethan manages to conflate *two* images. "He was the most striking figure in Starkfield, though he was but the ruin of a man. It was not so much his great height that marked him, for the 'natives' were easily singled out by their lank longitude from the stockier foreign breed: it was the careless powerful look he had, in spite of a lameness checking each step like the jerk of a chain" (3–4). For clarity's sake we must dissect fantasy from fact: Ethan is tall, as are most natives, and he walks with a pronounced limp; yet these simple attributes have been elevated by the narrator's language—"the most striking figure in Starkfield," "but the ruin of a man," "careless powerful look," "each step like the jerk of a chain." Ethan Frome becomes, in the eyes of the teller of his tale, an emblem of vanquished heroism, defeated strength, and foreclosed potentiality—not merely a crippled man, but Manhood brought low. " 'It was a pretty bad smash-up?' I questioned Harmon, looking after Frome's retreating figure, and thinking how gallantly his lean brown head, with its shock of light hair, must have sat on his strong shoulders before they were bent out of shape" (6).

The contrast preys upon the narrator's mind, and he finds himself compelled to pry into the matter. Relentlessly he questions those taciturn New Englanders, and he gets a series of enigmatic and taciturn replies. "Harmon drew a slab of tobacco from his pocket, cut off a wedge and pressed it into the leather pouch of his cheek. 'Guess he's been in Starkfield too many winters. Most of the smart ones get away.' 'Why didn't *he?*' 'Somebody had to stay and care for the folks. There warn't ever anybody but Ethan. Fust his father—then his mother—then his wife' " (6–7).[131] Too many winters. The phrase becomes a key to the puzzle. "Though Harmon Gow developed the tale as far as his mental and moral reach permitted there were perceptible gaps between his facts, and I had the sense that the deeper meaning of the story was in the gaps. But one phrase stuck in my memory and served as the nucleus about which I grouped my subsequent inferences: 'Guess he's been in Stark-field too many winters' " (6).

The narrator offers this phrase to us as a central clue to Ethan's dilemma and to his own investigation; then abruptly, the distance between those two narrows. The narrator becomes implicated in Ethan's fate, and his investigation must be presumed to include himself as well. "Before my own time there was up I had learned to know what that meant. . . . When winter shut down on Starkfield, and the village lay under a sheet of snow perpetually renewed from pale skies, I began to see what life there—or rather its negation—must have been in Ethan Frome's young manhood. . . . I found myself anchored at Starkfield . . . for the best part of the winter" (7–8). Was the speaker interested in Ethan Frome's history before he (like Ethan) had been constrained to spend a winter at Starkfield? There is no way, really, of knowing, for the entire tale is told retrospectively (and of course, the narrator is insistent—perhaps too insistent—that *anyone* would have felt an interest in the man, the interest that he felt immediately upon seeing him).

Who is the narrator? A busy man—we see the energy that he pours into his quest—a man of affairs: "I had been sent up by my employers on a job connected with the big power-house at Corbury Junction, and a long-drawn carpenters' strike had so delayed the work that I found myself anchored at Starkfield" (8). Nothing else would have brought such a man up here. Even marooned as he is in this desolate spot, he does what he can to keep his routines regular: he hires Denis Eady's horses to take him daily over to Corbury Flats where he can pick up a train, and when Eady's horses fall sick, he hires Ethan Frome. The man has a visionary side; we have already seen it in the language of his opening remarks. But surely he is at heart an active man, a man who is part of the larger world, a man who keeps his options open, a man who bears no essential similarity to these poor folk among whom he has been thrust. Spending one winter in Starkfield will surely mean nothing to such a man. "During the early part of my stay I had been struck by the contrast between the vitality of the climate and the deadness of the community" (8)—the observation of a confident outsider.

And yet, slowly, something within him begins to succumb to this insidious environment. "Day by day, after the December snows were over, a blazing blue sky poured down torrents of light and air on the white landscape, which gave them back in an intenser glitter. One would have supposed that such an atmosphere must quicken the emotions as well as the blood; but it seemed to produce no change except that of retarding still more the sluggish pulse of Starkfield. When I had been there a little longer, and had seen this phase of crystal clearness followed by long stretches of sunless cold; when the storms of February had pitched their tents about the devoted village and the wild cavalry of March winds had charged down to their support; I began to understand why Starkfield emerged from its six months' siege like a starved garrison capitulating without quarter. . . . I felt the sinister force of Harmon's phrase: 'Most of the smart ones get away' " (9). And as he begins to "feel" the force of the phrase—and of the environment which sucks his confidence and his independence away from him—and as his tale draws closer and closer to that crucial moment of transition when we move into the "vision," a peculiar thing begins to happen to his language. The brave assertion of heroic contingencies falters; what he limns now is capitulation, and at the heart of the experience is an unavoidable and dreadful image—"cold" and "starved."

Doggedly, the narrator persists in his quest. He sounds the finer sensibility of Mrs. Ned Hale, who rises only to the platitude that she seems fated to reiterate without explanation: " 'Yes, I knew them both . . . it was awful . . .' " (11).

And yet, it is not entirely clear what *would* satisfy him. He does not want facts alone; he wants something less tangible, something deeper. "No one gave me an explanation of the look in his face which, as I persisted in thinking, neither poverty nor physical suffering could have put there" (12). He wants an explanation for his own inferences and his own suppositions—we might call them the projections of his own morbid imagination. Harmon Gow, who is more loquacious, can be prodded to speak. The "facts" as he sees them look only to those causes which the narrator has already rejected as insufficient, poverty and physical suffering. But the language in which he speaks, language which the narrator records more completely than any other utterance in the frame, addresses itself to the deeper meaning and heightens the horror of the narrator's speculations by reinforcing those images of starvation: " 'That Frome farm was always 'bout as bare's a milkpan when the cat's been round; and you know what one of the old water-mills is wuth nowadays. When Ethan could sweat over 'em both from sun-up to dark he kinder choked a living out of 'em; but his folks et up most everything, even then, and I don't see how he makes out now. . . . Sickness and trouble: that's what Ethan's had his plate full up with, ever since the very first helping' " (14–15).

The narrator's next description of Ethan—drawn during their initial intimate contact as Frome drives him for the first time to the railroad junction—brings all of these themes together. The sight of Frome still calls up visions of ancient heroism and strength; but superimposed upon these images and ultimately blotting them out is a picture of Ethan Frome as the embodiment of some deep mortal misery. Not poverty, merely; not hard work, merely. But something intrinsic to human existence, something imponderable and threatening—something that might swallow up everything else. "Ethan Frome drove in silence, the reins loosely held in his left hand, his brown seamed profile, under the helmet-like peak of the cap, relieved against the banks of snow like the bronze image of a hero. He never turned his face to mine, or answered, except in monosyllables, the questions I put, or such slight pleasantries as I ventured. He seemed a part of the mute melancholy landscape, an incarnation of its frozen woe, with all that was warm and sentient in him fast bound below the surface; but there was nothing unfriendly in his silence. I simply felt that he lived in a depth of moral isolation too remote for casual access, and I had the sense that his loneliness was not merely the result of his personal plight, tragic as I guessed that to be, but had in it, as Harmon Gow had hinted, the profound accumulated cold of many Starkfield winters" (15–16). And, as we have already observed, this is a winter of the soul that the narrator must now share.

We can see the narrator attempting to assert a distance between himself and this foreboding figure; but in the palpable cold of the region of Starkfield, all things seem to contract. Instead of discovering reassuring distinctions, the narrator finds disconcerting and unexpected similarities. "Once I happened to speak of an engineering job I had been on the previous year in Florida, and of the contrast between the winter landscape about us and that in which I had found myself the year before; and to my surprise Frome said suddenly: 'Yes: I was down there once, and for a good while afterward I could call up the sight of it in winter. But now it's all snowed under.' . . . Another day, on getting into my train at the Flats, I missed a volume of popular science—I think it was on some recent discoveries in bio-chemistry—which I had carried with me to read on the way. I thought no more about it till I got into the sleigh again that evening, and saw the book in Frome's hand. 'I found it after you were gone,' he said. . . . 'Does that sort of thing interest you?' I asked. 'It used to.' . . . 'If you'd like to look the book through I'd be glad to leave it with you.' He hesitated, and I had the impression that he felt himself about to yield to a stealing tide of inertia; then, 'Thank you—I'll take it' " (16–18).

The winter landscape reduces the world and obliterates casual surface distinctions. The snow-covered fields lie about the two men, "their boundaries lost under drift; and above the fields, huddled against the white immensities of land and sky, one of those lonely New England farm-houses that make the landscape lonelier" (21). Unknown affinities emerge when everything that fleshes out man's daily existence is taken away—like the ice-age rocks that unpredictably thrust their noses through the frozen ground during winter heaves   shared mortal problems and shared mortal pain. A man must confront himself in such a world, and the narrator is brought to this terrible task in his journey with Ethan Frome. Frome is his Winterman, his shadow self, the man he might become if the reassuring appurtenances of busy, active, professional, adult mobility were taken from him.

The narrator is a man of science; he knows the meaning of cold. Cold is an absence, a diminishment, a dwindling, and finally a death. Everything contracts in the cold. The "place" of the novel is defined by this contraction: from the world to Starkfield; from Starkfield to the thickening darkness of a winter night, "descending on us layer by layer" (25); from this "smothering medium" (25) to the "forlorn and stunted" (22) farmhouse that is a castrated emblem of its mutilated owner. This relentless constriction of place accompanies a slow shedding of adult personae and leads finally to a confrontation with the core of self that lives beneath these and that would emerge and engulf everything else should the supporting structures of the outside world be lost, somehow. To this point is the narrator reduced—to the edge of nothingness: without identity, without memory, without continuity, without time. All these are outside and beyond. Now there is only the farmhouse. The two men enter it, enter into a small, dark back hallway. The movement is inescapably decreative, and it is captured in a perverse and grotesque inversion of the terms of birth. They move through the hall to the door of a small, warm room. Slowly, the door is opened, and as it opens, the narrator, who is poised on the threshold, starts to "put together this vision" of Frome's story (27). The fantasy begins.

The fantasy begins with an involuntary echo of the narrator's own world: Ethan Frome, a young man striding through the clear atmosphere of a winter night, "as though nothing less tenuous than ether intervened between the white earth under his feet and the metallic dome overhead. 'It's like being in an exhausted receiver,' he thought" (29)—an association that is plausible in the young Ethan Frome, who had been, so the fantasy postulates, at a technological college at Worcester, but which is much more probably related to the consciousness of the storyteller, who has been sent to Starkfield to work on a power plant. Perhaps the principal thrust of the image is to assert the similarities between the two. They are surely placed similarly. The story brings Ethan to the church where Mattie Silver has gone to dance. He waits for her—poised just outside and looking in—and his position recapitulates the modalities of the narrator's own placement in the framing story, the cold without and the warmth within. However, the implication here is inverted: in young Ethan's life the warmth of the dance represents gaiety, freedom, and love.

The motif of the threshold renders one of the most significant themes of the novel. The narrator's vision begins while he is poised at the edge of the kitchen with the door beginning to swing open. The long fantasy is spun out; it concludes with the terrible, abortive sledding accident, and we return to the framing world of the narrator. "The querulous drone ceased as I entered Frome's kitchen . . ." (187). The entire fantasy has been formulated in the instant that marks the passage from hall to kitchen—that timeless eternity of hesitation upon the threshold. In its essential formulation, the story is about that transition (or the failure to make it). The narrator's fantasy about young Ethan begins by placing him at the juncture of two worlds. Over and over again he is pictured thus. Ethan and Mattie return to the farmhouse, and they are greeted at the threshold by Zeena. "Against the dark background of the kitchen she stood up tall and angular, one hand drawing a quilted counterpane to her flat breast, while the other held a lamp. The light, on a level with her chin, drew out of the darkness her puckered throat and the projecting wrist of the hand that clutched the quilt, and deepened fantastically the hollows and prominences of her high-boned face under its ring of crimping-pins" (58). The next night, after Zeena has gone, the vision is reenacted with Mattie: "So strange was the precision with which the incidents of the previous evening were repeating themselves that he half expected, when he heard the key turn, to see his wife before him on the threshold; but the door opened, and Mattie faced him. She stood just as Zeena had stood, a lifted lamp in her hand, against the black background of the kitchen. She held the light at the same level, and it drew out with the same distinctness her slim young throat and the brown wrist no bigger than a child's. Then, striking upward, it threw a lustrous fleck on her lips, edged her eyes with velvet shade, and laid a milky whiteness above the black curve of her brows" (87–88). Since these threshold scenes with Zeena and Mattie are the only two significant passages that have been preserved from the Black Book *Ethan*, we must infer that Wharton chose to use them again because *only these* were appropriate to the story as it is told by the narrator, for only these echo his own spatial position and his own psychological dilemma.

We know what thresholds meant to Edith Wharton long ago, and though we need not have this knowledge to understand the novel, it greatly enriches our reading of it. The threshold of Lucretia's house was a moment of transition for the adolescent girl: at this juncture, the opposing demands of two distinct worlds were visited upon her—the world of adulthood, independence, freedom, and sexual maturity; and the world of childhood, obedience, limitation, and emotional starvation. Every passage of this threshold entailed a momentous and terrible struggle: here Edith Wharton, poised in unbearably protracted psychic conflict, was seized by "a choking agony of terror"—anxiety that took the almost palpable form of a ravening beast at her back. In adolescence, the implications of independence were apparently more frightening than the consequences of submission: the beast who embodied her fears stalked her only when she was outside, and her dreadful anxieties could be relieved by reentering Mother's house. Certainly for many years Edith Wharton did choose to submit herself to the rule of "Mother's house."

And yet, as Wharton eventually discovered, this retrogression had an even more appalling aspect than the dangers that had attended her excursions into the outside world. An adult who has chosen dependency must remain an incomplete and undeveloped human being. Even worse, once systematic diminishment of self has been begun, there is no natural limitation to the process. The only end to diminishment is nullity. The mature Edith Wharton recognized her adolescent mistake. The recovery from the illness of 1898 was a reiteration of this crisis at the threshold, a reenactment in which (given a second chance) the woman chose the outside world and all that went with it: autonomy and initiative. As time passed, her personal struggle opened to her a truth that inheres in the human condition. There is more than a little accuracy in the narrator's obsessive claim—"you must have asked who he was." We all harbor a "Winterman": it is always tempting to cast aside the complexities and demands of adulthood. Within every one of us there lurks a phantom self, not our "real" self, not the self that the world sees, but a seductive shade who calls us to passivity and dependency in a sweet, soft voice. Here is the greatest danger—to relax, to let go, to fall pell-mell, tumbling, backward and down. The horror of the void.

Such is the world we enter as the door to Ethan Frome's kitchen begins to swing slowly open: a world of irrecoverable retreat.

Central to such a world is an inability to communicate: its habitants are inarticulate, mute; and like the patient farm animals they tend to, they are helplessly bound by their own incapacities. The narrator has already experienced Ethan's parsimonious conversation, and his vision repeatedly returns to it. Ethan, walking with Mattie, longing to tell her of his feelings, admiring her laughter and gaiety: "To prolong the effect he groped for a dazzling phrase, and brought out, in a growl of rapture: 'Come along' " (49). Again and again Ethan "struggled for the all-expressive word" (53); and again and again he fails to find utterance.

Speech is the bridge that might carry Ethan Frome to a world beyond Starkfield, the necessary passport to wider activities and larger horizons. Without it, he is literally unable to formulate plans of any complexity because all such determinations are beyond his limited powers of conceptualization and self-expresson. Because he cannot think his problems through in any but the most rudimentary way, he is as helpless as a child to combat the forces that bind him. It is not that he does not feel deeply, for he does. However, one mark of maturity is the ability to translate desire into coherent words, words into action; and Ethan Frome is incapable of all such translations. "Confused motions of rebellion stormed in him. He was too young, too strong, too full of the sap of living to submit so easily to the destruction of his hopes. Must he wear out all his years at the side of a bitter querulous woman? Other possibilities had been in him, possibilities sacrificed, one by one, to Zeena's narrow-mindedness and ignorance. . . . All the healthy instincts of self-defence rose up in him against such waste" (142). Still, he cannot concoct his own plans. All thoughts of another life must come to him ready-made. He gropes among the meager scraps of his experience: there is the "case of a man over the mountain" (142), a man who left his wife and went West. His eye falls on a newspaper advertisement, and he reads "the seductive words: 'Trips to the West: Reduced Rates' " (145). But these solutions are no better than clothes bought through a mail-order catalogue: they do not fit his situation; they hang loosely on his lank frame, bearing only the general outline of the garment he desires; he must do the finishing work himself, must tailor the garment to fit. And he cannot do such work (how had that other man done it, anyway? how could *he*, Ethan Frome, scrape together enough money to make such a move?). Imprisonment is not inevitably inherent in the external conditions of his world. The example of the other fellow demonstrates as much. But Frome does not have any set of categories available to him that can explain how escape is possible.

It is not too much to say that the entire force of Ethan's life has been exerted merely to hold him at the level of primitive communication he does manage; and the balance of his life, even as he leads it, is precarious and dangerous. A more fully developed capacity to express himself might open avenues of escape. Any further dwindling of his limited abilities would lead in the opposite direction, propelling him down pathways that are both terrifying and fascinating. Further to lose the power of expression would be a diminishment of self; but though loss of self is an appalling specter, there is at the same time a sensuous attraction in the notion of annihilation—of comforting nothingness.

Why had he married Zeena in the first place, for example? Left with his mother after his father's death, Ethan had found that "the silence had deepened about him year by year. . . . His mother had been a talker in her day, but after her 'trouble' the sound of her voice was seldom heard, though she had not lost the power of speech. Sometimes, in the long winter evenings, when in desperation her son asked her why she didn't 'say something,' she would lift a finger and answer: 'Because I'm listening.' . . . It was only when she drew toward her last illness, and his cousin Zenobia Pierce came over from the next valley to help him nurse her, that human speech was heard again in the house. . . . After the funeral, when he saw her preparing to go away, he was seized with an unreasoning dread of being left alone on the farm; and before he knew what he was doing he had asked her to stay there with him" (74–76). Yet Ethan's own habitual tendency to silence is not relieved by Zeena's presence. The deep muteness of his nature seems to have a life of its own, spinning outside of him and recreating itself in his environment. After a year or so of married life, Zeena "too fell silent. Perhaps it was the inevitable effect of life on the farm, or perhaps, as she sometimes said, it was because Ethan 'never listened.' The charge was not wholly unfounded. When she spoke it was only to complain, and to complain of things not in his power to remedy; and to check a tendency to impatient retort he had first formed the habit of not answering her, and finally of thinking of other things while she talked" (77–78).

He knows that his silence (so like the silence of his mother who had been "listening" to unearthly voices) is but a short step from pathology. He fears that Zeena, too, might turn "queer"; and he knows "of certain lonely farm-houses in the neighborhood where stricken creatures pined, and of others where sudden tragedy had come of their presence" (78). But his revulsion from silence is ambivalent, for beyond insanity, there is another vision—the close, convivial muteness of death. Ethan feels its attractions each time he passes the graveyard on the hill. At first the huddled company of gravestones sent shivers down his spine, but "now all desire for change had vanished, and the sight of the little enclosure gave him a warm sense of continuance and stability" (55). On the whole, he is more powerfully drawn to silence than to speech. Over and over again, the arrangements of his life reinforce that silence. If his consciousness recoils from it in terror, some deeper inclination perversely yearns toward it.

It is always easier for Ethan to retreat from life into a "vision" (the word is echoed within the fantasy in a way that inescapably reinforces the narrator's deep identification with him). If Ethan is not able to talk to Mattie during that walk home from church, the deprivation is more than compensated for by his imagination. "He let the vision possess him as they climbed the hill to the house. He was never so happy with her as when he abandoned himself to these dreams. Half-way up the slope Mattie stumbled against some unseen obstruction and clutched his sleeve to steady herself. The wave of warmth that went through him was like the prolongation of his vision" (55–56). The force of such visions is indescribable: it is the appeal of passivity, the numbing inertia that renders Frome impotent in the face of real-world dilemmas. Like a man who has become addicted to some strong narcotic, Frome savors emotional indolence as if it were a sensual experience. In the evening he spends alone with Mattie he is ravished by it. They sit and talk, and "the commonplace nature of what they said produced in Ethan an illusion of long-established intimacy which no outburst of emotion could have given, and he set his imagination adrift on the fiction that they had always spent their evenings thus and would always go on doing so . . ." (97). In truth he is not listening to Miss Mattie Silver with any greater attention than he gives to Zenobia; he is listening to the mermaid voices within himself. Afterwards, the vision lingers. "He did not know why he was so irrationally happy, for nothing was changed in his life or hers. He had not even touched the tip of her fingers or looked her full in the eyes. But their evening together had given him a vision of what life at her side might be, and he was glad now that he had done nothing to trouble the sweetness of the picture" (106). As always, the uncompromised richness of the dream is more alluring than the harsher limitations of actual, realized satisfactions.

In electing passivity and a life of regression, Ethan Frome has chosen to forfeit the perquisites of manhood. The many images of mutilation throughout the story merely reinforce a pattern that has been fully established well before the sledding accident. Ethan flees sexuality just as he has fled self-assertion. When he loses his mother, he replaces her almost without a perceptible break in his routines; and the state of querulous sickliness to which Zeena retreats after a year of marriage might plausibly be seen as a peevish attempt to demand attention of some sort when the attentions more normal to marriage have not been given. It is not Zenobia's womanliness that has attracted Ethan: "The mere fact of obeying her orders . . . restored his shaken balance" (75). Yet the various components of this wife-nurse soon grate upon Ethan Frome's consciousness. "When she came to take care of his mother she had seemed to Ethan like the very genius of health, but he soon saw that her skill as a nurse had been acquired by the absorbed observation of her own symptoms" (77). Ethan and Zeena have been brought together by their mutual commitment to the habits of care-taking; now they have become imprisoned by them.

At first, Ethan's affection for Mattie seems to have a more wholesome basis. However we soon realize that the sensual component in that relationship is of a piece with the sensuality of death. It thrives on exclusions and cannot survive in the rich atmosphere of real-world complexities. Ethan features Mattie as someone who can participate in his visions, and he does not allow the banality of her actual personality to flaw that supposition. One evening they stand watching the blue shadows of the hemlocks play across the sunlit snow. When Mattie exclaims: " 'It looks just as if it was painted!' it seemed to Ethan that the art of definition could go no farther, and that words had at last been found to utter his secret soul . . ." (37–38). His imagination can remedy the deficiencies of genuine conversation; if worse comes to worst, he can ignore genuine conversation altogether (as he has in his relationship with Zeena) and retreat to the more palatable images of his fancy.

By far the deepest irony is that Ethan's dreams of Mattie are not essentially different from the life that he has created with Zeena; they are still variations on the theme of dependency. Mattie "was quick to learn, but forgetful and dreamy. . . . Ethan had an idea that if she were to marry a man she was fond of the dormant instinct would wake, and her pies and biscuits become the pride of the country; but domesticity in the abstract did not interest her" (39). The fantasies here are doubly revealing. As always he substitutes make-believe for reality—loving his vision of Mattie rather than Mattie herself. However, even when Ethan is given full rein, even when he can make any imaginary semblance of Mattie that he wants, he chooses a vision that has no sexual component. He does not see her as a loving wife to warm his bed in the winter. No. She is, instead, a paragon of the kitchen, a perfect caretaker, someone who can fill his stomach—not satisfy his manhood. She is, in short, just what he had imagined Zeena might be. And there is no reason, even at the beginning of the tale, to suppose that Mattie Silver would be any better in the role than Zeena.

Ethan and Mattie are never pictured as man and woman together; at their most intimate moments they cling "to each other's hands like children" (178). At other times, they envision a life in which they exchange the role of caretaker and protector: if Mattie might become the best cook in the county; Ethan longs " 'to do for you and care for you. I want to be there when you're sick and when you're lonesome' " (172). When they finally do come together in their momentous first kiss, even that physical contact is described in terms that remove it from the world of adult passion and reduce it to the modalities of infancy: "He had found her lips at last and was drinking unconsciousness of everything but the joy they gave him" (130).

The sled ride is a natural climax to all of the themes that have been interwoven throughout the story. It is, or ought to be, a sexual culmination—the long, firm sled; the shining track opening up before them; the swift, uneven descent, now plunging "with the hollow night opening out below them and the air singing by like an organ" (176), now bounding dizzily upward only to plunge again with sudden exultation and rapture past the elm until "they reached the level ground beyond, and the speed of the sled began to slacken" (177). The description of their long, successful first ride gives some intimation of the possibilities before them. Nevertheless, the language does not remain fixed; the vision is not steady. By this time the story has achieved such a palpable air of veracity that the reader is apt to accept this language as a more or less adequate description of what "really happened." Of course it is not. Even at this point—especially at this point—we must recollect that Ethan's world and all of the decisions in it (all the language that renders those decisions) is no more than the narrator's vision. We have finally reached the heart of that vision—the ultimate depths of the shadow world in which the narrator has immersed himself—and the inescapable implications of it crowd about us like the shades that gather dusk together and enfold the world in night.

The story becomes a vertitable dance around the notion of vision. Ethan's eyesight is keen. " 'I can measure distances to a hair's breadth—always could,' " he boasts to Mattie. And she echoes his thought: " 'I always say you've got the surest eye . . .' " (177). Yet tonight "he strained his eyes through the dimness, and they seemed less keen, less capable than usual" (181). Other visions are competing against his clear-eyed view. The couple discovers that each has ached throughout the long six months before, dreaming of the other, dreams defying sleep. This, too, is a climax; for the mingling of their love-fancies becomes the most explicit bond between them. It is a more compelling vision even than the long, smooth, slippery track before them, a vision that is compounded by the potent imagery of Mattie's despair. " 'There'll be that strange girl in the house . . . and she'll sleep in my bed, where I used to lay nights and listen to hear you come up the stairs . . .' " (180). Vision calls to vision, and Ethan, too, succumbs to the stealing softness of his own dreams. "The words were like fragments torn from his heart. With them came the hated vision of the house he was going back to—of the stairs he would have to go up every night, of the woman who would wait for him there. And the sweetness of Mattie's avowal, the wild wonder of knowing at last that all that had happened to him had happened to her too, made the other vision more abhorrent, the other life more intolerable to return to . . ." (180).

It is Mattie who suggests death (though her plea has the urgency of a lingering sexual appeal): " 'Ethan! Ethan! I want you to take me down again!' " (179). And he resists her—as he has always resisted any action.

In the end, he is seduced by the vision; her words do not even penetrate. "Her pleadings still came to him between short sobs, but he no longer heard what she was saying. Her hat had slipped back and he was stroking her hair. He wanted to get the feeling of it into his hand, so that it would sleep there like a seed in winter" (180). Not the violence of passion, but the loving, soothing release of sleep. Never has the silence been more profound (her words lost entirely into the cold and empty ether— that exhausted receiver of sky inverted over earth). The close conviviality of the grave has overwhelmed his imagination at last: "The spruces swathed them in blackness and silence. They might have been in their coffins underground. He said to himself: 'Perhaps it'll feel like this . . .' and then again: 'After this I sha'n't feel anything . . .' " (181). The indivisible comfort of nothingness.

The delicate balance has swung finally to the side of retreat; time and space rush forward, and Ethan Frome lapses back into the simplicities of childhood, infancy. Words will not suffice to reach him now. Nothing does, save one sound—"he heard the old sorrel whinny across the road, and thought: 'He's wondering why he doesn't get his supper . . .' " (181). Food—and then sleep—the very oldest memories, the persistent, original animal needs, nothing more. Mattie urges him, but he responds only to the "sombre violence" (181) of her gesture as she tugs at his hand. Slowly they take their places. But then, Ethan stops. " 'Get up! Get up!' " he urges the girl. "But she kept on repeating: 'Why do you want to sit in front?' 'Because I—because I want to feel you holding me,' he stammered, and dragged her to her feet" (182). This is how he must go, cradled in the embrace of her arms.[132]

The ride begins. Down the hill—no farewell but the gentle neighing of the sorrel. Down and down again, a "long delirious descent [in which] it seemed to him that they were flying indeed, flying far up into the cloudy night, with Starkfield immeasurably below them, falling away like a speck in space" (183). " 'We can fetch it' " (184); he repeats the refrain as the sled wavers and then rights itself toward the looming elm. "The air shot past him like millions of fiery wires, and then the elm . . ." (184).

Afterwards, there seems nothing left but silence; silence at first, and then "he heard a little animal twittering somewhere near by under the snow. It made a small frightened *cheep* like a field mouse. . . . He understood that it must be in pain. . . . The thought of the animal's suffering was intolerable to him and . . . he continued to finger about cautiously with his left hand, thinking he might get hold of the little creature and help it; and all at once he knew that the soft thing he had touched was Mattie's hair and that his hand was on her face" (185). He has come to the very verge, but he has not managed to go over. His own final threshold remains uncrossed. He has not quite died. He has only been reduced, irretrievably reduced, to the sparse simplicities of animal existence.

Having plunged thus far from the world of adult possibilities, having brought Mattie and Zeena with him, he is doomed, after all, to wait for the end—possibly to wait for a long time. The last words of the vision measure the level of reality to which he has consigned himself. "Far off, up the hill, he heard the sorrel whinny, and thought: 'I ought to be getting him his feed . . .' " (186). Thus the vision concludes, and the narrator steps finally through the kitchen door into the unchanging world of Ethan Frome, his wife, and Miss Mattie Silver. The condition of static misery that he infers, the life that has been Frome's scant portion, is an inevitable consequence of those dark impulses that lead past madness to the edge of oblivion.

We leave the narrator reflecting upon the tale he has told. It is not "true" except as an involuntary expression of his own hidden self; nevertheless, this purgatory of the imagination becomes ominously insistent, and the "self," having had life breathed into it, grows stronger even as the narrator assembles his story. Mrs. Hale's banal chatter falls upon deaf ears: he heeds her no more than Ethan has heeded Zeena or Mattie; and like Ethan, he has a parsimonious way with conversation. "Mrs. Hale paused a moment, and I remained silent, plunged in the vision of what her words evoked" (194). Insidiously, the vision possesses him.

Wharton issues a grisly invitation to compare this frozen horror with the works of the New England regionalists.[133] It is grotesque—this tale of appalling bleakness, this novel of the apocalypse measured against those wistful, nostalgic, sentimental evocations of "rural simplicities." The contrast is so bizarre that we might be tempted to rest with the obvious differences, and that would be a mistake.

Ethan Frome introduces us to terrible contingencies of the human condition; it also compels us to examine a nightmare that inheres in the deluding allurements of all literary embodiments of the Romantic vision. If we remove the accidents from the work of a writer like Sarah Orne Jewett (even one with such mastery), what will we find? What is the subject of her loving attention? In social terms, we must speak of a diminished world where all pleasure, all hope, all energy have been focused into the simplest acts of subsistence. We read of early-morning blueberries and succulent fresh fish, of hot tea and cold milk, and of long, chilly, dreamless summer nights. The disruptions in such a world are few (and they often come as unwelcome invasions from the world outside), but peace has been purchased at the price of passion. There is no rage, and the climax of sexual fulfillment has been indefinitely suspended. It is a twilight world; perhaps a world of senescence, but more probably an evocation of childhood. It recalls to the reader that time in his own life when days were longer and pleasures simpler. But—such an evocation is at base a sham. What we are invited to savor is a memory of childhood as it never was, as it never could be. Childhood is but one stage, a *real stage*, in a process of development. It is passionate, and it is constantly changing—its essence is change, its sanity resides in its capacity for change. Only adult memories of childhood are static. Only adult dreams and fantasies of childhood can invest that time with such a pleasing illusion of permanent happiness. And if by some terrible chance we should achieve the world of that dream—a world where our entire energies are focused into the acts of eating and sleeping and being taken care of, a world devoid of emotions powerful enough to change it or disrupt it, a world where man's deep harmony with nature makes his life virtually indistinguishable from the lives of simple animals (like Ethan's sorrel, whose hungry whinny is the only sound to penetrate the final moments of the vision, or like the small, cheeping field mouse into which Miss Mattie Silver has been transformed)—if we should sink into the oblivion of such a world, we would go mad. Taken seriously, the beckoning vision of the New England regionalists becomes a nightmare.

Ethan Frome is, of course, the explication of a private nightmare as well. Wharton never lost her fear of animals; but by the time she wrote *Ethan Frome*, she had a detailed understanding of the many meanings of that fear. It was among other things, the fear of muteness, of helplessness, of confinement to those elemental activities of eating and sleeping. Above all—and Wharton understood that it was above all—her nightmare was a fear of that part of herself that forevermore longed to retreat from adult complexities into the terrible diminishments of such a world. It was a terror of the desire to regress. Wharton had controlled that fear by repressing any feelings that might produce it—ultimately, by suppressing virtually all feeling. When she first began writing, she had postulated her private bondage as the necessary condition for *any* kind of coherent existence. Repression seemed an existential necessity of life; thus, when she made fictions, the worlds in them were landscapes of unrelieved desolation.

Now, at last, Wharton is able to recognize the horror *as* horror—and to reject it. The literary device of the "frame" in this story makes an important assertion: the narrator's "vision" is just that, a vision. The life of the young Ethan Frome that he has conjured is *not* a description of necessary human hopelessness; it is no more than a private nightmare (like Wharton's nightmare of twelve years past, perhaps). Beyond it and outside is a whole world—made "real" by multitudinous possibilities.

Finally, *Ethan Frome* is a statement of Edith Wharton's coming of age as a novelist. What had she meant when she said that "it was not until I wrote 'Ethan Frome' that I suddenly felt the artisan's full control of his implements"? One thing she might have meant was that she had finally learned to distinguish between a "vision" and a "fiction." By her own admission: "No picture of myself would be more than a profile if it failed to give some account of the teeming visions which, ever since my small-childhood, and even at the busiest and most agitated periods of my outward life, have incessantly peopled my inner world." [134] A vision must be hammered into shape. It is, perhaps, the germ of a fiction; but it is not yet a fiction. A vision is a primitive expression of self; a fiction is the creation of an independent world that stands apart from self. Within *Ethan Frome* the narrator lapses into a vision (the tale of Ethan which is, as we have seen, a terrified expression of the narrator's latent self—his *alter ego*, his "Winterman"). The *novel*, *Ethan Frome*, focuses on the narrator's problem: the tension between his public self and his shadow self, his terror of a seductive and enveloping void.

We might almost fancy Edith Wharton going back to her own first efforts—"Mrs. Manstey's View" or "The Fullness of Life"—and regarding them with a mature and critical eye. But these are only partial fictions, she might say; my own dilemmas intrude into them, my own need to find expression of self prevents them from standing independently of me. These are visions more than fictions—visions of reduction and isolation. I have grown beyond that now. Let me complete the cycle before I go on. Let me write a novel that captures the compulsive quality of vision-making. And so she did. And then, she went on.

Edith Wharton, 1897

Edith Wharton, 1905

Edith Wharton, 1907

Edith Wharton, 1910

III

Studies of Salamanders
The Fiction, 1912-1920

If a man's fate were as a forbidden fruit, detached from him, and in front of him, he might hesitate fortunately before plucking it; but, as most of us are aware, the vital half of it lies in the seed-paths he has traversed. We are sons of yesterday, not of the morning. The past is our mortal mother, no dead thing. Our future constantly reflects her to the soul. Nor is it ever the new man of today which grasps his fortune, good or ill. We are pushed to it by the hundreds of days we have buried, eager ghosts. And if you have not the habit of taking counsel with them, you are but an instrument in their hands.

George Meredith: *Harry Richmond*, XXXII
(Recorded in Edith Wharton's Commonplace Book in 1899)

When we understand the genuinely abysmal horror that *Ethan Frome* dares to examine, it is perhaps surprising to discover that Edith Wharton was extraordinarily happy while she was writing it. This was a turning point in her career. A sense of maturity and power lay at the root of her happiness, and she seized upon that maturity with voracious glee: "When she received the proofs of her 'winter's work' in April . . . she confessed to being in a 'state of fatuous satisfaction.' " [1] *Ethan Frome* proclaimed a final victory over the part of herself that had inclined so precariously in the direction of passivity and dependency; it was a psychological coming of age. It was, however, another kind of coming of age as well: its very structure (the importance of which Wharton stressed so repeatedly and emphatically) demonstrated Wharton's awareness as a writer of the seductive and artificial nature of fiction. "Though this world the artist builds about him in the act of creation reaches us and moves us through its resemblance to the life we know," she wrote some years later, "yet in the artist's consciousness its essence, the core of it, is other. All worthless fiction and inefficient reviewing are based on the forgetting of this fact. To the artist his world is as solidly real as the world of experience, or even more so, but in a way entirely different; it is a world to and from which he passes without any sense of effort, but always *with an uninterrupted awareness* of the passing." [2] Fiction grows inevitably out of life—Wharton's fictions would continue to grow out of reflections upon her own experiences—yet never again would fiction be confused with life.

When she concluded *Ethan Frome*, Edith Wharton brought one era of her creative life to a close. The contrast is striking. Every one of the early fictions had been preoccupied with the modalities of care-taking: even the short stories had been for the most part devoid of genuine adult passion. Moreover, scarcely one among all of these fictions (there are minor exceptions in the short stories) had offered a picture of man mastering his fate—or even a picture of what it might mean to master one's fate. To use Wharton's own vocabulary, the first fictional worlds had been dominated by evocations of coldness, suffocation, and slow starvation. *Ethan Frome* is the apotheosis of these fictional worlds, and at the same time it definitively rejects them. Despite the fact that the decade following 1911 would be tumultuously disrupted (by Wharton's divorce from Teddy after nearly thirty years of marriage and by World War I, which she experienced first-hand in Paris), it would nevertheless be the decade of her strongest and most confident work. Edith Wharton was forty-nine when she finished *Ethan Frome* in early 1911. Already well into middle age, she had finally hit her stride as a novelist.

The group of novels that begins with *The Reef* (1912) and concludes with *The Age of Innocence* (1920) leaves all those early fictional worlds behind. There is an abrupt and dramatic departure of tone—almost as if Wharton's creative life had begun anew and she had determined to plunge into the immensities of a dawning universe whose shapes and ways loomed unfamiliar and unclear in the half-light. This was a new day—not cold any more.

Suddenly, Wharton began to write about passion: sexual passion; the passions for acquisition, for experience, for love. Before, her central figures had been swayed and bent by the fortunes that beset them; now her main characters proclaim an almost muscular need to meet the forces that would shape their lives. They expand into the atmosphere that surrounds them and probe it and fill their lungs with hope. These are still not novels about man mastering his fate (for Wharton knew that one might grow to be a lover of life, but never, in the end, grow to be its master); yet they are novels about men and women who confront their fate, and the novels are suffused with the intensity of their quests.

In 1925 Edith Wharton wrote a short book about the composition of fiction. In it she cautions, "It is useless to box your reader's ear unless you have a salamander to show him. If the heart of your little blaze is not animated by a living, moving *something* no shouting and shaking will fix the anecdote in your reader's memory." [3] It is an interesting image that Wharton uses here to characterize good fiction—the figure of the salamander, that animal who can withstand fire, that ancient symbol of passion. We can see how directly it grows out of the patterns that had shaped her thinking since childhood. In its dramatic evocation of heat and passion, it is an image fully appropriate to the novels of this period when the exhilaration of mastery possessed her. Finally, she has salamanders to show us.

1

In the beginning, the affair with Morton Fullerton had enticed Edith Wharton to unloose her feelings with the reckless innocence of a girl too long confined in the uncongenial clothes of Victorian prudery. The Love

Diary echoes her sense of rapture, wonder, hesitation, and then joyous, abandoned, passionate delight. For many months Edith Wharton was sustained in a state of sublime intoxication: nothing else could so completely have absorbed the woman as this, her first emotional awakening. Yet love is always far from simple. The ultimate effect of Wharton's encounter with Fullerton was a more complete understanding of human experience than she had ever had before. Important problems of her past were settled and put behind her when she attained the adult strength to confront and repudiate those infantile yearnings toward passivity. At the same time, however, the rousing of her full womanly sensual potential plunged her back into other discreetly veiled recesses of the past where other specters, the ghosts of the unresolved sexual crises of childhood and adolescence, waited to receive her. Eventually she would have to come to terms with herself—again—and that would take almost another ten years. The first step involved coming to terms with the amorous provenance of the man she had chosen for her lover.

When William Morton Fullerton appeared on that chilly autumn afternoon in 1907, Edith Wharton knew little or nothing about him. They engaged in intense intellectual discussions (Fullerton was doing an essay on James at the time), but their talk was not intimate. They strolled the snow-dusted hills, pausing to pluck branches of witch hazel; they smoked their ruminative cigarettes together, and then Fullerton was gone. A figure in a dream, perhaps. In the first months of 1908 in Paris, Wharton saw Fullerton several times a week at public gatherings; she had more than enough opportunity to spar with his fiery intellect, but still nothing intimate passed between them. Even when the love affair was finally consummated, Wharton knew very little of Fullerton's other entanglements. Yet the correspondence with James suggests that at least by 1909 (and probably earlier) she had finally begun to penetrate the deep complexities of Fullerton's life. There was a great deal to learn.

Fullerton was the son of a Massachusetts clergyman. As a young man his interests had inclined naturally towards the spiritual; however, when he matured, the vaguely mystical, dreamy elements in his personality became focused into a talent for romantic idealization. And the talent was put to sensual, not religious, use. Fullerton was a short, compact man; he took exquisite pains with his appearance, dressing with superb taste and giving great attention to detail. He was a man of considerable intelligence and intellectual promise. However, the most distinctive thing about him was the compelling intensity of his personal presence. Every look, word, gesture took on a significance of almost unbearable force. The letters from several of Fullerton's amours survive (Wharton's, alas, do not), and all of them are written in a tone of almost hypnotized wonder. The voice is of one utterly enraptured by passion. To be sure, Fullerton was an experienced and accomplished connoisseur of the art of love-making. He was more than that, however; he was also a man who was capable of pouring the fierce energy of his entire nature into the affair of the moment (and, of course, that is the quality we hear echoing in the letters he received from his lovers). Nothing else mattered save this man and this woman: their experience epitomized a kind of voluptuous ideal; and in the very perfection of their love, they shared mystically in the experience of all who had preceded them. They might be Francesca and Paolo or Dante and Beatrice (such were the flights of fancy that Fullerton indulged in with his ladies); partaking as they did in the very essence of love, they moved in the immortal presence of all lovers, both sacred and profane. Fullerton offered a new religion of love; and whenever he was engaged in an affair, he wrote elaborate letters expounding his doctrines. The affair with Wharton was no exception.

The Love Diary captures her, luxuriating in her lover's persuasive eloquence.

A note comes almost every morning now. It is brought in on my breakfast tray with the other letters, and there is the delicious moment of postponement, when one leaves it unopened while one pours the tea, just in order to "savourer" longer the joy that is coming! —Ah, how I see in all this the instinctive longing to pack every moment of my present with all the wasted driven-in feeling of the past! One should be happy in one's youth to be happy freely, carelessly, extravagantly! How I hoard and tremble over each incident and sign! I am like a hungry beggar who crumbles up the crust he has found in order to make it last longer! . . . And then comes the opening of the letter, the slipping of the little silver knife under the flap (which one would never tear!), the first glance to see how many pages there are, the second to see how it ends, and then the return to the beginning, the breathless first reading, the slow lingering again over each phrase and each word, the taking possession, the absorbing of them one by one, and finally the choosing of the one that will be carried in one's thoughts all day, making an exquisite accompaniment to all the dull prose of life. . . . Sometimes I think the moment of reading the letter is the best of all—I think that till I see you again.[4]

Surely Fullerton's unique capacity to join the literary and the sexual was his highest aesthetic achievement.

It is not difficult to see why this combination would appeal to a woman like Wharton. Indeed, it not only appealed to her, it established a congenial set of conventions within which she might begin to express her own newly discovered feelings; almost certainly many of the self-consciously "literary" elements in the Love Diary (the allusions to Ronsard and Donne, for example) were responsive echoes of Fullerton's habitual style of passion. Wharton carried the custom even into her daily appointment book where significant encounters with her lover were indicated by cryptic allusions to Dante or appropriate quotations from *The Divine Comedy*. Basking in the spiritual glow of this relationship, Wharton must have been confused, at the very least, when she began to discover the prodigality with which her lover had spread his talents.

Fullerton was not a hypocrite: he conveyed an air of emotional absorption because he was genuinely absorbed—at any given monent. But he had a prodigious capacity for romantic involvement, and during the first two years of the affair with Wharton, he was being blackmailed by a woman named Henrietta Mirecourt. Fullerton had always had a naive compulsion to tell his current lover about his past, and the pressure of the blackmailing must have made him even more confidential than usual. Thus little by little, Wharton was constrained to descend from the spiritual plane on which she had begun the liaison into the rather more squalid depths of Fullerton's voluptuary past.

Fullerton had come to London from the United States in 1890; after his arrival, he had dallied in any number of casual sexual intrigues—some with men and some with women. During this early period, there were two serious entanglements, one with Lord Gower and one with Margaret Brooke, the Ranee of Sarawak—a woman quite literally old enough to be his mother. The affair with Margaret Brooke lasted for about three years, after which she resignedly gave him up because he was unable to stay out of the beds of younger women. For several years Fullerton seems to have kept clear of any binding entanglements; however, at some time around 1900, he again became seriously involved with a woman older than himself—Henrietta Mirecourt. They lived in the same apartment building, probably intermittently sharing an apartment. Then, without warning, in 1903 Fullerton married yet another woman—an actress named Victoria Camille Chabert—who almost immediately bore him a daughter. For nearly two years Fullerton was married to Camille while attending to his still engrossing affair with Mirecourt. In 1904 he was divorced (though he stayed on friendly, not to say intimate, terms with his former wife for many years), and at the same time he began trying to extricate himself from the affair with Mirecourt. However, at last he had met a woman who was not content to let the affair die: Henrietta Mirecourt was violently jealous and more than a bit vindictive; she let herself into Fullerton's apartment and rifled his papers, finding evidence at least of the affairs with Lord Gower and Margaret Brooke—and possibly finding much more. Thus in 1907 and 1908, at the very moment he was initiating the affair with Edith Wharton, Fullerton was being troubled with demands from Mirecourt.

During the spring of 1908 when Wharton and Fullerton became intimate, Henrietta seems to have suspended her threats; however, by the summer of 1909 the situation had again grown so sordid that Wharton herself concocted a plan to extricate her lover. It required the help of Henry James.

Fullerton had been writing to James for years in great agitation over the delicate and dangerous situations in which he so frequently found himself. James was genuinely fond of Fullerton, anxious to see him relieved, and undoubtedly titillated to be a part of the intrigue with Wharton and Fullerton that would succeed in dispatching Henrietta Mirecourt. In any case the three schemers perpetrated the following deception. Fullerton had been engaged by Macmillan's to write a little book about Paris, and he had received a £100 advance for the project. Now James was to write to the publisher, explaining that Fullerton was in particular need of money because of his father's illness; James was to send Macmillan's £100, urging them to give the money to Fullerton as an additional advance on the book without ever allowing Fullerton to know that the money had, in effect, been a gift from James. Then, so the plot went, Fullerton could use the money to pay Mirecourt and retrieve the incriminating evidence once and for all. Everything went according to plan, and Henrietta Mirecourt troubled Fullerton no more. However, the strangest element of the story had to do with the money. It was, of course, not really James's £100 that was sent to Macmillan's: Edith Wharton had given the money to James to forward in this circuitous way. Why had she not merely given the money directly to her lover? No one will ever know. However, we can speculate that she would have found it repugnant to do so. Wharton was willing to enter upon a Grand Passion; she was not willing to sink to the level of a demi-mondaine.

Nevertheless, it was increasingly difficult to maintain the credibility of those elegant, elevated, spiritual, and literary categories by which she had at first defined this new experience. Fullerton's colorful past made it difficult; even the mere particular details of their meetings tended to strain the spell. It may be, as Wharton recorded in the Commonplace Book in 1908, that a spiritual joining must descend to physical union "Which sense may reach and apprehend,/ Else a great Prince in prison lies." The practical truth was that the physical union had to occur *somewhere*—somewhere discreetly chosen, somewhere carefully planned. Wharton's longings in those early days had a romantic, almost girlish naïveté: "Sometimes I think that if I could go off with you for twenty-four hours to a little inn in the country in the depths of a green wood, I should ask no more. Just to have one long day and quiet evening with you, and then next morning to be still together—." But real life could not offer so simple and beautiful a fulfillment; they never went to the "little inn," and their sexual encounters most often took place in Edith's own apartment on the Rue de Varenne, the residence of Mrs. Edward Wharton. It made her queasy. It offended her sense of delicacy and decency. "Something gave me the impression the other day that we were watched in this house," she wrote in the Love Diary on May 13, 1908. "Commented on. —Ah, how a great love needs to be a happy and open love! How degraded I feel by other people's degrading thoughts . . ." [5]

When Wharton and Fullerton did travel together, their actual sojourns were at a far remove from the pastoral ideal of her early imaginings. Wharton has left a poignant reminder of the distance. In June of 1909 the lovers took a two-day holiday before Fullerton left on a short visit back to America to see his family. They went to England, where they saw Henry James; and on the second night they stayed at the Charing Cross Hotel—in a suite with "dull impersonal furniture . . . / And the low wide bed, as rutted and worn as a high-road,/ The bed with its soot-sodden chintz, the grime of its brasses,/ That has born [e] the weight of fagged bodies, dust-stained, averted in sleep." [6] In the morning, after Fullerton had left to catch the boat train, Edith propped herself among the pillows with her pens and ink and blue paper to spend the usual three or four hours writing. However, this morning she chose not to write fiction. Instead, she began a long erotic poem about the night that she and her lover had just spent together. She entitled the poem "Terminus." R. W. B. Lewis has suggested that the title has double significance: "a name chosen to indicate both that the experience occurred in a station hotel and that it marked a temporary end to their relationship." [7] There is, however, a third and even more significant implication.

The poem "Terminus" marks a conscious conclusion of that early period of the affair when Wharton's own renderings of her feelings so directly responded to the rhapsodic, idealizing, highly romantic language that was habitual with Fullerton. The elevated evocations of perfection are gone; in their place—the actual realities of the affair as Wharton knew it. Impersonal rooms appropriated for one or two nights; no garden below, only "the shaking and shrieking of trains, the night-long shudder of traffic." Nevertheless, "Terminus" is both erotic and deeply affectionate. Wharton may have rejected the categories in which Fullerton had defined their relationship, but she did not intend thereby to reject the man. Rather, there is an almost playful adaptation of his transcendent "religion" of passion: in her poem, the act of love still forms a mystical bond by which the lovers are joined with others who have preceded them. Yet the union now conjures no images of idealized love. Instead of rising above the ordinary, Wharton and her lover are postulated as having plumbed the very heart of common, human experience. "I was glad as I thought of those others, the nameless, the many,/ Who perhaps thus had lain and loved for an hour on the brink of the world,/ Secret and fast in the heart of the whirlwind of travel." [8] How many others have passed through these dingy rooms as we have? Whitman, not Dante, has become the ultimate authority.

If we consider the nunlike purity of Wharton's life before meeting Fullerton, we must marvel at her capacity to absorb the unsavory facts of his past and the furtive expedients that the affair required. These were the realities of life; as such, Wharton was determined to come to terms with them. Nevertheless, there was one discovery that seems to have touched Wharton's sensibilities deeply (it may even have facilitated the gradual decline of the affair in 1910)—and that was Morton's relationship with Katherine Fullerton. It is a bizarre tale.

Katherine Fullerton was Morton's cousin. Orphaned in infancy, she had been brought into Morton Fullerton's house when she was a baby and he an adolescent of fourteen. She was raised as his sister; and in fact, until she was a woman well into her twenties, she actually thought that she was his biological sister (though, of course, Morton and his parents knew otherwise). Even as a little girl, Katherine Fullerton had extraordinarily deep feelings of affection for her older "brother." The further she grew into adolescence, the more intense and confusing these feelings became (fueled, we must imagine, by Morton's more than brotherly attentions).

As one reads the letters that Katherine wrote to her "brother"—Morton kept more than forty of them until the day he died—it is impossible not to like and admire her; in many respects she resembled Edith Wharton. An exceptionally intelligent and sensitive woman (she went to Radcliffe College, became a teacher of English at Bryn Mawr, and eventually wrote a number of creditable novels), she was also deeply passionate and determined to confront the implications of her feelings as honestly as possible. At first, this meant that however much she was attracted to Morton, she must restrain her affection within the bounds of a sisterly attachment. The friendship "of brother and sister seems to me to contain the most elements of perfection," she wrote him valiantly in 1899.[9] Finally, when she was almost twenty-five, Katherine discovered the truth. She was not Morton's sister but his first cousin; they might marry (though his parents understandably opposed the match). As fate would have it, however, she made this discovery at just the time when Morton had involved himself in the short-lived marriage to Camille Chabert. Once again Katherine was forced to suppress her feelings. Nevertheless Morton eventually was divorced; there was no legal obstacle to the match, and like the hero in a romance, Morton returned to his patient admirer.

In that fateful autumn of 1907 when Morton Fullerton first visited The Mount, he preceded that visit with a trip to Bryn Mawr, where he declared his own passion for Katherine and they became engaged to marry. Thus—as Wharton was to learn several years later—at that momentous meeting when she and Fullerton first strolled and talked so intensely, so "personally," he was a newly affianced man. While Edith Wharton was making the first tentative entries in the Love Diary, Katherine Fullerton was writing letters to her fiancé that bore an uncanny resemblance to Wharton's own musings. By every standard entitled to express her feelings, Katherine finally did so. "Ah, my own, my own—! You know that I'm quite simply desperately in love with you: that in your own sacred words (only a week ago, my darling, and you so far away from me!) 'without marriage there is no life for you nor for me.' If you feel that too—and the words were yours before they were mine—life hasn't treated me without magnificence. . . ." [10] "Oh, my darling, my darling. I did not think I should ever want to marry anyone as much as I want to marry you. 'Terrible as an army with banners.' I have always known it was the only thing ever said that gave an inkling of what love is. That, and 'The Sacred Terror.' And that terror you have taught me, to the last shudder of it. There is something hopelessly and finally humiliating about being so at another person's mercy: but perfect love casteth out pride." [11]

Fullerton was perhaps intimidated by the force of Katherine's feelings; more probably, he was intimidated by the thought of committing himself to one woman for the rest of his life. In any case, he responded to her with the hesitant suggestion that they had been a bit too impetuous. Perhaps they should remain merely Platonic lovers: she might be his ideal—as Beatrice had been to Dante. (Remembering Wharton's habit only a few months after this time of alluding to the developing relationship with Fullerton by making cryptic references to Dante and *The Divine Comedy*, we might be excused for wondering whether he did not employ much the same vocabulary with all of his mistresses.) In any case, Katherine responded to this tactic vehemently. "Your note, read at dinner last night, broke my heart in twain. My darling, and my darling, I will not be your Beatrice, to triumph in some fantastic Heaven. You shall have me yet—flesh and blood, on earth. . . . But do not call me Beatrice: for there is no power either of my own instinct, or of other's violence, that I am not prepared to combat, rather than delude myself for one moment with the hope of a Heaven in which I do not believe. . . . I have always so hated the *Paradiso!* But I should have hated it more, had I foreseen that you would ever call me Beatrice. I am grateful, grateful for being a dream to you . . . for being 'idealized' as people say. But if you think that I am so aloof from the world that I do not wish to be loved quite otherwise, you do not know me—. I have always known that if I really loved a man, I should rather be to him Gemma than Beatrice. For Gemma must often have made him forget Beatrice." [12] Eventually, Katherine would have to be reckoned with!

For almost three years, however, Fullerton kept the arrangement with Katherine hanging fire. He visited America on several occasions and saw her just often enough to sustain her love for him; but when he was in

Europe, he would allow months to pass without so much as a word. Considering the situation, Katherine maintained remarkable equilibrium, though she was not above reminding Fullerton, "you've a power, my poor darling, of inflicting pain—." [13] Eventually, however, she determined that matters had to be resolved. Gordon Gerould, a young English instructor at Princeton, had asked her to marry him; Katherine was obliged to give him a reply. Thus on January 5, 1910, she composed an anguished letter of nearly two thousand words, begging the courtesy of a reply and asking her cousin either to release her or to marry her at once. "I am desperately anxious to be honest with myself, with you and with him," she wrote in part. "How can you not have written to me—whatever your feeling, your attitude and your position in regard to me and to others (for of course it would be mere foolish airs and graces on my part to pretend that some one else was not making you so inconsiderate of me) may be? One word: three lines on a page; almost any formula, saying almost anything, could have passed muster. But *nothing!* . . . You must free me, must give me peace, must speak some word. Good heavens, my dear, after all, you asked me to marry you. You had my promise, and you have never either taken back your request or released me from my promise—. I am not a conventional person; but one has one's sense of decency." [14] The engagement was terminated, and Katherine married Gerould on June 9, 1910.

When Edith Wharton eventually read these letters, they thrust upon her yet another aspect of the love affair—the matter of "one's sense of decency." Wharton had long ago accepted the essential rightness of physical passion and sexual love; that was not at issue. Even passion, however, had its social component. Here was a young woman, a woman whom Wharton could only admire—and a woman whom Wharton's affair with Fullerton had injured (never mind that Fullerton would almost certainly have entangled himself with someone else if Edith Wharton had not been there). The matter of individual fulfillment was inextricably tied to larger questions of emotional obligation. Edith Wharton's position in January of 1910 made her especially alive to such questions: only three weeks earlier, her own husband—whose mental balance had been steadily deteriorating for two years—had confessed that he had been involved in a rather ugly affair with an actress in Boston. Wharton had not been emotionally injured by Teddy's announcement; there had been no sexual contact between them for years. But her sense of decency had been offended. When she learned the details of Katherine Fullerton's destiny, she was particularly disposed to regard the case with sympathetic understanding.

A more complex notion of "love" had begun to appear in her fiction by the time Wharton published *Tales of Men and Ghosts* (October 1910). The sinister, parasitic relationship between Andrew Culwin and his protégés in "The Eyes" reflects a preliminary acquaintance with the darker side of passion. However, another story, "The Letters," most directly captures the drift of Wharton's interest. "The Letters" is about Lizzie West. It begins in Paris, where Lizzie has been employed for some time by Mr. and Mrs. Vincent Deering as a teacher for their young daughter; Mrs. Deering is an indolent semi-invalid, and poor Lizzie has been drawn into an innocent flirtation with Mr. Deering. She has just determined to leave the situation when to everyone's surprise, Mrs. Deering's illness becomes genuinely acute and she dies. Suddenly no obstacles stand between Lizzie and Vincent Deering; the two declare their love, and Lizzie agrees to wait in Paris while he returns to the United States to settle his wife's affairs. To seal the pledge of their love, they make a "pact." "That pact, as she reviewed it through a sleepless night, seemed to have consisted mainly, on his part, in pleadings for full and frequent news of her, on hers in the promise that it should be given as often as he wrote to ask it." Lizzie is inexperienced in articulating her feelings. Her confidence wavers: "All that she felt and said would be subjected to the test of comparison with what others had already given him: from all quarters of the globe she saw passionate missives winging their way toward Deering, for whom her poor little swallow flight of devotion could certainly not make a summer." She hesitates, but then she begins to pour her feelings onto paper, sustained by the conviction that "no woman had ever loved him just as she had, and that none, therefore, had probably found just such things to say to him." [15]

Deering responds to the first two or three letters, and then—unaccountably—he lapses into total silence. Lizzie is at a loss to explain her lover's behavior. "His had not been the attitude of the unscrupulous male seeking a vulgar 'advantage.' For a moment he had really needed her, and if he was silent now, it was perhaps because he feared that she had mistaken the nature of the need, and built vain hopes on its possible duration." Lizzie is sensitive to the possibility that she might be inflicting her affection on a reluctant suitor, and she becomes obsessed with the desire to release him entirely. "To make this clear to Deering became an overwhelming need, and in a last short letter she explicitly freed him from whatever sentimental obligation its predecessors might have seemed to impose." [16] However, even this last letter (for it is the very last she writes) remains unanswered, and Lizzie resolutely takes up the threads of her old life again.

Three years pass; Lizzie's situation has remarkably altered. Having come into a substantial inheritance, she now finds herself to be a woman of means. One day, unexpectedly, she encounters Vincent Deering. His conversation moves smoothly and easily back into their old familiar tone, and Lizzie is shocked. How can he behave thus when he has not answered her letters—never answered even that last pitiful plea? But Vincent Deering has lost none of his old agility. "His parries were incredible. They left her with a sense of thrusting at emptiness." [17] Ah—how could he have imposed upon her when he found that, after all, he was a pauper. A man without a competence cannot presume, even on a love so great as hers.

Lizzie finds herself at a loss. Deering's charm works on her again—as if no time had elapsed at all, really. They marry. Years pass. They have a child.

One day Lizzie is going through some of her husband's old trunks. The baby toddling at her side suddenly reaches into the depths of one of them and brings up a bundle of papers. Lizzie recognizes them at once: they are the letters that she wrote to Deering—now so many years ago. She is touched, knowing that he has preserved them for all this time. She puts out her hand to take them and read them over when she discovers that although he has kept them, he has kept them *unopened*. The truth flushes over her: he did not answer her letters because he had not read them—had not even opened them! "She knew so well how it must have happened. The letters had reached him when he was busy, occupied with something else, and had been put aside to be read at some future time—a time which never came. Perhaps on the steamer, even, he had met 'someone else'—the 'someone' who lurks, veiled and ominous, in the background of every woman's thoughts about her lover. Or perhaps he had been merely forgetful. She knew now that the sensations which he seemed to feel most intensely left no reverberations in his memory— that he did not relive either his pleasures or his pains. . . . She had learned by this time that she could not modify his habits; but she imagined that she had deepened his sensibilities, had furnished him with an 'ideal'—angelic function! And she now saw that the fact of her letters—her unanswered letters—having on his own assurance, 'meant so much' to him, had been the basis on which this beautiful fabric was reared." [18]

Lizzie meditates upon the man who has been for many years her husband, her faithful husband she is certain, the affectionate father of her child. She pictures him, as she has so often seen him, with a newspaper in hand: "He seemed to read little else, and she sometimes wondered when he had found time to store the material that used to serve for their famous 'literary' talks." He is, after all, just a man, a mortal man and no idealized lover. A weaker man than others, perhaps. But "she saw now, in this last wide flash of pity and initiation, that, as a comedy marble may be made out of worthless scraps of mortar, glass, and pebbles, so out of a mean mixed substance may be fashioned a love that will bear the stress of life." [19] So she puts the letters aside, for the final time, and turns to greet her husband.

It is no feat to tease the particulars of Katherine Fullerton's situation out of this little tale, nor even to discern Wharton's own half-indulgent, half-scornful revaluation of Morton Fullerton's character. Yet the story is slender, even melodramatic. Wharton has not confused fiction with life, but she has attempted to draw fiction rather too directly and simply out of real-world experience. It is a herald, nothing more, of things to come. The single most important notion in it is that of "a love that will bear the stress of life"; this is related to another notion, "one's sense of decency," that had emerged with some force in Wharton's considerations during the year 1910. Passion—even passion—can be construed correctly only by an exquisite refinement and extension of the sense of "place."

Inner and outer worlds—both were unbalanced by the complexities of the experience that had opened before her. Fullerton's language of romantic love was clearly insufficient; even Whitman's magnificent invocation of transcendent affection could not manage the problems she faced. Thus while Edith Wharton had known a full range of passionate experience by 1911, she had as yet evolved no set of categories to deal with it. On the one hand, it had become clear that no one can love privately. The vectors of passion travel with deadly silence and swiftness—out, beyond—who knows how far or in what quarters their devastating effect may be felt? Passion can disrupt and hurt and destroy; yet society has not the right to prohibit passion. And between these two truths lies an immensity of uncertainty. How can one, after all, mediate among the delicate and uncertain claims that strive to place passion in the larger scheme of things?

On the other hand, it seemed paradoxically clear that love is essentially private. The capacity for love, like the wellspring of every passion, reaches down into the uttermost depths of individual personality. Wharton knew this with a fine, intuitive sense of the configuration of human nature. Every adult experience creates anew; however, in many of its essential elements it also echoes that which has passed. Really to understand passion (really, that is, to understand the multiple implications of the affair with Fullerton), Wharton had to journey once again into the hidden recesses of her own inner self. She knew the perils of such a quest, and yet her sense of integrity as an artist demanded that she make it. As she wrote to Brownell during this period, "Plus je vais, more and more it becomes the essential thing for me that anyone who writes should be able to say: 'Gods of heaven and gods of hell have I looked on face to face, and adored them.' " [20] It was an enormous task to undertake, the task of "placing" passion.

2

The Reef, which was published in the late months of 1912, was Wharton's first major novel in the five years that followed *The Fruit of the Tree* (*Ethan Frome*, despite its virtuosity, was really a long novella). She wrote other things—short stories, a book of verses, a travel book—but her capacity to manage the sustained complexity of long fiction was definitively blocked for a time. Wharton tried to work this difficulty through: she had begun *The Custom of the Country* with great zest in 1907 and had pushed on despite her diminishing results. After a while, however, her efforts yielded almost nothing, and finally she reluctantly suspended work on it. At this point in her career, the obstacles were in no way related to her proficiency as a writer or her commitment to profession. Now the impediment had entirely to do with the choice of subject.

The clustering of novels at this point is significant, despite that misleading hiatus: three of them—*The Fruit of the Tree* (1907), *The Reef* (1912), and *The Custom of the Country* (1913)—address one or another aspect of the same configuration of problems. We have spoken of sexuality; we might more correctly speak of appetite, for in Wharton's life, the terms in which she experienced sexual passion were indelibly colored by the fearful shades of an earlier, more primitive, and more inclusive hunger. This successful woman of fifty had not yet banished that totem of childhood, the big bad wolf.

It would be simplistic and wrong to say that Wharton was beset by voracious sexuality (although the language of the Love Diary suggests that it was never easy or natural for her to modulate the intensity of her passion).[21] It would be more accurate to say that any awakening of sexual feeling, any attempt to address problems that were essentially sexual in nature, was always accompanied by a threatening resurgence of that infantile sense of unsatisfied, insatiable oral longing. Almost certainly it was easier for her to *act out* her adult impulses than it was for her to come to terms with the long-repressed but still unresolved crises attendant upon them. Thus she could, finally, experience sexual passion in the affair with Fullerton; for throughout that period she might focus entirely on the adult elements, keeping the dangerous childhood residue out of consciousness. However, for many years she could not bring herself to *write fiction* with an explicitly sexual focus because the act of writing by its very nature compelled regression. (Kris might call it "regression in the service of the ego"; Wharton, speaking less technically, might say that she traveled to "some secret region on the sheer edge of consciousness." Both would have the same mental processes in mind.) In this case, regression would compel her to confront the many fears and feelings and conflicts that had been associated with sexuality in her girlhood and adolescence. For many years, the prospect of such a journey was too difficult to face.

Many authors in such a situation might have satisfied themselves with the psychological victory asserted in *Ethan Frome*, the victory of denunciation. But Wharton had reposed a great trust in words and had thereby committed herself to a quest. Eventually, therefore, despite the resistance, she finally did succeed in treating sexuality in her fictions.

It is true that such writing forced Wharton to deal with the general problem of limiting appetite; however, other problems crowded upon her as well, now. Chief among them was the problem of initiative; for the awakening of sexuality and an upsurge of initiative always go hand in hand in normal development.[22] In Wharton's life—as in the life of every human being—a desire to engage in competition and a new sense of energy for attacking and conquering first appeared at about the age of four or five. This was the period during which the little girl conceived an intense and possessive love for her genial, affectionate father. Unfortunately, she never discovered suitable ways to focus or redirect the force of these feelings; hence she never mastered them, and all her tentative ventures (save "making up") were engulfed by waves of guilt, multitudes of fiercely felt and largely self-imposed injunctions that prohibited aggressive or assertive behavior. Thus, this crisis of childhood went unresolved.

As an adult, Wharton did much to repair the damage of that early failure; nevertheless, even now after the affair with Fullerton, the remnants of those unresolved feelings about sexuality (and initiative) remained. The fact that they persisted with such malignant force must be attributed in part to society's attitude toward all women during Wharton's youth. It was not "nice" for girls to have feelings; it was, of course, equally improper for girls to contemplate assertive, independent behavior. In this prohibition, even her class worked against her (as indeed, it did against the men as well): gentlepeople were not expected to have ambitions, drives, desires, professional commitments; to do so would be a violation of code—an offense against the norms of polite behavior.

The memory of all such forces and feelings (some conscious, many long pushed out of consciousness) lurked in the reticulations of any question of sexuality. It is a staggering fact, though a true one, that Edith Wharton could not begin to deal meaningfully with the subject until she could bring herself to resurrect these ancient bogeys of childhood and adolescence.

Given the burden of this tortuous past and given, furthermore, the complex adult problems that the affair with Fullerton had opened to her, Wharton can scarcely be faulted for her reluctance to commit herself to writing about sexual problems, nor for the relative clumsiness of her first efforts. *The Fruit of the Tree* had been an acknowledged failure. Although *The Reef* was immeasurably better, it was the least successful major novel of this period. For years afterward, Edith Wharton voiced her uncertainty about it; critics have found it difficult to handle. Yet, with all its faults, *The Reef* was a necessary beginning.

Edith Wharton was still working among the echoes of *Ethan Frome* when she wrote *The Reef*, for it shows a more heightened awareness of the artificial quality of fiction than any other of her major novels. There is something relentlessly barren at the heart of it. When Henry James read it, he was moved to speak of Racine in attempting to capture its essential quality, and the association is a natural one.[23] The principal characters are rendered with a chiaroscuro sharpness that articulates them almost as if they were specimens mounted against a backdrop. Everything about the work suggests that Wharton was intently concerned to bring her intellectual powers rigorously to bear on the problem that occupies it; and in the end, she fails by having been too rigorously limited and too thoroughly intellectual. The world of the novel never fully comes to life, and the characters seem altogether too much "points of view." Critics often speak of *The Reef* as the most "Jamesian" of Wharton's major works; in some respects this evaluation is valid. However, in adopting James's methods, Wharton failed to match his mastery. Instead, this uncharacteristic spareness was a sign of the difficulty she was having with the subject.

The subject that she wished to consider—sexuality—grew in too many divergent directions; Wharton discovered that she could not prune away its many offshoots, and despite her best efforts a tangled, confusing undergrowth remained. So, by compensation, she determined to simplify her method of presentation. In *Ethan Frome* she had offered a situation filtered through the categories of a single observer. In *The Reef*, she makes the minimal amplification of that method. The situation—the "problem" of the novel—is given to the reader only as it is perceived by one or the other of two main characters: the narrator in this novel (for unlike *Ethan Frome*, it is not told in the first person) is rigidly restricted to the consciousness either of George Darrow or of Anna Leath. Yet, perversely, the technique that had worked so brilliantly in *Ethan Frome* fails utterly here.

The structure of *Ethan Frome* had led us into a dream vision: the fictional world of that entire novella, then, was interior—a dizzying descent into the frozen depths of a soul in which passion had been extinguished—and for the presentation of such a world, Wharton's limitation of narrative vantage was not only workable, it was necessary. In *The Reef*, however, Wharton wants to move in quite the other direction; she wants to deal with the complex personal and social implications of sexuality. Now at the very core of Wharton's problem stands the difficulty of discovering a language and a set of categories that are sufficient to express both the subjective and the objective meanings of passion. It is a problem of multiple dimensions, and she tries to circumscribe it by limiting the scope of her investigation to the consciousness of only two individuals. That is a dangerous strategy. Of course, she might solve the problem in this manner if the understanding of the pair were large enough and supple enough to embrace the subject in all its shaded nuances. But if the characters are inadequate to the demands the fiction places upon them, this technique of presentation, this particular way of limiting the problem, is no more than a beautiful evasion. And so it is. George Darrow and Anna Leath have not the range for the task Wharton has set them. *The Fruit of the Tree* had perpetrated its subterfuge by giving us too much (too many obscuring plots); *The Reef* follows its path of malingery by giving us too little (too narrow a perspective of Sophy Viner). Yet merely by dangling Sophy so tantalizingly before us, Wharton moves closer to the truth here than in the earlier novel, *The Reef*, is an interesting and necessary failure.[24]

The plot is simple. George Darrow and Anna Leath are both ambassadors from genteel old New York. They dabbled together in romance when young, but Anna married another man and moved to France, acting as stepmother to his adolescent son and eventually bearing his daughter. Now, some fifteen years later, Anna has been widowed; she and George Darrow have chanced upon each other again; the romance has rekindled; and when the novel opens, Darrow is en route from London to France, intending to propose to her. The only obstacle is some shadowy reticence in Anna, a reservation that has caused her to ask him to delay the expected visit while giving no explanation for the request. The tale begins with Darrow wondering irresolutely whether to continue his journey or to wait for further word. In this peevish frame of mind, he chances upon Sophy Viner. Sophy is difficult to place: a young woman of good enough connections—now for many years an orphan, supervised by no one, so it would seem—making her living by acting in some vague social capacity in the large homes of the wealthy. Sophy has just lost her job and is traveling to join friends in France; on impulse, Darrow accompanies her. Little by little, once they have reached Paris, the two drift into an affair. It lasts but a few weeks, and then they part. Many months later, the novel again picks up the path of George Darrow; he finally joins Anna Leath, and the way seems clear for their marriage. Once again, however, Sophy Viner intrudes. Now, as Darrow discovers, she has taken a job as governess to Anna's little girl; worse still, she is engaged to Anna's stepson, Owen Leath. Darrow must come to terms with Sophy and with his casual affair; Anna, too, must find some way to understand what has happened—her lover's lapse in faithfulness and even more, a whole world of passion and ambition through which Sophy (but not Anna Leath) seems to move with ease and natural grace. It is not, primarily, a novel whose interest lies in the plot. Anna eventually decides that she cannot marry Darrow; Sophy leaves entirely—breaking her engagement to Owen. Yet these facts matter very little. What matters, always, is Sophy Viner.

Like the characters in the fiction, we are driven to define her, capture her essence, place her, somehow, in the larger categories of our lives. She is a glimmering, dancing jewel, a shaft of sunlight, perhaps; perhaps a malignant gleam in the eye of some beautiful predatory animal; she is at the mercy of all these enfranchised, secure people, and yet she is a force that twists their lives with (perhaps) no malicious intent. Furtive, flaunting, spontaneous, designing, feral. The most marvelous thing about Wharton's creation of Sophy Viner is that the girl manages to command our attention without ever being shown to us directly: we see her refracted through the imperfect judgment of Darrow (distorted, inevitably, by his limited ability to evaluate her); we see her even more obscurely through the shaded vision of Anna Leath. In the end, we realize with frustration that we have never seen into her nature (no further than her flawed interpreters); and before we can turn to catch sight of her again, she has darted out of the novel forever. The interest in the work lies almost entirely in Wharton's provocative conjuration of Sophy Viner; its failure lies in the fact that having declined to deliver Sophy directly, Wharton attempts to fix our attention instead on the mediating terms by which Darrow and Anna Leath perceive her, a subject which fails to dominate our interest. The novel sets itself up to address a "problem"; yet the abstract problem is immeasurably complicated by the reality of Sophy, with whom Wharton cannot come to terms.

It is no accident that Darrow encounters Sophy while they are both traveling (in fact, he literally bumps into her), nor that he knows he has met her before but cannot recall her name. He must grope to place her. "She was clearly an American, but with the loose native quality strained through a closer woof of manners: the composite product of an enquiring and adaptable race." [25] She has a quick, chirping manner, a habit of movement that prevents her from settling easily into any of his familiar categories. Her manner is refreshingly "free from formality" (14), yet is often in "doubtful taste" (15). Like Selden, Darrow has but a few ego-centric groupings when it comes to women: he "had a fairly varied experience of feminine types, but the women he had frequented had either been pronouncedly 'ladies' or they had not. Grateful to both for ministering to the more complex masculine nature, and disposed to assume that they had been evolved, if not designed, to that end, he had instinctively kept the two groups apart in his mind, avoiding that intermediate society which attempts to conciliate both theories of life" (25). Clearly Sophy will fit into neither of these comfortable compartments, principally because they are ways of construing the feminine nature that make it entirely ancillary to masculine needs. Women, even women who are not entirely "nice," will react but not act—so Darrow has always held. Yet Sophy has had experience, and "her experience had made her free without hardness and self-assured without assertiveness" (26). Little wonder, as Darrow gazes upon her, that his thoughts should drift into more consoling and familiar visions of Anna Leath.

Poor Anna, she has none of this girl's quick adaptability. "The reflection set him wondering whether the 'sheltered' girl's bringing-up might not unfit her for all subsequent contact with life. . . . [Anna] was still afraid of life, of its ruthlessness, its danger and mystery. . . . If she had been given to him [in the moments of their first love] then he would have put warmth in her veins and light in her eyes: would have made her a woman through and through. . . . A love like his might have given her the divine gift of self-renewal; and now he saw her fated to wane into old age repeating the same gestures, echoing the words she had always heard" (28–29). Thus Darrow sits musing, little conscious of the violence that will be done to this smug, self-congratulatory manner of construing life.

Darrow and Sophy reach Paris, and the girl steps into his life like the naiad of an ancient fable, "looking as if she had been plunged into some sparkling element which had curled up all her drooping tendrils and wrapped her in a shimmer of fresh leaves" (34). Her passion seems poised, entirely spontaneous, merely waiting with a splendid receptivity to be awakened. The theater awakens it—"great waves of sensation . . . beating deliciously against her brain. It was as though every starved sensibility were throwing out feelers to the mounting tide. . . . She was an extraordinary conductor of sensation: she seemed to transmit it physically, in emanations that set the blood dancing in his veins" (50). Darrow fancies he can play tutor to this childlike creature, and with a tolerant masculine sense of superiority, he tries to pity her total naiveté. Yet she eludes this move to fix her in his realm of knowables, and the natural force of her being cannot be entrapped—"the freshness of the face at his side, reflecting the freshness of the season, suggested dapplings of sunlight through new leaves, the sound of a brook in the grass, the ripple of tree-shadows over breezy meadows" (57). Darrow talks to her of "life." "The word was often on her lips—she seemed to him like a child playing with a tiger's cub; and he said to himself that some day the child would grow up—and so would the tiger. Meanwhile, such expertness qualified by such candour made it impossible to guess the extent of her personal experience, or to estimate its effect on her character. She might be any one of a dozen definable types, or she might—more disconcertingly to her companion and more perilously to herself—be a shifting and uncrystallized mixture of them all" (60).

She means to seize life. " 'I'm not so sure that I believe in marriage,' " she tells Darrow. " 'You see I'm all for self-development and the chance to live one's life. I'm awfully modern, you know' " (61)—*se ressaisir*. And above all, there is the unmitigated, elemental fact of her passion— available, receptive, confirmed. Passion that is consummated in the dingy, impersonal surroundings of a hotel room. The Terminus Hotel.

Only ten days after the affair has begun, Darrow already begins to recoil from it, loathing himself, Sophy, even the room in which their encounters have occurred. "There was something sardonic, almost sinister, in its appearance of having deliberately 'made up' for its anonymous part, all in noncommittal drabs and browns, with a carpet and paper that nobody would remember, and chairs and tables as impersonal as railway porters. . . . It seemed to have taken complete possession of his mind, to be soaking itself into him like an ugly indelible blot. Every detail pressed itself on his notice with the familiarity of an accidental confidant: whichever way he turned, he felt the nudge of a transient intimacy . . ." (73–74). Darrow is not an inexperienced man, and yet he has no categories sufficient for this interlude, surely no categories that will accommodate Sophy's open sensual appetite. There are, of course, certain "masculine" classifications that can be brought to bear on such women: repeatedly, almost compulsively, Darrow offers Sophy money—now and even much later—as if thus to discharge his "debt" and rid himself of the emotional encumbrance. But these maneuvers do not work: "The whole incident had somehow seemed, in spite of its vulgar setting and its inevitable prosaic propinquities, to be enacting itself in some unmapped region outside the pale of the usual" (74–75). Finally, Darrow puts an end to the problem by dissolving the relationship, and after only a little while, he returns to the reassuringly familiar paths of Anna Leath's life.

The reader enters Anna's consciousness just before Darrow reenters her life. She is presented to us in ways designed to heighten the contrast with Sophy. "In the court, half-way between house and drive, a lady stood. She held a parasol above her head" (81). Sheltered, secure, serenely and finely placed. Her maiden name had been "Summer—Anna Summer," and the course of her life has fulfilled the tender and genial promise of such a name. Indeed—we discover as we descend gently into the neat folds of Anna's mind—her expectation of Darrow's visit, of the proposal he will almost certainly offer, has a welcome thrill of the unfamiliar for her; perhaps—she moves to this conclusion with a slow and easy grace—perhaps her life has been too sheltered, too orderly. "She felt, saw, breathed the shining world as though a thin impenetrable veil had suddenly been removed from it. Just such a veil, she now perceived, had always hung between herself and life" (84). She recalls their first romance when "he wanted to kiss her, and she wanted to talk to him about books and pictures, and have him insinuate the eternal theme of their love into every subject they discussed. Whenever they were apart a reaction set in. She wondered how she could have been so cold. . . . But as soon as he reappeared her head straightened itself on her slim neck and she sped her little shafts of irony, or flew her little kites of erudition, while hot and cold waves swept over her, and the things she really wanted to say choked in her throat and burned the palms of her hands" (87). In the end she married a different man, someone who seemed to offer glimpses into a society at once freer and finer, filled with art and books and passionless order.

Anna's mind has remained as neat and fresh as a crisply ironed child's frock: the few, simple compartments into which she organizes her experience have no hidden recesses and no dark corners. This is her heritage, this clear, blank order. "In the well-regulated well-fed Summers world the unusual was regarded as either immoral or ill-bred, and people with emotions were not visited" (85). Anna had been aware of certain discreet absences, even as a girl. "She perceived, indeed, that other girls, leading outwardly the same life as herself . . . were yet possessed of some vital secret which escaped her. There seemed to be a kind of freemasonry between them; they were wider awake than she, more alert, and surer of their wants if not of their opinions. She supposed they were 'cleverer,' and accepted her inferiority good-humoredly, half aware, within herself, of a reserve of unused power which the others gave no sign of possessing. This partly consoled her for missing so much of what made their 'good time'; but the resulting sense of exclusion, of being somehow laughingly but firmly debarred from a share of their privileges, threw her back on herself and deepened the reserve which made envious mothers cite her as a model of ladylike repression" (85–86).* She had vaguely hoped for a release in marriage, but marriage had merely "had the effect of dropping another layer of gauze between herself and reality" (94). The life she has led has been in many ways a good life: she carries herself to Darrow with the supreme confidence of an unblemished ancestral porcelain. Her ideas of the possibilities for them are few and simple, but they are attractive. Her mind is filled with nothing but the most lovely images: " 'I want our life to be like a house with all the windows lit,' " she cries innocently to him; " 'I'd like to string lanterns from the roof and chimneys!' " (120).

What is more, Darrow is pleased and immeasurably reassured by Anna's lack of complication. "His imagination was struck by the quality of reticence in her beauty. She suggested a fine portrait kept down to a few tones, or a Greek vase on which the play of light is the only pattern. . . . He dwelt with pardonable pride on the fact that fate had so early marked him for the high privilege of possessing her" (126, 128). Their fantasies of self and other seem ideally suited. Until Sophy Viner reenters their lives.

---

* The stream of Anna's thoughts here gives some hint of one of the novel's defects. It is unlikely, to say the least, that a woman of Anna's habitual ignorance would use a word like "repression" to describe herself (the use of such a term, after all, implies at least the knowledge that there is something else—something more—and some inkling of what that "something" might be). The author or the author's wise narrator might have these thoughts; they are entirely consonant with the reflections of an Edith Wharton, especially an Edith Wharton who had known the belated passion of an affair in middle age. The intrusion of such implausible insights into Anna's narrative explains, perhaps, the readiness with which so many critics have identified her with her creator. This is an uncharacteristic lapse on Wharton's part, displaying more than anything else her discomfort with her subject.

When Darrow does join Anna, almost nothing stands between them—only that small thing, a period of time unaccounted for, a letter unanswered, the fact of Darrow's dalliance with Sophy Viner. Yet even this is abrasive, like a grain of sand rubbed against a tender organ, for Anna questions her fiancé with a candid wonder. And Darrow is forced to lie to her. She watches him; "he seemed to be honestly turning over his memories" (114). And yet he lies. What else can he do? How could Darrow find words to describe the experience correctly? How could Anna comprehend?

Next, there is Sophy herself, innocently enough employed, so it would seem, as the governess to Anna's daughter. Having pledged herself with apparently sincere affection to Owen Leath. Darrow's prior acquaintance with Sophy is made public; and so, he must lie again. " 'She was secretary, or something of the sort, in the background of a house where I used to dine.' He loathed the slighting indifference of the phrase, but he uttered it deliberately, had been secretly practicing it all through the interminable hour at the luncheon-table" (142). Sophy's behavior is even more troublesome than his own: she is frightened of him, frightened of the exile he can force upon her; yet she is unflinching where he is most inclined to avert his eyes. " 'Don't imagine I'm the least bit sorry for anything!' " she flings at him (149). What *had* the interlude meant to her? Darrow has no idea. "The girl's absolute candour, her hard ardent honesty, was for the moment the vividest point in his thoughts" (151). Yet there is not only Sophy herself to consider, nor even himself, but Anna and Owen and all the widely scattered family attachments. "The situation, detestable at best, would yet have been relatively simple if protecting Sophy Viner had been the only duty involved in it. The fact that that duty was paramount did not do away with the contingent obligations. It was Darrow's instinct, in difficult moments, to go straight to the bottom of the difficulty; but he had never before had to take so dark a dive as this, and for the minute he shivered on the brink . . ." (152). The kaleidoscope of the puzzle shifts, and he can exercise no mastery over it. And so, he continues to lie.

But he does not lie successfully. Even Anna, with her almost impenetrable purity, cannot fail to perceive that some truth has eluded her. She tries to approach Sophy, and as she looks at the girl, "so small, so slight, so visibly defenceless and undone, she still felt, through all the superiority of her worldly advantages and her seeming maturity, the same odd sense of ignorance and inexperience. She could not have said what there was in the girl's manner and expression to give her this feeling, but she was reminded, as she looked at Sophy Viner, of the other girls she had known in her youth, the girls who seemed possessed of a secret she had missed" (236–37). Anna muses upon the relationship between Darrow and Sophy, and having no other language with which to meditate, she lapses into a naive and girlish variant of Darrow's "masculine" categories: "He had met the girl in Paris and helped her in her straits—lent her money, Anna vaguely conjectured—and she had fallen in love with him, and on meeting him again had been suddenly overmastered by her passion" (277). But this is not enough; and as Anna recognizes that she has no way to verbalize the truth, Sophy begins to seem "the embodiment of that unknown peril lurking in the background of every woman's thoughts about her lover. Anna, at any rate, with a sudden sense of estrangement, noted in her graces and snares never before perceived. It was only the flash of a primitive instinct, but it lasted long enough to make her ashamed of the darkness it lit up in her heart . . ." (282).

Inexorably, little by little, Anna dimly senses "everything"; and for this moment, the two separate narratives converge briefly. " 'I don't even know what you mean by "everything," ' " Darrow tells her. " 'Oh, I don't know what more there is!' " she responds. " 'I know enough. I implored her to deny it and she couldn't. . . . What can you and I have to say to each other?' Her voice broke into a sob. The animal anguish was upon her again—just a blind cry against her pain! . . . 'What *is* she? What are you? It's too horrible! On your way here . . . to *me* . . .' She felt the tears in her throat and stopped. . . . 'I always thought her an adventuress!' " (289, 292, 293). Darrow fumbles to correct Anna's bitterness. " 'She's not an adventuress. . . . She had the excuse of her loneliness, her unhappiness—of miseries and humiliations that a woman like you can't even guess' " (293). Yet no words known to either of them can capture Sophy Viner. "What did he mean by 'a moment's folly, a flash of madness'?" Anna wonders miserably (294). " 'I don't think I understand what you've told me,' " she concludes, " 'I don't want to—about such things!' " (295).

There is no doubt that Darrow has been moved (as Selden never was) to see the inadequacies of his conventional habits of thought. " 'You've always said you wanted, above all, to look at life, at the human problem, as it is, without fear and without hypocrisy,' " he tells Anna, " 'and it's not always a pleasant thing to look at' " (292). Neither pleasant nor easily comprehensible, for though Darrow knows his insufficiencies, he has discovered no truths to replace them. " 'What complex blunderers we all are,' " he muses at his last visit. " 'How we're struck blind sometimes, and mad sometimes—and then, when our sight and our senses come back, how we have to set to work, and build up, little by little, bit by bit, the precious things we'd smashed to atoms without knowing it. Life's just a perpetual piecing together of broken bits' " (315).

Once Darrow has left, even the limited insights he has brought to the problem are no longer available, and Anna must muse alone. In her last encounter with Sophy, the girl pleaded that Anna dismiss Darrow's indiscretion from her mind and marry him; and Anna, blinded with indignity and rage, was mute. "She wanted to find a word, but could not: all within her was too dark and violent" (310). Now as this episode in her life winds slowly to its closing, Anna's thoughts revert once again to Sophy Viner, "with a mingling of antipathy and confidence. . . . But what indeed was the girl really like? She seemed to have no scruples and a thousand delicacies. She had given herself to Darrow, and concealed the episode from Owen Leath, with no more apparent sense of debasement than the vulgarest adventuress; yet she had instantly obeyed the voice of her heart when it bade her part from the one and serve the other" (320-21). Anna knows that Sophy has been to Darrow what she will never be, and she is torn between horror and envy. "Here they were, these dark places, in her own bosom, and henceforth she would always have to traverse them to reach the beings she loved best!" (353). She longs to throw off the veil of ignorance and specious innocence, but she has had no training, no experience. Darrow could not find the words to explain life—Anna rummages desperately through her little stock of alternatives. "It was only Sophy Viner who could save her—Sophy Viner only who could give her back her lost serenity" (361). Thus with the shining faith of a convert and a certainty that Sophy, at least, might be trusted to be true, Anna sets out on a quest to find her.

Sophy had mentioned a sister—vaguely connected with the theater, vaguely married—and she left the Leath household to join that sister. It is a shabby apartment, cluttered with faded roses, tumbled cushions, half-eaten chocolates; the door is answered by a pretty young man. His manner has the grace of infinite flexibility; he looks penetratingly at Anna. " 'Just a minute,' he smiled; 'I think the *masseur's* with her.' He spoke in a smooth denationalized English, which, like the look in his long-lashed eyes and the promptness of his charming smile, suggested a long training in all the arts of expediency" (364). After a while, Anna is escorted to a disheveled pink bedroom where a flush, fair woman lies amid the pillows. "In the roseate penumbra of the bed-curtains she presented to Anna's startled gaze an odd chromo-like resemblance to Sophy Viner, or a suggestion, rather, of what Sophy Viner might, with the years and in spite of the powder-puff, become. Larger, blonder, heavier-featured, she yet had glances and movements that disturbingly suggested what was freshest and most engaging in the girl; and as she stretched her bare plump arm across the bed she seemed to be pulling back the veil from dingy distances of family history" (365).

Sophy—ah, what a shame—Sophy has left Paris. Desolate? Destitute? Why no. She had a chance of a job as . . . companion . . . to a family that is traveling to India. Sophy has gone, whirled once more out of Anna's world. The curtain falls; the novel ends.

In speaking of the conclusion to *The Reef*, Blake Nevius has observed that "Edith Wharton may for the first time be accused of begging the question." [26] It is a valid indictment. We are left without even the means for assessing the dark suspicions raised by Anna's last visit: the essence of Sophy Viner eludes us entirely. It is not enough to say with Darrow merely that life is complex; this observation may be true, but it is an insufficient moral insight around which to structure a fictional world. When Edith Wharton sent the novel to Berenson, she wrote him apologetically. "I'm sick about it. . . . *Please* don't read it! Put it in the visitors' rooms, or lend it to somebody to read in the train and let it get lost." [27] Yet six years later, when Brownell wrote her a belated appreciation of the novel, she thanked him in an unusually personal tone. "You tell me you have re-read *The Reef* with growing approval (which goes to my inner-most heart because I put most of myself into that opus)." [28] There is little doubt that Wharton consciously thought of the novel as a nervous, insufficient, but immensely important experiment.

Aware of her power as a novelist, she daringly, though unsuccessfully, manipulated the narrative vantage; aware of the weight of her experiences as a woman, she audaciously scattered the accidents of her adult life throughout the novel. The lovers have their affair in the Terminus Hotel (no one would have known the significance of this save Fullerton and Wharton herself, of course); the evocation of the suite of rooms that floats through Darrow's anguished consciousness is a paraphrase of the language of that other description (in an entirely different tone) in Wharton's poem "Terminus"; Anna Leath's mother-in-law bears the Christian name Lucretia; and the characterization of Anna Leath herself borrows overtly from memories of Wharton's own girlhood. The novel is almost deliberately deluding. Even R. W. B. Lewis has been entrapped. "In the presentation of Anna Leath, Edith Wharton almost literally began to write her autobiography," he says. "The story of Anna's life to the moment when the novel's action begins is such that Ralph Curtis could say quite rightly that it was 'a masterly self-diagnosis, as I knew [Edith] at Newport.' " [29] But this is not—at least not in the usual sense—autobiography, for all its flirtatious allusiveness. (We can put Lewis's remark in context merely by reflecting that Anna Leath fails to grow; Anna Leath does not have an affair; Anna Leath could never write a novel.)

What is central both in Wharton's life and in this novel is the *problem:* the immensely convoluted, many-sided problem of sexuality. It is as if Wharton had taken the crystalline wholeness of her nature and sent it crashing to the floor to break into bright shards. Out of the largest of these, she fashioned a fiction. We can see elements of her nature (and more significantly, of her problem) in Anna; we can find them equally in Sophy and in Darrow. If Wharton might be Anna Leath, so might Katherine Fullerton: the mirrors shift, and the complex conjury continues; the superficies of the novel will never yield its truth. More important even than the characters here are the forces at work. There is an acknowledged need for sexual experience and a recognition of the naturalness of a woman's sense of initiative. Yet there is a simultaneous sense that sexuality and aggression have their darker sides, even, at their roots, some hidden horror. There is a renunciation of the suffocating hypocrisies of established Victorian society; yet there is an acute consciousness of the beauty and peace that inheres in the order of a society whose mores are deeply structured. Individual "right" is balanced inconclusively against social "need." And though the many components of the problem are reflected in the shifting mirrors of the novel, they are never resolved into a coherently focused image.

Throughout the next eight years, Wharton will labor at the problem she first examines in *The Reef*—dealing now with one element of it, now with another. Finally, in *The Age of Innocence*, she will pose it again in all its complexity; the same constellation of forces will be invoked, even the same balance of characters (a man torn between two women—one the self-conscious product of "old New York," the other an elusive outsider). Yet in the interim, she will have managed to sort out the many elements of the quandary. *The Reef* is tantalizingly imperfect; *The Age of Innocence* will be a brilliant success.

3

On April 16, 1913, Edith Wharton was divorced from her husband of almost thirty years. The wrench had been preceded by more than ten years of increasing anguish. Teddy—always cheerful, always reliable—Teddy, who had taken such good care of his wife during the nightmare of that twelve-year bout with nausea and depression: something had gradually happened to Teddy.

The first signs had appeared as early as 1902. After completing *The Valley of Decision*, Edith suffered the last real collapse of her protracted illness; surprisingly, Teddy was not able to stay and comfort her, for he had been forced to take himself off to North Carolina to recuperate from some malaise of his own. Again in the summer of 1903 Teddy was ill, depressed and full of vague symptoms; perversely, he improved when the couple resided on the coast at Newport (which Edith had come to hate), and he grew worse when they took up residence at The Mount (where Edith thrived). There was certainly no conscious contest of wills at this point, but the interests of the two had begun to diverge, markedly and unmistakably. Several years passed with only minor problems, but in December of 1907 (when, we must recall, Edith was in the initial phases of the affair with Fullerton), Teddy suffered a serious collapse. He hated the Paris rounds of salons and concerts and dramas that stimulated his wife; what is more, he almost certainly sensed the high pitch of an expectant mood that excluded him (for that mood is easily discernable in the letters to Sara Norton), even though he had no idea of its cause. In any case, he left Paris on February 12 to spend nine days in the country with friends; this time, however, a short vacation did not improve his health. Edith's appointment book for 1908 bears the notation: "March 21. T. W. sailed on Philadelphia, to take cure for gout at Hot Springs." [30] Never again did he fully recover his health.

Teddy was eventually diagnosed as a "neurasthenic"—a catchall term in those days for men with psychological disturbances; today, we might label his illness "manic-depression." At this distance, however, and with so few facts, no one can make a diagnosis. Nevertheless, one thing is clear. Edith Wharton's success (especially her growing assertiveness and independence) aggravated the symptoms of her husband's disorder, and for five years the marriage was a bitter irritation to Teddy and a constant drain on his wife. "I wonder," she wrote ruminatively to John Hugh-Smith in February of 1909, "among all the tangles of this mortal coil, which one contains tighter knots to undo, and consequently suggests more tugging, and pain, and diversified elements of misery, than the marriage tie—and which, consequently, is more 'made to the hand' of the psychologist and the dramatist?" [31] (*Ethan Frome*, written during the winter of the following year, certainly grew in part out of the grotesque irony of Teddy's illness—a malady whose depths were a mocking emblem of the possibilities that had been latent in her own behavior.)

Teddy's mother died in the summer of 1909, and he grew much worse. He had all sorts of physical complaints—pains in his joints, facial neuralgia, toothaches, insomnia—and his moods shifted from wild exhilaration to the most abject and groveling dejection. Sometimes a mood would possess him for days, weeks, even months; sometimes the shifts could occur in the space of time it took to walk across a room. There were periods when his temper seemed to be on a more or less even keel, but one could rely upon nothing. What was worse, the only environment in which he was able to function was one that denied Edith the atmosphere she felt she needed to develop as a novelist. Teddy remained in America in the fall of 1909 to clear up his mother's estate while Edith returned to Europe; and Teddy's sister, Nannie Wharton, sent Edith a series of twittering letters declaring that "Ted seems *perfectly* well, a *perfectly* normal man." [32] However, when Teddy arrived in Paris that November, Edith recognized at once that he was still in the grip of his old trouble. She had not reckoned, however, on the practical forms his illness had taken. While in Boston he had set himself up with an actress—so he confessed in early December—several actresses, in fact. His enthusiasms knew no bounds, and in a burst of exuberance, he had speculated on his own behalf with Edith's trust funds. To put the matter bluntly, he had stolen $50,000 from her. Yet one must not judge him harshly: life had been difficult for Teddy, too.

For years he had had no substantial income of his own at all. He did not work, and the family money was held by his mother. Edith had received a sizable inheritance; in addition, her income from writing supplied an enviable amount of money (even Henry James was not above expressing his envy of it). Teddy had been appointed one of the trustees who managed her inherited income; but that was all he did—he managed it, conservatively and with the cooperative supervision of others. Nothing in life made him feel terribly important (save, perhaps, the symptoms with which he countered his wife's successes). From 1909 until the divorce in 1913, the couple's disagreements would focus on two subjects: the method of treatment Teddy ought to undergo to alleviate his illness and—much, much more important—his capacity to manage Edith's money.

For a long while, Edith determined not to let the marriage founder. Teddy repaid the money he had appropriated (using virtually all of the inheritance from his mother to do so), and in the early months of 1910 Edith began investigating a variety of medical approaches to his illness. In all of this, however, she was opposed by Teddy's brother Billy Wharton and his sister Nannie. Certain members of Edith's own family, most notably her sister-in-law Minnie Jones, were supportive, but of course they exercised no authority over Teddy. On April 4, 1910, Edith wrote to Judge Robert Grant—a friend from happier days in Lenox—in a state nearing desperation. She describes herself as "worried and wearied and generally unhinged" and adds rather bitterly: "You need not be told that I don't know much work in these conditions! I believe some people can live in this kind of atmosphere and adapt themselves to it, or rather remain unconscious of it; but it colours my whole existence, and Teddy is never out of my mind, or *off* my mind, for an instant." [33] When Teddy was in Paris, he was seldom out of her presence, for his state was such that he could not be left alone. Peevish, irritable, querulous, sometimes very angry, other times morose and humble—his moods shifted in ways that defied normal interaction.

Edith pleaded with him to submit to a regular course of treatment (as, after all, she had done herself), but he refused. "Teddy has always been extremely self-willed," she wrote Grant, "and has done all his life, exactly what he chose; and it is hopeless to try to direct him now, unless all those about him unite in trying to carry out what the Drs. suggest." [34] Unfortunately, Teddy's family did quite the opposite. Sturgis Bigelow, a medical man (though no longer practicing) who came from a long line of doctors—began dropping by to take Teddy out for a motor jaunt, thereby giving Edith a few hours of welcome relief. Bigelow was a steadying influence on Teddy, and he may have helped induce him to take sensible steps. In any case, by June Teddy had finally decided to enter a well-known sanatorium in Switzerland, where he stayed until the end of July. Unlike his wife, however, Teddy was not permanently helped by this course of treatment. He was well enough afterwards to do a little traveling alone with friends, and he did so; but the symptoms persisted, and in August, Sturgis Bigelow wrote to Edith in considerable agitation. "I have been thinking over your affairs and this is the way they look to me. You are dealing with two separate and distinct problems. —1. Nannie. —2. Ted . . . [1.] Nannie. Her attitude since she came to Paris has been in the main one of persistent, dogged and indiscriminate opposition to all suggestions about Ted, no matter whether they were doctors' orders or not. —This cannot go on. . . . 2. Ted . . . *He ought to be put under restraint, and the sooner the better.* It ought to have been done a year ago. . . . Of course you will be careful about being alone with Ted with nobody within call." [35] Nevertheless, Edith continued to have more or less exclusive responsibility for Teddy until mid-October when, with his doctors' permission, he set off with friends for a long trip around the world. Until his return on April 6, 1911, Edith Wharton would lead a life of relative calm. But she was not deceived: she had only borrowed time (the reports that came to her during Teddy's trip were by no means reassuring); eventually some final arrangement would have to be made.

It is impossible to say how Edith's various successes and growing strengths affected Teddy. The dramatic and exaggerated quality of his shifts in mood gives evidence that he was suffering from a good deal more than merely a peevish reaction to Edith's behavior. Nevertheless, it is inescapably the case that Teddy chose to act out his illness principally in the two areas where Edith's life had most changed since 1900: sexuality and the ability to manage money. Edith entered upon a three-year affair in early 1908; simultaneously, Teddy's condition worsened, and he went back to America and set himself up with a chorus girl or two. We can follow a similar though much more complicated situation in the matter of finance.

Edith Wharton was an astute businesswoman despite the fact that there was every reason to expect that she would not be. "Even the men of her class were, as she describes them in many of her stories, too proud and too ignorant of the methods of money-making to apply their intelligence to augmenting an inherited wealth." [36] What is perhaps most surprising, she managed the contractual negotiations for her work herself, right from the beginning, even when she suffered most severely from depression (we have seen many of the letters in Section II): she never hid behind some masculine go-between. [37] Obviously, it was important for her to know that she was more than a genteel dabbler; characteristically, she became, therefore, the shrewdest of professionals. She was not in the least mean-spirited (the correspondence with Burlingame and Brownell is always cordial and usually very friendly), but she learned to market the product of her labors very, very well. Thus by the time she was making arrangements for the publication of *The Fruit of the Tree*, she demonstrated a justified confidence in her commercial skills. [38] Teddy cannot have been unaffected by this development. There is not the slightest evidence that she was anything but open and generous in their arrangements, but the fact was that husband and wife had somehow exchanged roles. She made the money; to a large degree, she held the purse strings. Could they ever, in these circumstances, be held loosely enough not to bind? It is hard to believe that both of them were not conscious of this unorthodox exchange (we might remember that *The Custom of the Country*, Wharton's "business novel," was begun as early as 1907).

Really, the final breaking point in the marriage came as much over money as anything else. Teddy steadfastly refused to admit the full extent of his illness; he was not content to submit to sustained and systematic treatment; and as proof of his mental competence, he demanded that he be allowed to resume his part in the management of Edith's inheritance—to take over, as well, the supervision of their major domestic affairs. In view of his health, that would never again be possible. On July 8, 1910, Edith wrote a long letter to Teddy, who was then in Kreuslingen Sanatorium: "As far as my personal efforts to cheer and help you are concerned, they have all been unsuccessful, and you are probably right when you say, in your letter of June 30th, that, for the present, at any rate, the sense of what you call 'having to be a passenger for the rest of your days'—that is, not being able to manage my money affairs and

decide about household matters—would make you dissatisfied and unhappy, whatever plan of life we tried to carry out together." [39]

Edith was beginning to be consistently firm now, but Teddy was in
no mood to give up. He came out of the sanatorium and went on the trip
around the world. In May of 1911 he wrote to Herman Edgar, Edith's
first cousin and chief financial adviser. In dangerously high spirits,
Teddy was rambling and incoherent.

> I should like you to send me a list of the three trusts and of Puss' individ-
> ual things and also will you tell me what changes you have made. I think it
> was a great mistake to have sold Tobacco common, as it was at its worst,
> and an adverse decision will have, they all tell me, no effect on its value, it
> has all been discounted. I hope you have sold nothing else. I think Harry
> and I, as the two Trustees, should be consulted before any other things are
> sold. In fact I must insist on this, otherwise you are not Agent, but sole
> Trustee. You see, dear boy, Tobacco yielded almost 10% and if you go on
> selling 10% things and putting them into 5% things, Puss' income will be
> much smaller. If you would kindly let me know the history of the various
> properties from the time of my collapse to date, letting me know how the
> money sent on by my brother, about $50,000 [i.e., the money covering
> Teddy's embezzlement] was invested and what things you have sold and
> what other investments made I shall be greatly obliged.[40]

Edgar forwarded this note with considerable bewilderment, and Edith
took immediate action. On May 30, 1911, she wrote to Teddy demanding that he resign his trusteeship. "During several of our talks in Paris,
and more definitely and specifically during our last talk, the day before
you sailed, I told you—in reply to repeated requests on your part to be
allowed to have control of my income—that I would not, at any time in
the future, go back to our former arrangement in this respect, or consent
to your having anything to do with the control of my money, whether
income or capital. . . . I must protect myself from the recurrence of the
wearing and unprofitable discussions about money which have made the
chief subject of our talk whenever we have been together lately." [41]

From this point, the marriage degenerated into black comedy. Teddy
and Edith entertained Henry James and several of his friends at The
Mount in the summer of 1911, and James described Teddy as both "sce-
nic" and "violent." Relations between husband and wife were strained,
and they came to a head one evening in late July. Edith recognized that

her husband was hopelessly unbalanced; yet she offered (probably feeling no little guilt in the matter) to let him salvage his self-respect. He might stay on at The Mount, which he had grown to love, exercising complete authority there; she would provide a liberal allowance for the purpose. He, in turn, would resign as trustee of her estate and would agree to cease all further demands for control over her money. Teddy agreed. That was at eight o'clock. At ten o'clock Edith suggested that she and Teddy sign a mutual agreement sealing their bargain, and Teddy lost control of himself completely—he raged, he threatened, he berated her, he accused her of lying to him. The agreement was off. Things dragged on for almost a month more; but later that year, preparations were begun for the sale of The Mount. Edith took up permanent residence in Paris, and eighteen months afterward the couple was divorced.

Yet even after at least six years of aggravation and eighteen months of explicit preparation, Edith Wharton was still deeply conflicted about the divorce. It is probable that nothing else she ever did—save perhaps the momentous commitment to her career as a writer—affected her with such deep and painfully contradictory feelings. One example gives some hint of her distress. Wharton was self-consciously careful about the contents of her private papers: she knew with justified certainty that they would eventually become the basis upon which a biography would be built (and she had an aversion to biography, by the way, steadfastly resisting it during her lifetime). In view of her unusual caution, it is interesting that she did not destroy either the Love Diary or the Beatrice Palmato fragment. Her final illness was merciful and slow heart failure; she had plenty of opportunity. Something in her seems to have whispered: let them discover that I, too, have lived. On the other hand, she did prepare a packet of papers labeled "for my biographer." It contained a variety of letters, many from doctors, and it constituted an almost formal brief defending her decision to obtain the divorce.[42] She did not feel the need to explain her affair; but she did her divorce. The ambivalence assumed a morbid quality.

Of course there was a good deal of real-world justification for her queasiness: in 1913, divorce was not readily accepted among Wharton's circle of genteel acquaintances; people were bound to talk, even if she *was* a flagrantly injured wife (and by 1913, she was). At her insistence, Bernard Berenson made tactful inquiries of his Harvard acquaintances in Boston, among them President Lowell, and brought back the reassurance that her plight had evoked understanding and sympathy; nevertheless, Teddy's Boston relations made free with her character and maligned her motives. Divorce resurrected the old-maid element in many natures. Her cousin Thomas Newbold wrote in April of 1913 with a prissy sort of support: "As you may imagine we have had innumerable conferences and have thoroughly thrashed out your affairs! [What comfort *that* image must have provided!] . . . Have you decided what you are going to call yourself? I told Herman [Edgar] that I thought we had better, for the present, address letters simply *Mrs. Wharton*. Would you prefer Mrs. E. W.? I object violently to Mrs. 'Edith' Wharton! Of course I would be proud to have the name Newbold shoved in, but that might be a mistake in your case . . . ?" [43] There is no doubt whatsoever that the divorce raised again the haunting problems associated with "niceness"; given Edith Wharton's person history, these problems were preternaturally troublesome.

In fact, we must assume that whatever real unpleasantness there was (and there was a good deal), the most relentless punishment came from within. [44] After all, Minnie Jones, the wife of Edith's brother Freddy, had been divorced for many years; Minnie and Edith were good friends, and society had not cast Minnie beyond the pale. Others of Wharton's acquaintance had survived the trauma of divorce. But for Edith Wharton, divorce reopened a number of conflicts that had festered unresolved since childhood. In the end, it was the discomfort of these that she could not banish. If throughout this period she was engaged in finally coming to terms with a complex network of problems, the particular problem that was increasingly thrust to the top of her mind was that of initiative. As a woman—a successful, ambitious woman—did she have the right to a self-determined, autonomous, even competitive life?

Society said no. (Society might be captured in Thomas Newbold's voice: now that you are no longer attached to a husband—"have you decided what you are going to call yourself?") Edith Wharton, however, had rejected the social imperative of feminine passivity; the vigor and assertion that had become so much a part of her life were the conditions for remaining free of the illness that had crippled her before. Central to this new sense of self was a pride in her vocation, not merely in writing, but in being a rather tough *professional* writer, making money, managing her affairs. All of this had clearly alienated her husband. He would certainly have been a sick man in any case, but his symptoms responded directly to his wife's growing strengths. Recognizing this—as her letters demonstrate that she did—what was she to do? Did she not have a *right* to the position she had earned with such effort? Suppose that she did— felt that she did. By what social standards might that right be defined? How did successful women, ambitious women, behave? Whose example did they follow? Sophy Viner had said: " 'I'm not so sure that I believe in marriage. You see I'm all for self-development and the chance to live one's life.' " But Sophy Viner ultimately eluded us, as she apparently eluded her creator: she appears like a genie from a bottle, tangles the lives of those she meets, and hurries on—to India—to meet some destiny, who knows what. Sophy yields no answers; she merely embodies a quandary. Divorce confirmed Edith Wharton's own right to "self-development and the chance to live one's life." Her problem lay in coming to terms with it.

The Reef touched tantalizingly on events in Wharton's present; it also summoned echoes from the past with painful immediacy. Anna Leath is certainly not Edith Wharton. However, swathed as she is in layers of gauze "between herself and reality" (94), she is a surprising visitation from "The Valley of Childish Things," Wharton's short story of twenty years earlier. "A model of ladylike repression" (86), she is Lucretia's image of propriety in young ladies, in gentlepeople of both sexes. She grows out of the memories of Wharton's adolescence when aggressive behavior was condemned; and these memories, in turn, build upon even earlier experiences. From the depths of Wharton's own "Valley of Childish Things" come the persistent voices of thoughts and feelings that have been largely pushed out of consciousness, remnants of those fearful, self-imposed injunctions against competition that had been formulated when she was a little girl of four or five. It is dangerous to reach out and grasp what you want (so the memories recite—remember the fateful effects of that "robber story"); opposition is dangerous (do not even think things about Mother that you could not say aloud!).

Eventually, Edith Wharton did write a fiction that required her to enter the forbidden areas where questions of initiative and competition had their origins; however, it was anything but an easy task.

The original sequence was clear enough: in *The House of Mirth* she had explored the nullity of "being"; next she wanted to invade the land of "doing," and Justine Brent was her beginning. However, the inadequacies of *The Fruit of the Tree* showed Wharton the limitations of her experience as a woman. Undine was to have been Justine's successor, but Undine's world glimmered mockingly out of Wharton's grasp. In 1907, she had not yet loosed her own feelings sufficiently to infuse that fictional world with life; *The Custom of the Country* had to be put aside. Meanwhile, the love affair with Fullerton revealed further complexities in the problem. By the time the affair was ended, Wharton had unloosed so many feelings that she could not understand them or give order and focus to the quandaries they posed. Hence the ultimate failure of *The Reef*, whose subject was too ambitious for Wharton in 1911. Yet Sophy Viner is a significant step beyond Justine Brent; a link, as it were, between Justine and Undine. If Sophy might be isolated, some element of Sophy, perhaps, then a coherent fiction could be built around it. Edith Wharton could not yet write a successful novel about the sinuous web of sexuality; she was ready, however, to spin off a significant segment of that web—the matter of feminine initiative.

She could have chosen no more brilliant mode of exploring it than a special, ironic adaption of the current craze in fiction—the money novel. Horatio Alger's myth had possessed the land. Dreiser said, "There was a singing, illusioned spirit. Actually, the average American then believed that the possession of money would certainly solve all his earthly ills. You could see it in the faces of the people, in their step and manner. Power, power, power—everyone was seeking power in the land of the free and the home of the brave." [45] (Recall Teddy's plaintive letter: a buffoon's cry for power.) A magazine entitled *Success* was entirely devoted to singing the litany of this new faith. The strongest young writers in America were composing new epics of business and money. No one knew the trends more intimately than Edith Wharton, who had begun to do the research for a projected novel to be entitled "Literature." [46] In her case, however, the research was almost unneeded. She had felt the exultant pulse within herself: the joyous mastery of profession, the drive and energy that distinguished those few who excelled, the management of money that gave such self-esteem and self-confidence. These were authentic, powerful feelings in her life. Yet—and here was the terrible discomfort of Wharton's situation—society offered no language, no categories by which she might define these feelings. Neither did literature.

Horatio Alger's myth in all its manifestations was for men, not for women. The new captains of industry were men, and the literature that celebrated their conquest was a saga of active men and passive women. Even the slow, sleepy motion of Carrie Meeber's rocker suggests a mute animal instinct for survival, not a coiled, hairspring reflex for ruthless, grasping success. Competition, conquest—these belonged to the Cowperwoods of the world (or even the Tom Sawyers—for capitalism in the young often began as a game, but a game in which no girls were allowed).

Thus Wharton found herself in a situation very like the one that had produced *The House of Mirth:* the language of heroism was insufficient to the breadth of her own experience. So, she would have to turn that language upon itself, making heroism one of the explicit objects of her scrutiny. *The Custom of the Country* is not about Edith Wharton's personal problem; Undine, despite her red hair, is not Edith Wharton. Yet there is a superb meshing of subjects. Wharton captures the surging imperatives of initiative and drive, and inspects them, all the while assuming that they are normal human (not merely masculine) traits. The enterprise allows her to gain full access to that reservoir of deepest feelings and to fuse those feelings with an artistically appropriate subject. Finally acknowledging their terrible force, she is able to draw upon their energy in the service of her fiction. The result is a novel infused with the woman's outrage and the long-suppressed fury of the girl whose deepest instincts had been engulfed by guilt. The object of that fury is a society whose norms are not equal to the range of experience that its members feel. An insensitive, effete, corrupt society; a society that might, without humor, produce a magazine entitled *Success;* a society whose "best" people have been frozen into stupefaction by the niceties of "propriety." In speaking of her method in writing *The House of Mirth*, Wharton had said: "A frivolous society can acquire dramatic significance only through what its frivolity destroys. Its tragic implication lies in its power of debasing people and ideals. The answer, in short, was my heroine, Lily Bart." [47]

She might have made a similar statement about *The Custom of the Country*, a novel that is in many ways a companion-piece to its predecessor. "Do you want an image of your corruption? Look at what you have produced! Look at Undine Spragg!"

4

Elmer Moffatt " 'strikes me as the kind of man who develops slowly, needs a big field, and perhaps makes some big mistakes, but gets where he wants in the end, ' " Ralph exclaims with unusual fervor. " 'Jove, I wish I could put him in a book! There's something epic about him— a kind of epic effrontery.' " [48] Someone might have written an American epic of Elmer Moffatt; it was the age for such efforts. Ralph didn't. Neither did Edith Wharton. *The Custom of the Country* furnishes enough subject for several tragedies, yet it is not an epic. Its sweep is gargantuan: the aim of its conquest is very nearly as large as the ambition of its heroine; its mood is martial, furious, and devastating. But it is not an epic. Wharton tantalizes us with the fact on every page. We might be with Becky Sharp in Brussels, the cannons booming just over the horizon and the generals passing back and forth from metropolis to battlefield. It is the cosmopolitan debacle that Wharton fixes upon with such ruthlessness; the epic is outside the walls, just within shouting distance.

Nor is the work even a satire of epic proportions. To be sure, the satirical element suffuses this novel: raucous laughter pursues us throughout Undine's chronicle, hollow, mocking, derisive. There is much to loathe in Poppleland, the strange world of this fiction. And yet, here too, Wharton is cunning. She commands objects to appear before us: lo!— they are easy to despise; we recoil from them and pass on; other objects, people, places, practices, events—they twist and turn under her deft management—now repellent, but now pitiable, and now even lovely. She dares us to scorn, taunts us with the simplicity of our impulsive eagerness to judge. Ultimately, she rejects the orderliness of pure satire.

Even the novel's realism is strained almost to the point of collapse. None of Wharton's other fictions gives us such an uncompromising vision; no quarter given, no sentimental attachments honored, no niceties got up for the occasion, no vulgarities left untouched. Still, it is a vision that slides precipitously close to caricature: the hilarity of names like Indiana Frusk and Claud Walsingham Popple and Mr. Urban Dagonet rises up almost (but not quite) to obscure the veracity of the tale, just as the riotous ceremony of divorce dissolving hastily and happily into the marriage of Undine Spragg Moffatt Marvell Chelles Moffatt tugs at credulity. Nevertheless, life is there—vibrant and virulent.

The secret of Wharton's most ambitious masterpiece is its perversity, its constant change. It is a difficult and disorienting novel. Reading it, we are challenged always to be mindful of what it is not (not epic, not pure satire, not caricature), constrained always to wonder whether our response has been correct. The relentless forward movement of the work is countered by a tidal undertow. Nothing is fixed. The relationships among the characters shift continuously as fortunes are won and lost, married and divorced. (How often we are tempted to suppose that the cosmopolitan society that fills this fiction is all merely a shadow world and that the substance of the novel is, somehow, really the stock exchange—its "place" really the pit!) Nothing is less certain than the moral relationships among the parti-colored crew, for there is no moral center within the world of this novel, no fixed set of principles according to which we may systematically evaluate its characters. We may sympathize now with one, now with another; but the final judgment of any individual must be ambiguous. The most reliable voice within the novel is that of the Marvells' family friend, Mr. Bowen. Yet even Bowen adopts the tone, almost, of a sociologist. He can tell us certain "facts" about this world, observe the ways in which social arrangements are faulty. But he cannot formulate a code by which to judge the jumble that he observes. Nor does the narrator offer much help in this matter. Following the general pattern, the narrator's vantage shifts—to Undine, momentarily to her parents, to Ralph, occasionally to Moffatt, very often to the position of solemn, impartial spectator. There are no clarifying summations: the language of praise is inconclusively balanced against the language of condemnation.

One thing and only one is genuinely fixed; and that is a preoccupation with energy. Psychic energy—power, assertion, drive, ambition. This, more even than Undine herself, is the subject of the fiction.

The novel is postulated in an era of titanic transition.[49] It is, perhaps, a Götterdämmerung; perhaps it is the triumph of a progressive, pioneering spirit, the dawning of a new age of strength and wisdom. The final verdict has not been rendered when the novel ends, and we cannot tell whether the world is dying or being reborn. We know only the fact of change—the nervous, restless movement that pervades the entire work—and at the heart of this change there is energy. Old orders must pass away. Some have grown enervated, their resources exhausted, the beautiful harmony of their proprieties resounding with a fainter and yet fainter echo. Others have become perverted, their energy misplaced, channeled into the preservation of empty forms whose content has been eroding for decades. By contrast the newcomers radiate energy. Their vitality is manifest in nothing so much as an apparently unending capacity to rebound from defeat, and their vigor thrusts them forward, ever forward; they are the wave of the future, these high-riding buccaneers. They swarm over the globe—never hindered by boundaries of country or continent—and, roaming at will, they plunder the castles of the rich, now become glorious tombs. Often they destroy, unmindful of the value of their spoils; just as often they preserve with a voracious need for beauty that suggests a capacity to become the preservers of the future: we cannot judge what final course these modern barbarians will ultimately follow. The novel is poised precariously upon the moment of change; the values that were revered have been sundered from the force needed to sustain them. This instant in the transition is characterized by an ominous, free-floating residue of power, and the Undine—a creature without a soul—is a perfect and monstrous emblem of the time. *The Custom of the Country* is a money novel, a business novel, that is true. However, above all, it is a novel of energy, of initiative.

The novel chronicles a poignant passage: there is much to admire in the cultures that are being laid waste. The Aboriginal house in Washington Square that "might have passed for [the] inner consciousness" (73) of old New York is an orderly place. "Its dark mahogany doors and the quiet 'Dutch interior' effect of its black and white marble paving" (73) emanate a sense of harmony and dignity that surpasses anything else in the world of this fiction. The ideals of the Dagonets and the Marvells have always been "small, cautious, middle-class" (74); however, when they are balanced against the "chaos of indiscriminate appetites which made up . . . modern tendencies" (74), the mores of that older world seem lofty and admirable. Clare Van Degen is a woman of little imagination and intelligence, but she is kind and genuinely sympathetic. "Slender and shadowy in her long furs, [bearing] a battered old Dagonet bowl that came down . . . 'from our revered great-grandmother'" (211–12), she seems the uncomplicated guardian of some hushed and dusky haven where peace still reigns.

Congenitally inclined to seek shelter from the storm of competition, the members of the old order are paying with their existence for the privilege of avoiding those things that are "common." Harriet Ray "knew by heart all the cousinships of early New York, hated motor-cars, could not make herself understood on the telephone, and was determined, if she married, never to receive a divorced woman" (78). When Mr. Spragg inquires whether Ralph has ever been taught to work, Mr. Urban Dagonet renders what might pass as a smile: " 'No; I really coudn't have afforded that' " (122). The black and white tiles and the paneled interior—these things are "real" to Ralph's clan, and they seek solace from such comforting "realities" when time passes them by and the world hurries to new assignations. A muscle that is never flexed, their moral fiber atrophies (for the inward movement requires very little effort), and they gradually become too crippled to rise to the demands that ordinary living makes upon them. They seek an elegant stasis, and in so doing, they deny themselves even the remnants of will and emotional strength. The energy that once infused their lives with meaning has been banished because it is vulgar.

All that seems so intrinsically attractive has gradually been contaminated by the hypocrisies that are necessary to sustain the lives of these graceful aristocrats. Harriet Ray's virginal resolutions grow ludicrous when they are exposed to the actualities of Ralph's misery. What help can such a family offer to a son who has become involved in something beyond the reach of their experience? "The affair was a 'scandal,' and it was not in the Dagonet tradition to acknowledge the existence of scandals. . . . Ralph suspected that the constraint showed by his mother and sister was partly due to their having but a dim and confused view of what had happened. In their vocabulary the word 'divorce' was wrapped in such a dark veil of innuendo as no ladylike hand would care to lift" (336–37). And those in the closed little world of old New York who manage to ride the cresting wave do so by living on the refuse of the invader whose habits they contemn. Clare grows substantially less attractive when the rectitude of her manner is subjected to scrutiny. "Poor Clare repented, indeed—she wanted it clearly understood—but she repented in the Van Degen diamonds, and the Van Degen motor bore her broken heart from opera to ball" (76–77). And so there they are—the last, etiolated remnants of a once-vital organism. Harriet Ray, Mr. Urban Dagonet, Clare Van Degen—all seem little more than fate's puppets in the end. The significance of their lives is absorbed into the grand sweep of history, and they interest us only insofar as they give substance to this chronicle of a vanquished race.

Yet, the novel as a whole will not allow us to rest with such easy disengagement. The movement of history may be inexorable, even inevitable; however, individual success and failure is not. Wharton adopts an almost reckless tone of caricature in her delineation of the crowd, but she excises the particular from the general with a rapier sureness of touch.

The reader is always aware of the restless tide of social transition, and the principal characters all play some essential part in the grand design that unfolds before us. We perceive them (correctly) as instruments of destiny or victims of change, and as such they resist our tendency to identify with them or to evaluate them. At the same time—so the perverse tensions of this fiction tax us—they assume a palpable breathing semblance of reality. Ralph, Undine, perhaps even Moffatt seem very much real people in the world of the novel. We perceive them (again correctly) as personalities whose complexity reflects the nature of actual human life. We feel that they are in some measure responsible for their fate, and thus an emotional and even judgmental response seems appropriate. (Few readers, for example, succeed in remaining indifferent to Undine.) Thus are the counter movements of current and undercurrent reflected in the author's method of characterization.

Ineptly managed, this insistent contradiction would prove fatal. In Wharton's hands it does not. The result is a deliberate unsettling of every comfortable conviction: the Marvell-Dagonet culture is beautiful and ugly; it is, genuinely, both—any simplification would falsify. Ralph is both admirable and pitiable; Undine both villain and victim. The fictional world of *The Custom of the Country* is a daring tour de force: view it head-on, you will draw one set of inferences; shift your vantage to a slightly different angle, it will become something altogether different.[50]

Of what value is this legerdemain? Wharton's answer might be that it compels her readers to examine mankind's precarious state. Any individual's options in life are limited—by the constraints of his time in history, of his place in society, of his sex, of his intelligence—by all the countless elements that combine to particularize existence. Within any given set of options there is choice; some lives, some sets of options, undoubtedly offer more choice than others. How much choice—for anyone—who can decide? Perhaps part of wisdom is discovering the range of one's choices; certainly that is one of the problems that this novel is designed to bring to our attention. By forcing the reader to respond to a mode of characterization that is paradoxical, double, and unresolved (individuals as the instruments and victims of fate; individuals as "real," more or less autonomous people who are culpable and pitiable), Wharton ultimately demands that we confront the complexity of human nature in the actual world. We are all at one and the same time free and not free; that is the impasse to which man is always brought.

Correctly read, *The Custom of the Country* should leave us with neither sympathy nor scorn, but terrible understanding.

The story of Ralph Marvell unravels one portion of the skein. Ralph has resisted unthinking acquiescence in the traditions of his forebears. He can smile dismissively at Harriet Ray's priggishness, and he "had never taken his mother's social faiths very seriously. . . . He had early mingled with the Invaders, and curiously observed their rites and customs" (78–79). Yet having made his cautious and tentative explorations, he has determined (so he would say) that the old ways are best, after all, and has elected to take up his life in the family house on Washington Square. "It must have been by one of the ironic reversions of heredity that [only after apparent rebellion] he began to see what there was to be said on the other side—*his* side, as he now felt it to be" (74). And the supple sensuousness of Undine's appeal is indistinguishable in Ralph's mind from a desire to affirm "his side."

At their first meeting he is charmed most by the absences in Undine's nature; she seems "still at the age when the flexible soul offers itself to the first grasp. That the grasp should chance to be Van Degen's—that was what made Ralph's temples buzz, and swept away all his plans for his own future like a beaver's dam in a spring flood. To save her from Van Degen and Van Degenism: was that really to be his mission—the 'call' for which his life had obscurely waited?" (82). Ralph is an artist by choice; his affection for Undine is the lust of a creator to shape and give symmetry; the categories of his courtship (and for a long time, of his marriage) are those of a lost chivalric age. "He had preserved, through all his minor adventures, his faith in the great adventure to come. It was this faith that made him so easy a victim when love had at last appeared clad in the attributes of romance. . . . He seemed to see her . . . like a lovely rock-bound Andromeda, with the devouring monster Society careering up to make a mouthful of her; and himself whirling down on his winged horse—just Pegasus turned Rosinante for the nonce—to cut her bonds, snatch her up, and whirl her back into the blue . . ." (83–84).

A vision. It is always a vision that Ralph pursues. He has fixed upon the reclusive refinement of his heritage and elevated it to the status of a consuming religion; the result is a "world of wonders within him" (75)—a world whose seductive cadences have drowned out everything beyond. "As a boy at the sea-side, Ralph, between tides, had once come on a cave—a secret inaccessible place with glaucous lights, mysterious murmurs, and a single shaft of communication with the sky. He had kept his find from the other boys. . . . And so with his inner world. Though so coloured by outer impressions, it wove a secret curtain about him, and he came and went in it with the same joy of furtive possession" (75–76). Fastidiousness has subtly been permuted into narcissism: the most glorious sound, the only sound his soul can tolerate, is the mysterious chant of the tides within; the only pleasures rare enough are self-induced and self-sustained. It is an inner kingdom in which a man might easily lose himself.

Others of his circle have made relatively successful monetary alliances with the progeny of the new class. Such bargains are not admirable; but they do, at least, betray a nice capacity on the part of the aristocracy to appraise the assets of their conquerors. Ralph has no such ability (though his grandfather, Mr. Urban Dagonet, does—as the interview with Spragg makes clear). His eyes see only the beauties that his fancy provides, and he never really sees Undine at all.

When the actualities of Undine's life thrust at his retreat, he flees the intrusion: it became "a point of honour with him not to seem to disdain any of Undine's amusements" (157). When indignation flickers momentarily into disgust, he is revived by the salvific force of his vision: "As quickly as it had come the sneer dropped, yielding to a wave of pity, the vague impulse to silence and protect her" (177). When her person is absent, the imagination of her is more potent and satisfying than her presence has ever been. A letter, brief and banal, conjures "the vision of their interlaced names, as of a mystic bond which her own hand had tied. Or else he saw her, closely, palpably before him as she sat at her writing table, frowning and a little flushed, her bent nape showing the light on her hair, her short lip pulled up by the effort of composition; and this picture had the violent reality of dream-images on the verge of waking" (308).

Thus it is that the climactic moment is not a moment of separation but one of revelation—the revelation that his fantasies have always been false. The real world discovers him at last, and he cannot bear it. "Her freshness, her fragrance, the luminous haze of her youth, filled the room with a mocking glory; and he dropped his head on his hands to shut it out. . . . The vision was swept away by another wave of hurrying thoughts. He felt it was intensely important that he should keep the thread of every one of them, that they all represented things to be said or done, or guarded against; and his mind, with the unwondering versatility and tireless haste of the dreamer's brain, seemed to be pursuing them all simultaneously. Then they became as unreal and meaningless as the red specks dancing behind the lids against which he had pressed his fists clenched, and he had the feeling that if he opened his eyes they would vanish, and the familiar daylight look in on him . . ." (471–72). Only daylight. It is not enough, and Ralph puts a bullet through his brain.

In some sense, this ultimate stasis has been the goal implicit in all of his maneuvers. The most malignant heritage of old New York is apathy. Energy is frowned upon; it is vulgar and common. There is, after all, no use to which energy can easily be put within the delicate, rigid structures of this fine and fragile system. People prefer even misery to exertion: Clare will not leave her husband for Ralph, though she might save both herself and Ralph by doing so. She "thinks divorce wrong—or rather awfully vulgar" (347) and has no strength to sift the facts and find some different conclusion.[51] Clare, like Ralph—like virtually every descendent of old New York—has lost the capacity for initiative.

The very attitudes of his body reveal Ralph's fundamental passivity. He returns from his first encounter with Undine at the opera and throws himself "into an armchair" (74). We discover him in the midst of a rapturous honeymoon "stretched on his back in the grass . . ." (139); his notion of artistic creativity embraces "a little place in Switzerland where one can still get away from the crowd, and we can sit and look at a green water-fall while I lie in wait for adjectives" (146). Sitting, leaning, waiting, reclining—these are Ralph's habitual postures.

The motions of his mind, too, have an air of unutterable fatigue. "He could do charming things, if only he had known how to finish them!—and, on the writing table at his elbow, scattered sheets of prose and verse; charming things also, but, like the sketches, unfinished. Nothing in the Dagonet and Marvell tradition was opposed to this desultory dabbling with life. For four or five generations it had been the rule of both houses that a young fellow should go to Columbia or Harvard, read law, and then lapse into more or less cultivated inaction" (75). Even if Undine had been susceptible to Ralph's romantic projections for them, his own stealing inertia might have ruined the scheme. The language by which he originally concocts this particular dream captures his ambivalence. He sees himself on Pegasus (turned Rosinante) whirling in to save her (perhaps—for even here the vision mocks itself). Yet in a more characteristic moment, he envisions himself waiting expectantly in the supernatural blue of his secret cave with "Undine Spragg . . . on its threshold" (77). In this second variant he does not venture out to capture her or rescue her; instead he crouches in his inner world, waiting for her to cross the threshold and "reign over it and him" (76).[52]

Even the most important transaction in Ralph's life is contaminated by this deadly lassitude. The details of the separation, where the interests of his son most intimately concern him, slip unnoticed through his limp fingers. He receives his wife's legal application for divorce and locks "it away in his desk without mentioning the matter to any one. He supposed that with the putting away of this document he was thrusting the whole subject out of sight" (343). Indeed, he is so eager not to be worried by the matter that he declines even to read it or to examine the terms that he has tacitly accepted. Much later, he realizes that his inaction has given Undine full custody of their son "and he, Ralph Marvell, a sane man, young, able-bodied, in full possession of his wits, had assisted at the perpetration of this abominable wrong, had passively forfeited his right to the flesh of his body, the blood of his being" (436). The son of the vanquished has been lost into captivity, and the last act of Ralph's tragedy has begun. Is Undine a despoiler? Perhaps. But perhaps the seeds of defeat have grown inexorably out of the same soil that bore the last generation of a loftier race.

Wharton wrote no more devastating comment on the world of her childhood and youth than this. Even here, however, her criticism is neither wholesale nor random. Like a surgeon who seeks to preserve by removing only diseased organs, Wharton focuses her satirical thrust with agonizing sharpness. Much in old New York has value. Two elements within it threaten to destroy all the rest; and from these two deadly faults, all other evils follow.

The first is the tendency to withdraw from the rest of society and to ignore everything that is difficult or "common" or "not nice": the adoption of a determinedly unrealistic attitude. In this novel, there are any number of casual allusions to the feminine token that has so often served as Wharton's emblem of this inclination—for instance, the "black cashmere and *two veils*" that Mrs. Marvell wears when she goes to see her ostracized divorced friend (old New York's general squeamishness on the subject of divorce was very much in Wharton's mind just now, and the

Aborigines' sense of scandal at it appears more than once in this novel). However, in *The Custom of the Country*, the principal, vast, grotesque representation of retreat is Ralph's secret world, his cavernous, sounding kingdom beneath the sea—weaving a "secret curtain about him"—eventually annihilating him in the isolated splendor of his broken dreams.

The second focus of Wharton's rage is the denial of normal, natural life energy. She draws for us a society where vitality has failed, a world that stifles initiative in children and encourages haphazard dilettantism in adults. The possession of energy and initiative is not sufficient to prove the merit of a social system. However, it is a necessary condition for any society's survival. Without it, all else—however valuable—will inevitably perish.[53]

Ralph takes a rather fatalistic view of his accumulated failures. He concludes wearily "that the weakness was innate in him. He had been eloquent enough, in his free youth, against the conventions of his class; yet when the moment came to show his contempt for them they had mysteriously mastered him, deflecting his course like some hidden hereditary failing" (437). It is typical of Ralph that he should construe his situation thus, for it removes from him the onus of striving to change. There is a large measure of truth in his conclusion, for the options offered by old New York are limiting indeed. Yet it is equally true that for whatever reason, Ralph has built his life around the most pernicious of those options. He has spent all his emotion in passive fantasy instead of manifesting the kind of genuine commitment to family that is intrinsic in his sister's sensitive and tender ministrations. He has allowed his powers of observation and judgment entirely to atrophy so that he has neither the rudimentary cunning of his grandfather nor the sensible analytic capacities of Mr. Bowen. Free and at the same time inevitably shaped by the conditions that particularize his life, Ralph is a haunting specter of the terrible possibilities that are latent in his venerable world.

The novel dwells upon Ralph's fate with a fascinated preoccupation; however, Ralph is not its hero—nor even its central character. When the final tally is rendered, Ralph's account is secondary: it is Undine (and with her, Moffatt) whose sweeping path we follow. As its title insists, this novel was written to display "the custom of the country." And Bowen rightly observes that Ralph is only "the victim and the exception" while Undine is the "monstrously perfect result of the system: the completest proof of its triumph" (208).

Undine seems monstrous indeed, especially when she is compared to Ralph; in fact, the novelistic device of measuring them against each other does much to extend our tolerance of Ralph. At the core of Undine's being is a void: she has none of the "softer" emotions, no capacity to feel sympathy for others. Even the close ties of marriage affect her very little. "Marvell, at first, had fancied that his own warmth would call forth a response from his wife, who had been so quick to learn the forms of worldly intercourse; but he soon saw that she regarded intimacy as a pretext for escaping from such forms into a total absence of expression" (151). She is by no means repressed in the usual sense; rather, all of the energies that might normally find sexual expression or even the expression of spontaneous affection have been channeled elsewhere, sublimated in the service of acquisition. "She had never shown any repugnance to [Ralph's] tenderness, but such response as it evoked was remote and Ariel-like, suggesting, from the first, not so much of the recoil of ignorance as the coolness of the element from which she took her name" (152). Her callousness during Ralph's illness appalls even Peter Van Degen. " 'It came over him gradually. . . . One day when he wasn't feeling very well he thought to himself: "Would she act like that to *me* if I was dying?" And after that he never felt the same' " (360).

Yet the relentless push and pull of the novel will not allow us to remain satisfied with the dreadful (and accurate) evaluations of a Peter Van Degen: neither life nor this novel may be so simply dispatched. Our relationship to Undine is superbly balanced. Wharton tosses the narrative vantage about with a virtuoso's nonchalance, and as our point of reference to Undine changes, so do our feelings toward her. While we linger in the echoing chambers of Ralph's long, last agony, we are almost certain to condemn her heartlessness: it is not necessarily the case that we are less aware of the implications of Ralph's weakness; but our sense of shared humanity overwhelms us—and we suffer, even as he does. On the other hand, when we plunge with Undine into that "deep community of insignificance" (363) where she so nearly loses herself after the divorce—or when we endure, with her, the droning hours of unbroken, damp monotony at Saint Désert, where "as far back as memory went, the ladies of the line of Chelles had always sat at their needle-work . . . while the men of the house lamented the corruption of the government" (514)—we are tempted to chafe with this bright spirit, whose radiant ebullience has been unnaturally eclipsed. It is not right for Undine to ignore husband and child with such wanton selfishness; yet we cannot rest comfortably with the thought that she should be ravaged by the grinding harshness of a dull existence. And so her character dances, like a thousand mocking angels, on the head of a pin—unresolved and unsolvable.

The truth is, of course, that Undine too has a heritage (though one less easy to discover and define than Ralph's); she too has been limited by the particularities that shape existence, and in her case, the limitation has been mutilating.

Like any storm bursting upon the horizon, Undine comes out of the West, from a state renowned for its tornadoes. As Ralph's failure and the failure of his race grow out of lassitude, so Undine's great strength emanates from the power and suppleness of her ceaseless movement. "She was always doubling and twisting on herself, and every movement she made seemed to start at the nape of her neck, just below the lifted roll of reddish-gold hair, and flow without a break through her whole slim length to the tips of her fingers and the points of her slender restless feet" (6).[54] Beautiful and awesome, she is rendered in a torrent of verbs. Her essence is energy. And everything in her upbringing has focused on the development of one thing—a terrible spirit of desire that lays waste about her with indiscriminate fury. Her parents come from a new breed of pioneer: simple, basically good people, they have been swept up in a tidal wave of money-making and seeking after "success." Life has prepared only limited goals for them, nothing that can absorb or justify the delirious upward movement in which they have been caught. In the best American way, they have decided that everything has really been "for the children"—in this case, for Undine. Thus she is burdened with the task of formulating all of their inchoate dreams and desires, justifying that blur of dizzying prosperity; she is to reap the harvest of their labor—that is her destiny, the end for which her youth has been the imperfect preparation. "Mrs. Spragg had no ambition for herself—she seemed to have transferred her whole personality to her child—but she was passionately resolved that Undine should have what she wanted" (11). And so that she might always "want" something, she has been trained as the embodiment of will as well. "As a child [her parents] had admired her assertiveness, had made Apex ring with their boasts of it" (43). Thus by a kind of perverse symmetry, Ralph and Undine have been contaminated in opposite ways: the Marvells have denied any direct expression of energy or aggression; and the Spraggs have taken the normal capacity for initiative and inflated it beyond reason. Their offspring are complementary anamorphoses, parables of defect and excess.

What does Undine want? " 'I want the best,' " she tells Mrs. Heeny, who chuckles reassuringly, " 'Go steady, Undine, and you'll get any- wheres' " (24–25). But what is best? *"Go steady, Undine!* Yes, that was the advice she needed. Sometimes, in her dark moods, she blamed her parents for not having given it to her. She was so young . . . and they had told her so little!" (25). The world into which she has been propelled (with the command that she should have whatever she wants) is a treach- erous maze that seems specifically designed to entrap her "baffled social yearnings" (22). "Unsuspected social graduations" (28) lurk to humiliate her. In Ralph's circle, for instance, "all was blurred and puzzling. . . . [It was a] world of half-lights, half-tones, eliminations and abbreviations; and she felt a violent longing to brush away the cobwebs and assert her- self as the dominant figure of the scene" (37). What other defense has she learned, after all, but assertion? Her future is all poised upon unrooted, "floating desires" (48) which alight now here, now there—but have no purposive intention. In her quest to discover what is "best" she has had to undergo a "terrible initiation" (54): Mr. Spragg has provided the money, but always Undine has been called upon to provide the direction of the family's destiny; and always her certitudes have paled and then mockingly vanished in the blaring daylight of possession. "There was something still better beyond, then—more luxurious, more exciting, more worthy of her! She once said to herself . . . that it was always her fate to find out just too late about the 'something beyond.' . . . Every- thing was spoiled by a peep through another door" (54).

This prospect is dreadful to Undine—a kind of Alice-in-Wonderland nightmare. However, of itself, it need not hold such horror; in Moffatt's life, the same prospect is glorious. He has no more rooted background than Undine: dropping into town like some capricious summer storm, routing the Sons of Jonadab (the local Temperance Society), he seems a figure of fun, almost a clown. "His head was always full of immense nebulous schemes for the enlargement and development of any business he happened to be employed in. Sometimes his suggestions interested his employers, but proved unpractical and inapplicable; sometimes he wore out their patience or was thought to be a dangerous dreamer" (553). He has no fixed goal, only "a great sweeping scorn of Apex" (555); yet even from the beginning, "something in his look seemed to promise the capacity to develop into any character he might care to assume" (108). Undine inclines to him instinctively—to the "loose-drifting power" (197) so like her own and to the "gleam of mocking confidence that had carried him unabashed through his lowest hours at Apex" (244). Thrusting and strutting, wearing the careless effrontery of his challenge like a brash suit of clothes, Elmer Moffatt is never a clown at all. Even the vanquished races respond to the "Homeric volume" (252) with which he recounts his victories. They have categories with which to understand this phenomenon, and they are not surprised by the "Olympian modesty" (451) that evolves to characterize his success. Elmer Moffatt is the hero of an unfolding American epic. The epic that Ralph did not write.

But this is an epic for men only, and Undine cannot live it. Not that her capacities are insufficient: she is a second-generation replica of her father's business acumen. "Mr. and Mrs. Spragg were both given to such long periods of ruminating apathy that the student of inheritance might have wondered whence Undine derived her overflowing activity. The answer would have been obtained by observing her father's business life. From the moment he set foot in Wall Street Mr. Spragg became another man. Physically the change revealed itself only by the subtlest signs. . . . It was only in his face that the difference was perceptible, though even here it rather lurked behind the features than openly modified them: showing itself now and then in the cautious glint of half-closed eyes, the forward thrust of black brows, or a tightening of the lax lines of the mouth" (119). Undine has honed her talent in numerous confrontations with the old warrior—throwing her head back, "plunging her eyes in his, and pressing so close that to his tired elderly sight her face was a mere bright blur" (30)—and now she is ready for other victories. Yet the battle will not receive her (our novel is set in riotous revelry, we must recall, and not where the generals live and die). Turn your talents to domestic affairs, so the piping voices of conventional decorum mock her, spend your initiative on palaces and gowns.

This is, as Bowen tells us, the "custom of the country" (206): women are banished to the shadow world. " 'The average American looks down on his wife. . . . How much does he let her share in the real business of life? How much does he rely on her judgment and help in the conduct of serious affairs? . . . Where does the real life of most American men lie? In some woman's drawing-room or in their offices? The answer's obvious, isn't it? The emotional centre of gravity's not the same in the two hemispheres. In the effete societies it's love, in our new one it's business. In America the real *crime passionnel* is a 'big steal'—there's more excitement in wrecking railways than homes. . . . And what's the result—how do the women avenge themselves? All my sympathy's with them, poor deluded dears, when I see their fallacious little attempts to trick out the leavings tossed them by the preoccupied male—the money and the motors and the clothes—and pretend to themselves and each other that *that's* what really constitutes life!' " (205, 206, 207, 208).

The tragedy of Ralph's life has been shaped by the fact that his world never encouraged the expression of energy; but Undine's life has been even more grotesquely perverted. Possessing the energy needed to conquer life (possessing it even as her counterpart Elmer Moffatt does), she has been debarred from the victory by reasons of sex. "Little as she understood of the qualities that made Moffatt what he was, the results were of the kind most palpable to her. *He used life exactly as she would have used it in his place*" (563, italics added). But she cannot use life thus because the options available to him have not been opened to her. The impracticality and inapplicability of Elmer's grandiose, nebulous schemes can be corrected by the rough-and-tumble encounters of the pit; however, Undine's desires never encounter such substantial limitation. Actuality eludes the chimerical world through which she makes her way.

Her father's eyes grow evasive whenever business matters arise: "*That* was man's province; and what did men go 'down town' for but to bring back the spoils to their women?" (44). Thus Undine's inferences about the "real" world have always, perforce, been secondhand: she must interpret the behavior of the men she observes, for they are the intermediators, the only link between herself and the life-giving element of money. "Ever since she could remember there had been 'Fusses' about money; yet she and her mother had always got what they wanted, apparently without lasting detriment to the family fortunes. It was therefore natural to conclude that there were ample funds to draw upon, and that Mr. Spragg's occasional resistances were merely due to an imperfect understanding of what constituted the necessities of life" (45). When some undefinable difficulty arises, the only part Undine can play in that battle beyond her ken is a vigorous and resolute exercise of will; and always, that part has sufficed. The lesson has been taught with lethal consistency—through a series of summer ventures and New York experiments. Even her marriage to Ralph confirms it. Undine enters that marriage with "a blind confidence that [money] will somehow be provided. If Undine, like the lilies of the field, took no care, it was not because her wants were as few but because she assumed that care would be taken for her by those whose privilege it was to enable her to unite floral insouciance with Sheban elegance" (149). Eager to play his "manly" part, Ralph seeks only "to guard her from this as from all other cares" (149). And thus the perversity of her education continues.

The consequence is a lonely, soulless sprite who breathes dreams like air, a creature whose desires have been loosened from the moorings of reality and sent drifting into some infinitude of fancied satisfaction. In the end, Undine is betrayed not so much by the excess of her energy, but by the treachery that has excluded her from real-world confrontations that might impose normal limitations upon her.

Shortly before their marriage, Undine asks Elmer what he wants. " 'Why—everything I can, I guess' " (538); the goals that he postulates are ultimately defined by his capacities. Early in their relationship, Ralph asks Undine what she expects. " 'Why *everything!*' she announced" (96)—and nothing in the vicissitudes of her travels has altered that ambition. Hence she is doomed to pursue the phantom of "everything" until her dream explodes with the knowledge that "there was something she could never get, something that neither beauty nor influence nor millions could ever buy for her" (594). "Everything" having eluded her, she is left with nothing.[55]

It is tempting to rest with the stories of these characters. Perhaps the novelist's interest is primarily vested in them: they come to life so palpably before us as "people," whose lives have been shaped by the limitations of their time and place in history. And yet, the restless panoramic imperative of this fiction pulls us, shifting the focus of our gaze away from individuals and back to the moment itself, that magically captured instant of transition when old orders pass away and new orders rise to take their place. This prospect demands our attention too, and as usual, Mr. Bowen is our most reliable guide. We discover him at the heart of the hubbub: the dining-hour at the Nouveau Luxe. He savors the entire view with the relish of a connoisseur, lingering over the "undisturbed amusement of watching the picture compose itself again before his eyes" (272–73). Here, in miniature, the moment of change is endlessly enacted. "As he sat watching the familiar faces swept toward him on the rising tide of arrival—for it was one of the joys of the scene that the type was always the same even when the individual was not—he hailed with renewed appreciation this costly expression of a social ideal. The dining-room at the Nouveau Luxe represented, on such a spring evening, what unbounded material power had devised for the delusion of its leisure: a phantom 'society,' with all the rules, smirks, gestures of its model, but evoked out of promiscuity and incoherence while the other had been the product of continuity and choice. And the instinct which had driven a new class of world-compellers to bind themselves to slavish imitation of the superseded, and their prompt and reverent faith in the reality of the sham they had created, seemed to Bowen the most satisfying proof of human permanence" (273). What lingers on the periphery of history, waiting to rush in and conquer all? A world of nothing but money.

The Custom of the Country.[56] It is a play by Fletcher and Massinger about some benighted land where women's virtue is no more than a piece of property—a parcel of goods that may be taken or sold at public auction when impending marriage is announced.

> . . . O the wicked Custom of this Country,
> The barbarous, most inhumane, damned Custom.
> . . . That when a Maid is contracted
> And ready to the tye o' th' Church, the Governour,
> He that commands in chief, must have her Maiden-head,
> Or Ransom it for money at his pleasure.
>
> . . . all
> Your sad misfortunes had original
> From the barbarous Custom practis'd in my Country.[57]

Like many Jacobean works, the drama is a lurid chaos of shifting identities and unsavory behavior—a world whose moral center has been lost—a world where everything is for sale. A world like that of Wharton's novel.

The women's lives reflect the perversions of this way of life most directly, of course, for what they market is simply themselves. Marriage and divorce are no more than their means of bartering. We can see the inescapable similarities between this world and the world of Lily Bart; for if Lily had simply decided to manage her career (instead of slipping into the comforting sleep of oblivion), she might have been like Undine. Both crave the reflecting reassurance of the mirror to assuage an otherwise intolerable inner loneliness, and both are immensely vulnerable to the standards of others—having no fixed standards of their own. Yet the difference is crucial: Undine can succeed where Lily has failed—because of her superb capacities for observation and mutation, and most importantly, because of the energy with which she ceaselessly renegotiates herself.

At first, Undine is awkward in her transactions: the merest apprentice in this vast exchange, she is too eager to flaunt her sense of "value" before the Dagonets: " 'I guess Mabel'll get a divorce pretty soon. . . . They like each other well enough. But he's been a disappointment to her. He isn't in the right set, and I think Mabel realizes she'll never really get anywhere till she gets rid of him. . . . Out in Apex, if a girl marries a man who don't come up to what she expected, people consider it's to her credit to want to change' " (94–96). She shifts her graceful form enticingly and thrusts her eager, glowing face towards them; and all the while, her voice is full of money.

However, inexperience does not long hinder Undine's progress. Like some idealized embodiment of the entrepreneur, she epitomizes the spirit of the age—"Success." Alert to others, mindful of the roles they expect her to play, Undine virtually always delivers with facility. By the time she encounters Ralph's family, "her quickness in noting external difference had already taught her to modulate and lower her voice, and to replace 'The *i*-dea' and 'I wouldn't wonder' by more polished locutions; and she had not been ten minutes at table before she found that to seem very much in love, and a little confused and subdued by the newness and intensity of the sentiment, was, to the Dagonet mind, the becoming attitude for a young lady in her situation. The part was not hard to play" (91). Eventually, Ralph is disturbed by his wife's habit of "adapting herself to whatever company she was in, of copying 'the others' in speech and gesture as closely as she reflected them in dress" (160). His unease is well founded, for as soon as she discovers that there are new vistas ahead, new stages on which her talent may be exploited, Undine drifts on. By the time she has been married for three years, "she had learned to make distinctions unknown to her girlish categories. She had found out that she had given herself to the exclusive and the dowdy when the future belonged to the showy and the promiscuous" (193). Unwilling to have her lot cast with a fallen race, she adopts the airs and graces of a new company and leaves Ralph Marvell's universe behind her.

Undine is not always immediately successful: like anyone just begun in business, she suffers short-term losses. Nevertheless, she plays each venture with an ever more adept parlaying of her assets; and in each stroke of her progress, she is miraculously rehabilitated in another and yet another guise. As protean as the swelling tide itself, she picks up an intonation here, a vocabulary there, a set of moral sensibilities of one sort, a set of aesthetic norms of yet another. She learns countless things that her less-talented competitors miss—"shades of conduct, turns of speech, tricks of attitude" (558). Capable of every distortion and any imitation, she becomes the perfectly commercial item: able to simulate anything the purchaser desires. Nothing is essential and unchanged but the energy that animates her.

As a human being, she has grown grotesque. Yet as an item of exchange, there is little doubt that her market value has immensely increased. Moffatt makes the ultimate appraisal: " 'You're not the beauty you were . . . but you're a lot more fetching' " (568).

The women all seem more hideously disfigured than their male counterparts in the money game. After all, the women sell directly; and the flesh that they deal in is—by "custom of the country"—always in the first instance their own. Having been dehumanized, they act with inhuman indifference to the feelings of others. They have never had the freedom to indulge the luxury of emotions—not the emotions of a wife nor those of a mother—and all that should be fertile has grown barren.

By contrast, the men generally deal in "shares"—not people—and there is a semblance of order and distance in the relationship between their lives and their work. Thus Elmer Moffatt has the time (briefly) to take pity on Undine, to feel pity for her little boy; he has time, even, to indulge his apparently innate sense of quality by collecting the things and people that earlier cultures had prized. He seems humane, by turns; almost likeable in the end. Yet the ethics of business and the relation between the public and private worlds of the men who make business are difficult to fathom. Ralph is puzzled when he tries to make sense—his kind of sense—out of Moffatt's manipulations; and all the tendencies in Ralph's nature incline him, finally, to avoid the perplexities of that world rather than to put his efforts into thinking them through.

We must not be lured into following Ralph's easy, meandering way. "Shares" and "parties"—these are obscuring abstractions. At the bottom of every "deal" there are always real people. The hygienic distance imposed by the convenience of a public exchange does not, in the end, confute this fact.

Almost all the men seem more appealing to us than the women: as *psychological* entities, they are more coherently developed and less grotesque. The goal of "everything I can" renders them human and keeps them within the bounds of reality, not spun into impossible, infantile expectations of "everything." However, precisely *because* society has offered them humanizing options and a greater degree of control over their own destiny, it adds a moral dimension to their natures that cannot reasonably be brought to bear upon their consorts. Thus as *moral* entities, the men must be judged to be even more repugnant than the women.

Yes, Moffatt can find the leisure to pity Undine and her multi-fathered son. We must not be misled by such instances of "kindness." When the moment comes to do business, he is as uncomplicatedly ruthless with her as she has ever been with others. And since Moffatt (unlike Undine) *chooses* ruthlessness—having kindness as a possibility within his repertoire—he reveals himself ultimately to be more dangerous and more satanically possessed even than she. "She knew she interested and amused him, and that it flattered his vanity to be seen with her, and to hear that rumour coupled their names; but he gave her, more than any one she had ever known, the sense of being detached from his life, in control of it, and able, without weakness or uncertainty, to choose which of its calls he should obey. If the call were that of business—of any of the great perilous affairs he handled like a snake-charmer spinning the deadly reptiles about his head—she knew she would drop from his life like a loosened leaf" (563).

Indeed, there are intimations throughout this chronicle that the corruptions of the private world is no less than a frighteningly accurate reflection of the essential evil that lies hidden at the root of all the public transactions. Spragg has good reason to understand the many implications of his agreement to sell out Rolliver, for example. The clean efficiency with which he handles the affair and his distance from his prey both tend to distract our attention from its sordid implications. Yet, if we look into the matter, can we genuinely suppose that the "deal" by which Indiana Frusk Binch "buys" Rolliver when his market value has gone back up is genuinely more reprehensible than Spragg's earlier transaction? Or is it not the case, as Wharton spins the moral complexities of this carnival world before us, that Spragg is *more* guilty than Indiana Frusk?

Domestic comedy and epic: with what hilarity Wharton shakes them out. In the "normal" order of things, the amusing diversion of domestic comedy glides on the assumption that all is basically well in the world without: we can turn our attention to household disruptions and feminine vanities and youthful romances because there is no pressing imperative commanding us to attend to the business of state. How mockingly Wharton dares us to rest upon that comfortable assumption now. Now, the black comedy of domestic life has become a distillation of all the infamy that contaminates the public world; and the ladies, with their mutilated selves and monstrously realized dreams, are as fully appropriate to a representation of the spirit of the age as the story of any of its generals might have been.

In the end, it was not necessary for Edith Wharton to write an epic. For the purposes of social commentary, domestic comedy has sufficed.

When Moffatt reclaims Undine, he regales her with the tales of his battles. "Absorbed in his theme, and forgetting her inability to follow him, Moffatt launched out on an epic recital of plot and counterplot, and she hung, a new Desdemona, on his conflict with the new anthropophagi. It was of no consequence that the details and the technicalities escaped her: she knew their meaningless syllables stood for success, and what that meant was as clear as day to her. Every Wall Street term had its equivalent in the language of Fifth Avenue, and while he talked of building up railways she was building up palaces, and picturing all the multiple lives he would lead in them" (537).

Still, Wharton is faithful to the imperatives of her fiction; she has determined to capture the moment of transition—nothing more. We conclude perched at the edge of the abyss: we do not yet feel the full force of terrifying descent.

5

The terms in which Wharton captures this American Dream turned nightmare are indescribably suggestive. Insofar as we are drawn to Undine and inclined to be sympathetic with her impatience at reversals, it is the splendid animal vigor in her nature that attracts us. It attracts us in

Elmer Moffatt—to some degree in all of the men who wrench victory from their world. Wharton never condemns energy: on the contrary, in some sense it is the ultimate hero of her tale. Only "free-floating" energy is monstrous. Energy that has become divorced from human concerns is vitiated; energy that has been contaminated with insatiable hungers is emotionally distorting: and in the precision of such fictional decrees, we may discover the final sources of the power of Wharton's satire.

Not surprisingly, the same ability to make precise distinctions in the matter of energy served the author's own emotional needs as well. In sorting through the problems of a corrupted world, she began, at last, to work her way through terrors that had haunted her personal life since childhood.

To begin with, we must recollect the little girl of four or five— pursued by that ravenous Wolf who threatened to devour her. The totem Wolf of Edith Wharton's childhood was, of course, a creature of her own imagination—a primitive method of representing her feelings and fears and of postulating them as outside herself so that she might try to escape them. Many children feel such terrors, but Edith Wharton's experiences clearly exceeded the usual bounds: in the life of *this* little girl, the natural and intense awakening of affection for her father was invaded by the persistent remnants of an earlier, more infantile yearning— a voracious need for comfort and a ravenous, insatiable quality of desire. Thus the first stirrings of sexuality and competition are contaminated by a sense of dangerous totality: the notion of "love" is coupled with images of incorporation or obliteration; the notion of "initiative" carries fearful threats of indiscriminate annihilation. Confronted as she was not merely by the crisis of childhood sexuality, but also by the unresolved elements of that earlier crisis of infancy, the child could not thread her way through the appalling complexities of her situation. And so she fled: she sought to evade her fears instead of confronting them; she ran to Mother or Doyley to escape the Wolf. And the effect of her decision was to relinquish initiative for a long time and to leave the many problems of sexuality unresolved.

Eventually, as we have seen, Edith Wharton was unwilling to continue her retreat. She spent many years coming to terms with her inclinations to dependency; and now, after the affair with Fullerton had thrust the problems of sexuality once more to her attention, she was willing at last to confront the totem Wolf.

The first successful move in that confrontation is made in *The Custom of the Country*. It would be easy to point to the particular dilemmas of the moment that found their way into this fiction—divorce, the question of managing money. Yet if these had been the only informing concerns of the novel, it would never have achieved the emotional intensity that elevates it to greatness. A more fundamental set of problems underlies these—problems that the author can reach only by an act of controlled regression "in the service of the ego."

One ultimate concern of *The Custom of the Country* is initiative. Finally, a part of the five-year-old child's terror is brought to light: Undine Spragg is initiative run amuck. The very embodiment of energy, dealing in sexuality with a cold-blooded capacity for calculation, Undine is the spirit of competition embued with a voracious appetite. Her capacity for destruction is almost beyond computation, and she travels like a whirlwind, leaving devastation everywhere in her wake. Nor is her scope limited. Undine Spragg wants "everything." That is her terrible desire—terrible because it is, by nature, unable ever to be gratified—a desire that ultimately consumes her. Thus it is that those boundless perspectives lurking beyond every horizon fill her with fear. From the beginning, even Undine seems to sense that insatiable needs inevitably carry the certainty of eventual disappointment. Always, then, her anticipation is clouded by impatience and a feeling of cosmic insufficiency. Surely it is not too much to say that Undine's willful, petulant nature recaptures many of the impulses and fears that we have already observed indirectly in Edith Wharton's youth.

Yet the adult author, Edith Wharton, is finally in command. She can confront this ghost of self and disentangle its various components. Energy is released from thralldom, for of itself, psychic energy is a positive quality. Without it—as the consideration of Ralph's tragedy makes clear—nothing can survive. What Wharton does condemn is the aspiration to "everything," that atavistic component of her own longing that had tied initiative to the ghost of an earlier and more primitive self. Now, that infantile self is enjoined to relinquish its claims. They have been exposed to scrutiny and found intolerable.

The delicate sorting process that permeates this fiction suggests that Wharton has finally succeeded in making a conscious decision concerning the quandary of initiative. Other elements of that early sexual crisis are revived and examined with equal care.

Remember the little girl of six or seven whose life is regulated by a rigorous set of "scruples." This is the child who has evolved the principle "that it was 'naughty' to say, or to think, anything about anyone that one could not, without offense, avow to the person in question." [58] We have already explored the implications of these rules. They betray the child's deep fear at the power of her rage—rage against her mother, primarily (as the dancing-school episode so poignantly suggests). And the only recourse that the little girl managed to devise was silence: thus was rebellion stifled.

Finally, the adult author unleashes the voice of rebellion that the little girl had so fearfully stilled. We have had hints of it before, of course: *The Decoration of Houses* took unmistakable aim at Mother's standards of taste; *The House of Mirth* denounced the "feminine" injunction to passivity. But neither of these earlier efforts draws upon that inner powerhouse so violently and definitively as *The Custom of the Country*. This is the most passionate attack that Edith Wharton ever made upon old New York, all the more passionate because it is made with the righteous indignation of a woman whose prohibitions against self (so long and so painfully endured) have been turned outward to excoriate the inadequacies of others. And what does this raging daughter decry? Certainly not everything in the venerable world of her youth. No, only those things that prohibit the normal expression of psychic energy and condemn individuals to the curtained recesses that suffocate activity. In short, the insufficiencies that Wharton denounces all relate to those injunctions against self-assertion that (rightly or wrongly) the child had supposed Lucretia's standards to require.

Finally, we discover in *The Custom of the Country* a poignant reiteration of the desolate rage at what it meant—in this society—to be "only a girl." Even more than her brothers, Edith was prohibited from explorations of any useful sort. Not given a tutor. Not sent to school. Not exposed to the real world in any way. Rummaging among her brother's books, the child had determined to mend these deficiencies: "How I was going to know all about life! how I should never be that helpless blundering thing, a mere 'little girl,' again!" [59] But of course she did not—not then, perhaps never completely to her own satisfaction. Thus did "the custom of the country" affect her own growth.

Little wonder that when the adult author, Edith Wharton, chose to represent the worst deformities that a corrupt society might inflict, she consistently chose to do so by demonstrating the plight of its women. Women had not even the potentially saving opportunities of striving and working in the outside world for real and realizable goals. Women were kept from a knowledge of practical things almost as if these were part of some mysterious rite of passage—available to men, but not to their prospective mates. Thus men might, if they had sufficient determination, work against the influences of a corrupt society to correct them or become independent of them; but women for the most part were destined to be no more than passive incarnations of the values of the world within which they were so tightly bound. They were more directly and inescapably at the mercy of social custom. Inevitably, society's deficiencies were most explicitly and grotesquely mirrored in the natures of its women. Such is the conclusion of much of Wharton's social satire: we have seen it in *The House of Mirth;* we shall see it again in *Twilight Sleep.*

There is a tone of inescapable rancor in the tormenting nuances of that phrase—"the custom of the country"—as it is cited in this fiction. The novel is, among other things, a wry and bitter commentary on the feminine possibilities for heroism in fiction. Consider the following literary puzzle. The portrait of Ralph is intended to display his faults; the reader is invited to measure the ways in which Ralph's behavior has been deficient, and one way of doing so might be to invoke a "corrected" or "improved" image of him—Ralph without moral vacillation or Ralph with a full quantum of energy. The characterization of Ralph is susceptible to such improvements: any reader can perfectly well imagine an acceptable man who is "Ralph as he might have been." The same holds true for Elmer Moffatt. He is vulgar; in the end, we can see that he is ruthless—even deadly. But here again, a reader can conjure images of a "corrected" Elmer Moffatt—a man with all of Elmer's energy and drive, but with a fuller measure of moral concern and a more sustained capacity for personal, emotional involvement. The literary traditions having to do with the presentation of a positive male character would not exclude either Ralph or Elmer, provided that they be sufficiently brushed up.

There is nothing similar to be done for Undine. We are certainly aware of her defects; the novel pivots upon them. Nevertheless, she is not intended to be perceived as intrinsically monstrous: too much effort has gone into making the reader intermittently sympathetic with her, and too much care has been taken to focus the satirical element on precisely those "customs" that have conspired to pervert her nature. (We can easily see the balance in Wharton's method if we compare the complexity of Undine's nature with the undiluted viciousness of her American predecessor Selma Babcock in Robert Grant's novel *Unleavened Bread*.) Yet if she is not *intrinsically* monstrous, then there ought to be some "improved" Undine—a woman with a full measure of power and energy and ambition—who could pass literary muster. But there isn't. Categories for heroism in the great fictional tradition did not allow for those qualities that come together in Undine Spragg.

It was true in 1913 when Wharton published this novel that most authors could think of very little to do with their heroines save to kill them or to marry them off (remnants of this frame of mind linger even today, of course). Wharton turns the fact rather maliciously upon itself in the proliferation of Undine's weddings, and in so doing she gives the reader an ironic insight into the inadequacy of this device as a way of "placing" her heroine. Yet if we are still to ask, as the novel urges us to, what language she might have invoked for a sympathetic portrait of a woman who seeks power, the answer returns with chilling clarity. No such language existed for her use. Undine reflects that Elmer Moffatt "used life exactly as she would have used it in his place," but precisely such thoughts as these compel a perceptive reader to reflect upon the limitations that hedge heroism. Wharton can delineate the nature of this ambitious woman by suggesting what she might have done *if she had been a man*; given that she is a woman, however, Undine's drive for conquest must be rendered by a series of domestic ventures. "Reader, I married him": this is the confession we have been taught to expect from heroines. Our literary habits concerning the portrayal of women, then, become but one more "custom" by which society's inadequacies are perpetuated.

The concern here is similar to one that emerged in the treatment of Lily Bart, but the real-world component in the difficulties offered by Undine makes this problem of femininity even more difficult to resolve than the earlier one. The Beautiful Death is an instance of literary hyperbole: actual women were not expected to die with exquisite convenience—even though actual women *were* expected to be passive (even to the point of infantilism) and to play the role of aesthetic object. However, the absence of a literary language adequate to portray femininity as compatible with energy and ambition bears a direct relation to the fact that in the real world, as well as in fictional ones, it has long been considered "unnatural" for women to possess these "masculine" traits. Actual women have been discouraged from pursuing activities that would develop their sense of assertiveness and drive: they have been expected, "by nature," to be receptive—not thrusting and ambitious. Wharton might have called a male protagonist "hard-driving" or "furious" or "fierce" or "dominant" or "powerful" without thereby turning the reader's sympathy away from him; yet she could not have used such terms to describe a heroine without alienating a large portion of her audience. Thus the very language that might capture the spirit and energy of a woman like Undine Spragg has been deemed "appropriate" to men— but not to women.

Wharton can mockingly call our attention to this insufficiency of literature and life, but she cannot correct it. Indeed, there is evidence that this aspect of femininity may have remained particularly vexing throughout her own career.

She was a person of great capability; by 1912–13 she had learned as much and had come to take pride in this trait. The fact was, of course, that her world offered little accommodation for such a woman, few categories within which to define her nature. Wharton's writing was acknowledged as praiseworthy; yet even her closest friends tended to regard it as something extra rather than as a central concern or profession. Bernard Berenson, traveling with her in August of 1913, found her demands regarding the proper placement of the bed with reference to the window "an absurd performance; but because Edith never harped upon the physical requirements of her literary life, he did not quite realize that she worked in bed every morning and therefore needed a bed which faced the light." [60] The anecdote is doubly suggestive: Berenson was unable to keep the demands of this woman's profession in mind; and Wharton herself was unable to insist upon them confidently as a necessity of her trade.

The more successful Wharton became in her vocation—and the more she thrived upon that success—the more difficult her position as a woman became. Her life combined a set of attributes that popular myth often held to be incompatible: she was pleased with her womanliness, desirious of being thought attractive, and certain of her sexual preference for men; yet at the same time she was increasingly aware of her own ambition and creative power. Possibly Wharton felt more comfortable with people whose notions of "masculine" and "feminine" were more flexible than those of society at large. Many of her closest friends were men whose sexual preferences tended to blur: Henry James, Howard Sturgis, Morton Fullerton. Yet even among these intimates, she remained an enigma of a woman. James, very much in awe of her, coined the famous epithets—"angel of devastation" and the like; yet there is a hint of unease, perhaps even of hostility, in such names. Wharton must have felt it. And other intractabilities of language often betrayed the delicacy of her position all too well. Morton Fullerton at times addressed her as "cher ami"; and "Henry James in a commentary would point to a certain masculinity, a toughness of mind, in the very texture of the novel." [61] Percy Lubbock would note that she liked the company of men because "she had a very feminine consciousness and a very masculine mind . . . and she liked to be talked to as a man." [62] Undoubtedly all of these men regarded it as a sign of approbation that Wharton's intellect might be described as "masculine." Probably Wharton herself often felt complimented by such language. But her management of the problems of heroinism suggests that occasionally it wearied her to have her strengths so consistently tabulated as borrowings from the other sex.

Later in her career, Wharton was to write several novels that focused on the problem of balancing love and work—the harmonious possession of which Freud himself would postulate as necessary to human happiness. However, when she did, she always employed a male protagonist. Never a woman. Perhaps this choice betrayed timidity on her part, a reluctance to unearth the particulars of her own life; we can never know her reasons with certainty. Yet it is at least possible to offer compelling literary motivation for her decision. Once we understand the forces that shape the world of *The Custom of the Country*, we must suspect that Edith Wharton could never have written a novel about the adjustment of love and work within a *woman's* life without making that novel an excoriation of the way in which the lives of *all* women had been savaged by the injunction to define "work" entirely in terms of "love." Wharton spoke violently about that particular indignity in *The Custom of the Country*, giving voice to her full personal anger and exposing society's malignancies. She had dispatched the monster; there was no reason to summon it again to battle. And there was every reason, now, to move on to other subjects in other fictions.

6

In the years just preceding the war, Wharton exerted her efforts to consolidate the strengths of her personal life. Walter Berry again became a central figure. Having spent some years with the International Tribune in Cairo, he returned to take up permanent residence in Paris in the summer of 1910. While looking for a place of his own, he was Edith Wharton's houseguest in the large apartment on the Rue de Varenne for almost six months, and they became close and affectionate comrades once again. In the long run, no man meant more to Edith Wharton than this finicky gentleman with the dry humor; and he, not Fullerton, became the true love of her life.[63] Certainly his friendship and support were invaluable during the months of anguished uncertainty that the divorce brought. Henry James, too, grew even more valuable as friend and confidant during these uneasy times. Marriage having failed, Edith Wharton set about almost deliberately to replace the continuing tie of matrimony with ties of friendship that went very deep.

In addition, she continued to seek ways of coming to terms with the energy that surged ever more to the surface in her nature. By the time *The Custom of the Country* was completed, Wharton was physically exhausted (for both the divorce and the writing of the novel had drawn upon her deepest reserves of strength). Nevertheless, in quick succession she embarked on lengthy trips to Italy, England, Germany, the United States, and North Africa. The restless mood of her novel had reflected something in her own consciousness. She was searching. In a literal sense, the mood of questing was upon her. She returned from the African trip (on which she had been accompanied by the young Percy Lubbock) in June 1914 and spent barely more than a month in Paris before once again setting off—this time on a jaunt with Walter Berry to Spain. The Spanish adventure would be the last for a while. On July 30, 1914, the small party was motoring north from Poitiers: "The air seemed full of the long murmur of human effort, the rhythm of oft-repeated tasks; the serenity of the scene smiled away the war rumours which had hung on us since morning." [64] But this serenity was the last she was to know for a long time. The cataclysm that had been anticipated in *The Custom of the Country* was at hand. When Wharton returned to Paris in the first week of August 1914, she returned to general mobilization—and war.[65]

At first she was uncertain what to do. After considerable string-pulling, she obtained the necessary papers and sufficient ready cash for a trip to England, where she went at the end of August. For more than a year Wharton had been engaged in desultory negotiations to buy a house there—toying with the notion of settling in the adopted country of Henry James. But once she reached England during that fateful August, she was dissatisfied. She received reports of the Battle of the Marne in early September; and as she watched the epochal conflict from this vexing distance, she became possessed by the imperative to return to Paris. Thoughts of a quiet English existence were put once and for all behind her, and by the end of September she was back in residence on the Rue de Varenne.

In the Great War, Edith Wharton found another outlet for her energies. As early as August 1914, she had already begun. Discovering that the outbreak of the war had thrown local seamstresses out of work, Wharton established a workroom for several dozen of them (eventually the number would swell to almost a hundred); each woman was paid for her work, and in addition she was given a free lunch, free medical attention, and a supply of coal when the winter months approached. By October, after Wharton's definitive return from England, refugees from Belgium began to pour into Paris. Together with a number of friends, Wharton set up the American Hostels for Refugees. Eventually she headed an enterprise that provided lodging for many, and food and medical attention for many more. Wharton started an employment agency so that the refugees might begin to support themselves; and she had another workroom fitted out so that the women refugees could produce the clothes so desperately needed by those who had fled home and country with nothing more than what they could carry with them. These women workers (along with the seamstresses for whom Wharton had found employment earlier) often had young children whom they could not leave during working hours, and Wharton set up a day nursery, "a big pleasant room opening onto a court where the young people could play. Singing classes were held there, and lessons in sewing and English." After just one year, the results of Wharton's work were astounding. "Near the end of 1915, the American Hostels clebrated their first birthday [and] Edith could announce the following results: 9,330 refugees had been assisted during the year, 3,000 of them on a permanent basis; 235,000 meals had been served, and 48,000 garments handed out; 7,700 persons had received medical care; jobs had been found for 3,400." [66] In twelve months, Wharton had collected more than $100,000 to support her work for these displaced people. Nor did her fervor diminish. She labored at an enormous variety of tasks to sustain the war effort in Paris; and on April 8, 1916, the President of France appointed Edith Wharton a Chevalier of the Legion of Honor—the highest honor that the country could bestow upon her.

There is no doubt that the sheer exuberance of this outpouring of genuinely useful work lifted Wharton's spirits in the wake of her depression over the divorce. People appreciated her efforts; she was useful; and questions of feminine propriety were put to one side (as they so often are during a war when the men have left home to fight). Outwardly, the daily course of Wharton's life was much altered during these four frantic years; yet the inward search that had begun even before the composition of *The Reef* was destined to continue. The questing mood that had assumed so many guises stemmed ultimately from deep-rooted urgencies: Wharton was committed to a sorting out of the residual problems of sexuality, and that commitment reigned over the inner world of her nature despite all the outward vicissitudes of history. Her participation in the war affected the course of her development, but the true effects must be sought in other than the superficial elements of her life. Thus we must ask: what did the war *mean* to her; how did she understand its importance.

A major clue can be found in the most unusual of Wharton's many travel books: *Fighting France*. Still restless, still possessed by the mandate of quest, Wharton was unable to remain contented with her work in Paris while the battle raged in the countryside beyond. Thus between February and August 1915 she made four long trips to walk the front and view the fighting firsthand. She wrote journalistic accounts of these which were published in *Scribner's Magazine*, and late in 1915 she collected the articles with two additional essays in a book entitled *Fighting France*. Not surprisingly, the language here seems directly related to the concerns that had dominated *The Reef* and *The Custom of the Country*. The war was many things to Edith Wharton; but one of the most important ways of construing it had to do with the relationship between energy or passion—in all its many forms—and the value of tradition.

It was common in those early days of World War I to speak of it in terms of a retrogression of culture—Rome falling before the barbarians

Wharton had anticipated such talk in *The Custom of the Country*. However, oddly enough, when the real war finally came to pass it was not culture that interested her, at least not in the narrow sense of a country's accumulated artistic and intellectual production. What consistently impressed her was the ravaged continuity of countless insignificant human lives. What the war destroyed—the Germans in their brutal march through Belgium deliberately so—was the simple piety of many pasts, the penates of countless hearths.

Wharton's initial encounter with German ruthlessness took place in the little village of Auve in the Argonne region, now no more than "a mere waste of rubble and cinders, not one threshold distinguishable from another. We saw many other ruined villages after Auve," Wharton relates, "but this was the first, and perhaps for that reason one had there, most hauntingly, the vision of all the separate terrors, anguishes, uprootings and rendings apart involved in the destruction of the obscurest of human communities. The photographs on the walls, the twigs of withered box above the crucifixes, the old wedding-dresses in brass-clamped trunks, the bundles of letters laboriously written and as painfully deciphered, all the thousand and one bits of the past that give meaning and continuity to the present—of all that accumulated warmth nothing was left but a brick-heap and some twisted stove-pipes!" (58).

Here was a riot of energy, of violence that was cruel, but not purposeless and not random. Germany had decided to break the spirit of its adversary (that is a familiar notion now, but in 1915 it seemed an innovation in the art of war); hence it fought not only, perhaps not primarily, against the soldiers in the field. It aimed in addition to destroy the homes and families of the nation, to disrupt all accumulated sense of individual continuity. It was this calculated rape of the nation's sense of self that so shocked Wharton in her travels; for more than many observers, she perfectly understood the enemy's real goal. In town after town, the same terrible results awaited her. "Every window-pane is smashed, nearly every building unroofed, and some house-fronts are sliced clean off, with the different stories exposed, as if for the stage-setting of a farce. In these exposed interiors the poor little household gods shiver and blink like owls surprised in a hollow tree. A hundred signs of intimate and humble tastes, of humdrum pursuits, of family association, cling to the unmasked walls. Whiskered photographs fade on morning-glory wallpapers, plaster saints pine under glass bells, antimacassars droop from plush sofas, yellowing diplomas display their seals on office walls" (153). The whole body of complex human existence had been garroted; ultimately, what the Germans had determined to sunder was that "poor frail web of things that had made up the lives of a vanished city-full" (153–54). Truly, this was a war against the traditions of an entire people.

Wharton came to these sights at a time when she was preternaturally inclined to be sensitive to the whole question of "tradition"; after all, her most recent fiction had taken devastating aim upon many of the customs of the world which had spawned her. She could not fail to be sensible of the significance of the spectacle that met her eyes, and the experience of walking the front in these early years of the war effected a monumental change in her way of thinking.

In all of her fiction thus far, Wharton had been inclined to identify tradition with one or another form of repression. When she had urged acceptance (as she did, say, in *The Valley of Decision*), she did so only because submission was postulated as the necessary alternative to a holocaust in which "all the repressed passions which civilization had sought, however imperfectly, to curb stalked abroad destructive as flood and fire." From the time of her first novel even until 1913 when she published *The Custom of the Country*, Wharton tended to view tradition as an external restraining force: it told you what you were not allowed to do or know; it prohibited rebellion or assertion of any kind because at best these were "not nice" and at worst they were dangerous. To use Wharton's own words, the function of civilization was "to curb." For a long time she had been unable to distinguish among various forms (and various degrees) of passion; hence in the almost Biblical evocation above, it is "*all* the repressed passions" against which civilization must guard.

Gradually, her attitude toward tradition had begun to change: she rebelled with increasingly articulate confidence against those elements in her heritage that had been so punitive—the nightmare of indiscriminate exclusions and thoughtless censures, the tyranny of venerable triviality. What is more, she began to disentangle absolute passional longings (those remnants of her earliest life that *had* to be relinquished or repressed) from legitimate passions that might be a part of satisfactory adult life. Yet, her notions of the role that civilization might play in the life of an individual were still essentially simple. It was not until she started on those long, sobering trips through the embattled French countryside that she began to manifest a more complex and sophisticated notion of the relationship between tradition and individual human growth.

Walking through the empty villages and towns, peering into houses where the debris of many lifetimes lay scattered like so much chaff blown by a careless wind, Wharton realized that in mounting an attack against French civilization, the enemy had not set out to obliterate those things that *repress* life. Quite the contrary. They had aimed to destroy those things that support life—the countless, habitual, humdrum associations and pursuits that give meaning to existence. Plodding grimly through the mud, her quick novelistic eye missing no detail, Wharton began to formulate a new notion of tradition: it is the matrix within which individual personality is defined—a delicate fretwork of familiarities and understandings by which man's sense of self is confirmed and reconfirmed in his many daily encounters. Civilization is not something external to each of us, nor is its primary function one of suppressing freedom and growth. Rather, the civilization of any given time and place becomes an integral element in the personality of all its members: it sustains them, informs their existence with meaning, and changes—even as their lives change—with a slow, measured continuity.

This was Wharton's conclusion as she traveled through France in 1915. Yes, life is limited; hopes and aspirations limited. The very fact that an individual belongs to one society rather than another is an inescapable limitation. Nevertheless, it is ultimately the force of tradition and civilization that permits us to establish that essential relation between ourselves and others. It permits us to place ourselves, to know ourselves; it gives sustenance to life. Wharton saw this truth in the behavior of the French people; she was to remark it later in English and American soldiers as well. "The war has shown the world what are the real values of France. Never for an instant has this people, so expert in the great art of living, imagined that life consisted in being alive. Enamoured of pleasure and beauty, dwelling freely and frankly in the present, they have yet kept their sense of larger meanings, have understood life to be made up of many things past and to come, of renunciation as well as satisfaction, of traditions as well as experiments, of dying as much as of living. Never have they considered life as a thing to be cherished in itself, apart from its reactions and its relations" (230).

What is the most vital function of tradition? To stifle feeling? No.

Tradition provides the structures through which we can render our deepest emotions. "Intelligence first . . . has helped France to be what she is; and next, perhaps, one of its corollaries, *expression*. . . . I naturally do not mean public speaking, nor yet the rhetorical writing too often associated with the word. Rhetoric is the dressing-up of conventional sentiment, eloquence the fearless expression of real emotion. And this gift of the fearless expression of emotion—fearless, that is, of ridicule, or of indifference in the hearer—has been an inestimable strength. . . . 'Words' are not half shamefacedly regarded as something separate from, and extraneous to, emotion, or even as a mere vent for it, but as actually animating and forming it. Every additional faculty for exteriorizing states of feeling, giving them a face and a language, is a moral as well as an artistic asset, and Goethe was never wiser than when he wrote: 'A god gave me the voice to speak my pain.' It is not too much to say that the French are at this moment drawing a part of their national strength from their language" (230, 231, 232). Tradition allows us to shape our energies, to feel our emotions and become strong. It gives us the necessary context for being and becoming. It gives us—WORDS.

Thus the strength to prevail in such a war derives from a conscious reawakening to the connections between a sense of emotional strength and the customs that inform life; the will to live becomes, among other things, a determination to reestablish all the trivialities of daily life that support one's sense of self. Wharton first noticed this fact when she saw that flowers had been planted among the ruins—"Along the edge of the chasms that were streets, everywhere we have seen flowers and vegetables springing up in freshly raked and watered gardens" (93). She writes, as she tells us, with a bunch of peonies sitting on the table beside her— not "to point the stale allegory of unconscious Nature veiling Man's havoc: they are put on my first page as a symbol of conscious human energy coming back to replant and rebuilt the wilderness . . ." (94).

Soldiers whose village homes were blistered open have created new hamlets carved out of trenches that convey the quotidian air of business-as-usual. "They are real houses, with real doors and windows under their grass-eaves, real furniture inside, and real beds of daisies and pansies at their doors. In the Colonel's bungalow a big bunch of spring flowers bloomed on the table, and everywhere we saw the same neatness and order, the same amused pride in the look of things" (120). Over and over again, Wharton records the determined domesticity of the front:

"other cheery catacombs" in which she discovered "neat rows of bunks, mess-tables, sizzling sauce-pans over kitchen-fires. Everywhere were endless ingenuities in the way of camp-furniture and household decoration" (126). One day she visited a sod-thatched hut bearing the rude inscription, "At the sign of the Ambulant Artisans." Inside she discovered Paris jewelers making rings of exquisite design from the aluminum of enemy shells, men working because they carried the imperatives of their craft within them. "There are many such ring-smiths among the privates at the front. . . . They seemed to be beating out the cheerful rhythm of 'I too will something make, and joy in the making' " (128). The essential calm of the front, its underlying sense of sanity, grew precisely from the accumulation of such incidents.

There were other incidents too; many that were horrifying. Wharton never indulged in the simpleminded illusion that war is tidy and uplifting. Often she was quite literally sickened by the evidence of maiming and cruelty and filth that filtered back from the trenches. But the arresting thing is that she did not choose to focus upon the rape and destruction; she was more interested in those things that provided unexpected coherence and continuity. It is this focus, after all, that suggests what war signified to her. And the final, deepest meaning of war was the revelation of the power of those traditions that had been internalized as a necessary part of the characters of the men who fought. Confronted with annihilation, soldiers sought to re-create the familiar routines of civilization. Thence sprang their energy.

And the energy of war was very great. Everywhere vitality was bubbling to the surface. Percy Lubbock speaks of Edith Wharton as a "new woman" in those days; "her enthusiasm was like a searchlight, sweeping the scene with a purposeful energy that clearly wouldn't long be contained." [67] Everything was felt more keenly. The war was almost unbearably agitating; it suffused everyone with an unmistakably sexual intensity. "Such a heightening of life," Wharton remarked when she visited the village of Cassel, "so visually stimulating and absorbing. 'It was gay and terrible,' is the phrase forever recurring in 'War and Peace'; and the gaiety of war was everywhere in Cassel, transforming the lifeless little town into a romantic stage-setting full of the flash of arms and the virile animation of young faces" (146).

When Wharton returned to Paris, she was even more palpably conscious of a buzzing excitement that hung over the city. The war, the trip to the front, the general activity around her—all these merely reinforced the urgency of the inner searching that had begun with *The Reef.* "The noting of my impressions at the front had the effect of rousing in me an intense longing to write," Wharton recollects. That is scarcely surprising, for Wharton had always coped with her most intense emotions through the medium of fiction. Yet for the moment, "my mind was burdened with practical responsibilities, and my soul wrung with the anguish of the war. Even had I had the leisure to take up my storytelling I should have had no heart for it; yet I was tormented with a fever of creation." [68] It is true that her productivity diminished: she did not turn out the steady sequence of short stories that everyone had come to expect from her. Nevertheless, when she was strongly moved, she found the time to write. Most notably, she poured forth another major novel.

Wharton wrote no other fiction in such a state of heightened tension and palpable excitation. The work that finally did emerge from this moment seems to be at a strange remove from it: *Summer* ("hot *Ethan*," as Wharton jokingly dubbed it in the letters to Gaillard Lapsley)—another tale of the Berkshire Hills. Yet the illusion of remove is deceptive; in many respects, this is a war novel. The conflict had made an indelible impression: Wharton's time at the front had suggested new ways of comprehending all the compromises and trivialities of everyday life; she had begun to develop a more ample notion of tradition as the preserver of life, not necessarily repressive at all. There was immense reassurance for Wharton in this conclusion; it freed her to share in the tremendous surge of passion that enveloped the country at war. *Summer* captures all that was "gay and terrible," recreates the unmitigated sexual intensity of those days with a swift sureness of tone. A novel of the season of youth, of sensual awakening: it is unquestionably the most erotic fiction that Wharton ever published.

Above all, it marks another stage in the author's private quest, drawing her ever closer to the goal of "placing" sexuality. She made this fiction in the midst of war because some inescapable inner imperative had decreed that she must. "I had carried about the subject for a long time," she confided to Brownell; it could wait no longer, and finally it burst upon her.[69] "The tale was written at a high pitch of creative joy, but amid a thousand interruptions, and while the rest of my being was steeped in the tragic realities of the war; yet I do not remember ever visualizing with more intensity the inner scene, or the creatures peopling it." [70]

7

Although Edith Wharton had never allowed herself to suppose that life could be uncomplicated, in the dawning months of her affair she had longed for a *love* that was simple—"twenty-four hours" in "a little inn" in the country in the depths of a "green wood." Unfettered, Arcadian, serene. However, by the time she published *Summer* in 1917, Wharton had come with increasing wisdom to recognize that a genuine sensual awakening is none of these things: only the dream of love can be simple. The novel as it finally stands was undeniably influenced by the war; yet its origins went deeper. "I had carried about the subject for a long time." How long? In one sense for nine years, for all the time that she had groped to discover a language that was adequate to capture the essence of her relationship with Fullerton; in another sense for much longer, for all the time that sexual passion had clamored to find expression in her life. Love is not simple because it has its ancestry in dark and primitive impulses, ancient desires and primeval woes. This is the insight that informs *Summer*. The novel is the very antithesis of every sentimental, pastoral idyll that has ever been written about love. It deliberately disenchants Arcadian expectations. Here is "summer" from within—a myth of creation, capturing the violence of Nature's immutable plan. It is a tale of initiation, a record of the rites of passage, an ecstatic agony of understanding.

It seems clear that by the time she was completing *The Custom of the Country*, Wharton had already become interested in the violence that lies beneath smooth social surfaces. But in spite of all the talk about "barbarians" in that novel, its tone is the giddy calliope of swirling social commentary. The primordial grandeur of *Summer* is yet to come. Nevertheless, hints of it turn up in the notebooks as early as 1913.

On May 29, 1913, Edith Wharton was present at a signal event—the balletic premiere of Stravinsky's *Le Sacre du Printemps*. It shocked the conservative audience who had come to witness a tribute to spring—principally, so Stravinsky was later to claim, because it failed to satisfy their Romantic expectations. Instead of a melodious cascade of florescence, the audience was greeted with rhythmic, mocking cacophony. Wharton's friend Jean Cocteau described it as "a symphony impregnated with a wild pathos, with earth in the throes of birth, noises of farm and camp, little melodies that come to us out of the depths of the centuries, and panting of cattle, profound convulsions of nature, prehistoric georgics." [71] The performance was a rout: the audience whistled and stamped and tried to hoot the dancers off the stage. Edith Wharton, however, was not offended by it; indeed, she found it interesting—"extraordinary"—and in her notebook for 1913 there are quivering resonances to the primitivism that was sweeping Paris, echoes that may have grown explicitly out of that memorable musical event. For the first time she records an impressionistic response to music—the last movement of Beethoven's Fifth Symphony. On the next page of the notebook, an even more suggestive (and more novelistic) fragment: "Under their civil interchange of phrases one felt the mutter of old unsatisfied hates, like the whine of animals waiting to be fed." [72] She seems to have been preparing to confront the beasts again—but this time, they represent the hungers of sexual passion.

The story of Le Sacre du Printemps as Stravinsky describes it is suggestive. "I had a fleeting vision. . . . I saw in imagination a solemn pagan rite: sage elders, seated in a circle, watched a young girl dance herself to death. They were sacrificing her to propitiate the god of spring." [73] The ballet captures the abandon of adolescent passion (different movements were entitled "Dance of the Youths and Maidens," "Mystical Circle of the Adolescents," and so forth) and juxtaposes this to the restrictive domination of elders. As choreographed by Nijinsky, the generational contrast was heightened, made utterly stark and brutal. And underlying the entire conceit was the terror of mankind confronted with some force that is unknown and unknowable—a spring that may capriciously decide never to return without a sacrifice of dreadful proportions—a force that is wantonly ruthless and destructive. The Nature of Creation—Man's Nature.

In the fall and winter of 1913 Edith Wharton read The Secret Sharer (the first of Conrad's novels to fall into her hands) and was entirely captured by it. She wrote to him, praising the work unstintingly; and then she went out, purchased everything that he had written, and set about reading it at once, fascinated by his management of the primitive element in man. (A friendly relationship grew up between the two authors, and five years later, Conrad was to express *his* unbounded admiration for *Summer*—his favorite of all the novels she wrote.) In the first several months of 1914, Wharton set out on a journey to North Africa to view the primitive at first hand. "In Algiers the natives had seemed possessed of a noble beauty; [in Tunis and southern Tunisia] she was confronted by a vision of 'effeminacy or obesity or obscenity or black savageness.' In the sun-sprinkled depths of the vaulted bazaars in the native quarter, she felt she had stumbled into an 'unexpurgated page of the Arabian nights' and reveled in the fantastic variety of types. The crowded scene, constantly astir, seemed to her charged with sexuality. She responded by purchasing several erotic gifts: a phial of essence of sandalwood and sycamore, 'which diluted with the purest alcohol, is said to—*mais ne précisons pas!*'; some perfumes; and from a black prostitute in Sfax, a love charm in the form of an ambergris necklace." [74]

Her own scattered recollections of the trip (in the notebook for 1914) are curiously reminiscent of the forces and themes that had been dramatized in Stravinsky's ballet. "The brown hands of the native girls flutter perpetually, like tied birds," she muses. And in a longer meditation:

> In the native quarter at Biskra under a full moon, the scene (from the roof terrace of the hotel) is like a Carpaccio: two streets converging, one gay and thronged, with latticed balconies, green and yellow, and at the farther end, closing its perspective, the open door of a dancing house, in front of which white-draped figures are continually passing. From it comes a wailing clattering music, and now and then against the light, a dancing-girl's brown arm flings a red scarf and disappears.
>
> Other girls in yellow tunics and black headdresses come to the doorways, linger and go in; the white throng, with here and there a dark blue cloak, or a Turkish jacket, moves perpetually, restlessly, under the cafe lights, with an air of youth, adventure, vivacity. In the other street, against the wall of a long cafe, mats are spread, and motionless white groups cower on them at cards or dominoes. Other groups, against a dull iris-yellow wall with a vaguely seen parapet, move slowly—majestically, confer, break up and pass on. The turbans are larger, the white robes ampler, the gestures rarer and slower: on this side there are no women and no music. The picture is a symbolic diptych of the two ages of man. [75]

How long had Wharton carried the primordium of *Summer?* Surely it had entered her conscious mind by 1914 when Europe burst into war, for this was now only two years before she actually began writing it. "Dance of the Youths and Maidens"; a confrontation with the secret sharer (that uncivilized, unsocialized self within); conflict between generations, the two ages of man; the primitive in North Africa; the war: all of these—themes and journeys and events—must be understood as a part of the preparation for this novel. And in the end, all were atomized in the furnace of her imagination, absorbed into the fictional whole: the story of Charity Royall.

Wharton delivers her heroine in the very first words of the novel, yet the offering is curiously anonymous at its beginning: we do not learn Charity's name until we are several pages into the story. The first three or four pages "place" her with exquisite precision, thereby introducing the major theme in terms that have been deliberately generalized. She is, as we eventually discover, a highly particularized person; but her tale captures the essence of a moment in all human lives. She is the Adolescent. Her initiation, the rites of passage that she must endure and the wisdom she must learn, are a part of the universal human experience. She makes her journey for all of us.

Thus the novel begins.

A girl came out of lawyer Royall's house, at the end of the one street of North Dormer, and stood on the doorstep.

It was the beginning of a June afternoon. The springlike transparent sky shed a rain of silver sunshine on the roofs of the village, and on the pastures and larchwoods surrounding it. A little wind moved among the round white clouds on the shoulders of the hills, driving their shadows across the fields and down the grassy road that takes the name of street when it passes through North Dormer. The place lies high and in the open, and lacks the lavish shade of the more protected New England villages. The clump of weeping-willows about the duck pond, and the Norway spruces in front of the Hatchard gate, cast almost the only roadside shadow between lawyer Royall's house and the point where, at the other end of the village, the road rises above the church and skirts the black hemlock wall enclosing the cemetery.

The little June wind, frisking down the street, shook the doleful fringes of the Hatchard spruces, caught the straw hat of a young man just passing under them, and spun it clean across the road into the duck-pond.

As he ran to fish it out the girl on lawyer Royall's doorstep noticed that he was a stranger, that he wore city clothes, and that he was laughing with all his teeth, as the young and careless laugh at such mishaps.[76]

"A girl," "a young man," "a stranger," an early June day that constitutes "the beginning." The day is so thoroughly drenched in sunlight—the entire small town with its one narrow street so utterly exposed to the genial radiance of the afternoon—that the shadows scuttling before the wind seem scarcely to impinge upon it. Shadows, surely, belong beyond, down the road and up the hill within "the black hemlock wall enclosing the cemetery." The road leads inexorably there, of course, into a finality of shade. But the girl who stands poised upon this threshold does not concern herself with the far end of the road; her gaze encompasses neither the cemetery nor the possibility of death. She has just stepped into the sunlight; she is concerned with life and warmth. Why should she think of death? It is much more absorbing to watch the young man who laughs "with all his teeth, as the young and careless laugh."

Even this simplified vision of her world displeases her. Ready to be dismissive, she rejects it all with a single impatient gesture. " 'How I hate everything,' she murmured"—her very first words (9). Oh, there had been a time (a time of ignorance that seems long ago) when she had supposed North Dormer "to be a place of some importance" (9). But now, walking jauntily along the street, "swinging her key on a finger, and looking about her with the heightened attention produced by the presence of a stranger in a familiar place" (9), she finds it completely insufficient. Her discontent began with a visit to the larger hamlet of Nettleton where she went with the minister and a group of young people to hear an illustrated lecture on the Holy Land. There she "looked into shops with plate-glass fronts, tasted cocoanut pie, sat in a theatre. . . . This initiation had shown her that North Dormer was a small place. . . . It had no shops, no theatres, no lectures, no 'business block.' . . . 'How I hate everything!' she said again" (10–12).

Her adolescent harshness derives in part from inexperience and ignorance: she has never been tested, and she knows almost nothing about the outside world. However, in large measure it is a sign of apprehension. When we meet her at the beginning of the novel, Charity is not coherently aware of her feelings. Nevertheless, she harbors a distressing suspicion of personal insufficiency. She is shy, and she suffers (when she cannot shake it out of her head) from a painful "sense of inadequacy" (61) that all too often mocks her ambitions. She is not even a native of the town she disdains: she was born obscurely in an outlaw community; and when she was five years old, "she had been 'brought down from the

Mountain'; from the scarred cliff that lifted its sullen wall above the lesser slopes of Eagle Range, making a perpetual background of gloom to the lonely valley. . . . Charity was not very clear about the Mountain; but she knew it was a bad place, and a shame to have come from, and that, whatever befell her in North Dormer, she ought, as Miss Hatchard had once reminded her, to remember that she had been brought down from there, and hold her tongue and be thankful" (11–12). Even her name—"Charity"—is intended as a constant injunction to be thankful (and serves as a constant betrayal of her disgraceful origins). Fearful always that she might be ridiculed, how much easier and safer it is to take the initiative in resentment and rejection.

That crossing of the threshold into sunlight with which the novel begins is a representation of the girl's commitment to self-discovery, her embracing of the quintessential quest of adolescence. We find her glancing eagerly into dim mirrors and listening expectantly to the vagrant murmurs of still-nascent emotion; and the arrival of this strange young man has merely made her even more painfully self-conscious. Things that she had comfortably pushed out of her mind before can no longer be ignored. "She knew nothing of her early life, and had never felt any curiosity about it: only a sullen reluctance to explore the corner of her memory where certain blurred images lingered. But . . . she had become absorbingly interesting to herself, and everything that had to do with her past was illuminated by this sudden curiosity. She hated more than ever the fact of coming from the Mountain; but it was no longer indifferent to her. Everything that in any way affected her was alive and vivid: even the hateful things had grown interesting because they were a part of herself" (59). Eventually, when she is ready, Charity will have to confront this heritage of the Mountain; however, other things must come first.

The reader sees this world entirely through Charity's consciousness. It is never difficult to make more sophisticated inferences than she does from the material that she gives us, for her mind is blanketed in the absolute naiveté of the young. However, the compass of her observation is small: she is so completely possessed by the exhilarating and terrifying process of establishing the nature of her own identity that for the moment everything outside herself seems trivial and unimportant. The terms of her emotional economy do not permit her to afford the luxury of a sympathetic interest in others.

Thus, for example, the life of her guardian, lawyer Royall, is a matter of almost complete indifference to her. "He had been to her merely the person who is always there, the unquestioned central fact of life, as inevitable but as uninteresting as North Dormer itself, or any of the other conditions fate had laid on her. . . . She had regarded him only in relation to herself, and had never speculated as to his own feelings" (110). When his wife died, several years after he had carried the child down from the mountain into their home, Charity had sensed that "he was a dreadfully 'lonesome' man; she had made that out because she was so 'lonesome' herself. He and she, face to face in that sad house, had sounded the depths of isolation; and though she felt no particular affection for him, and not the slightest gratitude, she pitied him because she was conscious that he was superior to the people about him, and that she was the only being between him and solitude" (25). There was talk of sending her away to boarding school then; but for some indefinable reason, she chose to stay with him. Not an act of kindness, nor affection, nor understanding. Charity did not know, really, why she stayed. It was a youthful whim as much as anything. " 'I ain't going,' " she had breezily decreed, "swinging past him on her way up to her room" (27). He had been splendid that day—had "shaved, and brushed his black coat, and looked a magnificent monument of a man; at such moments she really admired him" (27). But she has not the maturity to understand him.

Both may be "lonesome"; however, the terrain of lawyer Royall's isolation has contours that Charity cannot fathom. Unconsciously, she withdraws from the implications of his taciturnity—just as she ignores the many implications of his kindness. And she is hard, with the startled, inexperienced harshness of one who has only just begun the process of initiation. For his part, Royall does not violate her ignorance. Once, only once, when she was seventeen, he had weakened. "She was awakened by a rattling at her door and jumped out of bed. She heard Mr. Royall's voice, low and peremptory, and opened the door, fearing an accident. No other thought had occurred to her; but when she saw him in the doorway, a ray from the autumn moon falling on his discomposed face, she understood. For a moment they looked at each other in silence; then, as he put his foot across the threshold, she stretched out her arm and stopped him. 'You go right back from here,' she said, in a shrill voice that startled her. . . . 'Charity, let me in. . . . I'm a lonesome man,' he began, in the deep voice that sometimes moved her. Her heart gave a startled plunge, but she continued to hold him back contemptuously. 'Well, I guess you made a mistake, then. This ain't your wife's room any longer.' She was not frightened, she simply felt a deep disgust; and perhaps he divined it or read it in her face, for after staring at her a moment he drew back and turned slowly away from the door. . . . She crept to the window and saw his bent figure striding up the road in the moonlight. Then a belated sense of fear came to her with the consciousness of victory" (28–30). She is shocked more than anything else: although Royall is merely her guardian (and not her father), the taint of incest hangs over the entire episode. Charity muses on that fact later, conjuring him as a "hideous parody of the fatherly old man she had always known" (34).

More shocking still is the spectacle of this man still fired with the lusts of youth. Lawyer Royall is "old"—perhaps in his late forties—old to a girl of Charity's age. It is difficult enough that she should have to bear the tensions of her own emergent feelings; it is intolerable to suppose that they might have anything in common with the dark moods and deep needs of this creature whose nature she refuses to comprehend. Thus when a few days later he asks her to marry him, she explodes with derision. " 'Marry you? Me?' she burst out with a scornful laugh. 'Was that what you came to ask me the other night? What's come over you, I wonder? How long is it since you've looked at yourself in the glass?' She straightened herself, insolently conscious of her youth and strength" (34).

But even this rejection is not enough to satisfy the violence of Charity's revulsion. The encounter on the threshold of her bedroom captures one element, a central element, of the more general task of self-discovery that is implied by her unhesitating venture into the sunlight in the first few lines of the novel. The adolescent quest for identity compels a confrontation with the many implications of sexuality. For a woman, any consideration of this problem must focus specifically on the consequences of penetration. Thus lawyer Royall's attempt to intrude into Charity's bedroom gives palpable focus for a whole network of possibilities and problems that attend the acceptance of adult, feminine, genital sexuality. The individual incident—as incident—is shocking to Charity; but the larger implications are even more frightful. It is the confrontation with her own developing instincts more than anything else from which she recoils, not frightened but "disgusted." Afterwards, she knows that she is perfectly safe from a repetition of the event: lawyer Royall will not approach her again. Nevertheless, she demands that he have a hired woman so that she will not be alone in the house with him; and "it was far less for her own defense than for his humiliation. She needed no one to defend her: his humbled pride was her surest protection. He had never spoken a word of excuse or extenuation; the incident was as if it had never been. Yet its consequences were latent in every word that he and she exchanged, in every glance they instinctively turned from each other" (38).

The presence of that other woman is the continuing echo of Charity's derision.[77] (She has learned this particular piece of meanness, perhaps, by having lived with the implications of her own name for so long.) And here, as in her scornful hatred for "everything" in North Dormer, she ridicules most mercilessly where she feels herself to be most vulnerable. The elaborate cruelty of her retaliation bespeaks the extent of her discomfort with the stirrings of her own feelings. By creating an atmosphere of constant, unspoken reproof, she can deny the complex implications of passion, remain distanced from all that is difficult or distasteful. Thus she clings tenaciously to ignorance and innocence for yet a while; and she is free to saunter into the pristine clearness of a sunlit June day with the simple hope of encountering a fine young man.

By her own lights, Charity has good reason to hate North Dormer: her imagination sings with unformed but ambitious dreams of herself, and her environment offers little scope for such bright expectations. Even her employment as local librarian seems perversely designed to immerse her in the damp and gloom of a uselessly accumulated past. As she sits at her desk under the water-stained steel engraving of the library's founder, she often wonders "if he felt any deader in his grave than she did in his library" (13).

So she feels this day with the impudent sun abroad when the door opens to admit the young stranger. An architect who has come to study old houses in the neighborhood, Miss Hatchard's cousin (Lucius Harney by name), he has little in common with Charity Royall, and they find almost nothing of significance to say to each other. In fact, verbal communication founders distressingly. " 'Have you a card catalogue?' he asked. . . . 'A *what?*' 'Why, you know—' He broke off, and she became conscious that he was looking at her for the first time. . . . 'No, I don't suppose you *do* know,' he corrected himself. 'In fact, it would be almost a pity—' She thought she detected a slight condescension in his tone, and asked sharply: 'Why?' 'Because it's so much pleasanter . . . to poke about by one's self—with the help of the librarian.' . . . 'I'm afraid I can't help you much.' 'Why?' he questioned in his turn; and she replied that there weren't many books anyhow, and that she'd hardly read any of them" (15–16). The young man inquires conversationally about houses in the area, but the more he talks, the more "her bewilderment was complete: the more she wished to appear to understand him the more unintelligible his remarks became. He reminded her of the gentleman who had 'explained' the pictures at Nettleton, and the weight of her ignorance settled down on her again like a pall" (17). He is interested in "old" houses. Now what could that mean and why would anyone want to make distinctions and gradations among all those outdated things? " 'Old houses?' " she brings out in wonder. " 'Everything's old in North Dormer, isn't it? The folks are, anyhow' " (18).

Yet there is more to this stumbling exchange than the broken bits of conversation. Charity and Lucius share their youth, and they call to each other (very softly and gently now at first) in a sweet, unspoken language of eyes and laughter. "The fact that, in discovering her, he lost the thread of his remark, did not escape her attention, and she looked down and smiled. He smiled also" (15). Afterwards, Charity hugs the memory of that moment: "She remembered his sudden pause when he had come close to the desk and had his first look at her. The sight had made him forget what he was going to say; she recalled the change in his face" (39). This more fundamental language sinks deeply into her being, and she leaves the library early that day, instinctively seeking the warm element of the sunny afternoon.

For a long while Charity has been listening to a host of half-heard and faintly comprehended murmurings. "She was blind and insensible to many things, and dimly knew it; but to all that was light and air, perfume and colour, every drop of blood in her responded. She loved the roughness of the dry mountain grass under her palms, the smell of the thyme into which she crushed her face, the fingering of the wind in her hair and through her cotton blouse, and the creak of the larches as they swayed to it. She often climbed up the hill and lay there alone for the mere pleasure of feeling the wind and of rubbing her cheeks in the grass. Generally at such times she did not think of anything, but lay immersed in an inarticulate well-being" (21). Always she has abandoned herself to this simple sensuosity, like a young animal nestling against its mother, and until now her feelings have been simple and uncomplicated. Today is different, however, for today her imagination lingers over the memory of the young man—his smooth sunburnt hands, his grey eyes, the suggestive sinewy strength of his flesh.

And the memory pursues her, gathering blurred visions of indefinable, expectant romance. That night, lying in the warmth of the June evening, she recalls the change in his face once again, "and jumping up she ran over the bare boards to her washstand, found the matches, lit a candle, and lifted it to the square of looking-glass on the white-washed wall. . . . A clumsy band and button fastened her unbleached nightgown about the throat. She undid it, freed her thin shoulders, and saw herself a bride in a low-necked satin, walking down an aisle with Lucius Harney. He would kiss her as they left the church. . . . She put down the candle and covered her face with her hands as if to imprison the kiss" (39–40). Perhaps this is the girl whose image she has been seeking, a girl who is suffused with the blush of a first kiss. Charity stands transfixed for the moment—and then the dream is broken. She hears Mr. Royall moving through the house, a "horrible old man" (40), and her fancies are contaminated by the memory of that ugly moment, by the fumbling base needs of this lonesome creature who can be no part of her joyous, innocent dream. "Until then she had merely despised him; now deep hatred of him filled her heart" (40).

The lazy days lengthen before her, and Charity slowly becomes acquainted with Lucius Harney. He suggests that she might be his guide on trips into the countryside looking for architectural "finds"; they are comrades, nothing more. A decorum of hesitation more rigorous than any formal rules modulates the friendship. One day, unthinkingly, he takes her hand in his, and Charity realizes that "she was feeling the smooth touch that she had imagined . . . before on the hillside" (51). She brings a petty problem to him, and he seeks to comfort her: "He looked straight into her eyes with his shy grey glance. 'You can trust me, you know—you really can' " (52). Nothing significant has passed between them—the brush of hands, a tender glance—yet "all the old frozen woes seemed to melt in her" (52). It is as if they share a delicious, unspoken secret, the secret of youth and summer.

It is a fragile season. "There had never been such a June in Eagle County. Usually it was a month of moods, with abrupt alternations of belated frost and mid-summer heat; this year, day followed day in a sequence of temperate beauty. . . . On such an afternoon Charity Royall lay on a ridge above a sunlit hollow, her face pressed to the earth and the warm currents of the grass running through her. Directly in her line of vision a blackberry branch laid its frail white flowers and blue-green leaves against the sky. Just beyond, a tuft of sweet-fern uncurled between the beaded shoots of the grass, and a small yellow butterfly vibrated over them like a fleck of sunshine" (53). Everything is at once beautiful and delicate, caught up in a tremulous equilibrium. Charity, too, is a part of this expectant moment: "She felt . . . the strong growth of the beeches . . . the rounding of pale green cones . . . the push of myriads of sweet-fern. . . . All this bubbling of sap and slipping of sheaths and bursting of calyxes was carried to her on mingled currents of fragrance . . . and all were merged in a moist earth-smell that was like the breath of some huge sun-warmed animal" (54). She yields to the feelings, but she does so with an artless desire that this time of anticipation might be indefinitely suspended.

She hangs back from Lucius, often wandering into the fields and woods on their trips, only to watch from a distance while he sits drawing. "It was partly from shyness that she did so: from a sense of inadequacy that came to her most painfully when her companion, absorbed in his job, forgot her ignorance and her inability to follow his least allusion, and plunged into a monologue on art and life" (60–61). Partly she suffers from a confusion about how to represent her murky antecedents. She has already fallen into the habit of holding herself contemptuously aloof from village love-making "without exactly knowing whether her fierce pride was due to the sense of her tainted origin, or whether she was reserving herself for a more brilliant fate" (61). Above all, however, the appearance of Lucius Harney—the surge of strange and inarticulate longings that his presence evokes—has caused another kind of shyness to be born in her: "a terror of exposing to vulgar perils the sacred treasure of her happiness" (62). One step further in their relationship would signal the end to those safe and innocent dreams of girlhood; she might discover in herself the same dark passions that had moved lawyer Royall, and that is a terrible prospect.

Yet the movement of the season carries her inexorably forward. She trails her young man into sun-bleached valleys ringed in blue heights "eddying away to the sky like the waves of a receding tide. . . . The sun had grown hot. . . . Behind them . . .—the noonday murmur of the forest. Summer insects danced on the air, and a flock of white butterflies fanned the mobile tips of crimson fireweed" (79). One day she is moved to confess that she comes from the Mountain. " 'How curious!' " he replies. " 'I suppose that's why you're so different . . .' " (67). He drops a casual, light kiss upon her sunburnt knuckles—and that is all. Only once does he call her by her Christian name: they "restricted their intercourse to the exchange of commonplaces; but there was a fascination to Charity in the contrast between these public civilities and their secret intimacy" (90). The sweet, unspoken language of eyes and laughter calls ever more insistently now.

One evening Charity leans meditatively upon her window sill, yearning after Lucius' presence; shortly, she sweeps down the stairs and out of the house, drawn by the call of some inaudible force. She has no fixed destination—through the gate, down the hill—until she discovers herself at Miss Hatchard's house, pausing before the one lighted square that is Lucius' room.

Entirely without realizing it (for her memory will not render the comparison), her attitude reiterates the position that Royall took on that fateful evening outside her bedroom: she stands just beyond the window looking in, and gradually, her vigil lengthens into a vivid sensual indulgence. She admires Lucius' long, smooth hands as they play nervously with a pencil; she luxuriates in the warm nearness of his body. "He had taken off his coat and waistcoat, and unbuttoned the low collar of his flannel shirt; she saw the vigorous lines of his young throat, and the root of muscles where they joined the chest" (103). Everything in his appearance suggests to her a subtle, phallic strength; and while she is unutterably drawn to him, she is again restrained by a "kind of terror, as if he had been a stranger under familiar lineaments" (103). The genial safety of their friendship is lost for this moment in the frank call of his manhood, and Charity lingers, suspended between attraction and reluctance—watching him and quickening to the throb of his movement. "One motion of her hand, one tap on the pane, and she could picture the sudden change in his face. In every pulse of her rigid body she was aware of the welcome his eyes and lips would give her; but something kept her from moving. It was not the fear of any sanction, human or heavenly; she had never in her life been afraid. It was simply that she had suddenly understood what would happen if she went in. . . . [She knew] exactly what she would feel if Harney should take her in his arms:

the melting of palm into palm and mouth on mouth, and the long flame burning her from head to foot" (105–6). The blurred, suggestive images of romantic love have been supplanted: Charity is compelled to acknowledge the sexual implications of crossing this threshold; and while she understands them now, she is not yet prepared for the initiation. "A long time passed in this strange vigil" (107); Harney flings himself upon the bed and slowly relaxes into sleep. And Charity "rose and crept away" (107).

She carries the flame of her feelings with exquisite care—like some member of a primitive race bearing fire wrapped in clay across a prehistoric plain. It is essential to Charity to believe that she is undefiled; and she attempts to sequester her love from everything that is common and familiar. However, she is not always successful; even her own associations throw unwholesome images into mind. If she understands "what would happen if she went in," her ecstatic visions are briefly overshadowed by murky and distasteful recollections. "It was the thing that *did* happen betweeen young men and girls, and that North Dormer ignored in public and snickered over on the sly. . . . It was what had happened to Ally Hawes's sister Julia, and had ended in her going to Nettleton, and in people's never mentioning her name" (105). She does not calculate specific consequences; she cannot, for her understanding of them is dim and she resists enlightenment. Yet she is pursued by an inescapable sense that there *are* common consequences even to so rare and beautiful a thing as her nascent yearnings. It is an unwelcome specter, and she rejects it—much as she has rejected the implications of the first fumbling attempts at spoken conversation between herself and Lucius—and looks instead for truth to the deep, unspoken language that they share with the budding season. Her decision to turn away is in part a matter of pride: "If he wanted her he must seek her" (106). In larger measure, it is a way of maintaining the distance between the life of her budding passion and the demeaning commonalities of everyday exchange.

And still she fails. The next morning lawyer Royall confonts her: " 'I've got something to say to you' " (110). At first she recoils; and then she turns to face him, demanding to know whether he has sent Harney away. " 'Didn't he have time to answer some of those questions last night? You was with him long enough!' he said. Charity stood speechless. The taunt was so unrelated to what had been happening in her soul that she hardly understood it. . . . 'Who says I was with him last night?' 'The whole place is saying it by now.' . . . Charity listened in a cold trance of anger. It was nothing to her what the village said . . . but all this fingering of her dreams!" (111–14). The inexorable intrusion of the ordinary into the fancies of this newly discovered self grows insufferable. She begins to stammer an explanation, and then "she felt her voice breaking, and gathered it up in a last defiance. 'As long as I live I'll never forgive you!' she cried" (115).

Royal stands like some prophet of the Old Testament—a residuum of accepted custom, a giver of laws. He is old. In Charity's eyes he seems ancient and thereby entirely unable to comprehend the language that she can hear, but cannot speak. "Age seemed to have come down on him as winter comes on the hills after a storm" (115). What does he know of the fevers of summer? And yet he drones on. " 'If he'd wanted you the right way he'd have said so.' Charity did not speak. . . . Mr. Royall rose from his seat. . . . 'You've always known I loved you the way a man loves a decent woman. I'm a good many years older than you, but I'm head and shoulders above this place and everybody in it. . . . If you'll marry me we'll leave here and settle in some big town, where there's men, and business, and things doing. It's not too late for me to find an opening.' . . . Charity made no movement. Nothing in his appeal reached her heart" (116–17). She starts toward the door, and lawyer Royall moves to check her impetuous flight. "He stood up and placed himself between her and the threshold. He seemed suddenly tall and strong" (117). For a terrible moment they stand eyeing each other. " 'Do you want him to—say? I'll have him here in an hour if you do. I ain't been in the law thirty years for nothing' " (118). But law is not what Charity craves now. She wishes only to be left alone to nurse her feelings. "Something transient and exquisite had flowered in her, and she had stood by and seen it trampled to earth" (118).

The Fourth of July: Independence Day. No feast of the year is celebrated more fervently in the hills than this holiday in the radiant midsummer heat. "Charity sat before the mirror trying on a hat which Ally Hawes, with much secrecy, had trimmed for her" (124). It is a new self whose reflection she admires—a girl who has contemptuously thrown off the small-minded, constricting customs of lawyer Royall and North Dormer. She smiles at the vivid image that the mirror returns to her. She has seen Lucius Harney again—many times; she has promised to continue as his guide, and for a full fortnight, they have roamed the hills each day in "happy comradeship. . . . [Lucius] had never put his arm about her, or sought to betray her into any sudden caress. It seemed to be enough for him to breathe her nearness like a flower's" (129). What further proof does she need to suppose that she can swirl entirely free from all the demeaning conventions that seem gathered together in the figure of her guardian? She is going to celebrate the holiday in a delicious excursion with her young man, "and if she stooped to fib . . . it was chiefly from the secretive instinct that made her dread the profanation of her happiness" (126). Youth and warmth and a day-long trip to the splendor of Nettleton. Fireworks, crowds, lunch under the trees—with insidious innocence, the rites of passage have begun in earnest.

The wagon ride to the junction where they will pick up the train: they do not have much to say, "but it did not greatly matter, for their past was now rich enough to have given them a private language; and with the long day stretching before them . . . there was a delicate pleasure in postponement" (128). The close crowd at the station, people pressing the pair together: "The haze of the morning had become a sort of clear tremor over everything, like the colourless vibration about a flame. . . . But to Charity the heat was a stimulant: it enveloped the whole world in the same glow that burned at her heart" (131). The lurching train, and through the sleeve of his muslin shirt, the suggestive pressure of Lucius' strong, smooth-muscled arm: "She steadied herself, their eyes met, and the flaming breath of the day seemed to enclose them" (131). Nettleton and all the recollected wonders of the city: cocoanut confections and dusty raspberries piled high in boxes are set on the sidewalk for sale. A glittering tray in a jeweller's shop: the next moment a shining pin with a deep blue stone is pressed into Charity's hand. Noon: lunch crowds spill onto the sidewalk and out into the street. A moving-picture exhibition: "All the world has to show seemed to pass before her in a chaos of palms and minarets, charging cavalry regiments, roaring lions, comic police-men and scowling murderers; and the crowd around her, the hundreds of hot sallow candy-munching faces, young, old, middle-aged, but all kindled with the same contagious excitement, became part of the spec-tacle, and danced on the screen with the rest" (139). A lingering after-noon ride on the lake under a heat-veiled sky, the water throbbing with light. And in the evening, fireworks!

Charity and Lucius arrive late at the grandstand, and they are obliged to take seats on the end of two planks, one above the other. "Presently there was a soft rush through the air and a shower of silver fell from the blue evening sky. In another direction, pale Roman candles shot up singly through the trees, and a fire-haired rocket swept the horizon like a portent" (146). Over and over again, the night sky is irradiated for a moment with fire: up and over their heads and falling down, down into darkness again. "Charity had taken off her hat . . . and whenever she leaned back to follow the curve of some dishevelled rocket she could feel Harney's knees against her head" (146–47). The display moves to its climax, and Charity loses herself entirely in wonder. The final panorama of lights. " 'Oh-h-h,' Charity gasped: she had forgotten where she was. . . . The picture vanished and darkness came down. In the obscurity she felt her head clasped by two hands: her face was drawn backward, and Harney's lips were pressed on hers. With sudden vehemence he wound his arms about her, holding her head against his breast while she gave him back his kisses. . . . He passed his arm about her waist, steadying her against the descending rush of people; and she clung to him, speechless, exultant, as if all the crowding and confusion about them were a mere vain stirring of air" (148–49).

Finally, at last, she is free—spun utterly beyond the cares of a world that degrades and demeans—she floats in an aura of purified rapture. And then, as suddenly as it had come upon her, the moment of ecstasy is shattered. Lawyer Royall, himself in the company of a coarse girl from Nettleton, catches sight of Charity. "He drew himself up with the tremulous majesty of drunkenness, and stretched out his arm. 'You whore— you damn—bare-headed whore, you!' he enunciated slowly" (151). Afterwards—at night alone in her room, the next morning as the early sun sends tentative fingers of light into the sky—Charity can think of little save an unmixed animal pain. The gates of ignorance have shut behind her, and she has no categories with which to take measure of her situation. Her one resort is flight (for the neat regulations of life in North Dormer can scarcely guide her), and the only place she knows to go is the Mountain, that brooding, unknown wilderness from which she came.

Thus it is that she finds herself on the road that afternoon, climbing with the intention of reaching by nightfall a little deserted house halfway to her destination. Thus it is that she encounters Lucius again.

" 'Where were you going?' " he expostulates. " 'I was going away—I don't want to see you—I want you should leave me alone,' she broke out wildly. . . . As she spoke she became aware of a change in his face. He was no longer listening to her, he was only looking at her, with the passionate absorbed expression she had seen in his eyes after they had kissed on the stand at Nettleton" (163–64). As if in a dream, she follows him to the little house, halfway up to the Mountain; they cross the threshold and sit alone in its frail shelter. "Inside . . . wind and weather had blanched everything to the same wan silvery tint; the house was as dry and pure as the interior of a long empty shell" (166). Isolated: they have risen above everything. Only the Mountain remains, penetrating the view from the window, "thrusting its dark mass against a sultry sunset" (167). In the stark power of its brooding presence, the Mountain assimilates all those other intimations of phallic insistence and moves Charity to a flood of recollection. She tries to explain to Lucius about that night long ago when Royall had come to the door of her bedroom. "But once more, as she spoke, she became aware that he was no longer listening. He came close and caught her to him as if he were snatching her from some imminent peril: his impetuous eyes were in hers, and she could feel the hard beat of his heart as he held her against it. 'Kiss me again—like last night,' he said, pushing her hair back as if to draw her whole face up into his kiss" (169). The final hesitation fails, and Charity surrenders herself to the deep eddying currents of unexplored passion.

And having surrendered, she finds that life is simple once again: there is no reticence, no sense of the constriction of a network of social conventions. All of the priorities of her former existence are merely reversed. She has agreed to remain with her guardian; however, reality breathes in the halfway house that has become the trysting place, and the time spent in North Dormer seems entirely "suspended in the void . . . a mere cloudy rim about the central glory of their passion. . . . [It] made her life something apart and inviolable, as if nothing had any power to hurt or disturb her as long as her secret was safe" (174–76). Charity has reduced her being to its most elemental components; and when she returns from the hill, she soars through the still evening air "like one of the hawks she had often watched slanting downward on motionless wings" (178). This love is not confused and furtive, but bright and open as the summer air. "For two golden rainless August weeks he had camped in the house, getting eggs and milk from the solitary farm in the valley. . . . He got up every day with the sun. . . . And in the afternoon

Charity came to him. . . . He had caught her up and carried her away into a new world" (180–82). Now, as at the moment of their very first meeting, they are no more than "a girl" and "a young man"—reenacting the endless ritual of summer.

Down below, the world inexplicably continues the buzzing routines of common life. Ever since the Fourth of July, North Dormer has been preparing for its Old Home Week, a simultaneous celebration of reaping time and of the return to this hamlet of those who have left to make their way elsewhere. There is to be a gathering at the Town Hall; the girls will form a chorus; lawyer Royall will speak; and afterwards, there will be a gala ball. Charity prepares for the fete with sparkling eyes, her fingers more nimble at their sewing than usual. Primarily it is her secret that fires such high good humor: what a rare delight to stand on stage looking boldly into the eyes of her lover in the audience—and all the world ignorant of their bliss. Thus does she feel as the evening begins. "It was a joy to Charity to sing: it seemed as though, for the first time, her secret rapture might burst from her and flash its defiance at the world" (191).

However, as the evening wears on, things do not follow as Charity has supposed. She has difficulty catching sight of Lucius in the murmuring, dusky crowd beyond; when lawyer Royall ascends the steps of the stage, he interposes himself between Charity and the audience. And his presence is intimidating. She cannot help observing that "his gravely set face wore the look of majesty that used to awe and fascinate her childhood. . . . His appearance struck her all the more because it was the first time she had looked him full in the face since the night at Nettleton, and nothing in his grave and impressive demeanor revealed a trace of the lamentable figure on the wharf" (191–92). At first she pays no attention to his speech: it floats to her in mere sonorous scraps of sentences. Yet the ponderous gravity of the rising and falling inflections gradually presses insistently into her consciousness. The oration is an appeal for reverence, for respect of one's heritage. Even those who have made their lives away from North Dormer nevertheless carry it within; many of the collected assembly have come back for precisely that reason—a pious pilgrimage paying honor to the past; others have ventured into the world only to have the high hopes of youth dashed, and these too have come back to North Dormer, disillusioned, perhaps. In either case, Royall entreats, let us come back " 'for good.' . . . He looked about him, and repeated gravely: 'For *good*. There's the point I want to make. . . . Our very experiments in larger places, even if they were unsuccessful, ought to have helped us to make North Dormer a larger place. . . . If you ever do come back to [the homes of your youth], it's worth while to come back to them for their good" (194–95).

He concludes with quiet dignity, and Charity hears the minister, Mr. Miles, murmur, " 'That was a *man* talking—' " (195); yet the effect of the speech is lost upon her, for at its conclusion when lawyer Royall steps back from the podium, she catches sight of Lucius Harney, bending solicitously over an elegantly dressed young lady. "The vision of their two faces had blotted out everything. In a flash they had shown her the bare reality of her situation. Behind the frail screen of her lover's caresses was the whole inscrutable mystery of his life: his relations with other people—with other women—his opinions, his prejudices, his principles, the net of influences and interests and ambitions in which every man's life is entangled" (196–97). The pieces of reality fall fatally back into place; the focus of Charity's comprehension shifts, and the last eight weeks blur into indistinction. "She had given him all she had . . . but [her] all was not enough" (198). Having based the relationship on the universal feelings that spring up between "a girl" and "a young man," they have nothing in particular to bind them, nothing to say to each other, no common language save the unspoken whispers of youth. It had seemed so entirely sufficient just two months ago—so important—and now it seems an empty mockery, not love at all.

Still, youth is resilient; the festive dance restores Charity's spirits, and the next day she lies waiting for her lover with her "arms folded beneath her head, gazing out at the shaggy shoulder of the Mountain" (202). When she hears someone fumbling at the door, she springs up expectantly to greet him; and instead she finds herself confronting lawyer Royall. Once again he interposes himself between the pair. When Harney comes in, Royall asks coolly: " 'Is this the home you propose to bring her to when you get married?' There was an immense and oppressive silence. . . . 'Ask him when he's going to marry you, then—' There was another silence, and he laughed in his turn—a broken laugh. . . . 'You darsn't!' " (206–7). After Royall leaves, Charity hears Lucius' voice as from a great distance: " 'I shall have to go off for a while—a month or two, perhaps . . . and then I'll come back . . . and we'll get married' " (210). The lovers' eyes do not meet, and Charity's imagination is entirely possessed by images of the other life that Lucius leads—his real life among people like himself, a life of accumulated associations and common interests. She scarcely attends to his soft pleading voice. She clings desperately to him, and they sink back together as if they were being sucked down "into some bottomless abyss" (211).

When he has gone, she recognizes that the bridge of their passion has always been as insubstantial as a rainbow: the complicated social nexus to which he belongs will never release him, and it is an arrangement in which she can play no part. "She would be compared with other people, and unknown things would be expected of her" (213). Once or twice she attempts to write him, but she can manage no more than a colored postcard with the simple inscription: " 'With love from Charity.' She felt the pitiful inadequacy of this, and understood, with a sense of despair, that in her inability to express herself she must give him an impression of coldness" (214). Ally Hawes brings the gossip that he is engaged to the elegant lady who was his companion during Old Home Week—Miss Annabel Balch—and in her despair Charity finally pens a short, miserable note:

> I want you should marry Annabel Balch if you promised to. I think maybe you were afraid I'd feel too bad about it. I feel I'd rather you acted right.
>
> Your loving
> CHARITY (221)

Then she discovers that she is carrying his child.

After the long anticipation, after the moment of ecstasy—the long night of anguish. This, too, is a part of the initiation, part of "what happens." Not delirium merely, but the slow, inexorable patterns of the ritual harvest. Charity has spun herself entirely outside of the social context only to discover that Nature's ways do not provide for the isolated individual adventure. She is alone now—and (paradoxically) not alone, never to be alone now that the child is deeply buried within her. North Dormer seems remote and cold: she can envision no place for herself and the child there. A desperate visit to Nettleton to see a smirking doctor— a large, dark, oleagenous woman—who offers to "help her out" and exacts as payment for this abhorrent insinuation the prize of Charity's gold pin with the blue stone: no help again. All these things flash before her in a distracting confusion of images; and now, truly, there seems no place to go save the Mountain. Once there, she intends to see her mother. "She herself had been born as her own baby was going to be born; and whatever her mother's subsequent life had been, she could hardly help remembering the past, and receiving a daughter who was facing the trouble she had known" (240). Here is another, starker mirror of self; no longer the girl who seeks a flushed vision of passion fulfilled, she is searching for a deeper and more distant identification. Ultimately, if she wants to complete the task of discovery herself, she must return to the first causes of her life, that aboriginal place from which she came.

Thus we discover her again stepping out the door of Royall's house to begin another stage in her quest. This time, however, she does not stride into the warm sun of midday; instead she creeps into the cold, autumnal light of dawn. For hours she trudges until unexpectedly Mr. Miles pulls alongside in his buggy: " 'I'm going to see my mother,' " Charity tells him simply (241). " 'You know, then—you'd been told? . . . Your mother is dying. . . . Get in and come with us' " (241). Finally, she arrives at the uttermost point.

What she finds is horrifying. Pure animal impulse rules in this place. No constrictions—that is certainly true—no binding social framework to define and limit relationships. Nothing but rude, mute instinct. Charity arrives too late to speak with her mother, for that woman has died, and the most her daughter can do is keep watch over the body. But what a disfigured, inhuman creature it seems to have been. She had "fallen across her squalid bed in a drunken sleep, and [had] been left lying where she fell, in her ragged disordered clothes. One arm was flung above her head, one leg drawn up under a torn skirt that left the other bare to the knee: a swollen glistening leg with a ragged stocking rolled down about the ankle" (248). A woman mutters, " 'She jus' dropped off' " (248). A dribbling old man protests: " 'I says to her on'y the night before: if you don't take and quit, I says to her . . .' " (249). Someone pulls him back and hurls him against a bench. Silence. An insolent young girl strolls out of the shadows and points to Charity: " 'Who's the girl?' . . . Mr. Miles spoke. 'I brought her; she is Mary Hyatt's daughter.' 'What? Her too?' the girl sneered" (249). A young man hurls oaths at her. Again, silence. And in the mother's face, "there was no sign . . . of anything human: she lay there like a dead dog in a ditch" (250). The funeral service begins.

There is no coffin. " 'I am the Resurrection and the Life.' . . . There was a sudden muttering and a scuffle at the back of the group. 'I brought the stove,' said the elderly man with lank hair, pushing his way between the others. 'I wen' down to Creston'n bought it . . . n' I got a right to take it outer here . . . n' I'll lick any feller says I ain't . . .' " (251–52). " 'Man that is born of woman hath but a short time to live and is full of misery. . . . He cometh up and is cut down . . . he fleeth as it were a shadow' " (254). Half-frozen clods of dirt are tossed into the pit; Charity's mother returns to earth.

Late that night, Charity lies on the floor on a mattress as her mother's corpse had lain, and she is overwhelmed by troublesome thoughts. The body—she has so recently discovered its many splendors—so soon to be brought to an awareness of decay. Vile body, inescapable mortality. A more mature vision of life is forced upon her, one that must encompass shadow as well as sunlight now, death, the huddled cluster of hemlocks at the end of North Dormer's single road. Thus cruelly does Nature circumscribe our possibilities. And freedom. She had thought to know freedom—exhilarating, heady, wonderful freedom—in those two months "suspended in the void." Now truth intrudes upon such fantasies. There *is* no freedom from the constrictions of custom—no freedom save the "savage misery of the Mountain farmers" (259)—and that is not freedom, but chaos. It is not even that these people are fired by a primitive vitality: they are brutal; but their brutality erupts only as a sporadic interlude in the more general atmosphere of endless, fruitless inertia. Their passions have no meaning because they are inarticulate and unformed by tradition of any sort. "As she lay there, half-stunned by her tragic initiation, Charity vainly tried to think herself into the life about her. But she could not even make out what relationship these people bore to each other, or to her dead mother; they seemed to be herded together in a sort of passive promiscuity" (259).

She cannot remain here: she does not belong to the Mountain; that dream was only a part of the youthful fantasy of perfect independence, an illusion that must fade before the frosts of autumn. "The morning was icy cold and a pale sun was just rising above the eastern shoulder of the Mountain. . . . Charity paused on the threshold" (262–63). One final glance, and then she crosses it to begin the slow descent back down to the realities of civilization.

She has gone but a short distance when she encounters a wagon bearing lawyer Royall, informed of her whereabouts by Mr. Miles. "Their eyes met, and . . . he leaned over and helped her up into the buggy" (265). He has come to marry her. " 'Come to my age,' " he ruminates, " 'a man knows the things that matter and the things that don't; that's about the only good turn life does us.' His tone was so strong and reso- lute that it was like a supporting arm about her" (271). She glances at this man—only a man, with a simple sense of dignity and a full share of human weakness—mortal like herself. Barely, just barely, she can recall the breathless hours of mid-July, but "she could no longer believe that she was the being who had lived them; she was someone to whom some- thing irreparable and overwhelming had happened, but the traces of the steps leading up to it had almost vanished" (274). And she is prepared, as she had not been before her initiation, to relinquish her expectations of absolute joy for the uncertain happiness of mortal life.

They are married quietly, and Royall escorts her to a hotel. " 'You go right along up to bed—I'm going to sit down here and have my smoke,' he said. He spoke as easily and naturally as if they had been an old couple" (282). Exhausted by her ordeal, she drifts into sleep. Once dur- ing the night she awakens to see Royall seated in a rocking chair: "He had not undressed, but had taken the blanket from the foot of the bed and laid it across his knees. . . . He knew, then . . . he knew . . . it was because he knew that he had married her, and that he sat there in the darkness to show her she was safe with him. A stir of something deeper than she had ever felt in thinking of him flitted through her tired brain, and cautiously, noiselessly, she let her head sink on the pillow . . ." (283–84).

The next afternoon, they start back to North Dormer. " 'You're a good girl, Charity.' Their eyes met, and something rose in his that she had never seen there: a look that made her feel ashamed and yet secure. 'I guess you're good, too,' she said, shyly and quickly" (290–91). It is not ecstasy. Never again will the fever of summer possess her; for ecstasy depends upon the illusion of perfect freedom, and that is a dream that only youth may cherish. But it is, perhaps, the beginning of love. "Late that evening, in the cold autumn moonlight, they drove up to the door of the red house" (291). Charity Royall has discovered herself, her capaci- ties, her limitations, the associations that will give her life meaning; she is ready, as Royall would say, to come back "for good."

Although it is by no means her most ambitious work *Summer* may well be Wharton's most balanced novel. The language has a shimmering, pellucid quality; and the natural rhythms of the passage of time and of the season are reflected with harmonious resonance in the structure of the novel. Above all, we might say that the "meaning" of the work *is* its structure—that crescendo, forte, diminuendo; that pure intensity of youthful fire, fading into the golden embers of adulthood. There is a sense of natural necessity in the imperatives of this fiction—and of exquisite artistic unity. Charity concludes the novel as she has begun it, at the threshold of the Royall home; but she can enter now out of choice, with the knowledge of maturity to guide her. In order to come back "for good," one must go away for a while. That is the dictum of adolescent growth. Wharton understands as much—for Charity Royall, perhaps for herself as well.

The tone of *Summer* is so entirely different from that of *The Custom of the Country* that at first it seems difficult to perceive a relationship between them. However, it is safe to venture that Wharton might never have written *Summer* without having written *Custom* first. Again it is a matter of fictional decision. In *The Custom of the Country* Wharton figured forth the embodiment of unrestrained appetite: never mind that Undine has no specific sexual component; it is the underlying problem that interests us here. If *Custom* could be said to prove anything, it proves that appetite (or energy) of itself is necessary to life and that only ungoverned and insatiable appetite must be rejected. *Summer* builds upon this conclusion by transferring it into explicitly sexual terms: passion is a component in all life; during the season of youth, passion may reign despotically for a time, but it does so at the expense of other things—"in a void"; eventually, even passion must submit to social injunctions; if it does not, it will destroy. In *Summer* such destruction—the consequence of promiscuous passion—is demonstrated by the Mountain people; and it is interesting that Wharton postulates it primarily as a destruction of the integrity of character. The Mountain people are weak as compared even to the citizens of North Dormer: they are less than human, not fully formed.

We can see the lesson of the war at work here, too. The "fearless expression of emotion" depends upon an animating and shaping cultural heritage; passion without order will be inarticulate and weak, as the Mountain people are weak, capable of no more than random acts of disruption. It is undeniable that we relinquish something significant—glorious—when we submit to the repressive process of civilization; specifically, we give up the fleeting ecstasy of unmitigated sensual indulgence. Yet in the end, we gain more than we lose: love, a kind of emotion that finds many different meanings and that may be sustained throughout a lifetime.

Wharton's absolute ease with the language of passion here suggests how completely she had absorbed this lesson in terms of her art. In some sense the novel recapitulates and resolves her own restless need to define the experience of love. The yearning for simplicity, for freedom, for Romantic fulfillment can be seen now as one stage in the complex process of maturation: it is entirely natural to someone first discovering sexuality; it is a language of wonder, quintessentially youthful. Yet growth demands that we move beyond this stage of verbal rapture and place the expression of love within the network of larger emotions that structure our lives and give them meaning. Sexual love will always be something important; it can only be "everything" for the brief season of youth.

Ultimately, this novel of Summer is a hymn to generativity and marriage. The fact of Charity's pregnancy forces the meaning of harvest time upon her; but this fictional event is merely a convenient mode of representation. We are clearly not meant to read it as an example of Nature's oppression: Charity is not Tess of the D'Urbervilles. Pregnancy is not the inevitable "punishment" for sexual indulgence; it is an opportunity to participate in the social and Natural continuum that informs our lives with meaning.

Edith Wharton, who never had a child and who (so far as we know) never had a pregnancy, nevertheless felt deeply about the importance of marriage itself. Charles Du Bos recollected a poignant moment in 1912 when she spoke out: " 'Ah, the poverty, the miserable poverty, of any love that lies outside of marriage, of any love that is not a living together, a sharing of all!' " [78] It is, perhaps, not too much to say that now finally in 1917 she had gone far toward completing that crisis of sexual identity that had been prematurely discontinued in her own girlhood and adolescence.

Like *Ethan Frome, Summer* is a drama of the threshold; but unlike the earlier work, the later novel explores the many implications of going out—declaring freedom, accepting the advent of genital sexuality. The two novels taken together offer a brilliant example of the way in which representation in Wharton's fiction is overdetermined: even with a complete understanding of the psychological complexities of her life, one could never say that the threshold means just this or that—and nothing more. In *Ethan Frome* the threshold divided regression from the rest of life: the phantasmagoria of frozen emotion that constitutes the narrator's vision in that work is a spelling-out of the consequences of failing to grow, a demonstration of emotional atrophy and living death.

Summer begins with the threshold and moves in the other direction: it shows the consequences of a search for autonomous adult identity. And even in this context, the threshold is immensely suggestive and open to many meanings. To go out is to accept the responsibility for growth. Growth has a sexual component—for a woman, the delights and fears of being penetrated by another individual, in the act of intercourse initially and secondarily in the state of pregnancy. Thus the yielding of one's body to another is also figured in the image of the threshold; and we can understand Charity's inclination to delay consummation of the affair with Lucius Harney (her lingering outside his window, for instance, and then deciding not to go in) if we realize that consummation implies such consequences.

Ultimately, if a woman is to develop completely, she must cross the threshold and go out for a while—and then, willingly and with fully informed adult knowledge, return and *recross* it—"come back for good." This second crossing is the acknowledgment that no one can be free of her social heritage, that she carries it within her in stored memories and associations that may never be expunged. One may return to reject what is bad and accept what is best (surely that is the implication of returning "for good"); and such a return is no surrender and no regression, but the act of a mature adult. Thus Charity pauses again on a threshold when she leaves the Mountain for her return to North Dormer.

Thinking back once more to *The Custom of the Country*, we can infer yet another link between this novel and *Summer*. The purpose of the violent satirical component in *Custom* had been precisely to identify the malignment elements in old New York and excoriate them. Surely one liberating effect of so ruthlessly condemning the destructive part of that society was to release Wharton from its bondage so that she might begin to appreciate and accept what had been good. Her own search for an integrated sense of self had contained many separate steps: in real life, the development of a career, the affair with Fullerton, the divorce. However, we cannot discount the importance of the step taken by the fictional denunciation in *The Custom of the Country*. *Summer* suggests that Wharton, too, was preparing to come back "for good." The opening page of the 1918 notebook is indicative: on it she inscribed the message, "I want the idols broken, but I want them broken by people who understand why they were made, and do not ascribe them to the deliberate malice of the augurs who may afterwards profit by them." [79]

Before she could complete this move, one last part of the puzzle of her background remained to be dealt with; it is the last piece in the puzzle of sexuality as well. Repression is a necessary element of all societies; however, the society that had produced Edith Jones Wharton had developed the art of repression to an excessive degree. We might say that in her personal activities Wharton had liberated herself from its malignant force insofar as she was able; nevertheless, if she was ultimately to accept the particularities of her own past, she would have to come to some understanding of the meaning of the repression she had known (since it had been so central to her experience). To put the question differently, we might say: yes, order is necessary, order that gives substance to life; but why repression—and why, ever, such painfully punitive repression. What function does it serve? Her initial answer to this question—in *The Valley of Decision*—had been that *all* emotions must be suppressed lest the beast in man assert himself and wantonly destroy everything. However, by the time she was writing *Summer* in 1917, such an answer no longer sufficed. And so, the puzzle of repression remained—the primary obstacle to a return "for good."

One sign of Wharton's restlessness during this period is the fact that she started so many things and left them hanging. As early as 1916 she had begun to work a little on *The Glimpses of the Moon*, a novel about an opportunistic "modern" couple, but she did not finish it for publication until 1922. In 1917–18 she spread her talents in several directions: she published a short—and very inferior—sentimental war novel entitled *The Marne*; and she began two other novels, *The Necklace* (which she never finished—another novel of modern society, not unlike *Twilight Sleep*) and *A Son at the Front*, which she did not publish until 1923. In 1919 she published a superficial study of French society, *French Ways and Their Meaning*. But the significant thread of self-discovery is to be found in none of these.

Wharton speaks of her own inability to settle down in *A Backward Glance:* "Before I could begin to deal objectively with the stored-up emotions of those [war] years, I had to get away from the present altogether; and though I began planning and brooding over 'A Son at the Front' in 1917 it was not finished until four years later. Meanwhile I found a momentary escape in going back to my childish memories of a long-vanished America, and wrote 'The Age of Innocence.' " [80] This novel—which many would claim is her best work—finally marks an end to the questing that was begun in *The Reef*. It is a novel of maturity—acceptance and not submission—and it signals Wharton's truce with the specters of childhood. However, before we can understand the terms of this truce, we must take a look at two unlikely intermediate works: the travel book *In Morocco* and the unpublished "Beatrice Palmato" fragment.

In Morocco has very much the mood of *Summer*, and it demonstrates Wharton's continuing fascination with the primitive. In 1917, while the war still raged, Wharton longed again to take off from Europe and cast herself into an exotic and remote land. Accordingly, in September of that year, accompanied by a suitable retinue of servants, Edith Wharton and her now (and forever more) most beloved friend Walter Berry set off for a several-month tour of Morocco. Were they lovers? We can never know. But this deep relationship, drawing together so many threads of a long-shared lifetime, was the closest thing that Wharton ever had to a happy marriage.

The journey must have provided Wharton with a delightful sense of contrast. After World War I was over, Morocco was opened to the vast tourist invasion that followed upon peace; however, during the war it was still relatively untouched by European or American incursions. Many parts of it had not been open to them at all until a year or two preceding Wharton's visit. It was, as she remarks wonderingly in the first sentence of *In Morocco*, "*a country without a guide-book*." [81] There they were, two relics of old New York cast into a still-barbarous and uncharted land. What would they discover?

The pilgrimage began in the cosmopolitan center of Tangiers, a city well known to European visitors and thus not very interesting to Wharton. She was eager to get under way—out into the wilderness, "the immense waste of fallow land and palmetto desert: an earth as void of life as the sky above it of clouds" (9). Soon after the beginning, an ominous event: the car broke down. "The heat is mortal at the moment. . . . All around is the featureless wild land, palmetto scrub streching away into eternity. . . . [Still] it is a good thing to begin with such a mishap, not only because it develops the fatalism necessary to the enjoyment of Africa, but because it lets one at once into the mysterious heart of the country: a country so deeply conditioned by its miles and miles of un-cities wilderness that until one has known the wilderness one cannot begin to understand the cities" (12–14). This is, perhaps, the key to Wharton's own journey: one has to know the wilderness to understand the cities.

Certainly it seemed a land on the very bourne of reality. Over and over again, Wharton remarks this sense. "The light had the preternatural purity which gives a foretaste of mirage: it was the light in which magic becomes ieal, and which helps to understand how, to people living in such an atmosphere, the boundary between fact and dream perpetually fluctuates. . . . Overripeness is indeed the characteristic of this rich and stagnant civilization. Buildings, people, customs, seem all about to crumble and fall of their own weight: the present is perpetually prolonged past. To touch the past with one's hands is realized only in dreams; and in Morocco the dream-feeling envelopes one at every step" (38–39, 85). One day in Fez, peering into the court of ablutions of El Kairouiyin, Wharton mused: "It is so closely guarded from below that from our secret coign of vantage we seemed to be looking down into the heart of forbidden things" (99). A Conradian thought, to be sure, but such were the associations that colored this trip for her. It was more than an interesting diversion; it was a trip into the primitive mind of man.

This primitivism manifested itself in violent blood ritual. One deceptively radiant afternoon, she came upon a sight rarely seen before by a Christian woman. "The beauty of the setting redeemed the bestial horror. In that unreal golden light the scene became merely symbolical: it was like one of those strange animal masks which the Middle Ages brought down from antiquity" (53). At one end of the public square, a group of musicians on a stone platform; below them, dancers; in the center, a creature with black ringlets whirling about on his axis, his cheek-muscles twitching convulsively. "The dancers were all dressed in white caftans or in the blue shirts of the lowest classes. In the sunlight something that looked like fresh red paint glistened on their shaved black or yellow skulls and made dark blotches on their garments. At first these stripes and stains suggested only a gaudy ritual ornament like the pattern on the drums; then one saw that the paint, or whatever it was, kept dripping down from the whirling caftans and forming fresh pools among the stones; that as one of the pools dried up another formed, redder and more glistening, and that these pools were fed from great gashes which the dancers hacked in their own skulls and breasts with hatchets and sharpened stones. The dance was a blood-rite, a great sacrificial symbol, in which blood flowed so freely that all the rocking feet were splashed with it" (54–55). Mutilation, blood, death—these capture one aspect of man's nature that layers of European culture had merely covered over. They were erupting in a world war even as Wharton saw them here in their native state; and this eerie fact of double violence merely served to confirm the eternal insistence of man's uncivilized self.

More prevalent than violence was the air of sensuous indulgence. This, too, was part of the hidden heart of things—often literally hidden, for the opulent quarters in which the harem was housed could usually be reached only through a labyrinth of passages and dusky stairways. In Marrakech, the European Resident General had taken over the palace of the Grand Vizier, and Edith Wharton found herself lodged in the apartment of the Grand Vizier's Favorite. "This lovely prison, from which all sight and sound of the outer world are excluded, is built about an atrium paved with disks of turquoise and black and white. . . . On each side of the atrium are long recessed rooms closed by vermilion doors painted with gold arabesques and vases of spring flowers; and into these shadowy inner rooms, spread with rugs and divans and soft pillows, no light comes except when their doors are opened into the atrium" (131). In other cities, she was allowed to visit the women's apartments and converse (through an interpretress) with "the Sultan's 'favorites,' round-faced apricot-tinted girls in their teens, with high cheek-bones, full red lips, surprised brown eyes between curved-up Asiatic lids, and little brown hands fluttering out like birds from their brocaded sleeves" (173). The atmosphere is cloying and claustral; sexuality hangs like heavy incense upon the air.

Most insidious of all was the effect upon the children. "Ignorance, unhealthiness and a precocious sexual initiation prevail in all classes. Education consists in learning by heart endless passages of the Koran, and amusement in assisting at spectacles that would be unintelligible to western children, but that the pleasantries of the harem make perfectly comprehensible to Moroccan infancy. At eight or nine the little girls are married, at twelve the son of the house is 'given his first negress'; and thereafter, in the rich and leisured class, both sexes live till old age in an atmosphere of sensuality without seduction" (194–95).

Wharton returned from this excursion towards the end of 1917, and a year later began putting her notes in order for publication (they appeared serially in *Scribner's Magazine* from July through October of 1919 and in book form in 1920). During this time or somewhat later, she began to make the first plot outlines of a novel about the New York of her own girlhood. Tentatively entitled "Old New York," in 1919 it was rechristened *The Age of Innocence*. The work is strangely but unmistakably influenced by the Moroccan adventure: there is an acute awareness of the barbarism, taboos, and ritual sacrifice that lie just beneath the surface of even this apparently bland society; she had been reading *The Golden Bough* as background for the trip to Africa, and her insight into the complexities of the cult of Diana emerges subtly in the work as well.

But the surprising missing link between *In Morocco* and *The Age of Inocence*—between *The Age of Innocence* and *Summer* (the major novel that immediately preceded it) can be found in the outline of a projected short story entitled "Beatrice Palmato" and an "unpublishable" fragment of it, both of which were written sometime in 1919.[82] The very name "Palmato" carries whispers of the burning desert wind; and the incestuous subject of the piece echoes the horrified observation of that "precocious sexual initiation" that Wharton had observed as prevalent throughout Moroccan life. Even the characters carry exotic hints of the lands beyond the Mediterranean—for the father, Mr. Palmato, is half Levantine. Furthermore, one might quite justifiably assert a linear relationship from this fragment, through the Moroccan essays, back to the marriage between Charity Royall and her foster father. However, the piece becomes most important when we consider it in terms of the problem that remained for Wharton to resolve in her own voyage back "for good" to the heritage of old New York, the problem of understanding the repressive quality of that society. The "Beatrice" fragment allows us to comprehend the function of such repression, in society as a whole and in the particular life of the little girl who had been paralyzed by it for so many years.

"Beatrice Palmato" was evidently designed as a kind of ghost story; a cover sheet reads:

POWERS OF DARKNESS—

———

Vol. of Short Stories.
I. Beatrice Palmato [83]

And it becomes a good deal easier to understand the strange contents of the story and the peculiar combination of documents that make up the fragment if we realize that Wharton herself conceived the work as belonging to the same genre as her supernatural tales.

Virtually all of Wharton's ghost stories focus on one of two themes. The first is the problem of the spectral double—a secret self or alter-ego who is the reflection of some evil or forbidden impulse in the individual who is haunted.[84] The second has to do with a jealous love triangle, and in these the ghostly confrontation has explicitly to do with romantic competition: there is a married couple, and there is a rival—an intruder, an interloper.[85] "Beatrice Palmato" seems clearly to belong to this second group; however, it has tentacles that reach into the first group as well.

Actually, it is strange that Edith Wharton should ever have written ghost stories at all, for when she was an adolescent, they inspired a deathly, choking terror in her. Dating from the beginning of her extended period of trepidation on the threshold, there was a lesser, accompanying phobia having to do with ghost stories. "With my intense Celtic sense of the supernatural, tales of robbers and ghosts were perilous reading," she recalls in "Life and I." "How long the traces of my illness lasted may be judged from the fact that, till I was twenty-seven or eight, I could not sleep in the room with a book containing a ghost-story, and that I have frequently had to burn books of this kind, because it frightened me to know that they were downstairs in the library!" [86] Of what was she so excruciatingly terrified? The fact that she links "ghost stories" and "robber stories" suggests that the fear had to do with her immensely powerful feelings of affection for her father and with the complex set of associations that danced menacingly "on the threshold." Whatever the source, there is no doubting the fear.

Late in her life, Wharton wrote a short essay on ghost stories, and she asserts (now in her capacity as creator and controller, not reader and victim): " 'Do you believe in ghosts?' is the pointless question often addressed by those who are incapable of feeling ghostly influences. . . . The celebrated reply (I forget whose): 'No, I don't believe in ghosts, but I'm afraid of them,' is much more than the cheap paradox it seems to many. To 'believe,' in that sense, is a conscious act of the intellect, and it is in the warm darkness of the prenatal fluid far below our conscious reason that the faculty dwells with which we apprehend the ghosts we may not be endowed with the gift of seeing. . . . The only suggestion I can make is that the teller of supernatural tales should be well frightened in the telling; for if he is, he may perhaps communicate to his readers the sense of that strange something undreamt of in the philosophy of Horatio." [87]

The "Beatrice Palmato" fragment consists of three parts: the cover sheet (cited above), a summary of a projected short story, and a piece of fiction entitled (in Wharton's own hand) "unpublishable fragment of Beatrice Palmato." The summary and the fiction are reprinted below.[88]

BEATRICE PALMATO
(plot summary)

Beatrice Palmato is the daughter of a rich half-Levantine, half-Portuguese banker living in London, and of his English wife. Palmato, who is very handsome, cultivated and accomplished, has inherited his father's banking and brokering business, but, while leaving his fortune in the business, leads the life of a rich and cultivated man of leisure. He has an agreeable artistic-literary house in London, and a place near Brighton. The wife is handsome, shy, silent, but agreeable. There are two daughters and a son, the youngest. The eldest, Isa, who looks like her mother, commits suicide in mysterious circumstances at seventeen, a few months after returning from the French convent in which she has been educated. The mother has a bad nervous break-down, and is ordered away by the doctors, who forbid her to take little Beatrice (aged 12) with her. After a vain struggle, she leaves the child in the country with an old governess who has brought her up, and whom she can completely trust. The governess is ill, and is obliged to leave, and Beatrice remains in the country with her father. He looks for another governess, but cannot find one to suit him, and during a whole winter takes charge of Beatrice's education. She is a musical and artistic child, full of intellectual curiosity, and at the same time very tender and emotional: a combination of both parents. The boy, whom Mrs. Palmato adores, and whom her husband has never cared for, is a sturdy sensitive English lad. He is at school, and spends his holidays with his tutor. Mrs. Palmato is still abroad, in a sanitorium. The following autumn (after a year's absence) she comes home. At first she seems better, and they return to London, and see a few friends. Beatrice remains with them, as neither parent can bear to be separated from her. They find a charming young governess, and all seems well.

Then suddenly Mrs. Palmato has another nervous break-down, and grows quite mad. She tries to kill her husband, has to be shut up, and dies in an insane asylum a few months later. The boy is left at school, and Mr. Palmato, utterly shattered, leaves on a long journey with Beatrice and a new maid, whom he engages for her in Paris. After six months he returns, and re-engages the same governess. Eighteen months after his wife's death he marries the governess, who is a young girl of good family, good-looking and agreeable, and to whom Beatrice is devoted.

The intimacy between father and daughter continues to be very close, but at 18 Beatrice meets a young man of good family, a good-looking rather simple-minded country squire with a large property and no artistic or intellectual tastes, who falls deeply in love with her.

She marries him, to every one's surprise, and they live entirely in the country. For some time she does not see her father or the latter's wife; then she and her husband go up to town to stay for a fortnight with the Palmatos, and after that they see each other, though at rather long intervals. Beatrice seems to her friends changed, depressed, overclouded. Her animation and brilliancy have vanished, and she gives up all her artistic interests, and appears to absorb herself in her husband's country tastes. The Palmato group of friends all deplore her having married such a dull man, but admit that he is very kind to her and that she seems happy. Once her father takes her with him on a short trip to Paris, where he goes to buy a picture or some tapestries for his collection, and she comes back brilliant, febrile and restless; but soon settles down again. After 2½ years of marriage she has a boy, and the year after a little girl; and with the birth of her children her attachment to her husband increases, and she seems to her friends perfectly happy. About the time of the birth of the second child, Palmato dies suddenly.

The boy is like his father, the little girl exquisite, gay, original, brilliant, like her mother. The father loves both children, but adores the little girl; and as the latter grows to be five or six years old Beatrice begins to manifest a morbid jealousy of her husband's affection for this child. The household has been so harmonious hitherto that the husband himself cannot understand this state of mind; but he humours his wife, tries to conceal his fondness for his little daughter, and wonders whether his wife is growing "queer" like her mother.

One day the husband has been away for a week. He returns sooner than was expected, comes in and finds the little girl alone in the drawing-room. She utters a cry of joy, and he clasps her in his arms and kisses her. She has put her little arms around his neck, and is hugging him tightly when Beatrice comes in. She stops on the threshold, screams out: "Don't kiss my child. Put her down! How dare you kiss her?" and snatches the little girl from his arms.

Husband and wife stand staring at each other. As the husband looks at her, many mysterious things in their married life—the sense of some hidden power controlling her, and perpetually coming between them, and of some strange initiation, some profound moral perversion of which he had always been afraid to face the thought—all these things become suddenly clear to him, lit up in a glare of horror.

He looks at her with his honest eyes, and says: "Why shouldn't I kiss my child?" and she gives him back a look in which terror, humiliation, remorseful tenderness, and the awful realization of what she has unwittingly betrayed, mingle in one supreme appeal and avowal.

She puts the little girl down, flies from the room, and hurries upstairs. When he follows her, he hears a pistol-shot and finds her lying dead on the floor of her bedroom.

People say: "Her mother was insane, her sister tried to kill herself; it was a very unfortunate marriage."

But the brother, Jack Palmato, who has become a wise, level-headed young man, a great friend of Beatrice's husband, comes down on hearing of his sister's death, and he and the husband have a long talk together—about Mr. Palmato.

The End

UNPUBLISHABLE FRAGMENT

"I have been, you see," he added gently, "so perfectly patient—"

The room was warm, and softly lit by one or two pink-shaded lamps. A little fire sparkled on the hearth, and a lustrous black bear-skin rug, on which a few purple velvet cushions had been flung, was spread out before it.

"And now, darling," Mr. Palmato said, drawing her to the deep divan, "let me show you what only you and I have the right to show each other." He caught her wrists as he spoke, and looking straight into her eyes, repeated in a penetrating whisper: "Only you and I." But his touch had never been tenderer. Already she felt every fibre vibrating under it, as of old, only now with the more passionate eagerness bred of privation, and of the dull misery of her marriage. She let herself sink backward among the pillows, and already Mr. Palmato was on his knees at her side, his face close to hers. Again her burning lips were parted by his tongue, and she felt it insinuate itself between her teeth, and plunge into the depths of her mouth in a long searching caress, while at the same moment his hands softly parted the thin folds of her wrapper.

One by one they gained her bosom, and she felt her two breasts pointing up to them, the nipples as hard as coral, but sensitive as lips to his approaching touch. And now his warm palms were holding each breast as in a cup, clasping it, modelling it, softly kneading it, as he whispered to her, "like the bread of the angels."

An instant more, and his tongue had left her fainting mouth, and was twisting like a soft pink snake about each breast in turn, passing from one to the other till his lips closed hard on the nipples, sucking them with a tender gluttony.

Then suddenly he drew back her wrapper entirely, whispered: "I want you all, so that my eyes can see all that my lips can't cover," and in a moment she was free, lying before him in her fresh young nakedness, and feeling that indeed his eyes were covering it with fiery kisses. But Mr. Palmato was never idle, and while this sensation flashed through her one of his arms had slipped under her back and wound itself around her so that his hand again enclosed her left breast. At the same moment the other hand softly separated her legs, and began to slip up the old path it had so often travelled in darkness. But now it was light, she was uncovered, and looking downward, beyond his dark silver-sprinkled head, she could see her own parted knees and outstretched ankles and feet. Suddenly she remembered Austin's rough advances, and shuddered.

The mounting hand paused, the dark head was instantly raised. "What is it, my own?"

"I was—remembering—last week—" she faltered, below her breath.

"Yes, darling. That experience is a cruel one—but it has to come once in all women's lives. Now we shall reap its fruit."

But she hardly heard him, for the old swooning sweetness was creeping over her. As his hand stole higher she felt the secret bud of her body swelling, yearning, quivering hotly to burst into bloom. Ah, here was his subtle fore-finger pressing it, forcing its tight petals softly apart, and laying on their sensitive edges a circular touch so soft and yet so fiery that already lightnings of heat shot from that palpitating centre all over her surrendered body, to the tips of her fingers, and the ends of her loosened hair.

The sensation was so exquisite that she could have asked to have it indefinitely prolonged; but suddenly his head bent lower, and with a deeper thrill she felt his lips pressed upon that quivering invisible bud, and then the delicate firm thrust of his tongue, so full and yet so infinitely subtle, pressing apart the close petals, and forcing itself in deeper and deeper through the passage that glowed and seemed to become illuminated at its approach . . .

"Ah—" she gasped, pressing her hands against her sharp nipples, and flinging her legs apart.

Instantly one of her hands was caught, and while Mr. Palmato, rising, bent over her, his lips on hers again, she felt his firm fingers pressing into her hand that strong fiery muscle that they used, in their old joke, to call his third hand.

"My little girl," he breathed, sinking down beside her, his muscular trunk bare, and the third hand quivering and thrusting upward between them, a drop of moisture pearling at its tip.

She instantly understood the reminder that his words conveyed, letting herself downward along the divan till her head was in a line with his middle she flung herself upon the swelling member, and began to caress it insinuatingly with her tongue. It was the first time she had ever seen it actually exposed to her eyes, and her heart swelled excitedly: to have her touch confirmed by sight enriched the sensation that was communicating itself through her ardent twisting tongue. With panting breath she wound her caress deeper and deeper into the thick firm folds, till at length the member, thrusting her lips open, held her gasping, as if at its mercy; then, in a trice, it was withdrawn, her knees were pressed apart, and she saw it before her, above her, like a crimson flash, and at last, sinking backward into new abysses of bliss, felt it descend on her, press open the secret gates, and plunge into the deepest depths of her thirsting body . . .

"Was it . . . like this . . . last week?" he whispered.

Perhaps the most important thing to bear in mind in any discussion of such a provocative piece is that it is *fiction*—a fact hardly worth noting but still essential. Suggestive as the piece is, it justifies no certainty of inference about Edith Wharton's own love-making; certainly it tells us absolutely nothing about the relationship between Edith as a little girl and her rather stodgy father. (If anything at all, it provides only an aperçu into the wellsprings of the girl's fantasy life.) What this fragment does present is a rather striking insight into the way Edith Wharton *conceptualized* love and sexuality; and since we are engaged in studying the evolution of her fiction, that is our principal concern in any case.

If we read the fragment with *Summer* in mind, it is impossible to miss the verbal echoes. Both render passion in an exquisite emanation of the language of heat, and both hint subtly of the emergence of a primitive animal self. Given Wharton's lifelong habits of representation, neither of these facts is surprising. More than this, however, particular phrases in the "Beatrice" piece seem directly related to the earlier novel: Beatrice sensing "the secret bud of her body swelling, yearning, quivering hotly to burst into bloom" is a rather franker presentation of the nascent genital sexuality in Charity, who shares "all this bubbling of sap and slipping of sheaths and bursting of calyxes. . . . All were merged in a moist earth-smell that was like the breath of some huge sun-warmed animal." The "strong fiery muscle" that is Palmato's "third hand" recalls Charity's phallic vision of Lucius' throat—"the root of the muscles where they joined the chest." Palmato's manipulation of the vulva, "a circular touch so soft and yet so fiery that already lightnings of heat shot from that palpitating centre all over her surrendered body, to the tips of her fingers, and the ends of her loosened hair," recapitulates Charity's fantasy "if Harney should take her in his arms: the melting of palm into palm and mouth on mouth, and the long flame burning her from head to foot." In both fictions, the climactic penetration is anticipated by a symbolic penetration of eyes: in *Summer*, "his impetuous eyes were in hers, and she could feel the hard beat of his heart as he held her against it"; in "Beatrice," "he spoke, and looking straight into her eyes, repeated in a penetrating whisper: 'Only you and I.' " Yet, most striking of all: the most genuinely erotic novel that Wharton ever published concludes with a young girl marrying her "father"; the one piece of explicitly sexual fiction that she left is a description of an incestuous relationship between father and daughter.

We might infer from the existence of the fragment—and from the fictional use to which Wharton evidently intended to put it—that the powerful element of incestuous romance in *Summer* had not escaped her attention.

The incest motif per se does not figure prominently in *Summer;* it is not a "bad" thing that Charity eventually marries lawyer Royall. Quite the contrary. Yet the truth is that both the first sexual encounter (on the threshold of Charity's bedroom) and the sexual conclusion (when Charity reenters Royall's house as his wife) are essentially incestuous: when Wharton sought, in that novel, to capture sexuality, her method of representing it was to depict a liaison between daughter and father-figure. That is the most significant fact. Instinctively, perhaps—unthinkingly (since the violated taboo is never brought to the surface of the novel and condemned)—Wharton has plunged back to her own crisis of the threshold once again, now to resurrect not the chilling, immobilizing, regressive passivity and dependence on Mother that had served as the basis for the horror in *Ethan Frome*, but its converse. The longing from which the girl had run—against which she had deployed regression as a defense—is a flaming, consuming love for the father, a fear of penetration that is inextricable from a desperate yearning for it.[89] This, too, is implicit in that complex phobia of the threshold; and this, too, is a kind of horror. In some sense (to the extent that the incestuous relationship is deployed unself-consciously in *Summer*), Wharton as author was at the mercy of her own past in that novel. In the "Beatrice Palmato" fragment, she is not.

For here, the incest *is* the horror. This was to have been a ghost story, we must remember (Beatrice haunted—possessed—by the insistent specter of her mother's suicide and by the familial history of perversion and insanity). How do you write a convincing tale of the supernatural? Wharton herself gives the answer: the teller should be well frightened in the telling. Now if we look at the fragment and compare it with the outline of the projected story, we discover that there is no place in the story where the fragment might have appeared: it was—could only have been—the suppressed horror that lay *behind* the action of the tale and made it understandable. And the most striking thing of all is that this "horror" is in *no way* abhorrent. It is a glowing, glorious, satisfying experience. Not sadistic, not shaming: a delightful erotic fantasy, if you will. And therein lies its real terror.

Incest, as Edith Wharton renders it, is irresistibly attractive.*

* How eerily the accounts of Wharton's life come into balance. Reflect for a moment that in *A Backward Glance* she went back to the first episode that she could remember—a walk that she took with her father when she was almost four years old. And what does she recollect *mainly* about that walk? The little girl's hand which lay "in the large safe hollow of her father's bare hand; her tall handsome father, who was so warm-blooded that in the coldest weather he always went out without gloves." And, of course, a kiss from a little boy whom they met while out walking. Palmato's organ is construed as his "third hand"—bare now for the first time to his daughter's passionate gaze. It is unlikely that Wharton herself made the connection consciously; but we can venture with some certainty that the little girl attached more than casual phallic significance to the warm, bare hand that held hers. What is more, the sensation must have stimulated her excessively (for she went to such phobic lengths to repress it) and persisted in her imagination—coloring many subsequent fantasies of sexuality. Charity Royall, for instance, attaches phallic significance to Lucius Harney's strong fingers—and the very name "Palmato" suggests the jest of the "third hand." When the core fantasy emerges, it bears these unmistakable signs of its origin.

Of course, in the story itself, the outcome was to have been cata-strophic: madness and death—inevitable punishment (imposed by the author) for this violation of social strictures. Nevertheless, it remains the case that the scene between Beatrice and her father becomes repellent only when society's customs and injunctions are invoked; and perhaps strangest of all, what prevents us from seeing the tale as a general dem-onstration of inevitable "natural" justice is that the author inflicts punish-ment only upon the women. The mother, the older sister, Beatrice her-self. The father, who is seen in this tale as the ultimate source of evil and perversion, dies a peaceful and not untimely death. This more than any-thing else—more even than the fact that the sexual encounter is told in terms of the woman's physical sensations—suggests how entirely "femi-nine" the narrative vantage is. It is a fiction that combines an exquisite rendering of a woman's sexual sensibility with an equally powerful ex-pression of a woman's sense of guilt: the first of these was consciously in-tended; the second less consciously so.

Again it is a matter of fictional decision: it was Wharton's story; she could have chosen to manipulate the plot in any way, and she chose to "punish" the women. Almost certainly she did not bring any of the implications of this decision to conscious level. As she says herself, the process of story-telling "takes place in some secret region on the sheer edge of consciousness," and the impact of ghost stories in particular is felt "in the warm darkness of the prenatal fluid far below our conscious reason." Yet we must not thereby suppose that the decision was without intent. It was certainly deliberate—the violent authorial retaliation for behavior that offends our sense of "decency"—retaliation that has be-come necessary because the usual mechanisms of repression have failed.

Thus we return to the problem of repression, the last puzzle that Wharton had to solve before understanding the mosaic of her childhood and accepting its heritage, the penultimate stage in the journey she had embarked on when she set out in *The Reef* to "place" sexuality. Why must society be repressive? Because at the very core of social organization, within the innermost circle of the family itself, there lurks such attractive temptation. Repression is necessary both because the temptation is there and, more important, *because it is so attractive.* (We need not, after all, submit ourselves to painful denial if the impulses that must be checked are ones whose consequences are sufficient to deter us anyway!) The more tempting and powerful the attraction of the forbidden action, the more vigorous repression must be. In the New York of Wharton's girl-hood, social custom tended toward excessive strictness: all emotion was officially frowned upon, not merely those emotions that are almost universally tabooed. Yet as Wharton matured and grew more sophisticated, she noticed that no social system manages to sustain a perfect balance between repression and indulgence; and she seems also to have concluded that deviation in the direction of repression is not necessarily worse than excess in the opposite direction. The Moroccan trip was enlightening. The most persistent image that Wharton carried away from that voyage was the recurrent face of unnatural initiation—a slave girl of seven or eight with her "grave and precocious little face. . . . And behind the sad child leaning in the archway stood all the shadowy evils of the social system that hangs like a millstone about the neck of Islam." [90]

This is not to say that old New York grew benevolent in her eyes; it did not. It *was* a pinched and cold and suffocating world; but it was, nevertheless, a world that could be coped with, could even produce good. After all, Edith Jones Wharton's experience of it may not have been entirely typical. (At some level she began to comprehend this fact.) Old New York may have been exceptionally repressive, but the little girl whose yearning for affection was so great that it fixed upon her father with voracious and terrifying intensity was probably much more than usually susceptible to the repressive influences about her. In considering her childhood we have noted as much: over and over again, when other children, less frightened children, discovered ingenious ways to mitigate the effects of this arid emotional climate, Edith did not. Even with the example of a mother who had braved the rigors of disapproving parents and entered upon an engagement during secret dawn meetings with her beloved—even with *this* heritage, Edith chose to become the perfect model of propriety and "niceness." Partly she did so because Lucretia was an unsympathetic and harsh woman. However, even more of her motivation in this regard came from within. She embraced old New York's customs of repression because they helped to support her resistance against the clamoring of unsuitable internal emotions. Indeed, the fantasy of forbidden intimacy was so appealing that she added a full complement of rigid, idiosyncratic private phobias to reenforce the usual prohibitions.

Perhaps old New York was really not so bad as it had once seemed to the child whose personal problems had encouraged her to emphasize its worst elements. Certainly it had given her the most precious gifts of all, the beautiful instrument of her language and a set of traditions that informed her thoughts with meaning. Order. Ultimately the capacity to give precise expression to her deepest emotions. The New York of Wharton's childhood would remain imperfect in her judgment of it, less nearly perfect than many other worlds. It would always be remembered as a world that gave little encouragement to its most promising individuals. Yet it had its values, not negligible values. Someone else, someone without the crippling private difficulties of an Edith Wharton, might turn these values into public benefit.

Thus it was, after all, a world to which one might return "for good." Such is the message implicit in her portrait of Newland Archer, a man who manages to preserve his sense of larger meanings and who finally understands life to be made up of many things past and to come, "of renunciation as well as satisfaction, of traditions as well as experiments, of dying as much as of living." [91]

That vastly imperfect story, "The Letters," had been an assertion of coming to terms with the Fullerton affair; yet the story's precipitate closure had militated against acceptance of the truth that Wharton so obviously wished the reader to accept. The truth of a "love that can bear the stress of life." Now in *The Age of Innocence*, we are introduced by slow degrees to such a love, and now we can comprehend what it entails. Sexual intensities are not ignored—merely "placed"; the limitations of old New York are deplored—but now with even humor and not bitter, biting satire. In less than a decade, Edith Wharton has returned to the problem that she had set for herself in *The Reef*—the problem of sexuality in *all* of its complexity. This time, she has finally resolved it to her own satisfaction.

9

Writing *The Age of Innocence* was a nostalgic act: "I showed it chapter by chapter to Walter Berry," Wharton recollects.[92] Like old times at the very beginning—like composing *The Decoration of Houses* under his keenly critical eye. But so many years had passed; the war was over, and things would never really be the same again. Although she still had Walter Berry, others were gone. Dear comrades of the heady wartime days had died: Ronald Simmons, for instance, a young American of whom she had become terribly fond, had perished in 1918; Newbold Rhinelander (from the younger generation on her mother's side of the family) had been shot down over Germany in September of 1918. Vigorous and vital men losing their lives—it wrenched her heart. Even worse, however, was the fragmenting away of that tight group of old friends who had stood in place of a family for so long in her life. Howard Sturgis died peacefully in his sleep in the first month of 1920. And worst of all, in 1916 she had lost Henry James. She didn't even have the chance to bid him good-by, for they had been separated by that raging holocaust of the war. "Yes,—all my 'blue distances' will be shut out forever when he goes," she wrote Gaillard Lapsley in 1915 as James's illness grew worse. "His friendship has been the pride and honour of my life. Plus ne m'est rien after such a gift as that—except the memory of it." [93] Ready at last to come back "for good"—only to have lost so many of those who might meaningfully share the journey with her. She was entirely conscious of the scope of the privation. In 1920, Henry James was still on her mind. Again, she wrote to Gaillard Lapsley in anguish. "My longing to talk with you about Henry is getting *maladive*. No one can *really understand* but you and me—to the extent to which we understand—so four-dimensionally." [94]

Thus she found herself very much in the midst of her memories of James while she was engrossed with *The Age of Innocence*. She and Edmund Gosse had become involved in extensive and complicated negotiations with James's family over the editing of his letters in 1920. Wharton's and Gosse's candidate to supervise the work was James's young friend, Percy Lubbock, but Mrs. William James so thoroughly detested Edith Wharton that negotiations had to be carried out with appalling subterfuge. Wharton, therefore, was forced to hold herself uncomfortably aloof from the memorial proceedings. Nevertheless, she was an inventive woman. She was making a spiritual pilgrimage home, and she was going to take her old friend Henry James with her. Why not? He "belonged irrevocably to the old America out of which I also came." He had spent his entire adult life as a European exile, even adopting British citizenship in the last year of his life (which Wharton deplored). They had shared the writing of fiction; they had shared countless hours of fun, that quality so impossible to preserve in a written biography—"the quality . . . of sheer abstract 'fooling'—that was the delicious surprise of his talk. . . . From many of the letters to his most intimate group [letters that Wharton was helping to edit in 1920] it was necessary to excise long passages of chaff, and recurring references to old heaped-up pyramidal jokes, huge cairns of hoarded nonsense." [95] Now, for the last time, the Angel of Devastation would swoop down and carry him off again with her. They would go back "for good" together.

The Age of Innocence had many meanings for Edith Wharton. It borrows more extensively from the ambiance of her childhood world than any other novel she published; [96] and it is explicitly called to the reader's attention that Newland Archer is fifty-seven at the conclusion of the novel, Wharton's own age in 1919 when she began writing it. Yet perhaps the central meaning grows out of the complex way in which the novel beckons to Wharton's dearest friend, Henry James.

The communication begins, most fittingly, with a complicated joke: *The Age of Innocence* is the title of a well-known portrait by Reynolds which hangs in the National Gallery; it is the portrait of a lady—a very young lady, to be sure, a little girl in fact. Nevertheless, the reference converts Wharton's title into a private pun. James's novel *The Portrait of a Lady* was Wharton's favorite among his many books (the only one ever to appear on her list of "favorite books"). In the name of her own novel, Wharton announces the antiphonal relationship between her work and James's in the way that *he* would have understood best. There is no mistaking her intention, for at the same time that she converted the working title of "Old New York" into "The Age of Innocence," she also changed the name of her hero to "Newland" Archer, an American who elects to remain at home in the New World only to have Old World temptations and knowledge come to him. That Newland Archer is intended as a parallel to Isabel Archer is further emphasized by Ned Wimsatt's remark to him: " 'You're like the pictures on the walls of a deserted house: "The Portrait of a Gentleman." ' " [97]

These resemblances are merely verbal plays, casual allusions meant to convey deeper connections between Wharton's work and James's. Wharton intended neither parody nor one-to-one borrowing: Newland is not Isabel's exact counterpart—nor is Ellen, though Ellen's marriage and her tragic knowledge certainly do recall Isabel's. Rather, Wharton used these allusions to James much as eighteenth-century satirists used references to classical epics as a way of conveying a sense of moral seriousness and a similarity of concern. If "The Age of Innocence" describes the stable pre–World War I society of old New York to which Wharton was making a private pilgrimage, it also describes a prelapsarian state. Thus while James explores the notion of a "fortunate fall" in *The Portrait of a Lady*, in *The Age of Innocence* Wharton examines the value of choosing not to be corrupted. Moreover, Wharton and James focus their intense moral scrutiny on similar concerns, particularly the problem of the right to individual "freedom" as measured against the binding sanctity of the commitment to the institution of marriage.

In the end, however, Wharton's novel is a balancing companion piece to James's; for while James is interested in exploring the world an American Puritan might discover by moving away from New World prejudices, Wharton's thrust is in the opposite direction, back into the shaping culture in which her American hero was born. Implicit in the imperative to come back "for good" is a notion of maturity very similar to the one that Erik Erikson has articulated for our generation: the full development of self is "a process 'located' *in the core of the individual* and yet also *in the core of his communal culture*, a process which establishes, in fact, the identity of those two identities." [98] Wharton, a self-conscious product of the old New York she recreates, had finally come to realize that the children of that time and place must forever bear its mark, cherish its values, and suffer in some degree its inadequacies. Growth, then, must proceed from an understanding of one's background—a coming to terms with one's past, not a flight from it.

The persuasiveness of Wharton's view is nowhere more powerfully rendered than in her handling of tradition. Wharton had accepted what Charity Royall and Newland Archer were to learn: that "each human life begins at a given evolutionary stage and level of tradition, bringing to its environment a capital of patterns and energies; these are used to grow on, and to grow into the social process with, and also as contributions to this process. Each new being is received into a style of life prepared by tradition and held together by tradition, and at the same time disintegrating because of the very nature of tradition. We say that tradition 'molds' the individual, 'channels' his drives. But the social process does not mold a new being merely to housebreak him; it molds generations in order to be remolded, to be reinvigorated by them." [99] The growth of any society depends upon the growth of the individuals who comprise it. Thus, since social change is inevitably tied to the individual struggle to achieve maturity, social change is, ironically, always rooted in the past;

no man can achieve maturity until he has accepted the particular conventions and traditions that have shaped him. If he wishes to alter these conventions and traditions, he can do so *only* by drawing on the strengths of his heritage: he cannot choose his heritage, and he cannot repudiate it without repudiating himself; "an individual life is the accidental coincidence of but *one* life cycle with but *one* segment of history." [100]

The particular traditions of old New York threaten to obscure the reader's vision, even as they threaten to suffocate the hero in *The Age of Innocence.* The crowded collage of drawing rooms and Worth gowns and opera evenings and Newport outings all evoke a compelling illusion of "place," and Wharton's eye for detail is seductive.[101] Yet to focus on place as extrinsic to character is, in the end, to miss the point of the novel. Wharton's narrative vantage is carefully chosen (it is similar to James's in *Portrait of a Lady* and even more like Austen's in *Emma*): the narrator may step outside of Newland Archer's mind to make judgments or draw conclusions; but when we see old New York, we almost always see it through his eyes. The world that seems at first a novelistic tour de force becomes, on closer examination, a mirror of Newland's mind and the very condition of his being. This is his "one segment of history"; these are the traditions that have "molded" him and "channeled his drives." The center of this novel is Newland's problem of being and becoming, given the unalterable traditions of this portion of history, this "place."

The Age of Innocence is Wharton's most significant *bildungsroman* (surpassing even *Summer*). In it she traces Archer's struggle to mature, to become in some continuous and authentic way—himself. She lays before us the present and the possible in such a way that the middle-aged man who concludes the novel seems an admirable and significant outgrowth of the untried youth at the beginning. Her profound acceptance of the kind of limitation described by Erikson is mirrored in the creative use to which she puts the *bildungsroman* tradition; her master was Goethe, whose works she was once again rereading in this postwar period. The theme of *The Age of Innocence* might be captured in the most famous line of *Wilhelm Meister:* "*Here or nowhere is America!*"

Newland Archer does have choices, but they have been limited by the nature of his one portion of history. Thus while Wilhelm's search (and that of most *bildungshelden*) is pursued in a journey, Newland's search is entirely internal. He cannot flee the provincial world of old New York; he must learn to transmute it into something valuable. Newland perceives himself as alienated and without vocation; his ordeal by love teaches him the lessons that Wilhelm learned—acceptance of reality and dedication to generativity. In this novel, the ultimate place is the little rock cottage at Skuytercliff: that home stands for the values that will endure—values of family and honor. Newland is here when he decides not to become involved with Ellen, and later he spends his wedding night with May here. It is not a lofty dwelling—narrow, unaesthetic, almost primitive—it scarcely answers the visions of a romantic adolescent. Yet it is such a place as this that Newland must "find."

The journey is not an easy one. Our first glimpse of him tells us that like Ralph Marvell he is, perhaps by inclination, perhaps by training, an onlooker—indeed, but one in a society that trains its young people to be no more than onlookers, members of an audience that stands to the side of life's great struggles and does not participate in them. To meet him as he prepares to watch a production of *Faust* is consummately, ironically appropriate.[102] Having no occupation sufficient to his energies, Newland has turned them to fantasy: "He was at heart a dilettante, and thinking over a pleasure to come often gave him a subtler satisfaction than its realization. This was especially the case when the pleasure was a delicate one" (2). There is a dangerous vitality in this inner life; his considerable passion, finding no satisfactory outlet, has been sublimated into extraordinary palpable fantasies (old New York gave men like Newland little else to do with their passions).

Unknown to Newland, however, the fantasies that have been nourished by the rich passional needs channeled into them slip quietly back into his perceptions of the actual world, distorting these perceptions and deluding his expectations. " 'We'll read *Faust* together . . . by the Italian lakes,' he thought, somewhat hazily confusing the scene of his projected honeymoon with the masterpieces of literature which it would be his manly privilege to reveal to his bride. . . . If he had probed to the bottom of his vanity (as he sometimes nearly did) he would have found there the wish that his wife should be as worldly-wise and as eager to please as the married lady whose charms had held his fancy through two mildly agitated years; without, of course, any hint of the frailty which had so nearly marred that unhappy being's life, and had disarranged his own plans for a whole winter. How this miracle of fire and ice was to be created, and to sustain itself in a harsh world, he had never taken the time to think out" (5).

Archer's naiveté about the configuration of his emotional life is coupled with an empty adherence to convention. With a little effort he might become a good man, for there is nothing vicious in his nature and much that is generous. However, never having examined the rules by which his society lives, his notion of "duty"—as in "the duty of using two silver-backed brushes with his monogram in blue enamel to part his hair" (3)—is a thing easily to be confounded with Larry Lefferts' notions of "form." His reading and his active imaginative life have brought other worlds and other customs to his attention; but his reflex for conformity has been too strongly developed to permit him easily to measure his own traditions against these others. "He had probably read more, thought more, and even seen a good deal more of the world, than any other man of the number . . . but grouped together they represented 'New York,' and the habit of masculine solidarity made him accept their doctrine on all the issues called moral. He instinctively felt that in this respect it would be troublesome—and also rather bad form—to strike out for himself" (6). Thus the life of his spirit is infused with only the vaguest apprehension of purpose. There is no self-consciousness in his virtue, and he cannot be said to be "moral" because his admirable acts are informed by no continuous inner sense of conscience.

When we first meet Newland, we may be most impressed by his deficiencies—the absence of available passion and the habit but not the substance of "correct" behavior. Yet these apparently empty places in Newland's life contain the possibility of change. His innate vigor has been shaped but not hardened by the traditions of his background; the final inclinations of his character have yet to be formed, and the eighteen months of the novel's principal duration comprise the period of that transformation. Newland is nearing the conclusion of his apprenticeship in old New York. His adolescence and young adulthood have been times for experiment, for casual alliances and intellectual curiosity. Marriage represents commitment, an irrevocable assumption of his adult roles and an affirmation of the society in which he lives. Newland is not prepared for this commitment, and the moment of the crisis is complicated by "the case of the Countess Olenska" (40).

Ellen is the catalyst that forces Newland's self-confrontation, for had she not appeared, he might have spent his whole life attaching his deepest emotions almost entirely to fantasy. Ellen offers him the opportunity to test his capacity to fulfill these fantasies. She draws forth his passion into a warm flesh-and-blood attachment, and she quickens his dormant emotional life. If he is ever to be the man he fancies he might become, he can be that man with Ellen Olenska. And yet, his reactions to her are deeply ambivalent.

It is typical of Newland's thinking that he should construe Ellen as a "case"; and this is of a piece with all those other habits of mind that push aside the ordinary complexities of actual human life for the grander sweep of the romantic imagination. He evaluates her exotic plight and her "foreign" appearance with nervous interest: her "pale and serious face appealed to his fancy as suited to the occasion and to her unhappy situation; but the way her dress (which had no tucker) sloped away from her thin shoulders shocked and troubled him" (12). Such a vision embodies the mystery of the unknown and represents all the world that lies beyond the familiar boundaries of Archer's experience. The "case" of a woman so intriguingly distressed appeals to his visionary sense, and his musings on her situation become fused in indefinable ways with his unutterable yearning for a larger realm of experience. Ironically, Ellen in person makes him uncomfortable (just as the fashionable nudity of her gown had unsettled his notions of propriety): her frankness, her wry sense of the absurd, and her easy assumption of intimacy all unbalance him. "Nothing could be in worst taste than misplaced flippancy" (15). Thus while the actual freedom of her manner is distasteful, the abstract "right" to "freedom" that her situation justifies is infinitely appealing to him.

Though Ellen's arrival has had the objective effect of hastening Newland's public commitment to May, it has at the same time made that commitment seem a sentence to death by asphyxiation. When Newland retreats to his study to sort out the various effects of Ellen's appearance, he finds that her case has "stirred up old settled convictions and set them drifting dangerously through his mind" (40). His image of Ellen balances conveniently and simplistically against an image of May as "the young girl who knew nothing and expected everything" (40); and the larger vistas of the twilight world from which Ellen has come diminish the appeal of a marriage that seems no more than "a dull association of material and social interests held together by ignorance on the one side and hypocrisy on the other" (41). Central to these images of the women in Archer's life is some picture of what he is to become himself. This scene in his study is but the first in a series of increasingly terrifying invocations of self; the future stretches before him, "and passing down its endless emptiness he saw the dwindling figure of a man to whom nothing was ever to happen" (228). In fearing acceptance into the "hieroglyphic world" of old New York, Archer really fears anonymity and personal insignificance.

Yet he is hindered more by his own habits of thought than by insufficiencies in the society around him, for his impatience with specific details and intractable actualities follows him in his quest for personal identity. Just as it is easier to deal with the "case" of Ellen than with Ellen herself, so it is easier to pursue an image of personal fulfillment that is uncomplicated by the details of everyday living. Throughout much of the novel Archer longs for a life that moves well beyond the charted realms of the familiar, a life of high emotional intensity and sustained moral and intellectual complexity. The kind of life he only hazily conjectures is a life that is, given the "harsh world" of human experience, available to only a very few; and Archer seems an unlikely candidate for the life that his imagination yearns toward.

Ironically, the danger that his life will be insignificant lies not so much in the probability that he will fail to fulfill these fantasies as in the more immediate possibility that, having failed to fulfill them, he will lack the capacity to give *any* aspect of his life authenticity. Not all things are possible for a man of Newland's time and place; some ways of life that are unavailable to him are, perhaps, better than any that are. But every real life involves compromises and relinquished hopes—even though some lives require more in the way of sacrifice than others. The problem that Newland faces without fully comprehending it is that his desire to create an ideal self substantially hinders him from infusing some *genuinely possible* self with meaning.

To be specific, if the passion that Ellen has finally released in him is eventually thwarted by his failure to effect a relationship with her, then he might not manage to attach these emotions to any part of the life he actually leads. Like Ralph Marvell, he might drift back into idle, empty dreaming. He might never attain the capacity for sustaining deep and meaningful bonds with others. He might become a hollow man altogether. This danger is the central problem that he faces.

And in this respect, Newland's quandary captures the quintessential problem of all who grew to maturity in the repressive society of old New York. Perhaps he will settle for a set of highly stereotyped personal relationships that serve only to mask a deep sense of isolation and incompleteness. Perhaps he will even go through his entire life never feeling that he is really "himself"—even though everyone else seems to think that he is "somebody." It is a horrifying specter.

Newland's yearning for transcendent experience is, from the very beginning, inseparable from his passion for Ellen; the longing for them suffuses the novel with an exquisite pain. And yet Wharton lets us know, though it becomes fully apparent to Newland only at the end of the novel, that precisely those capacities in Ellen that most attract him are capacities leading to behavior that his innermost being cannot tolerate. Throughout the earlier portions of the fiction, Newland drastically simplifies his notions of Ellen (indeed, as he does those of May as well) so that he need not deal with the complexities of her complete person. Newland fancies her world and the outrages she has experienced in it with convenient imprecision: it is "the society in which the Countess Olenska had lived and suffered, and also—perhaps—tasted mysterious joys" (102).[103] He conjures Ellen outside of any coherent social pattern: she has the "mysterious faculty of suggesting tragic and moving possibilities outside the daily run of experience. She had hardly ever said a word to him to produce this impression, but it was a part of her, either a projection of her mysterious and outlandish background or of something inherently dramatic, passionate and unusual in herself" (113). She is the vague embodiment of all that is lacking in his own life.

Yet Archer and Ellen have not one meeting in which the deep and fundamental antipathies between their ways of life are not apparent. Archer may romanticize Ellen's past in blurred and indefinite terms, but Ellen herself has a complete and quite precise complement of habits, manners, and tastes which are the product of her world; Wharton sets the pattern for an ironic juxtaposition of these habits against Archer's in the initial chapter and continues it throughout the novel. During Archer's first visit to Ellen's home, for example, he is enchanted with the artistry of her drawing room, "intimate, 'foreign,' subtly suggestive of old romantic scenes and sentiments" (69); and in some way (the connection is surely not one of decorative affinity) he is moved to ponder his own highly "American" insistence on " 'sincere' Eastlake furniture" (70). He is charmed by her experienced, casual manner and offended by her being "flippant" (72). He is deeply outraged by her association with Beaufort, and he naively supposes that he can terminate the association by making "her see Beaufort as he really was, with all he represented—

and abhor it" (75). He claims that she makes him "look at his native city objectively. Viewed thus, as through the wrong end of a telescope, it looked disconcertingly small and distant" (74); yet he leaves in a fury when she greets the Duke and Mrs. Struthers (who is not "received" by the polite world) with as much composure as she had greeted him. Each visit before Archer's marriage is tainted by Ellen's affinity for Beaufort— an attachment which he comprehends fitfully and totally detests.

Even at those times after his marriage when Archer seems most unambivalently to press Ellen to an elopement, he continues to view her more as a "case"—"the compromised woman"—than as another complex human being. Thus on the day of their outing in Boston, Archer marvels at Ellen's self-possession, and then reflects that "a woman who had run away from her husband—and reputedly with another man—was likely to have mastered the art of taking things for granted" (240). Still later, when he greets her on her return from Washington, she shocks him by asking: " 'Is it your idea, then, that I should live with you as your mistress—since I can't be your wife?' . . . The crudeness of the question startled him: the word was one that women of his class fought shy of, even when their talk flitted closest about the topic. He noticed that Madame Olenska pronounced it as if it had a recognized place in her vocabulary, and he wondered if it had been used familiarly in her presence in the horrible life she had fled from" (292–93).

Unable to accept her social accommodations, Newland unrealistically rejects society altogether. " 'I want—I want somehow to get away with you into a world where words like that—categories like that—won't exist. Where we shall be simply two human beings who love each other. Who are the whole of life to each other; and nothing else on earth will matter' " (293). However, if Ellen has learned nothing else, she has learned the terrible and inexorable toll that tradition takes: "She drew a deep sigh that ended in another laugh. 'Oh, my dear—where is that country? Have you ever been there?' " (293).

Ellen has a motley background; she was born of old New York, but has spent her childhood as a European vagabond. These bizarre antecedents give her more flexibility than anyone else in the novel, and though Newland is most vividly impressed with her European connections, Ellen herself is oddly imbued with an admiration for what could only be termed May's world. Ellen's view of this world is naive at first: she sees it simplistically as a place that is " 'straight up and down—like Fifth Avenue. And with all the cross streets numbered!' " (74). But she learns of its cruel social isolations, and she learns of the loneliness of living among the " 'kind people who only ask one to pretend,' " who don't want to " 'hear anything unpleasant' " (75)—and still she respects the complex morality that she (but not Archer) can so accurately calculate.

The young Newland Archer evaluates his world harshly and superficially. He sees its innocence as a stifling and destructive element—"the innocence that seals the mind against imagination and the heart against experience" (145)—and it weighs insignificantly against Ellen's world of intrigue. Yet there is much in the novel that suggests intricate harmony where Archer perceives only emptiness and silence. There are silences, to be sure; but they are rich with communication—a kind of totality of understanding that is possible precisely *because* the world of old New York is small and limited. It is a world where one can understand, without being told, that Mrs. Beaufort's presence at the opera on the night of her ball indicates "her possession of a staff of servants competent to organize every detail of the entertainment in her absence" (16); a world where Archer strolling abroad in the evening can ascertain that Beaufort must be about on an errand of "clandestine nature" because "it was not an Opera night, and no one was giving a party" (99). This depth of understanding concerns grave things as well as trivial. The very first action Archer takes in the novel is that of joining May at the opera to show his support of her and the family in behalf of Ellen. It is a kind, emotionally generous gesture, and May understands it without a word's being uttered: "As he entered the box his eyes met Miss Welland's, and he saw that she had instantly understood his motive, though the family dignity which both considered so high a virtue would not permit her to tell him so. . . . The fact that he and she understood each other without a word seemed to the young man to bring them nearer than any explanation would have done" (14). And so, in many ways, it does.

The novel is filled with instances of May's intuitive flashes of deep understanding. Occasionally these are verbalized, but usually they are not. Her penetration into Archer's growing attachment for Ellen, for instance, is more often revealed in a failure to include him in the family's discussions or in a question that discovers him in a lie. Their relationship is filled with a profound silence, but the very limitations of the code that governs their marriage fill the silence with meaning. The most remarkable instance of this mute dialogue occurs one evening when Archer tells

May he must go to Washington and May enjoins him to "be sure to go and see Ellen."

> It was the only word that passed between them on the subject; but in the code in which they had both been trained it meant: "Of course you understand that I know all that people have been saying about Ellen, and heartily sympathize with my family in their effort to get her to return to her husband. I also know that, for some reason you have not chosen to tell me, you have advised her against this course, which all the older men of the family, as well as our grandmother, agree in approving; and that it is owing to your encouragement that Ellen defies us all, and exposes herself to the kind of criticism of which Mr. Sillerton Jackson probably gave you, this evening, the hint that has made you so irritable. . . . Hints have indeed not been wanting; but since you appear unwilling to take them from others, I offer you this one myself, in the only form in which well-bred people of our kind can communicate unpleasant things to each other: by letting you understand that I know you mean to see Ellen when you are in Washington, and are perhaps going there expressly for that purpose; and that, since you are sure to see her, I wish you to do so with my full and explicit approval—and to take the opportunity of letting her know what the course of conduct you have encouraged her in is likely to lead to" (269).

It is true, as Ellen has observed, that old New Yorkers don't like to talk about "unpleasant" things. But what a wealth of shared knowledge their reticences permit!

Newland perceives May's moments of understanding as mere flickers of light in an otherwise unillumined darkness. The evocation of her as a young Diana is, in Archer's mind, a reductive vision of empty, unknowing, unsoiled virginity. He can deal with her primitive complexity no more than he can deal with the consequences of Ellen's experiences with Old World culture. He supposes that her "faculty of unawareness was what gave her eyes their transparency, and her face the look of representing a type rather than a person; as if she might have been chosen to pose for a Civic Virtue or a Greek goddess. The blood that ran so close to her fair skin might have been a preserving fluid rather than a ravaging element; yet her look of indestructible youthfulness made her seem neither hard nor dull, but only primitive and pure" (189). He doesn't hear or understand even her spoken disclaimer: " 'You mustn't think that a girl knows as little as her parents imagine. One hears and one notices—one has one's feelings and ideas' " (147–48).

Given Archer's own abysmal innocence, he is unprepared to counter the marshalled forces of the moral world that May commands. For Diana is the divinity of childbirth and fertility; she presides over the generation of life itself. May might well be ignorant of the more refined customs of decadent European culture; but in her "primitive" purity, she is committed to the most fundamental human processes, and in this commitment she is as ruthless as nature itself. May's devotion to an order by which the family can perpetuate itself is absolute; she is willing to release Archer from his engagement to her (for she is a generous woman), but once he rejects that offer, she dedicates herself to the task of holding him to the morality implicit in old New York's regulation of the process of generation.

Archer knows the rules of this morality; he recites them to Ellen much as a child recites a catechism by rote. Old New York has " 'rather old-fashioned ideas. . . . The individual . . . is nearly always sacrificed to what is supposed to be the collective interest: people cling to any convention that keeps the family together—protects the children' " (109–10). And yet they are meaningless to him throughout much of the novel. He sees himself not as an active force in this world—indeed, it is a world whose deep moral structures he little comprehends—but as the victim of its well-mannered brutalities, "a wild animal cunningly trapped" (66). The escape that Ellen seems to offer is, given his romanticized vision of her, not the liberty to choose an alternate moral system; it is a seductively blurred vision of "freedom" in an artistically and intellectually stimulating world whose constraints and moral ambiguities he little imagines.

Ellen's view is altogether different. Her contact with Old World corruption enables her to appreciate the pious primitivism of her American cousins. Even New York's rigidities have meaning for her. " 'Under the dullness there are things so fine and sensitive and delicate that even those I most cared for in my other life look cheap in comparison. I don't know how to explain myself . . . but it seems as if I'd never before understood with how much that is hard and shabby and base the most exquisite pleasure may be paid' " (243). Much of Ellen's affection for Newland stems from her supposition that he really does embody the goodness of a society she has come to respect. She imputes to him, perhaps, a more self-consciously principled mind than he possesses; the creed he recites in attempting to dissuade her from the divorce acquires in her understanding of it a meaning that Archer cannot yet feel. The Newland Archer who is beloved of Ellen Olenska is a "self" whose emotional commitments are integrally linked to the sentiments he has uttered. " 'I felt there was no one as kind as you; no one who gave me reasons that I understood for doing what at first seemed so hard and—unnecessary. The very good people didn't convince me; I felt they'd never been tempted. But you knew; you understood; you had felt the world outside tugging at one with all its golden hands—and yet you hated the things it asks of one; you hated happiness bought by disloyalty and cruelty and indifference. That was what I'd never known before—and it's better than anything I've known' " (172).

We might be tempted to judge Ellen's appraisal of Newland to be as uninformed as his is of her. Certainly she demands a kind of moral substance from him that he cannot yet recognize in himself, for the only Newland Archer that Ellen can admire is a man whose felt sense of duty would not permit him to betray those who have rested their confidence in him. Ellen has taken empty words and imputed significance to them; yet hers is not an act of such wistful longing as we might suppose. She may love a man who does not yet fully exist, but she has fixed her affections on what is potential and possible in Newland; and if he is not yet the man she judges him to be, there are clear indications that he has already committed himself to becoming that man.

The center of Newland's early pieties, the grave enduring traditions of his life, all have to do with family; when he acts without thinking, his automatic behavior affirms the bonds of kinship and familial affection. For May, and in a different way for Ellen, this loyalty is part of a coherent ethical framework; however, Newland does not feel the moral component in his behavior, probably because it is so familiar, so much a part of the "given" of his world, that he can become conscious of it only with great difficulty. The strength of his moral reflex is shown at the beginning of the novel when he rushes to May's box "to see her through whatever difficulties her cousin's anomalous situation might involve her in; this impulse had abruptly overruled all scruples and hesitations, and sent him hurrying through the red corridors to the farther side of the house" (14). The same deep instinctive tie to the norms that sustain the family can be seen in his involuntary revulsion from the "sordid" aspects of Ellen's right to "freedom." His social (and moral) inflexibility is confirmed by the splendid, parochial isolation of every European journey he makes. His inability to envision any realistic alternative to this life is captured in his groping visions of a life with Ellen—somewhere, "his own fancy inclined to Japan" (307).

Yet throughout much of the novel Archer has no emotional contact with that part of his nature (by far the greater part) that is so irrevocably wedded to the customs of New York. Because so little affect attaches to this "self," he cannot experience it as truly and authentically himself; because he so little understands it, he cannot respect or admire it.

What May and Ellen do together in a remarkable unvoiced conspiracy is confront Archer with the realities of his situation and thereby confirm the integrity of his life. Ellen does this by awakening his slumbering sentient self and wrenching his passional life away from pure imagination to an actual person (however romantically construed) and a series of particular situations within which he can measure his true capacities. May does so by offering her own "innate dignity" (196) as a worthy object of his emotional and moral allegiance: "Whatever happened, he knew, she would always be loyal, gallant and unresentful; and that pledged him to the practice of the same virtues. . . . She became the tutelary divinity of all his old traditions and reverences" (196–97). Thus his growing involvement with Ellen both awakens his deepest passions and ruthlessly outlines his personal limitations. May offers if not passion at least a "glow of feeling" (43) that becomes an "inner glow of happiness" (194) after the marriage; even more, she offers a way of life that is worthy of the passion he has discovered in himself. "She would not disappoint him"; she represented "peace, stablility, comradeship, and the steadying sense of an unescapable duty" (208). Eventually, she offers a true and honorable life when his dreams of Ellen are confounded.[104]

Newland is not a stupid man, and he is to some degree aware of the emotional distance between himself and Ellen. As we have seen, all of his encounters with her are marked by the fundamental differences in their natures; and though Archer's longing for Ellen usually blinds him to these differences, he is sometimes able to put their relationship into focus. The most significant readjustment of his values occurs during and after their meeting at Skuytercliff. He is always jealous of Beaufort, consistently plagued by a desire to "correct" Ellen's views of him. When Beaufort interrupts their meeting at Skuytercliff, the old jealousy emerges. Yet this time, the outrage is tempered by an even-minded appraisal of their situation.

Madame Olenska, in a burst of irritation, had said to Archer that he and she did not talk the same language; and the young man knew that in some respects this was true. But Beaufort understood every turn of her dialect, and spoke it fluently: his view of life, his tone, his attitude, were merely a coarser reflection of those revealed in Count Olenski's letter. This might seem to be to his disadvantage with Count Olenski's wife; but Archer was too intelligent to think that a young woman like Ellen Olenska would necessarily recoil from everything that reminded her of her past. She might believe herself wholly in revolt against it; but what had charmed her in it would still charm her, even though it were against her will.

Thus, with a painful impartiality, did the young man make out the case for Beaufort and Beaufort's victim (137).

Having confronted this painful reassessment, Archer makes what must in part be understood as a conscious decision: he immediately journeys south to see May.

May's sympathetic understanding of his emotional conflict contrasts markedly with the distance that has just been demonstrated between himself and the Countess Olenska, and her offer to release him makes him aware, perhaps for the first time, of the depths of her basic goodness. It is a genuine offer, and when Archer refuses it, his refusal constitutes a pledge to May's world as well as to May. Once the pledge has been made, May and Ellen conspire to hold him faithful.

Terrified by the finality of his acceptance of old New York, Archer impetuously turns to Ellen for some escape, but she answers him now as she is to answer him for ever after: " 'In reality it's too late to do anything but what we've both decided on' " (171). Ellen convinces the family to hasten the marriage, and then she moves to Washington, out of Archer's sight. In every subsequent meeting, her theme is the same. She reveres the narrow pieties of old New York, and her faith in Archer's own fidelity is the significant force keeping her safely in America: " 'If you lift a finger you'll drive me back: back to all the abominations you know of, and all the temptations you half guess' " (245–46). She actively wills that his love for her be realized not in their union but in a continuing separation that gives substance to Archer's own moral life. She conjures him to " 'look, not at visions, but at realities' " (292). Thus when at their last private meeting he urges her to consummate their love, she protests: " 'Don't let us be like all the others' " (314). She could no longer respect him or the code of his world, and she would, as she resolutely tells him, be forced back to the indignities of life with her husband—a betrayal of her own renewed moral commitment as well. Little wonder that at that moment when they are closest to the finality of a physical union, "they looked at each other almost like enemies" (316).

The news of May's pregnancy is the final force that drives the would-be lovers apart. Yet there is a real decision implicit in this penultimate act of the drama; for a man without firm moral commitments may almost as easily leave a wife and child as a wife alone. Newland is restrained from leaving not by any objective and external force—but by the deep-rooted conviction that his own moral duty must ultimately be defined by family obligations. The child that May is carrying represents a felt demand that has been internalized and thus that he cannot ignore.

Wharton never supposed that Newland could find happiness with a woman like Ellen; and though there are earlier outlines of the novel in which he does break his engagement to May and marry Ellen, he and Ellen are not happy together. There is no shared sense of reality: she misses the life in Europe that she has always known; he misses the familiar amenities of old New York; and finally they separate and return to their different worlds.

Throughout the novel as finally written, Newland repeatedly tries to define the nature of his "realities." Often he presumes Ellen to have known the real world in her life outside of New York, and his own real experiences are featured as lying outside of May's world and his marriage to her. Yet just as often he finds reality in May's world: "Here was truth, here was reality, here was the life that belonged to him" (140). His renunciation of May's offer of release is a final determination of the limitations of his *real* life (though his doubts continue); and his behavior towards Ellen, especially after his marriage, betrays the fact that he has genuinely chosen to cast his life in terms of old New York morality. His yearning for Ellen is indescribably intense, yet for the most part it belongs to another world. "That vision of the past was dream, and the reality was what awaited him" (216). He searches out the house that Ellen lives in much as one might visit the hermitage of some transfigured saint. "She remained in his memory simply as the most plaintive and poignant of a line of ghosts" (208); he sustains a private shrine to the man he might have been at a different time and in a different place, "and he had built up within himself a kind of sanctuary in which she throned among his secret thoughts and longings" (265).

His passion is still deeply attached to her, and meetings with her reawaken his longing. Nevertheless, his marriage marks the beginning of a process of distancing; and for the most part Archer is more comfortable with this process as he becomes increasingly conscious of his moral estimation of any other course. "In Archer's little world no one laughed at a wife deceived, and a certain measure of contempt was attached to men who continued their philandering after marriage. In the rotation of crops there was a recognized season for wild oats; but they were not to be sown more than once" (308). The imagery suggests the degree to which Newland has actively accepted the values of May's primitive, natural order, and his humiliation when Larry Lefferts casually includes him into a fellowship of deceiving husbands is vividly acute, for "in his heart he thought Lefferts despicable" (309). In the end, he is forced to realize that there can be no *real* life for Newland Archer and Ellen Olenska together. And the magnitude of his sacrifice measures for him the value of what he has preserved. He relinquishes his Faustian dreams for the more realistic understandings of a Wilhelm Meister and turns his energies from imagination to the process of generation.

In taking this step, Newland accepts the responsibilities that necessarily precede maturity and individual integrity. He has rejected notions of narcissistic self-fulfillment for the responsibility of "establishing and guiding the next generation"; [105] and in solving the problems of love, he has accepted the problems of care. The final results of that choice are evident only at the conclusion of the novel.

The last chapter begins with a confirmation of the values that Archer has chosen. He is seated alone in the library. "It was the room in which most of the real things of his life had happened. There his wife, nearly twenty-six years ago, had broken to him, with a blushing circumlocution that would have caused the young women of the new generation to smile, the news that she was to have a child; and there their eldest boy, Dallas . . . had been christened. . . . There Dallas had first staggered across the floor shouting 'Dad,' while May and the nurse laughed behind the door; there their second child, Mary (who was so like her mother), had announced her engagement to the dullest and most reliable of Reggie Chivers's many sons; and there Archer had kissed her through her wedding veil. . . . But above all—sometimes Archer put it above all—it was in that library that the Governor of New York . . . had turned to his host, and said, banging his clenched fist on the table and gnashing his eye-glasses: 'Hang the professional politician! You're the kind of man the country wants, Archer' " (347–49). Not a great life, perhaps, but a good life and a productive life, a life whose goodness has grown naturally and fruitfully out of the best that Newland Archer's time and place had to offer.

The emotions that Ellen freed have flowed bountifully into family affection, and beyond family into community concerns: he has not been crippled by repression, after all. No longer a Romantic visionary, Newland understands himself, now, with the graceful tolerance of a man who reveres the achievements of his special place in history. "It was little enough to look back on; but when he remembered to what the young men of his generation and his set had looked forward—the narrow groove of money-making, sport and society to which their vision had been limited—even his small contribution to the new state of things seemed to count, as each brick counts in a well-built wall. He had done little in public life; he would always be by nature a contemplative and a dilettante; but he had had high things to contemplate, great things to delight in; and one great man's friendship to be his strength and pride" (349).

The process of distancing himself from Ellen that began directly after his marriage has continued; but he can contemplate that process with a reflective, poignant sense of an irrecoverable loss that has in the end been overbalanced by the value of what has been saved. "Something he knew he had missed: the flower of life. But he thought of it now as a thing so unattainable and improbable that to have repined would have been like despairing because one had not drawn the first prize in a lottery. . . . When he thought of Ellen Olenska it was abstractly, serenely, as one might think of some imaginary beloved in a book or a picture: she had become the composite vision of all that he had missed" (350). Newland is content, even knowing that his life, like all meaningful lives, has compromised his sense of the ideal. He is not the man he had once dreamed of becoming, but he is a man at peace with himself and a man who has the satisfaction of having become most truly himself in the ways that were available to him. He has not betrayed his own capacities. "Looking about him, he honored his own past, and mourned for it. After all, there was good in the old ways" (350).

And old New York has changed; it had contained the seeds of change all along, in old Catherine Spicer's journey up through society or in Mrs.

Struthers' increasing respectability. However, the change has not come wrenchingly, as Archer had once thought it must. Instead, it has developed continuously out of the traditions that molded his youth. In his acceptance of the imperatives of his own life, Archer has helped to shape this change, by loving and guiding the son so like himself and by being what New Yorkers came to call "a good citizen." Above all, there are meaningful connections for Newland Archer between the past and the present: his children know freedoms that he never knew as a youth; but he is an unaffected comrade to his own son, who shares his fundamental decency. May was not entirely wrong in assuming that "whatever happened, Newland would continue to inculcate in Dallas the same principles and prejudices which had shaped his parents' lives, and that Dallas in turn (when Newland followed her) would transmit the sacred trust to little Bill" (351). The new ways have grown out of the old ways, and "there was good in the new order too" (352).

This moment of acceptance speaks directly to the problems that Wharton was finally resolving during the period when she was writing this novel. For her, too, one might say that "there was good in the old ways" and that "there was good in the new order too." The young people she had come to know through her work during the war were, like Newland's children, more candid and less limited by the rigidities of custom. Yet Newland's experience suggests that the validity of old New York's morality could withstand changes—even the more violent changes wrought by World War I. There is continuing value in loyalty, in commitment to family, and in undertaking responsibility for the generation that is to follow. Newland's self-confrontation substantially parallels Wharton's; and the placid man whom we meet at the beginning of the last chapter seems entirely to have come to terms with his own life.

However, for Newland one final test of the integrity of his identity is left. It comes when he has the opportunity once again to meet Ellen Olenska.

Newland is a widower, and Ellen has never remarried; there is no external obstacle to the consummation of the dream they shared almost thirty years earlier. Newland is intoxicated with the possibilities implicit in their meeting—"I'm only fifty-seven," he reminds himself while standing before "an effulgent Titian" (361). Yet at the same time he is overcome with doubts; he has felt his life to be "held fast by habit, by memories, by a sudden startled shrinking from new things" (354). He may feel "his heart beating with the confusion and eagerness of youth" (356) when he contemplates Ellen Olenska, but the image he conjures seems cruelly to mock the man he has become, "a mere gray speck of a man compared with the ruthless magnificent fellow he had dreamed of being" (357).

The anticipated visit to Ellen is overwhelming in its significance; for when Newland ponders it, he can at first find only two possible meanings for him. Either he will discover, at long last, that Newland Archer and Ellen Olenska can make a real life together; or his meeting with her will serve only to prove that he is, indeed, no more than a "mere gray speck of a man." Both of these possibilities would deny the validity of the good, decent, binding commitments that have shaped his life for the intervening years. If he is genuinely insignificant, then he has wasted his life; but if he can *now* find a viable world to share with Ellen, then he might have accepted his freedom thirty years before when May offered it. The quandary seems impossible thus postulated, but Newland is saved from despair by a final and redemptive visitation from the past.

The great strengths in the tradition of old New York lay in its powerful, unspoken capacity for complex communication (and with that—understanding, even compassion) and in its insistence upon the importance of the family above all else. Newland has reaped the fruits of the second of these in his loving fellowship with his son Dallas. Now Dallas, outspoken embodiment of the "good" new ways, enables his father finally to understand the magnitude of the first.

Dallas wonders aloud whether Ellen wasn't " 'the woman you'd have chucked everything for: only you didn't. . . . Mother said . . . the day before she died . . . she said she knew we were safe with you, and always would be, because once, when she asked you to, you'd given up the thing you most wanted' " (359). Newland, astounded that May knew his secret sorrow all along, astounded that she has told Dallas, can only reply "in a low voice: 'She never asked me.' 'No. I forgot. You never did ask each other anything, did you? And you never told each other anything. You just sat and watched each other, and guessed at what was going on underneath. A deaf-and-dumb asylum, in fact. Well, I back your generation for knowing more about each other's private thoughts than we ever have time to find out about our own' " (359–60). May has again managed to live up to the height of her intuitive strength. Archer had once presumed to suppose that she would never fail him, and now he discovers that she never did. "It seemed to take an iron band from his heart to know that, after all, someone had guessed and pitied. . . . And that it should have been his wife moved him indescribably" (360).

One vindication of old New York's code is Dallas himself, the son whose affection for his father encompasses even that father's deepest sorrow. This second vindication, the depth of genuine communication that has informed Archer's life with his wife, causes him to look at the meeting with Ellen in a somewhat different light. He has become, inexorably over the years, the man that he is now—a man who has had an affectionate but not passionate marriage, a man who has been a good father, a man who has used the strengths in his own tradition to mold the traditions that followed him. He has become a gentleman, in the truest usage of old New York. It is an identity that has been infused with renewed meaning for him by Dallas's communication. Madame Olenska, too, has been formed by the traditions of that complex European community to which she fled. "For nearly thirty years, her life—of which he knew so strangely little—had been spent in this rich atmosphere that he already felt to be too dense and yet too stimulating for his lungs. . . . More than half a lifetime divided them, and she had spent the long interval among people he did not know, in a society he but faintly guessed at, in conditions he would never wholly understand. During that time he had been living with his youthful memory of her" (362). If his youthful and more flexible self could not live with the "real" Ellen Olenska, then even less can the man that he has become. Yet this recognition need not bring sorrow or self-doubt.

Ellen had loved him for his honor, had loved him for being different from herself—committed to what he had called " 'rather old-fashioned ideas . . . any convention that keeps the family together.' " When she loved him, these things had not yet been fully formed in him, and she had loved the potential and the possible. Now at fifty-seven, Newland has become the man Ellen saw in him; any attempt to recapture the past would be a repudiation of the love that she gave him so long ago and of the man he has finally become. Thus he decides, in the end, not to see her. His message, " 'Say I'm old-fashioned: that's enough' " (364) is a tribute to the course he has committed himself to, a private reference to that night long ago when he championed family loyalty. Then the words had been hollow in his mouth. Now the slow accretion of his own life has finally given them substance.

So he waits below her apartment, envisioning her as she was not at their first meeting nor at their last, but at the meeting when he "explained" old New York's code to her. Of all their moments in the past, this one has become the most real to him: she will always be the woman she was that night. Thus it is that he pictures her—"a dark lady, pale and dark, who would look up quickly, half rise and hold out a long thin hand with three rings on it" (364).

Archer can acknowledge that Ellen will always be an unattainable dream for him; he accepts it with nostalgic sentiment, and in this recognition, he confirms the value of his own life as he has led it. He has finally discovered the reality he sought, and it rests in the man he has become; for the rest—" 'it's more real to me here than if I went up' " (364).

In the end he has gained more than he has lost: he has not rejected his unique moment in history; he has taken the best of it and built upon it. His final act affirms the coherence of his own identity, and in this assertion of "self," Newland achieves genuine maturity. At this moment he shares the wisdom of all men, past and present, who have achieved integrity: he understands his "one and only life cycle as something that had to be and that, by necessity, permitted of no substitutions; . . . he knows that an individual life is the accidental coincidence of but one life cycle with but one segment of history; and that for him *all* human integrity stands or falls with the one style or integrity of which he partakes." Newland has escaped the narrow limitations of old New York in the only way that was ever *really* available to him, by achieving an inner peace that transcends time and place altogether. For "a wise Indian, a true gentleman, and a mature peasant share and recognize in one another the final stage of integrity." [106]

He watches Ellen's apartment, content to be no more than a spectator to the play of high passions. "At length a light shone through the windows, and a moment later a man-servant came out on the balcony, drew up the awnings, and closed the shutters" (365). The drama is over, and Newland is free to go.

The Age of Innocence began with a sly, good-natured jest—a legerdemain with titles, a playing-off of this novel against James's great early work *The Portrait of a Lady*. Now it concludes with another kind of apostrophe to the master—more gentle and private. A tender reminiscence that James had shared with only a very few of the elect is recapitulated in Newland Archer's final vigil; Edmund Gosse has left a rare published record of James's experience:

> I was staying alone with Henry James at Rye one summer and as twilight deepened we walked together in the garden. I forget by what meanders we approached the subject, but I suddenly found that in profuse and enigmatic language he was recounting to me an experience, something that had happened, not something repeated or imagined. He spoke of standing on the pavement of a city, in the dusk, and of gazing upwards across the misty street, watching, watching for the lighting of a lamp in a window on the third storey. And the lamp blazed out, and through bursting tears he strained to see what was behind it, the unapproachable face. And for hours he stood there, wet with the rain, brushed by the phantom hurrying figures of the scene, and never from behind the lamp was for one moment visible the face. The mysterious and poignant revelation closed, and one could make no comment.[107]

The unapproachable face, that eternally elusive specter. Below, the anguished, lonely sentinel, waiting, waiting. One imagines Edith touching his shoulder affectionately. Dear friend, come home. It's more real down here.

Edith Wharton, early 1920's

Edith Wharton, early 1920's

Edith Wharton, 1925, "The Author": Frontispiece to *A Backward Glance*

Edith Wharton, c. 1936

IV

Diptych–Youth and Age
The Fiction, 1921-1937

Who made the room so mean and bare—
Where are the chairs, the tables where?
It was lent for a moment only—

From Goethe's *Faust*
Quoted in *The Children* (1928)

T he *Age of Innocence* radiates a mood of equilibrium and acceptance. There is satire in the novel, of course, a gentle mockery of the trivialities that have assumed such importance in the world within which Newland Archer has been constrained to seek his destiny —and a more acidulous commentary upon that society's tendency to encourage its members into unproductive dreaming. Still, it was a world where a meaningful life was possible (above all, that is the message of Newland's story). Built upon the values of family and honor, traditions as sturdy as the small rock cottage at Skuytercliff, it was a society that could absorb and utilize passion in the perpetuation and protection of those values. Not as benign as other, more enlightened societies, perhaps, old New York was nevertheless a world where one might achieve personal dignity. A man like Newland Archer could honor his own past, honor the realities of his life as he had lived it.

Old New York had been Edith Wharton's world as well, and we might justifiably understand this nostalgic novel as her own homecoming: acceptance, finally, of the imperfections in her shaping past and a willingness to revere the virtues of such a world.

There is no tragedy in this novel: Newland has been forced to come to terms with the limitations in his nature during his young manhood in the late 1870's and early 1880's; when we encounter him at the end of the novel in 1905, he can contemplate the integrity of his character, the realization of his nature and of his finite happiness as it extends backward over those many years that return to the moment of crisis and even beyond it. Having acknowledged the claims of his time and place in history *in* that time and place, he has a coherent sense of being and having been, and he is contented with the notion of the future as a legacy for his children, who will carry a part of his nature forward with them. He has had a full measure of his own epoch; he can leave other epochs to other men. In the end, much as Newland Archer shares with his creator, in this aspect they remain sadly distinct; and if there is no tragedy within the novel, there may well have been tragedy in the aftermath of writing it.

Unlike the lives of Newland Archer and Charity Royall—whose adolescent impatience led them to reject their worlds as insufficient and whose ordeals convinced them, at the end of adolescence, to come back to those worlds "for good"—Wharton's own life was painfully out of joint. She came back to her origins at last, but she did not return until her middle age was ending. Too late. Too late for so many things.

There is something consummately ironic in accepting the validity of "old-fashioned" ways at the end of a war that had definitively uprooted those ways. Having learned to respect the pieties of her background only in 1920, Edith Wharton had forever lost the opportunity of acknowledging the claims of her special time and place in history while that time and place were still present to engross her energies. If Newland Archer's triumph is that he manages to become a man in his time, Wharton's ineradicable sorrow was that she discovered and accepted her time only after it had passed her by. Newland's circumscribed life has the rhythms of organic development and unity; Wharton's life—considerably less circumscribed and more completely fulfilled in many respects—is a series of struggles and failures and successes, rejections and capitulations. In one sense it is a model of the will to survive—more, to triumph. In another sense, however, it is a haunting embodiment of the inevitable limitations of delayed maturity. She had succeeded in "placing" sexuality, and she had placed it within the context of continuity and generativity. The mellow quality of the conclusion to *The Age of Innocence* bespeaks her feeling of the essential rightness of that conclusion; at the same time, however, the implications of the novel cruelly mock the absences in her own life.

So rich in the offspring of her creative intelligence—"my children," she used to call her fictions as she scolded them into compliance and dressed them and spanked them into shape (these were *her* terms in letters to her friends)—she was barren of biological progeny. Having finally affirmed the value of family, she had no family of her own on which to focus the wealth of her feelings. How much she felt the absence may be inferred from the direction of her fictional interests.

The shift is striking. The novels beginning with *The Reef* and concluding with *The Age of Innocence* had all focused rather precisely on one or another aspect of sexual energy, and they are rebellious and fiery and passionate in tone. The novels that follow concentrate on quite another set of problems; merely the names of a few will suggest the difference: *A Son at the Front*, *The Mother's Recompense*, *The Children*, *Twilight Sleep* (the anaesthetic that permits a woman to drift into "motherhood as lightly and unperceivingly as if the wax doll which suddenly appeared in the cradle at her bedside had been brought there in one of the big bunches of hot-house roses that she found every morning on her pillow" [1]). These are novels about families—about parents and children, youth and age—

and for the most part, it is the older generation that commands Wharton's imaginative sympathies.

As a group, these novels are not as strong as her earlier work, although there are exceptions like *The Mother's Recompense, The Children*, and a number of the shorter fictions. One way to explain these failures would be to notice that now more than ever before Wharton wrote because she needed the money; another might be to suggest that as she aged, her powers diminished. There is some truth to both claims. However, the falling-away between a novel like *The Age of Innocence* (1920) and *The Glimpses of the Moon* (1922) or *A Son at the Front* (1923) cannot be accounted for entirely in terms of such considerations; other factors contributed.

The emotional problems that had dominated Wharton's earlier fictions—the sense of desolation, the need to place sexuality—had been problems that she knew at first hand. Now that is no longer the case. She may have felt driven to write repeatedly about the feelings of parents toward their children; however, she could only infer the nature of such feelings. She may have longed for family (the tone in fiction after fiction suggests as much), but she had none. In fact, although she made wholehearted efforts to get to know "les jeunes," she was more and more alone, and she felt increasingly alienated from the manners and practices of the younger generation. The inability to marshal her energy efficiently in these works bespeaks her uncertainty, and the tone in many of them is mixed. When she is at her best, Wharton captures the poignancy of aging. At other times, her management of the fiction grows less felicitous: increasingly, her satire lapses into an uncharacteristic querulousness, and everything about the postwar world is dismissed as vulgar and cheap; there is an inauthentic groping for the damning comment—for example, in the novels after 1925 she often alludes to "druggers," and the reader is moved to wonder whether Wharton was personally acquainted with many young people who took drugs or whether this is merely an imprecise, captious generalization.

In her last novels, for the first time, if we do not read carefully, we might be misled into accepting the stereotype of "Edith Wharton: The Author" that has prevailed since her death: a haughty woman, cold, faintly supercilious, with the imperious remove that only breeding and great wealth can confer. That persona is there sometimes, on the surface; yet below, there is someone quite different. Defensive and wary, with desperate (and hopeless) longings, loneliness, and apprehension. Wharton's own epoch had passed, and she had never truly lived in it; now, too late for reconciliations, it was gone forever.

Loss. That was to be her last challenge. How would she confront the losses of her life—the particular losses that her abnormally protracted psychological struggle had inflicted upon her and the normal losses that every aging human must manage? As always, she was more than a little aware of her situation. In the end, she straightened her shoulders and confronted it. She had never expected existence to be easy and probably would never have chosen an easy path, given the option. "Life is always either a tight-rope or a feather bed," she observed briskly to her diary in 1926. "Give me the tight-rope!" [2]

I

As the war drew to a close, Edith Wharton began a conscious effort to resettle her life; for the first time since the sale of The Mount, the author of *The Decoration of Houses* wanted a house of her own. With the help of Elisina Tyler, an attractive young woman with whom she had worked closely during the war, Wharton discovered the eighteenth-century Pavillon Colombe in the northern suburbs of Paris. Like almost every home in the district, it was for sale in early 1918 because it was in the direct line of the German approach to the city. When Wharton first saw it, it was filthy and in great disrepair; nevertheless, by her own admission, she fell instantly in love with the place. It was spring; "the orchards were just bursting into bloom, and we seemed to pass through a rosy snow-storm to reach what was soon to be my own door. . . . At last I was to have a garden again—and a big old kitchen garden as well." [3] The next year she leased the ancient chateau of Ste. Claire in Hyères on the French Riviera, which she soon purchased as well. Thus she embarked upon the routine that was more or less to describe the rest of her life: winter and spring in Hyères; summer and autumn at the Pavillon Colombe. The years of renovation and refurbishing were taxing, yet they brought a sense of buoyancy and palpable rejuvenation. " 'I am thrilled to the spine,' " she was to tell Royall Tyler (Elisina's husband). " *'Il y va de mon avenir;* and I feel as if I were going to get married—to the right man at last!' " [4] This period (1919–20) coincided with her writing of *The*

Age of Innocence, and it is easy to understand her triumphant sense, at last, of bringing things definitively together.

Yet by the time her next novel was published in 1922, Edith Wharton was sixty. What a strange juxtaposition—these feelings of renewal coupled with the inexorable dwindling of her life. " 'Sometimes,' " she was wont to say, " 'when I am dressing, I find myself wondering who is the ugly old woman using my glass.' " [5] She was not ugly (the photographs demonstrate that); perhaps merely the advance of years seemed ugly. Certainly old age crept stealthily closer to this woman who could still feel the exultations of youth so vividly. One suspects that she was often startled by the tolls time had taken of her—life's last surprise.

The reception of *The Age of Innocence* was overwhelmingly positive. Even so, there were a few disquieting voices. The young critic Edmund Wilson complained that her English was growing more and more awkward, and she knew it was true that she now spent a good deal of her time speaking either French or Italian (and not colloquial American). "I wonder if he's not right," she mused jokingly to Gaillard Lapsley, "when he says I can't write English any more?—I shall take up my pen with a distrustful hand tomorrow at 8 A.M." [6] Just the hint of a nagging doubt. Was she—could she be—growing stale? It was a concern that had never worried her before.

When she became the first woman to win the Pulitzer Prize in May of 1921 (for *The Age of Innocence*), Wharton was very much reassured by the honor—though somewhat less so when she discovered that the committee's first choice had been *Main Street* by Sinclair Lewis, a novel that had been rejected by Columbia University's board of trustees on "moral grounds." Nevertheless, the occasion provided an excuse for the two authors to exchange courtesies, to begin what was to be a continuing casual friendship. Lewis had admired Wharton's novels since his undergraduate days at Yale,[7] and when he wrote to congratulate her for the Pulitzer Prize, he voiced genuine respect for her work. Such tribute was received gratefully by Wharton: "Your letter touched me very deeply. . . . What you say is so kind, so generous, and so unexpected, that I don't know where to begin to answer. It is the first sign I have ever had— literally—that 'les jeunes' at home had ever read a word of me. I had long since resigned myself to the idea that I was regarded by you all as the—say the Mrs. Humphry Ward of the Western Hemisphere." [8]

Her next two full-length novels are strangely transitional works; both were begun before the publication of *The Age of Innocence* and in some respects are clearly related to the period before 1920. At the same time, both contain elements that look forward to suggest the themes that will preoccupy Wharton's final novels. Neither is very successful.

Her correspondence with Appleton during 1919 and 1920 suggests the sources of some of the failures in the first of these, *The Glimpses of the Moon*. Appleton was eager to have a novel "along the lines of *The House of Mirth*"—by which they meant a novel set before the war. Wharton had been working on *A Son at the Front* (one of her editors received four chapters of that novel in July of 1919), and she grew very impatient with Appleton's insistence that there was no longer any market for a war novel. But they were resolute: they wanted a novel like *The House of Mirth*. Wharton had sent them an outline of *The Glimpses of the Moon;* surely, she insisted, this novel would meet their demands. It was, to be sure, about a "modern" couple; nevertheless, it was set in some rather nebulous prewar time. But no. Appleton wanted a period novel. Then, out of the blue, Wharton proposed that they do "Old New York" (soon retitled *The Age of Innocence*), which she had apparently been working on along with these other pieces. And of course they did. Only after they had published *The Age of Innocence* with such great success in 1920 did they publish *The Glimpses of the Moon* (in 1922). They never did publish *A Son at the Front;* Scribner's published it in 1923.

The reiterated references to *The House of Mirth* in this exchange, along with Wharton's insistence that *The Glimpses of the Moon* could, despite its modernity, be acceptable as a prewar novel, reinforce the careful reader's uneasy sense that Wharton has begun—probably entirely without realizing it—to borrow from her own earlier work. Nick Lansing and Susy Branch are almost caricatures of Selden and Lily Bart.

The plot of the novel is simple enough: Nick and Susy are both well-born young people who have no money; Nick has an unprofitable literary bent, and Susy has a talent for making herself useful as a companion to her rich women-friends. The two fall in love, and they agree to marry on only one condition—that if either should get a "better chance," he or she should take it, without regrets and without recriminations. At first their honeymoon is ecstatic (they live on the largess of friends—borrowed homes and the money that they have requested in lieu of wedding presents); however, all too soon, doubts set in. Nick is inclined to be censorious of Susy's habit of manipulating their lives so successfully, and

Susy becomes jealous of his attentions to a rich American girl. Each begins to think that the other has been offered that "better chance" and wants to take it; they part under the force of this misunderstanding, and the main portion of the novel traces the period of unhappy separation. Each of them does have the chance to marry for money, and in the end, each rejects that chance and chooses instead to make the best of a penniless marriage based on true love.

We cannot infer a great deal from the melodramatic nature of the story: Wharton's novels can almost always be made to seem trite if they are rendered merely in terms of a plot summary; her strengths as a novelist resided in her ability to re-create the psychological complexity of human nature. That is exactly what this novel misses completely, and the fact that Wharton lapses into borrowing from her earlier novel contributes substantially to this failure. We are never introduced into the genuine depths of either Nick or Susy Lansing: their natures are sketched quickly, almost carelessly, with a facile, glossy, verbal shorthand. Wharton picks up a good many turns of language and situation that had been used meaningfully in *The House of Mirth* (undoubtedly they rang in *her* ear with significant resonance); in this novel, however, the verbal tricks do not coalesce into a meaningful fictional whole.

The tone of the work hovers between satire and sympathy, and perhaps nothing reveals its fundamental flaws more directly than the pat, sentimental denouement: in need of money, Susy has been persuaded to supervise an obstreperous family of five children while their parents take a vacation; Nick happens to catch sight of her with the baby, "a red-cheeked child against her shoulder." [9] Suddenly his doubts vanish. "His Susy, the old Susy, and yet a new Susy, curiously transformed, transfigured almost, by the new attitude in which he beheld her. . . . For an instant she stood out from the blackness behind her, and through the veil of the winter night, a thing apart, an unconditioned vision, the eternal image of the woman and the child" (319). Why these worldlings should be moved by *this* experience escapes us. The transformation bears no relation to anything in the novel that has preceded it. One answer is that Wharton herself must have found the episode of surrogate mother-and-child plausible and moving, and that is perhaps the best account of her allowing this saccharine conclusion to stand.

Wharton's growing friendship with Elisina Tyler and her husband had introduced her to the vagaries and delights of little children, for the couple had a son, William, who was only two in 1912 when Wharton first met his parents. She was close to the child—and very fond of him. [10] Given Wharton's increasing commitment to tradition as reflected both in *Summer* and in *The Age of Innocence*, it is not surprising that she was especially receptive to the attractions of this delightful group. Conversely, the many pleasant hours that she spent with them might well have reinforced her inclination to affirm the values of domestic life (she did, after all, appropriate the name of her friend Royall Tyler for lawyer Royall). *The Glimpses of the Moon* signals Wharton's increasing interest in families; *A Son at the Front* shows it even more clearly.

A Son at the Front is a vexing novel: one feels that it should have been better; Wharton certainly wanted it to be a good novel, for she cared deeply about the war and had yearned for a long time to capture the "stored-up emotions of those years." [11] It was dedicated (as *The Marne* had been) to Ronald Simmons, the young American with whom she had formed such a close, brief friendship before he was killed. Yet it is not among her best work; the emotions that compelled her to record this historical moment of crisis might have been better satisfied by another piece of frankly journalistic writing (like *Fighting France*). [12] As it is, the cinematic representations of home-front activity merely clutter the novel. Beneath them is a psychological drama that is too much lost sight of to command the fiction: the plight of an artist-father, "tired, disenchanted, and nearing sixty" (7), who does not know how to acquaint himself with his son.

We meet John Campton on the opening page of the novel in his "bare studio in Montmartre" (3), musing upon the now-famous portrait of his son George; and as is so often the case in Wharton's novels, this physical placing of Campton fairly accurately captures the tone of his life. That, too, is bare—devoid of emotional entanglements, carrying no baggage of accumulated familial ties. He rashly acquired a wife once; but not long after their marriage it had "come home to him that she was always going to bore him" (17). When boredom finally overshadowed everything else, Campton's wife left him, taking their infant son and later marrying a respectable and suitably dull Parisian businessman, Anderson Brant. Eventually, Campton noticed the absence, but it was more a relief than anything else. "His misfortune had been that he could neither get on easily with people nor live without them; could never wholly isolate himself in his art, nor yet resign himself to any permanent human communion that left it out, or, worse still, dragged it in irrelevantly. He had tried both kinds, and on the whole preferred the first" (40). Thus the novel opens with Campton musing on that portrait of his son now hanging in the Museum of the Luxembourg. It made his reputation, capturing so brilliantly the nuances of plane and shadow and lurking depth of character. He knows it intimately, knows all of the drawings and sketches of his son exceedingly well (there is a large portfolio of them). How strange to think, as he does later that night, that "if war came, if George were not discharged, if George were sent to the front, if George were killed . . . [the] things the father did not know of might turn out to have been the central things of his son's life!" (79).

We cannot suppose that the plight of this aging artist was indifferent to Wharton. Too many of its consequences echo portions of her own life. Above all, perhaps, the loneliness.[13] Campton has his art; others have family. Usually, he is unthinkingly satisfied with his lot. But occasionally, when he stumbles by accident into an intimate gathering, he recognizes "how frail a screen of activity divided him from depths of loneliness he dared not sound" (68). As a youth "he had imagined flights . . . with the woman who was to fulfill every dream. 'Well—I suppose that's the stuff pictures are made of' " (8). But he realizes that the woman has never materialized; none of the dreams have come true, and now he has only his pictures. The loneliness of living among *replicas* of life.

Most painful of all is his isolation from the son who was born of his blood but whom he has never known in any real measure. "At home" for George always meant "at the Brants'." Campton had never thought much about the implications of this fact until one day when George, a schoolboy of twelve, had one of his bad colds. Usually the maid fetched him to his father's studio one day each week; this week Campton was forced to go to his son's "home." When he enters his son's bedroom, he discovers that "the boy was reading as only a bookworm reads. . . . It was clear that he regarded the visit as an interruption. Campton, leaning over, saw that the book was a first edition of Lavengro. 'Where the deuce did you get that?' . . . 'Didn't you know? Mr. Brant has started collecting first editions. . . . He lets me have them to look at when I'm seedy. I say, isn't this topping?' " (29). The son of this artist, developing his own sense of art and of the past, with the father no more than an intrusion in the process. So it has been with everything important in the boy's life. Even now, at this tardy time, Campton is still "trembling for the chance to lay the foundation of a complete and lasting friendship with his only son" (11–12); and he is still clumsily failing.

Their talk is amiable, courteous, even friendly. But not frank, certainly not close. The youth feels easy with his father, but there is an ineradicable distance, a restraint between them. It lasts throughout this first evening that they have spent together in a long time—until the boy drifts off to sleep. Then the artist's faculties become fully concentrated: Campton "stole back to the sitting-room, picked up a sketchbook and pencil and returned. He knew there was no danger of waking George, and he began to draw, eagerly but deliberately, fascinated by the happy accident of the lighting, and of the boy's position" (53). It is Campton's only mode of intimacy.

His case is put to him rather bluntly by an old friend to whom he complains of the stepfather's intrusions: " 'Well, poor Anderson really *was* a dry-nurse to the boy. Who else was there to look after him? You were painting Spanish beauties at the time. . . . Life's a puzzle. I see perfectly that if you'd let everything else go to keep George you'd never have become the great John Campton: the *real* John Campton you were meant to be. And it wouldn't have been half as satisfactory for you—or for George either. Only, in the meanwhile, somebody had to blow the child's nose, and pay his dentist and doctor; and you ought to be grateful to Anderson for doing it' " (117).

For almost the entire novel, we watch John Campton trying to assure his son's safety in the uncertain dangers of the war; in the end, he fails. George Campton dies as the result of injuries sustained in battle. And only at this point can Campton feel success. The boy's mother and stepfather had never "had anything, in the close inextricable sense in which Campton had had his son. And it was only now, in his own hour of destitution, that he understood how much greater the depth of their poverty had been" (421). He has been asked to design a monument for the boy's grave, and the novel concludes with him alone in his studio, trying to decide whether to do the work: "He had always had a fancy for modelling—had always had lumps of clay lying about within reach. He pulled out all the sketches of his son from the old portfolio, spread them before him on the table, and began" (425–26).

Is the ending of this novel meant ironically? It does not sound like irony; yet by resting with Campton's sense of success, Wharton has shamefully pulled away from the question. Since George can continue in some measure to live in spirit for his father even though his death has made it impossible for him to live in fact for anyone else, Campton's sense of gratification at the end of the novel is understandable.[14] But the question that Wharton has raised with such tortured indirection is a question of living people. By shifting her focus, she brings the novel to a closure that is false in the specific terms within which the fiction has been postulated. (Surely we are no more encouraged to believe that it is good for George to have died so that his father might make a monument for him than we are supposed to be satisfied with Lily Bart's death as a tribute to the quality of Selden's capacity to "appreciate" her.)

How much must an artist rob from everyday actuality to feed his art? Too much for any other sustained and draining emotional tie? Wharton refuses to focus upon the puzzle for now. She turns her back upon it; and though she begins and ends her novel with the artist-father alone in his studio, she injects so many distractions in between that the problem his situation poses may well be lost in them.

Nevertheless, despite the evasions, what dominates this novel is a protracted sense of loss and sorrow. It would be facile and completely wrong-headed to suppose that Wharton was explicitly regretting the course of her own life here. She is not to be confused with her creation, John Campton: Wharton's life had been too full of complications for such an easy transposition; and the protracted illness at the beginning of her marriage rendered all simple questions of "choice" between art and family infinitely complex. Furthermore, if we wished to traffic in specific speculations, we would have to remember that Edith Wharton did not publish a novel until she was almost forty years old and that all other things being amenable (which they were not), she might have had a family and her fictions both. But even to raise such complicated calculations suggests how far they are from the heart of this work.

Let us say, merely, that the novel mourns for what has not been, mourns for the unrealized closeness of child and parent; it is a theme that will be treated with increasing clarity and strength in other fictions of this period.

Certainly it runs throughout the four novellas that were published collectively under the title *Old New York* in 1924.[15] If these tales trade upon the nostalgic success of *The Age of Innocence*, they inject the backward glance with an acrid sense of disappointment and loss; and in none is the anguish more relentlessly drawn than in "The Old Maid." At the time of

its publication, many critics found it (after *Ethan Frome*) the most powerful of her short fictions. The plot is tightly drawn, although it skirts
perilously close to sentimentalism,[16] and it captures the complexities of
parenthood with more painful precision than any of Wharton's fictions
thus far.

"The Old Maid" tells the story of not one woman, but two; and its
title reverberates ironically, for the old maid's state is cruelly delineated
by casting it against "marriage and babies," the joyous expectations that
dance in hopeful girlish eyes. Delightful visions that fade into warm
realities: "the startled puzzled surrender to the incomprehensible exigencies of the young man to whom one had at most yielded a rosy cheek in
return for an engagement ring . . . the large double-bed; the terror of
seeing him shaving calmly the next morning, in his shirt-sleeves, through
the dressing-room door; the evasions, insinuations, resigned smiles and
Bible texts of one's Mamma . . . a week or a month of flushed distress,
confusion, embarrassed pleasure; then the growth of habit, the insidious
lulling of the matter-of-course, the dreamless double slumbers in the big
white bed, the early morning discussions and consultations through that
dressing-room door which had once seemed to open into a fiery pit
scorching the brow of innocence. And then, the babies; the babies who
were supposed to 'make up for everything,' and didn't—though they
were such darlings, and one had no definite notion as to what it was that
one had missed, and that they were to make up for." [17]

The cousins, Delia and Charlotte Lovell, have not conformed exactly
to society's prescriptions for young women (the Lovells, a daring and adventurous lot, never quite did). Nevertheless, Delia at least was eager
enough to establish herself in a brownstone; and though she had fallen in
love with romantic, careless Clement Spender, who refused to settle
reliably into law and a home in Gramercy Park (that was the Lovell in
her), she married reliable Jim Ralston when she was twenty. By twenty-
five, she is a contented mother of two, with only a vagrant memory to
sting her imagination into images of what love with Clem Spender might
have been.

Now cousin Chatty seems destined for the same safe harbor; for
though she has lingered until twenty-five, she has at last become engaged
to Jim's second cousin, Joe. It is a relief all around; one worried about
Chatty—so Delia muses as the tale begins, wondering why her cousin
has demanded with such urgent insistence to see her that afternoon.

Chatty was always a difficult case, one of the "poor" Lovells, with hair that was too red and eyes that were too pale. And then, she had been ill—lung disease like her prematurely deceased father, they said—and was hastily bundled off to a remote village in Georgia to recover. When she came back, she was more unpromising than ever, wearing plain Quakerish clothes and devoting a terrible energy to the care of indigent orphans. It was then that everyone decided that Chatty was destined to become an old maid; and just when people had settled comfortably into the notion, Chatty manifested the Lovell perversity and engaged herself to Joe Ralston. Delia was happy for her, of course, but wary of Chatty's unpredictable moods; and her anxiety is well-founded. The purpose of Chatty's visit that day is to announce that she cannot be married after all.

Joe insists that she give up her orphans; he fears that her contact with them might bring contamination home to their own children. She can never relinquish her foundlings—she insists upon that with feverish excitement—she cannot give them up because one of them is her own. Her own and Clem Spender's. A disillusioned young man whose sweetheart has decided to espouse security, and a lonely girl with so few expectations. One could imagine it. "Yes, that was Clem Spender all over," Delia muses, "tolerant, reckless, indifferent to consequences, always doing the kind thing at the moment, and too often leaving others to pay the score. 'There's something cheap about Clem,' Jim had once said in his heavy way" (36–37). And now here is Chatty, begging for admission to the happy estate: " 'I want to marry—to be a wife, like all of you' " (37). Delia can feel the force of that plea.

Somehow, Chatty must keep her baby. Standing there with one red spot staining each pallid cheek, trembling with insistence, Chatty makes her priorities clear. But she cannot have the baby and also have marriage. "The idea of Charlotte's marrying Joe Ralston—her own Jim's cousin—without revealing her past to him, seemed to Delia as dishonourable as it would have seemed to any Ralston. And to tell him the truth would at once put an end to the marriage; of that even Chatty was aware. Social tolerance was not dealt in the same measure to men and to women, and neither Delia nor Charlotte had ever wondered why: like all the young women of their class they simply bowed to the ineluctable" (66). So, Chatty must relinquish her dream of marriage (that is the sacrifice she knowingly lays at Delia's feet), and her cousin must contrive to find the money to support Chatty and "one of her foundlings."

Deftly, Delia negotiates the exchange. Chatty is rumored to have had a recurrence of her illness; marriage is impossible, and by compensation, Chatty is allowed one little girl. Even Delia's husband Jim recognizes that " 'a woman *must* have children to love—somebody else's if not her own' " (75); and "it was said—Dr. Lanskell was understood to have said—that the baffled instinct of motherhood was peculiarly intense in cases where lung-disease prevented marriage" (86).

Charlotte takes her little girl, then, and goes into seclusion. Little by little, all signs of illness leave her; she grows "robust and middle-aged, energetic and even tyrannical" (87). And as the transformation in her character takes place, she becomes "more and more like the typical old maid: precise, methodical, absorbed in trifles, and attaching an exaggerated importance to the smallest social and domestic observances" (87). It is her fate; people have been right all along. Years pass. Chatty and the girl, Clementina, might remain forever removed from Delia's world were it not for the accident of Jim Ralston's early death. The widow is left alone with her own two children; it seems only natural that she should offer to take in her cousin and the cousin's ward. And so they come together into a peculiar menage—the mother and the children and the old maid.

Almost from the first, Chatty's orphan calls "Delia Ralston 'Mamma,' and Charlotte Lovell 'Aunt Chatty' " (88–89). Nothing else seems quite natural in the presence of Delia's ample affection and Charlotte's disciplined austerity. As Tina grows older, she withdraws bit by bit from Aunt Chatty, whose ways seem "so dreadfully old-maidish. . . . 'But she *is*,' " the girl protests whenever Delia tries to mediate between them, " 'in her inmost soul, I mean. I don't believe she's ever been young— ever thought of fun or admiration or falling in love—do you?' " (91–92). Chatty merely purses her lips and remains silent, and only occasionally with a quick leap of intuition can Delia enter into the other woman's soul and for a moment once more measure "its shuddering loneliness" (94). Even worse, her own easy intimacy with the girl quite unintentionally accentuates Chatty's plight. Delia "always knew beforehand exactly what her own girl would say; but Tina's views and opinions were a perpetual delicious shock to her. Not that they were strange or unfamiliar; there were moments when they seemed to well straight up from the dumb depths of Delia's own past. Only they expressed feelings she had never uttered, ideas she had hardly avowed to herself: Tina sometimes said things which Delia Ralston, in far-off self-communions, had imagined herself saying to Clement Spender" (101–2).

Out of the blue one day, Charlotte insists that her bedroom be moved downstairs, into the small room next to Tina's. At first, just for a moment, Delia suspects her of jealousy and possessiveness; but then she reasons that "Charlotte, as Tina's mother, had every right to wish to be near her, near her in all senses of the word; what claim had Delia to oppose to that natural privilege?" (102–3). But it is not privilege, after all, that has motivated Chatty; she has discerned the need to keep an unobtrusive watch over the girl's bedroom. Clementina is of marriageable age now, and she has a bewitchingly charming manner. Yet she is not really eligible to marry any of the young men who escort her, for her background is clouded. One young man in particular has been taken with her, Lanning Halsey, who is "handsomer and more conversable than the rest, chronically unpunctual, and totally unperturbed by the fact. Clem Spender had been like that" (110). And only Chatty realizes that a young man may persuade a girl like Tina to let him follow her into the house when he brings her home, that Tina's very existence is the result of such a clandestine meeting. Delia, so much the mother in other ways, is ignorant on this score. " 'I can't imagine, Charlotte, what is gained by saying such things—even by hinting them. Surely you trust your own child.' Charlotte laughed. 'My mother trusted me,' she said" (119).

Later the same night, Delia lies awake thinking about the safe life she chose when she married Jim Ralston. How has Clementina figured in that life? The relationship has had nothing to do with Clement Spender himself (he was pursued and domesticated years ago by a plain, determined cousin who now obliges all of New York to buy his pictures as they pass through Rome). No, the affinity is less tangible; Tina embodies something of Delia's "one missed vision, her forfeited reality" (130). Tina is hope—hope for the future, hope that a beloved someone will enjoy the opportunities that Delia has relinquished. This, then, is what babies were "to make up for": the things that their parents have missed.

And what of Tina herself? As things stand, she has no future; Chatty has proposed to take her away, someplace obscure without the temptations of young men like Lanning Halsey. Delia can give Tina an alternative to that exile: if she adopts the girl, Clementina will acquire all the respectability that the Ralston name can bestow. Is this a selfish desire on Delia's part? Or is Chatty's plan merely a sacrifice of Tina to the natural mother's own jealous "desire for mastery" (155)? Once more the two women confront each other as they did the afternoon when Chatty had sought Delia's help to keep her baby; now Delia must beg this woman to relinquish the child at last. Another exchange is negotiated; and Chatty "hid her face in the cushions, clenching them with violent hands. The same fierce maternal passion that had once flung her down upon those same cushions was now bowing her still lower, in the throes of a bitterer renunciation" (155).

The adoption is accomplished. Tina is engaged to Lanning; the preparations for the nuptial have been made; and the two women are left alone together for the last evening with the daughter they have so strangely shared. As the shadows lengthen, Delia rises. " 'You were going up now to speak to Tina?' Charlotte asked. 'I—yes. It's nearly nine. I thought . . .' " (176). All of the unvoiced antipathies find expression now. The girl should have a mother's counsel—" 'Yes; I feel that.' Charlotte Lovell took a hurried breath. 'But the question is: *which of us is her mother?* . . . Just tonight,' Charlotte concluded, *'I'm* her mother' " (177–78). Charlotte's fury boils to the surface. Hate—" 'it's the word that's been between us since the beginning—the very beginning! Since the day when you discovered that Clement Spender hadn't quite broken his heart because he wasn't good enough for you; since you found your revenge and your triumph in keeping me at your mercy, and in taking his child from me! . . . That was what I gambled on, you see—that's why I came to you that day. I knew I was giving Tina another mother' " (178–81). Delia recoils from the assault; it is on her lips to denounce the withered old woman who has spoken so poisonously. "Then the evil mist cleared away, and through it she saw the baffled pitiful figure of the mother who was not a mother, and who, for every benefit accepted, felt herself robbed of a privilege" (181). Of course Chatty must go to Tina; and the lonely woman slowly climbs the stairs to her daughter's room.

Yes, Delia muses, "there was a strange element of truth in some of the things that Charlotte had said. . . . All these last days she had been living the girl's life, she had been Tina, and Tina had been her own girlish self, the far-off Delia Lovell. . . . She had made her choice in youth, and she had accepted it in maturity; and here in this bridal joy, so mysteriously her own, was the compensation for all she had missed and yet never renounced" (184–85). Her thoughts wander drowsily, and then she realizes that Chatty has come back downstairs. " 'I haven't been in—but there's a light under her door.' 'You haven't been in?' 'No: I just stood in the passage, and tried— . . . to think of something . . . something to say to her without . . . without her guessing . . .' A sob stopped her, but she pressed on with a final effort. 'It's no use. You were right: there's nothing I can say. You're her real mother. Go to her. It's not your fault—or mine' " (188). Thus the tale draws to a close.

More clearly, perhaps, than in any other of the fictions before 1925, Wharton sounds here the stark note of loss. The two cloistered women at the conclusion of "The Old Maid" capture the essence of age: the knowledge that each life is bitterly incomplete. And on the other side of age is youth, the flushed girl upstairs. For some (here, only for Delia, who has been the "real mother" after all), a child can become that other self, the one who pursues our lost dreams, who is not yet bound by the commitments that slowly root each life—give it foundation and at the same time forever fix its possibilities. We dream dreams for our children in which we suppose that the insufficiencies of our lives will be remedied in theirs.

And hope can mitigate our sense of loss: Wharton has shown us as much in the portrait of Newland Archer; she lets us glimpse it again here in Delia Lovell. However, optimism does not command her fiction now. Although we see the world of "The Old Maid" through Delia Lovell's tranquil eyes, the tale is dominated by the passion of Chatty's despair. Like John Campton, she is the parent who was never—really—a parent at all; and for her, the spectacle of youth brings not renewal and comfort, but a bitter recollection of everything that has been snatched from her.

Wharton unstintingly sounds the mournful cry of age and of hopeless longing now; and the strength of this novella grows out of her bold recognition of the plight that had lurked so elusively in A Son at the Front. To grow old and to be lonely—with all life's options already taken and all life's expectations harshly foreclosed. One must understand the full force of such feelings before one can begin to understand why those who grow old sometimes cling so tenaciously (and unrealistically) to the youth that has passed them by. A Son at the Front was a very partial success; "The Old Maid" is much better; however, both might best be seen as necessary precursors to Wharton's strongest novel of this period, The Mother's Recompense.

2

In some form, Edith Wharton carried the fictional world that is finally realized in The Mother's Recompense for twenty-five years; it was the most persistent, the most firmly tenured of all the residents in the shadow world from which her novels emerged. We have already encountered one treatment of it in "Disintegration," the unfinished first New York novel of 1901. Yet even from the beginning, Wharton recognized that the situation was susceptible to several interpretations (that truth is inescapably brought home by the fact that in her first Donnée Book she recorded the two titles—"Disintegration" and "The Mother's Recompense"—on immediately sequential pages and separated them by only one stark phrase: "Anne's impenetrable purity" [18]). In those far-off days when she was just embarking on her fictional career, it had been the daughter's plight that most decisively captured her imagination, and so "Disintegration" had focused on the lonely little girl. Now this first perspective serves as a measure of the aging artist's shifting interest and greater maturity: the problems of infancy and dependency have been left behind—treated elsewhere and banished from the fictions. Still, Mrs. Clephane and her daughter remained, stubborn specters, and Wharton was increasingly driven to examine the fate not of the child, but of the mother. [19]

How doggedly the case followed her. To begin with, there are the early notations in the first Donnée Book and the unfinished novel. The Second Donnée Book offers little, only a few jottings to intimate that she might have kept the tale in mind. And the contents of the 1918–23 notebook suggest that she had entirely given the story up, for there appears to be no mention of it whatsoever. Yet a closer examination yields more encouraging results: pages 27–33 are missing (lost, one might infer at first); however, a search discovers them where Wharton herself left them, carefully inserted into the 1924–28 notebook. They contain a detailed outline of *The Mother's Recompense*, and they have been placed in that portion of the later notebook where the plot of the novel as it was finally written has been thoroughly worked out. For all these years, then, the tale slipped in and out of Wharton's imagination: over and over again she made a stab at fashioning it; repeatedly, she abandoned it. Yet it never left her entirely, and finally in 1924–25 she was ready to render it, sensing, perhaps, that at last it was time to examine the problems presented by a Kate Clephane.

Foolish, impulsive Kate Clephane; pretty—yes, still pretty when the light is kind. She is so determined to look only ahead; there is no way that we could properly meet her save when she is "awakened, as usual, by the slant of Riviera sun across her bed." [20] Her nature seems like a vast canvas on which have been dashed a few brilliant but scattered daubs; all the rest is blank, an immensity of whiteness waiting hopefully for the strokes of Fortune that will fill it in. Such an un-Whartonian heroine, Kate comes almost entirely without a past: she married (it seems, now, so long ago and distant); she was unhappy; and she ran away, leaving her husband and infant daughter. If she had a girlhood and parents, they have vanished in the mists of forgetfulness. Always bad at remembering, Kate is best at beginnings. Each day is a new beginning for her, and she always chooses her room so "that the morning sun came in at her window, and yet . . . didn't come too early" (3).

Nevertheless, the expectant opening of this fiction is deceptive—just like all of Kate Clephane's beginnings. She wakens to sunlight, but not to sunrise: "No more sunrises for Kate Clephane. They were associated with too many lost joys" (3). And if she wills herself to be born anew each morning, she is born into illusion and not reality. "Reality and durability were attributes of the humdrum, the prosaic and the dreary" (5); these were the characteristics of the world from which she had fled to become a creature living in the perpetual half-light of new days. Now, she exists "in a chronic state of mental inaccuracy, excitement and inertia, which made it vaguely exhilarating to lie and definitely fatiguing to be truthful" (27). Thus it is that she holds so tenaciously to her youthful charm, to the girlish elasticity of her bearing, walking lightly, humming a snatch of melody with "her thoughts waltzing and eddying like the sunlit dust which the wind kept whirling round the corners in spasmodic gusts" (13).

The curse of this perpetual quest for renewal is that the illusion threatens always to dissolve into nightmare. Determined to launch into every day as if it were her first (well, practically her first), Kate has no sustained grasp upon her past; and with no coherent sense of the past, she cannot keep track of the present. Thus her world pivots upon disjunctions of time and space, and each day becomes an uncertain process of forgetting and trying to remember. Her age, for example, so discreetly veiled, has at last become a matter for conjecture even to Kate herself; she is "forty-two or so (or was it really forty-four last week?)" (4). The image of the daughter left behind these eighteen years is unchanged: she is always, in her mother's imagination, "little Anne." What would it be like to see her again, Kate wonders: " 'My daughter . . . my daughter Anne . . . Oh, you don't know my little girl? She *has* changed, hasn't she? . . . My daughter . . . my daughter Anne . . . let me introduce you to this big girl of mine . . . my little Anne' " (15).

Most disconcerting of all is Kate's effort to manage her memories of young Chris Fenno; for her interlude with him is the one jewel-like memory that shines through all those other uncertainties in the past. How old would Chris be now? Thirty-three? "No, thirty-one, he couldn't be more than thirty-one, because *she*, Kate, was only forty-two . . . yes, forty-two . . . and she'd always acknowledged to herself that there were nine years between them; no, eleven years, if she were really forty-two; yes, but was she? Or, goodness, was she actually forty-five? Well, then, if she was forty-five—just supposing it for a minute—and had married John Clephane at twenty-two, as she knew she had, and little Anne had been born the second summer afterward, then little Anne must be nearly twenty . . . why, quite twenty, wasn't it? But then, how old would *that* make Chris? Oh, well, he *must* be older than he looked . . . she'd always thought he was. That boyish way of his, she had sometimes fancied, was put on to make her imagine there was a greater difference of age between them than there really was. . . . And of course she'd never been that dreadful kind of woman they called a 'baby-snatcher' " (10–11). How difficult it is for Kate to keep track of these things. " 'My looking-glass, please,' " she calls out to her maid. "She wanted to settle that question of ages" (11). And yet some things spring out from the past like living entities. If she cannot recall Chris Fenno's age, she can recall his jaunty manner—the way they loved. She can recall, though she would ever so much rather not, that he left as good-naturedly as he ever did anything else, and that she has been waiting for a word "for two years, three years; yes, exactly three years and one month—just a word from him to say: *'Take me back!'* " (8).

The time with Chris was the most brilliant improvisation on the canvas of her life; no wonder she is still expecting that magic message, *"Take me back."* By comparison, everything now is dreary and aimless. All sense of continuity sacrificed to the ritual of renewal, Kate must manufacture and organize the contents of each day. Her rounds are recorded securely in her engagement-book; it is essential to have an engagement-book, for it is thus that she measures the moments of her existence—by notations to try on a dress, to visit the milliner, to take a slow, solemn drive with old Mrs. Minity. A precarious business, this buzzing confusion of endless beginnings that lead precipitously close to oblivions; it compels such a constant touch on the orienting landmarks of life. As for being alone, "she had never, for years at any rate, been able to bear it for long; the crowd, formerly a solace and an escape, had become a habit, and being face to face with her own thoughts was like facing a stranger. Oppressed and embarrassed, she tried to 'make conversation' with herself; but the soundless words died unuttered, and she sought distraction in staring about her at the unknown faces" (21–22).

Most of her memories have blurred into indistinction: her husband, now dead, has become the most transparent shade; his imperious mother is no more than a vanished annoyance who is difficult to call to mind any more. Even Hylton Davies, with whom she fled on that improvident early morn, "had become to her, with his flourish and his yachting clothes . . . the highly coloured hero (or villain) on the 'jacket.' From her inmost life he had vanished into a sort of remote pictorial perspective, where a woman of her name figured with him, in muslin dresses and white sunshades, herself as unreal as a lady on a 'jacket' " (17). A creature without a past. Who is she then? Gratefully, Kate can answer *that* question. She came into existence when she met Chris Fenno: "At thirty-nine her real self had been born; without him she would never have had a self" (18). That is why she must cling fast to the memory of Chris if to no other at all. Perhaps the affair was a mere passing thing for him; he was so young (though one didn't like to think it—no, surely it was more, much more). But to Kate Clephane, it was everything: the recollection of it—the hope, the daily expectation that he will return—is the only thing that sustains her sense of self. If it be a fantasy, then she needs the fantasy, able to endure the newness of each morning only because it might be *the* morning.

Today she has received a telegram. "For her? It didn't often happen nowadays. But after all there was no reason why it shouldn't happen once again—at least once. There was no reason why, this very day, this day on which the sunshine had waked her with such a promise, there shouldn't be a message at last, the message for which she had waited for two years, three years" (8).* Quivering with excitement, the urgency to

---

* In this passage as in many that render Kate's thoughts, there is an eddying of language that mirrors her inability to understand or accept the linear nature of time. Masterfully, Wharton has captured the essence of Kate's confusions in the linguistic structures that are habitual to her. Thus she repeats certain phrases—"happen once again—at least once" or "this very day, this day on which the sunshine had waked her" or "a message at last, the message for which she had waited"—almost as if she is backstitching a fine seam. It is a

be born again into that "real self" filling every fiber of her body, she tears open the blue fold. " 'Mrs. Clephane dead—' A shiver ran over her. *Mrs. Clephane dead?* Not if Mrs. Clephane knew it! Never more alive than today. . . . What was the meaning of this grim joke?" (9).

When Kate has pulled herself together, she can recognize that the telegram refers to her mother-in-law and that her daughter is now entreating her to come back to New York. Nevertheless, Wharton intends the macabre irony of the message.

Mrs. Clephane, Kate herself, is dead—amid all these determined new days, extinguished indeed. The nirvana into which she has cast herself, avoiding change and artfully eluding the effects of time's progress, has obliterated all ties, all responsibilities, all continuity in life. If it has conferred "freedom," its gift constitutes an exemption from the very things that might confirm her sense of self. She is hollow, then, monstrously empty, and all her delights are built on insubstantial fantasies. The delusion of constant renewal and endless beginnings is itself a denial of the essence of life; its consequence is a terrible death of the soul.

Thus it is that Kate seizes the chance to return, for occasionally she can actually assess her situation—"always pretending that she felt herself free, and secretly knowing that the prison of her marriage had been liberty compared with what she had exchanged it for" (73). To return is to initiate another beginning: "Anne's mother [could be] born again . . . on the gang-plank of the liner that . . . [brought] her home" (71). And the birth is such an easy one, everybody so eager to welcome her: "Smoothness, Kate Clephane could see, was going to mark the first stage of her re-embarkation on the waters of life" (72).

Like some consummate actress who can get herself together for a role, Kate works at the illusions that make her seem actually to *be* "the Mother." She purchases an inobtrusive (but definitely elegant) dark dress to make a decorous bow in the direction of Anne's grandmother's decease; she listens to her girl (she can call this unknown young adult "my girl" without the slightest tremolo); and she begins to dine with the middle-aged group of people whom she had called friends so long ago. All at once, she seems anchored and real. "To be with Anne, to play the part of Anne's mother—the one part, she now saw, that fate had meant her for—that was what she wanted with all her starved and world-worn

---

manner that creates an echo, reiterates the past, making past into present as if time *could* repeat itself or even stand still.

soul. To be the background, the atmosphere, of her daughter's life; to depend on Anne, to feel that Anne depended on her; it was the one perfect companionship she had ever known, the only close tie unmarred by dissimulation and distrust. The mere restfulness of it had made her contracted soul expand as if it were sinking into a deep warm bath" (87). She will return as if nothing whatsoever had happened, as if "they had never been disjoined—as if Anne were that other half of her life, the half she had dreamed of and never lived. To see Anne living it would be almost the same as if it were her own; would be better, almost; since she would be there, with her experience, and tenderness, to hold out a guiding hand, to help shape the perfection she had sought and missed" (75–76). Optimistic Kate Clephane, dreaming the dreams so many mothers dream—of the babies who make up for everything else. And yet for her, these visions have a more urgent significance—the assurances of life against those revenants of death, the expectation that having been reborn as Anne's mother, she can continue to *be*, so long as she participates in Anne's reality. A frightening, cannibalistic variant of "mother's dreams."

Wharton's language here reinforces our sense of the hopelessness and deformity of Kate's eternal quest. Her needs are insatiable: the yearning for confirmation and reassurance is infinite—an enveloping quicksand for all who venture near her.

Thus even motherhood, which had seemed such a sure thing, is elusive; and from the beginning Kate has difficulty conforming to her latest identity. She has memories of a daughter, but they are echoes of a chubby child crying out through the nursery, " 'Mummy—Mummy—I want my *Mummy!*' " (22). When she meets Anne, she tries to discern "the round child's body she had so long continued to feel against her own, like a warmth and an ache, as the amputated feel the life in a lost limb" (37), but all she can see is the "tall black-swathed figure" (37) of the young woman. The interim is a mystery. How has the transformation between baby and young woman occurred? "It was as if one had set out some delicate plant under one's window, so that it might be an object of constant vigilance, and then gone away, leaving it unwatched, unpruned, unwatered—how could one hope to find more than a dead stick in the dust when one returned? But Anne was real" (75). However, if Kate attempts to drop a veil of ignorance over the events of her child's growth, the simple facts will not support her. Anne gives evidence of having been tended by others—in the swift finality of her voice, for instance, that sounds so disconcertingly like her grandmother's. Kate's long absence resounds in awkward pauses and sudden silences between mother and daughter, for they have almost nothing to say to each other. Often, Kate lapses into loneliness, oppressed by the fact that "there were hours when the sense of being only a visitor in the house where her life ought to have been lived gave her the same drifting uprooted feeling which had been the curse of her other existence. It was not Anne's fault; not that, in this new life, every moment was not interesting and even purposeful, since each might give her the chance of serving Anne, pleasing Anne, in some way or another getting closer to Anne. But this very feeling took a morbid intensity from the fact of having no common memories, no shared associations to feed on" (103–4).

Who is she then (the question arises once again)? Anne's Mother. She was born into selfhood when she crossed the gangplank and became Anne's Mother. Yet even Kate is occasionally troubled by the likeness of this relationship to "that other isolated and devouring emotion which her love for Chris had been" (104).

Kate cannot bring herself to acknowledge what we are so clearly meant to infer: that this identity, too, can subsist only on a deliberate disjunction of normal processes. In New York as on the Riviera, time must stop to accommodate Kate Clephane. "To keep Anne for the rest of her life unchanged, and undesirous of change—the aspiration was inconceivable. . . . Only she did not want her to marry yet—not till they two had grown to know each other better, till Kate had had time to establish herself in her new life. So she put it to herself; but she knew that what she felt was just an abject fear of change, more change—of being uprooted again, cast once more upon her own resources" (86). The Motherhood of Kate Clephane can be a plausible charade only when it is played in a vacuum: she has no friends her own age—"was it because she was too much engrossed in her daughter to make any? Or because her life had been too incommunicably different from that of her bustling middle-aged contemporaries, absorbed by local and domestic questions she had no part in?" (104). In actuality, mothers obtrude less and less into their children's lives as the children grow up—eventually, "a real mother is just a habit of thought to her children" (194). Thus Kate cannot afford the real thing: without Anne's conscious and continuous acknowledgment, Kate's new-found self would evaporate. Who would she be then?

All of Kate's difficulties are cast into vivid relief by the appearance of Chris Fenno as Anne's suitor. The thing seems preposterous to her, her former lover and her daughter. Beyond her instinctive recoil, Kate cannot think; her feelings are too perversely intertwined. Everyone knows, of course, that Kate was acquainted with the boy, years ago, when he traveled in Europe before the war, but no one suspects the truth. No one would, for Chris Fenno has changed. There is no doubt that we are meant to credit this change: he has matured. Sobered by his experience in combat, he has become more meditative and responsible. He has not sought the complications, for he fell in love with Anne before he knew that Kate was her mother. When he found out, he tried to leave her; but he could not because the girl's passion for him so clearly matched his for her. He has honestly searched for the honorable and just course: indeed, one might say that he has outgrown Kate Clephane—and grown into a man who is appropriate for her daughter.

Yet Kate cannot confront these facts. She must manage this difficulty as she has managed all the others, by behaving as if time could be bent to her whimsy, ignored and stopped in the service of her peace of mind.

At first, time seems indeed to be her servant, and she fancies that Chris has reentered her life only to claim the self that was born when she was thirty-nine. When she learns the truth, she has nothing but her precarious identity as Anne's mother to support her. What is her duty as Anne's mother? What guides can Kate use to define duty? "Her duty—how he used to laugh at the phrase! He told her she had run away from her real duties only for the pleasure of inventing new ones, and that to her they were none the less duties because she imagined them to be defiances" (124). The duty she invents now is that of keeping the lovers apart, dissimulating with her daughter and threatening to reveal Chris—to Anne, to his own family. It should be a ghastly ordeal, but to her surprise, Kate finds that she is rejuvenated by the project. "She had to deceive Anne, to lull Anne's suspicions, though she were to die in the attempt. And she had not died— That was the worst of it. She had never been more quiveringly, comprehensively alive. . . . They said grief was ageing—well, this agony seemed to have plunged her into a very Fountain of Youth" (160). Never more alive; Mrs. Clephane is not dead, of course not. By keeping Chris and Anne apart, she can seem to halt time's progress once again and preserve her sense of self, both as Chris's lover and as Anne's mother. And when Chris leaves—sending a telegram that "Kate opened with bloodless fingers. 'I am going.' That was all" (179) —it is almost as good as reading the words *"Take me back"* for which she had yearned for so long. "The bitterness of death was passed," she thought gratefully to herself, "yes—but the bitterness of what came after?" (178).

New York is not a village suspended in time on the Riviera; from the moment she set foot on shore, Kate has been confronted by evidences of time's domination here. To begin with—even before she left—there were unfamiliar and disconcerting intrusions of death-thoughts into her bright beginnings; now death's shade haunts her ever more relentlessly in New York. Take the case of Fred Landers, such a dear old friend, still unmarried, still pining after Kate. She has practiced her first words to him: " 'Fred Landers! Dear old Fred! Is it you, really? Known me anywhere? Oh, nonsense! Look at my gray hair. But *you*—' She had said the words over so often in enacting this imagined scene that they were on her lips in a rush" (37). But they are never uttered. Fred Landers has become a "heavy grizzled man with a red and yellow complexion and screwed-up blue eyes whom Time had substituted for the thin loose-jointed friend of her youth" (37). Protestations that he is unchanged would make Kate look ridiculous; she must remain silent. Indeed, the evidences of time's indisputable power are everywhere here—even in that triumphant interview with Chris when she wins back her girl, her "little Anne," "a clock she had not noticed began to tick insistently. It seemed to be measuring out the last seconds before some nightmare crash that she felt herself powerless to arrest" (174).

Kate can ignore time, perhaps, but Wharton's reader cannot. Its passage is the foundation upon which the novel is structured. Book I begins in the morning. Book II picks up with a meditative midday stroll during which Kate reflects upon the delicacy of her situation "for the thousandth time as she turned into the Park one afternoon" (105). Book III continues the progression into evening: Kate and Anne are traveling now—desolately wondering whether there was "never any night, real black, obliterating, in all these dazzling latitudes" (185). And Kate's final, horrifying glimpse of Anne and Chris together comes when the dark of night has definitively fallen. The novel ends with a new day, of course—morning again. But it is a nightmare beginning outside real time, not morning at all, no more than a mockery of mornings.

So no matter what course Kate pursues, what apparent victories she wills in the matter, there must be the bitterness after—"the time to come, when mother and daughter were left facing each other like two ghosts in a gray world of disenchantment" (178–79). Kate has not beaten time (could never beat time); she has merely pulled her girl out of the normal run and into the shadow world which has been Kate's realm for so long—both ghosts now. They travel; running away has always been Kate's best balm. But all the while Anne grows distant and quiet, and "her soul seemed to freeze about its secret" (186). One day, Anne breaks into speech—more bitterness and now more than a touch of her mother's soul-starvation: " 'All this beauty and glory in the world—and nothing in me but cold and darkness' " (188). Anne is in mortal peril of becoming her mother's daughter now, and she turns in bitter revolt. " 'You want me to go on suffering, then? You want to kill me?' " (192). Finally everything returns to the matter of death—Anne's or Kate's—and Anne chooses life; she decrees that they will return to New York, to the normal courses of generation and the passage of time.

Chris Fenno returns, too; for a brief rapturous moment Kate fancies that she will hear the words *Take me back* at last: "He had come to her, then—had come of his own accord! She felt dizzy with relief and fear" (218). But time has moved on; he has come for Anne, definitely and obstinately. Only Kate is doomed to repeat the episodes of their brief past: "All at once in her own cry she heard the echo of other cries, other entreaties. She saw herself in another scene, stretching her arms to him in the same desperate entreaty, with the same sense of her inability to move him, even to reach him" (222). The battle for Anne is over, and Kate has lost. Chris is willing to brave every threat that Kate can offer. "Well—perhaps it also made her own course clearer. She was as much divided from them already as death could divide her. Why not die then—die altogether?" (231–32).

Yet Anne's view is more lenient; given that she guesses the truth for one brief moment—and then rejects it—it is a view that she might have held even if Kate had decided to confess every nuance of difficulty: " 'After all, we've all got to buy our own experience, haven't we? And perhaps the point of view about . . . about early mistakes . . . is more indulgent now than in your time' " (234). A rather different conception of duty from the one Kate has invented, and one which is confirmed in Kate's anguished interview with Dr. Arklow. " 'It is [the mother's] duty to tell her daughter . . . Unless,' the Rector continued uncertainly, his eyes upon her, 'she is absolutely convinced that less harm will come to all concerned if she has the courage to keep silence— always. . . . As far as I can see into the blackness of it . . . the whole problem turns on that. I may be mistaken; perhaps I am. But when a man has looked for thirty or forty years into pretty nearly every phase of human suffering and error, as men of my cloth have to do, he comes to see that there must be adjustments . . . adjustments in the balance of evil. Compromises, politicians would call them. Well, I'm not afraid of the word. . . . The thing in the world I'm most afraid of is sterile pain' " (265–66). Let the child have *her* life in her time—not tied to a mother whose lifeblood must be extracted from the child's filial reverence. Let Anne make her mistakes, have her imperfect freedoms.

Kate is strongly moved by the plea. "Legally, technically, there was nothing wrong, nothing socially punishable in the case. And what was there on the higher, the more private grounds where she pretended to take her stand and deliver her judgment? Chris Fenno was a young man—she was old enough to be, if not his mother, at least his mother-in-law" (275). Thus considerations of time begin to invade Kate's meditations as she wanders noiselessly about the house looking for Anne. She is not in the sitting room (Kate looks in and sees only her memory of the little Anne who used to sit by that same fire trying to coax the red birds through the fender). Is she in the bedroom? The mother treads quietly across the deep rug. Yes, Anne is there—looking at the dress she will wear at her wedding—and Chris is with her. "Kate Clephane stood behind them like a ghost. It made her feel like a ghost to be so invisible and inaudible. Then a furious flame of life rushed through her; in every cell of her body she felt that same embrace, felt the very texture of her lover's cheek against her own, burned with the heat of his palm as it clasped Anne's chin to press her closer. . . . Jealous? Was she jealous of her daughter? Was she physically jealous? Was that the real secret of her repugnance, her instinctive revulsion?" (278–79).

Devastation could not have come more decisively. "If some incestuous horror hung between them" (279), as Kate must now acknowledge, it is she—the Mother—who has violated Nature's taboos. She has been jealous of Chris's devotion to Anne; that is one horror. But she has been jealous of Anne's devotion to Chris, too—perhaps a more damning indictment—had been willing, almost willing, to sacrifice Anne on the altar of her own propitiations to time by attempting to engross all of the girl's affections into herself. Kate can feel the force of these dizzying condemnations. Now what is her duty? "She must put the world between them—the whole width of the world was not enough. The very grave, she thought, would be hardly black enough to blot out that scene" (279). How characteristic it is of Kate to postulate death—once again death—as the only response.

Anne, Dr. Arklow, Fred Landers have all suggested other alternatives, for death is not the dark angel that haunts their thoughts. In fact, they even offer a new beginning but not a beginning that Kate can accept. Kate might live not far from Anne and become the occasional mother that most women with married daughters are. Or Kate might marry Fred Landers; she is certainly fond of him. Nevertheless, "she winced a little at being so definitely relegated to the rank where she belonged. Yes: he and she were nearly of an age. She remembered, in her newly-married precocity, thinking of him as a shy shambling boy, years younger than herself. Now he had the deliberate movements of the elderly, and though he shot, fished, played golf, and kept up the activities common to his age, his mind, in maturing, had grown heavier, and seemed to have communicated its prudent motions to his body. She shut her eyes for a second from the vision. Her own body still seemed so supple, free and imponderable. If it had not been for her looking-glass she would never have known she was more than twenty" (298–99). And so, even though she knows Fred Landers loves her with the comfortable, unhurried love of a man who has outgrown capricious changes of affection, even though he can accept all the horrors of Kate's situation when she confesses it to him (as she eventually does), she cannot bring herself to marry him. Still time's fool, Kate prefers death—her kind of death—to middle age.[21]

Thus the novel ends as it had begun. "Kate Celphane was wakened by the slant of Riviera sun across her bed" (328). Only "the hotel was different; it was several rungs higher on the ladder than the Minorque et l'Univers. . . . So much was changed for the better in Mrs. Clephane's condition. . . . She had the feeling of having simply turned back a chapter, and begun again at the top of the same dull page" (328). A new hotel, but the same carefully manufactured day that allows Kate to measure the moments of her existence; flirtations to "fill certain empty hours" (336). This particular day, Dr. Arklow arrives, bringing a message from Fred Landers. " 'He would be prepared to begin his life again anywhere . . . It lies with you . . .' There was a silence. At length she mastered her voice enough to say: 'Yes; I know. I'm very grateful. It's a comfort to me . . .' 'No more?' . . . 'I don't know how to tell you—how to explain. It seems to me . . . my refusing . . .' she lowered her voice still more . . . 'the one thing that keeps me from being too hopeless, too unhappy.' She saw the first tinge of perplexity in his gaze. 'The fact of refusing?' 'The fact of refusing' " (340–41).

A new hotel, a new fantasy. All hope of Chris is gone; Anne too, not gone, but never close, never life's comrade—nevermore "little Anne" to enfold and comfort. Who, then, is Kate Clephane? She is the woman who has refused Fred Landers. If she were to accept him, she would be plunged into time and change and the compromises of reality. And the ritual of renouncing an absent lover can stop time almost as magically as the ritual of awaiting a lover who will never return.

We take our leave of her, a lady lost in mists of her own making, the dreams that give an illusion of anticipation to each day. Sterile pain, so Dr. Arklow would define it. " 'But is this really your last word; the very last?' 'Oh, it has to be—it has to be. It's what I live by' " (341). Pain, too, can confirm existence. Kate is cursed—to the end, we must suppose—to shun the human satisfactions of flesh-and-blood relationships, hugging to herself the consoling, unchanging memory of one "grand" gesture. "Nothing on earth would ever again help her—help to blot out the old horrors and the new loneliness—as much as the fact of being able to take her stand on that resolve, of being able to say to herself, whenever she began to drift toward new uncertainties and fresh concessions, that once at least she had stood fast, shutting away in a little space of peace and light the best thing that had ever happened to her" (342).

3

Like *Ethan Frome*, *The Mother's Recompense* does not tie the disintegration of individual character to larger communal issues: thus its thrust is not satirical, and Kate's predicament must be understood as a response to the general human condition and not to a specific social problem. The delicate treatment of Kate Clephane is so fine that one might be tempted to class this novel among Wharton's best, and that would be a mistake—principally because she does not manage to focus her vision unwaveringly upon Kate, as she did upon Ethan's narrator or Charity Royall. Even though there is no clear object of social satire in this novel, the beckoning presences of New York, the old New York of Kate's married days and the up-to-date New York to which she returns, seem to distract Wharton's attention; and they do so without justifying the intrusion.

Thus although we are casually informed that Kate's marriage was endured in an atmosphere of stifling rigidity, we are not meant to infer that the limitations she confronted in any way justified her impetuous dash, though in some measure they explain it. Kate's condition is not an inevitable product of the system from which she fled, and any inference that it might be is explicitly denied. Still, Wharton's narrator dwells upon the defects of that vanished world with distracting frequency, and to some extent this preoccupation clouds our understanding of Kate.

Even less integral to the real business of the novel is the picture of modern New York. The world to which Kate returns is clearly flawed. The young women (save Anne, who is inexplicably sensible and pure) are a loose, insolent crew, and their parents are scarcely better. We see them, through Kate's eyes, at dinner parties and social gatherings. Enid Drover, for example, with her monstrous daughter, is rendered almost as a caricature. "After eighteen years [she] seemed alarmingly the same—pursed-up lips, pure vocabulary and all. . . . Yet the mere fact of her daughter Lilla profoundly altered her—the fact that she could sit beaming maternally across the table at that impudent stripped version of herself, with dyed hair, dyed lashes, drugged eyes and unintelligible dialect" (64). Lilla Gates, her daughter, *is* is a caricature, with her hyped-up vocabulary—" 'Ain't there going to be any more furniture than this? . . . Oh, but I see: you've kept the place clear for dancing. Good girl, Anne! Can I bring in some of my little boys sometimes? Is that a pianola? . . . I like this kindergarten' " (99)—and her degenerate habits. Even thrice-married Nollie Tresselton, who is Anne's best friend, seems to have come from some alien species. Kate watches her at dinner with interest: "One felt her perpetually ordering and storing and marshalling things in her mind, and the fact, Kate presently perceived, now and then gave an odd worn look of fixity to her uncannily youthful face. Kate wondered when there was ever time to enjoy anything, with that perpetual alarm-clock in one's breast" (68).

Wharton's problem here has several components. First, Kate is our observer; we know Kate's deficiencies, the inescapable confusions that char-

acterize her thoughts, and they make her an altogether unsuitable com-
mentator. The calm and occasionally insightful perceptions with which
Wharton endows her (as above in the comments regarding Nollie) are
simply not of a piece with the waltzing, eddying habits of mind that
Kate exhibits elsewhere. She might be the object of our pity, sympathy,
and censure; or she might be a reliable onlooker and evaluator. However,
she cannot comfortably be both, and the double role falsifies the characterization. Second, the criticism of youth throughout the novel is too
sweeping. Like scattershot, it covers a large area without tearing into
anything in particular with telling force. The tone is, perhaps, grudging,
perhaps even querulous; and it verges on both of these without achieving the sure edge of satirical devastation. This more than anything
(more, even, than Wharton's tin ear for the vernacular of youth in the
jazz age) betrays the novel. Published in the same year as *The Great
Gatsby*, *The Mother's Recompense* was no match for the work of the younger
writers when it came to capturing the mood of that strange era. Still able
to dissect the secrets of human misery with appalling accuracy, Wharton
was beginning to show her age in the matter of social commentary.

The reviewers often hit upon this fact, however obtuse they were
about the central meaning of her works, and she found it vexing because
while their remarks were often stupid, at the same time they were often
dangerously close to the mark. In May of 1925, she wrote to John Hugh-
Smith regarding *The Mother's Recompense*. "It *is*, of course, what an English reviewer (I forget in what paper) reviewing it jointly with Mrs.
Woolf's latest, calls it: an old-fashioned novel. I was not trying to follow
the new methods, as May Sinclair so pantingly and anxiously does; and
my heroine belongs to the day when scruples existed. One reviewer, by
the way, explained the title (incidentally remarking that I am always a
moralist!) by saying that Kate's reward for sparing her daughter useless
pain is 'the love of a good man'!" [22] The comparison with Virginia Woolf
galled her. They were often reviewed together these days; and while
Woolf was lauded for her innovative methods, Wharton was consigned
to the dustbin of "old-fashioned." Of course, Edith Wharton kept up
with new experiments in literature. In 1922 she read Joyce's *Ulysses* and
Eliot's *The Waste Land*; but she didn't like either one. "It's a turgid welter
of pornography (the rudest school-boy kind)," she wrote to Berenson of
Ulysses, "unformed and unimportant drivel. . . . The same applies to
Eliot." [23] Changes were taking place everywhere; her generation was

being supplanted, and the experience was not a pleasant one. When she had completed the last proofs of *The Mother's Recompense*, she sighed, "I feel rather as if I'd made my last will and Testament and were waiting for the feet of the young men." [24]

More important, she was growing dangerously out of touch with the world that she felt forevermore to be *her* world—American society, the society of fashionable New York especially. Ever since the publication of *The Glimpses of the Moon*, Wharton had been talking with her editors at Appleton about returning to the United States for a fresh examination of the language and customs of the people she so tenaciously thought of as her own. But she put the trip off. "America?" she wrote to Lapsley in 1923. "No—I'm *afraid*. I'd love the two voyages with you; enough, almost, to risk the rest! But when I think of publishers, relations, friends, invitations—and see how little I can do without great intervals of rest and monotony—I quail at the thought. I wish I didn't. . . ." [25] She did return in June of that year to receive an honorary degree at Yale, but not for long. In all, she spent only eleven days on American soil; and much of that time was taken up with visiting Minnie Jones, Beatrix Farrand, and other old friends in New York and on Long Island. Scarcely time for a thorough inventory of postwar New York. And what she did see, she didn't much like—as those scant satirical passages in *The Mother's Recompense* suggest. Yet one must ask, at this point, whether Wharton's animus is justifiably directed at things she actually saw (or read about, for she was an avid reader of newspapers and journals) or whether her indictments of the new and the young were not really of a piece with the terrible, poignant longings and angers that advancing age brought to her.

Having no immediate family, she was increasingly isolated. The letters of the years after 1921 are filled with invitations to friends to come and visit, letters that chide when an anticipated excursion must be postponed, letters that bespeak loneliness. Her autobiography (published in 1934) begins with this reflection. "Years ago I said to myself: 'There's no such thing as old age; there is only sorrow.' " [26] For Edith Wharton, the sorrow had begun long, long ago, in the childhood she recalled with such pain; however, the particular sorrows of old age were beginning now in the mid-1920's—the sorrows of exclusion and estrangement that gave rise to the theme of the would-be parent in these later fictions. It is cold, perhaps, to have marked the passage of the seasons of one's life with nothing more than the writing of a series of novels, even if the novels have been very good. And now, one senses an attitude of resentment that has even begun to infect her work—manifest in a tone of righteousness and a too-prompt condemnation of the modern world. It is evident in certain passages of *The Mother's Recompense*, and it dominates her next novel, *Twilight Sleep*.

In early 1927, Wharton read *Elmer Gantry* with indignation. It was a "pitiful production," she declared to Lapsley. "America *is* like that, no doubt, but not all and only like that. I said to Walter [Berry] the other day, the trouble with them all is that they don't know what a gentleman is, and after all it was a useful standard to get one's perspective by. . . . I do despair of the Republic, as it is, and without wanting any more reason for it!" [27] Perhaps Wharton had her own "gentleman," Newland Archer, in mind when she made the acquaintance of those creatures who populated current American fiction; certainly her standard for comparison when it came to "the Republic" was the well-ordered world from which she had come. Old New York had been a narrow place—no one was more willing than Edith Wharton to testify to that—and it had produced incalculable pain. Still, it had been a world with certain values; those of its progeny who best exemplified its virtues had led lives of honor and dignity. Now postwar America seemed entirely to have reversed the values of old New York. To what end? The attempt to achieve perfect freedom from pain—that was Wharton's judgment. " 'Being prepared to suffer is really the way to create suffering,' " Pauline Manford tells her daughter. " 'And creating suffering is creating sin, because sin and suffering are really one. We ought to refuse ourselves to pain.' " [28] *Twilight Sleep* is a satirical examination of a society that refuses itself to pain; and Pauline Manford, whose whole life "had been a long uninterrupted struggle against the encroachment of every form of pain" (306), is the ultimate product of such a world, a world where "people's lives [are] disinfected and whitewashed at regular intervals, like the cellar" (19). Pauline succeeds: she does not feel pain. But then, she does not feel anything. As the title suggests, the goals of modern society can be achieved only by general anaesthesia—of emotions and of moral sensibilities as well.

The principal pain from which Pauline is attempting to isolate herself is age. "Rejuvenation! The word dashed itself like cool spray against Pauline's strained nerves and parched complexion. She could never hear it without longing to plunge deep into its healing waters" (319). With determination and boundless energy, this woman of uncertain middle age devotes herself to "plans for a rest-cure, for new exercises, for all sorts of promised ways of prolonging youth, activity and slenderness" (95). If she senses the threat of unhappiness (never more than a threat), she seeks a new healer or spiritual counselor, certain that there is "a cure for everybody's frustrations" (139). That is the great thing about modern life: "America really seemed to have an immediate answer for everything, from the treatment of the mentally deficient to the elucidation of the profoundest religious mysteries. In such an atmosphere of universal simplification, how could one's personal problems not be solved?" (226)..

Like stainless steel, Pauline's life combines efficiency with an attractive appearance; its only defect is that it has none of the components of humanity. Her children, for instance, are a constant source of pride, products of the most up-to-date methods of scientific rearing. But she never has time to talk to them, for she is too busy with her exercises and her cures; thus she does not know and does not want to know that her son's marriage is on the brink of disaster and that her daughter is wretchedly unhappy. These are the victims of the new age of miracles. Nona, Pauline's serious daughter—so often compelled to take the responsibilities that her mother has artfully eluded—reflects sometimes upon the curious inversions of American society. "It was as if, in the beaming determination of the middle-aged, one and all of them, to ignore sorrow and evil, 'think them away' as superannuated bogies, survivals of some obsolete European superstition, unworthy of enlightened Americans, to whom plumbing and dentistry had given higher standards, and bi-focal glasses a clearer view of the universe—as if the demons the elder generation ignored, baulked of their natural prey, had cast their hungry shadow over the young. After all, somebody in every family had to remember now and then that such things as wickedness, suffering and death had not yet been banished from the earth; and with all those bright-complexioned white-haired mothers mailed in massage and optimism, and behaving as if they had never heard of anything but the Good and the Beautiful, perhaps their children had to serve as vicarious sacrifices" (47–48).

Those of the younger generation who have not committed themselves to the premature gravity of a Nona Manford have aped their parents' efforts to avoid pain; and the principal pain of youth is boredom, which they combat with a "perpetual craving for new 'thrills' . . . some insidious form of time-killing . . . drinking or drugging" (14). The hopes of youth are fixed upon "making it" in the movies; and their homes are graced with obscenities, tolerated because they are the "latest thing" in modern art.

Only occasionally do other values permeate the foul air of this world. Dexter Manford, Pauline's second husband, can remember the life of his boyhood. "He had a vision of his mother, out on the Minnesota farm, before they moved into Delos—saw her sowing, digging potatoes, feeding chickens; saw her kneading, baking, cooking, washing, mending, catching and harnessing the half-broken colt to drive twelve miles in the snow for the doctor" (79). Of course that life is all rubbish now—but then, what sort of a life does he want, if not the one of busy, streamlined comfort which his wife has concocted? "What he really wanted was a life in which professional interests as far-reaching and absorbing as his own were somehow impossibly combined with great stretches of country quiet, books, horses and children—ah, children! Boys of his own . . . and girls. . . . In that other world, so ringing with children's laughter, children's wrangles, and all the healthy blustering noises of country life in a big family, there would somehow, underneath it all, be a great pool of silence, a reservoir on which one could always draw and flood one's soul with peace" (80–81). No more than his wife is Dexter capable of confronting pain: the visions of his own mother's drudgery are engulfed in this glossy, magazine image of "family life" that becomes his impossible goal. And having failed to achieve that goal, he settles for illusions of youth and an affair with the wife of his stepson.

Twilight Sleep is chaotically plotted; some of this anarchy is undoubtedly intended as a reflection of the disjointed quality of life in postwar America. Nevertheless, Wharton does not manage to prevent the novel from falling into dreadful melodrama at the end when Pauline's first husband invades Dexter Manford's home one night, brandishing a pistol and preparing to redeem the family's honor. Even worse than the plot, however, is the sloppy management of the social criticism.

Edith Wharton, a product of New York's upper class, has worked herself into a position where she is sentimentalizing the hardships of prairie farming (the authentic life of pain that Dexter's mother led) while she takes potshots at such modern conveniences as good dentistry and efficient plumbing. She has anything but a lethal hold upon the object of her satire. The book is strident with protest, but it sputters instead of dealing death blows; and underneath, never honestly brought into focus, are the problems that occupy so much of Wharton's late fiction. How does one come to terms with the pain of advancing age? When old age comes and one has never experienced the rewards of family, what happiness can life offer? Probably these concerns were more immediately distressing to Edith Wharton now than the decay of American society, seen from her homes across the Atlantic; and probably it was these against which she was flailing so bitterly in *Twilight Sleep*. She had courageously confronted one element of them in *The Mother's Recompense* and had vehemently denied one sort of "solution." But insights into the stark misery of a Kate Clephane gave little consolation; and they offered Wharton no way to deal with her anger—for it is angering, too, to grow old. "Life is the saddest thing there is, next to death," Edith Wharton was to muse in *A Backward Glance*.²⁹ How, indeed, to reconcile oneself to such sorrow?

From the tone of some of the fiction written during this period, it would be easy to infer that Edith Wharton had adopted an attitude of disdainful remove from the world, like a widowed queen wrapping herself in resentment and mournfulness. Occasionally, she *could* stoop to hauteur; there is no doubt about it. But she was far from being that remote figure—"Edith Wharton: The Author"—that has so often been her image.³⁰

If she was snappish in her judgment of *Ulysses* or *The Waste Land* or *Elmer Gantry*, she was immensely admiring of *Main Street* and *Babbitt*; and when *The Great Gatsby* was published, she wrote F. Scott Fitzgerald a letter of such insight and understanding that it "meant more to him than all the others."³¹ She sustained a long-term acquaintance with Sinclair Lewis, not an easy man by most accounts. On her own initiative she began a friendship with the young novelist William Gerhardi by writing him an enthusiastic letter of praise for his novel *Futility;* she even allowed her commendation to be used in the English advertisements (something she virtually never did), and she badgered an American firm into bringing the novel out in the United States. Another young novelist, Geoffrey Scott, the author of *The Portrait of Zelide*, was included in her closest circle of friends; and his early death in 1929 was one of the many deep sorrows that she had to bear as her own life drew to its close. There were others whom she did not know so personally, but admired deeply. The poetry of A. E. Housman moved her to exultant shouts of praise in the letters to Lapsley. She ardently recommended *Susan Lenox* (the unexpurgated version) to her friends. Her penetrating appreciation of Proust's genius is amply recorded in the long essay on his work that is the final chapter of *The Writing of Fiction* (1925). She had known and respected Gide's work since the years during the war when they first met. Not easily classified—this Edith Wharton, who was so sensitive on the subject of "les jeunes."

The truth is that advancing age plagued her most of all because she still felt such an eagerness for life and new experience. Lady Aberconway, one of John Hugh-Smith's friends, recalls a dinner spent with the "formidable" Mrs. Wharton: "I began to anticipate with some dismay those inevitable moments later in the evening when she and I would be left to entertain each other. Her dress, I then noticed, was quite perfect: black satin—elegant yet suitable. . . . Then my eyes wandered downwards and I looked at her feet. What entrancing shoes she was wearing, exquisitely cut, with large sparkling buckles. And they covered such *very* pretty feet. And then I became aware that the feet were jutting out just a little further than was necessary from beneath the hem of her dress." Edith Wharton, sixty-five or seventy, still conscious of her pretty shoes and pretty feet. And with such a ravenous curiosity. Lady Aberconway continues: "She questioned me about my children, asking what it was like to *talk* to a child, to talk often, indeed every day, to a really *young* child." [32] The personal diary begun in 1924 records many moments of unhappiness. Yet there are shivers of joy, too. "I love to be with my friends," she wrote in July of 1925. "With four or five of them I feel my wings; but, oh, when I'm alone how good the talk is!" And—"Back again [at Ste. Claire] after 8 months away. Oh, the joy of being alone—alone; of walking about in the garden of my soul!" The month of May could still play upon her emotions as if she were the merest girl. "The song of nightingales: a spring Gale through the orange blossoms." [33] And she could be girlish in company too. Sir Kenneth Clark, who met Wharton in her later life, recalls the "warm welcome that greeted us every time my wife and I went to stay at one of her houses, the talk and laughter, not to say giggles—for Edith, like her great namesake, Dame Edith Sitwell, was a confirmed giggler." [34] In fame she hid behind shyness and reserve—much as she had hidden behind it that night so long ago when she had first "come out." The same timidity; and beneath it, still, the same bubbling capacity for rapture.

" 'Who is the ugly old woman using my glass?' " Perhaps this involuntary exclamation best captures Edith Wharton's feelings as she moved from sixty to seventy. Still to *feel* so young—and repeatedly to discover one's real age. It was such a surprise. Who could believe that the party would be ending so soon, that dear friends had already begun to depart, that it actually was too late to "marry the right man" and to have the children that she asked about with such intensity? Most likely she did not feel that the time had yet come to leave youth's perquisites entirely to the young, even if her mirror and her calendar told her otherwise. It was hard—very hard—for Edith Wharton to acclimate herself to old age.

It is in the light of these complexities that we must understand the last major motif to appear in her fiction: incest, or more correctly, liaisons between generations. The theme of incest had appeared much earlier in Wharton's work, of course, in *Summer* and in the "Beatrice Palmato" fragment. However, in those cases it was explicitly associated with the awakening of feminine sexuality, and it had betrayed the persistence of certain unreconciled fantasies and fears from childhood and adolescence which were specifically (and rather narrowly) related to the process of initiation.[35] "Incest" as it appears in the late novels has an altogether different implication—even though it springs from the same tortured origins.

As always we must distinguish between Wharton's life and work; however, fully to understand this element in her work, we must begin with the life, with the little girl who had developed such powerful emotional hunger. She was left with many legacies, among them a voracious need for affection; as she grew older, she carried this intense need into her attachment to her father; and that crisis, too, was incompletely resolved. We have already seen the evidence for such a pattern. However, one thing is worth recalling: a woman who has had such a past can never completely eradicate its effects. Despite the resolute determination with which she attacked the impeding remnants of her early failures, Edith Wharton would always carry certain emotional habits with her: an inevitable residuum from those early traumas remained to complicate the dilemmas of adult life. Just as the little girl's unresolved feelings about her father might affect all subsequent *sexual* relationships, so the same persistant ghost of oedipal uncertainty might resonate in any *cross-generational* relationship. An adult role that could be construed as an invitation to rehearse the feelings of "amorous child" would be made more difficult by the relics of past conflicts; and so would any demand to assume the role of "parent." [36] The tatters of those early crises lingered with remarkable persistence—even into old age—and the powerful reticences and ambivalences that characterized Wharton's twilight years are of a piece with the problems that had impeded her earlier life.[37]

Given that the implications of incest touched so many elements in Wharton's life, it is scarcely surprising to discover that the *theme* of incest was integrated into the apparatus of her fictions. Like those evocations of starvation and suffocation and cold—even more like the suggestive and many-faceted image of the threshold—"incest" was absorbed into Wharton's fictional vocabulary as a significant mode of representation. Initially, as we have already seen, it was associated with the intensity of nascent sexuality (this during the years when Wharton was dealing with the feelings generated by the affair with Fullerton). In the last novels it is put to quite different use. Now it becomes a way of demonstrating that something has gone awry in the attitudes of the elders toward their inheritors; and as we might expect, in the works of Wharton's old age, incest is seen from the vantage of the parent—not the child.[38]

What does it signify here? Many different things: a desperate yearning for rejuvenation; the desire to go back and do things over; envy of those who *are* young—and competition with them; admiration for the young—and a desire for their comradeship and approval; the inability (or unwillingness) to assume the role of parent; even a confusion of parental affection with sexual love. Wharton chose to render the complications of plot in her later novels in terms of the incest motif because that way of representing them seemed instinctively appropriate—a distinctive figure in a fine fabric, a recurrent signal of disharmony in the relation of generations. Thus the hollowness of Kate Clephane's life is a result of her inability to accept her place in the "old order," and this, in turn, is manifested in her persistent longing to maintain the sexual relationship with Chris Fenno. In *Twilight Sleep*, Dexter Manford's affair with his stepson's wife is one evidence of his own unsatisfied hungers for youth and "family."

Wharton was ambivalent about growing old; that is, perhaps, only to be expected. The remarkable thing about her vitality as an artist is that she brought herself to focus on the problems of old age as subjects for her fictions: thus despite the fact that she clearly felt resentment, she managed to identify resentment and envy as enemies of life; she recognized the problems of age *as* problems, and she developed a fictional mode in which to render them. The finest completed novels of this period, *The Mother's Recompense* and *The Children*, both focus with exact precision on the crises of generativity and ego-integrity.

There is much to admire in the courage of such a woman; and yet, there is an inescapable undertone of sorrow, too. Despite the keenness of her insight, Wharton seems at last to have exhausted her capacity for discovering solutions. None of her fictions since "Bunner Sisters" sink more perilously into despair than the best novels of her last years, especially, perhaps, *The Children*.

4

The Children had an unusual birth. That is, by the way, the only correct term: Wharton's previous novel had been entitled *Twilight Sleep;* to follow that fiction with a novel entitled *The Children* indicates a quite conscious "birthing" metaphor that suggests the childless author's determination to indicate the nature of the progeny she *had* produced (Wharton delighted in making such private jokes with her fictions—as we have already seen).

The eight-page typed outline of the novel that Wharton sent to Appleton in February of 1927 gives an accurate account of the plot as it was realized in the completed work—with one crucial exception. Originally, the novel was to have ended with Boyne's marrying Judith. As Wharton explains, the conclusion would "be made up of the struggle on Judith's part to keep her children together, of Boyne's struggle against his growing love for a girl who might be his daughter, and of Mrs. Sellars's struggle to keep Boyne, and detach him from Judith. . . . Judith keeps her little group together for about a year, during which poor Terry dies. Then the Wheaters again divorce. . . . The heart-break is terrible for Judith, and she turns in despair to Boyne's sheltering and understanding love. She is now nearly 17, and she agrees to marry Boyne if he will let her adopt [the other children]. He sees the folly of the marriage, and yet is so frightened by her loneliness . . . that, having obtained the consent of her parents, Boyne marries her—but as if he were taking a little sister home. Scopy and the 'steps' and she are always to live under his roof with her. The story ends on this note of quiet emotion, sad yet hopeful." [39] The completed work concludes quite differently; however, there are several things about this original plan worth noting.

It makes concessions (as neither *The Mother's Recompense* nor *Twilight Sleep* had) to the older generation's fantasy of rejuvenation through a sexual union with youth. It permits the confusion of affection for "a girl who might be [a] daughter" with love for an appropriate partner in marriage. And having given these dispensations, the story is to end "on a note of quiet emotion, sad yet hopeful." Now the finished version of the novel is anything but hopeful. The tone of its resolution is one of renunciation and bleak resignation, a finality of loneliness. No one can ever know with certainty what made Wharton change her mind about the book; however, one catastrophic event did take place in the interval between the conception of the novel in February of 1927 and its completion on January 17, 1928.[40] An event that inexorably brought home the devastations of old age and the inescapable erosions of time. The death of Walter Berry.

Berry's decline had begun in late 1926 with an operation for appendicitis. Weakened by surgery, Berry suffered a mild stroke in January of 1927. After her initial fright, Wharton was consoled by his rapid progress. Berry was depressed by the episode, and he made very difficult company for Wharton, who had urged him to come to Ste. Claire for convalescence; nevertheless, he sustained very few aftereffects, and soon he was virtually back to normal. A tentative lull followed as they both resumed normal activities. Months passed. Then, without warning, Berry was stricken again in early October 1927—this time fatally. Both Berry and Wharton were in Paris; and as soon as she received news of his illness, Wharton rushed to his side, seeing him as often as the doctors would allow, keeping a faithful and loving attendance for the long ten days during which his life dwindled away.

Two lifetimes were slipping into eternity now, for Walter Berry had truly become Edith Wharton's other self. "I suppose there is one friend in the life of each of us who seems not a separate person, however dear and beloved, but an expansion, an interpretation, of one's self, the very meaning of one's soul," Wharton recollected in *A Backward Glance*. "Such a friend I found in Walter Berry, and though the chances of life . . . separated us . . . for long years put frequent intervals between our meetings, yet whenever we did meet the same deep understanding drew us together. That understanding lasted as long as my friend lived; and no words can say, because such things are unsayable, how the influence of his thought, his character, his deepest personality, were interwoven with mine." Forty-five years of her life had been shared with him; and now, she had only the last privilege of watching him die. "Whatever I saw with him in the many lands we wandered through, I saw with a keenness doubled by his. . . . I remember that, summoned to him at the first attack of his fatal illness, I found him lying speechless, motionless and barely able to look up, but yet able to whisper, as he recognized me: 'Bamberg—in the hall.' After a moment's bewilderment I guessed that he must be speaking of a new book . . . and going out into the hall I found a newly published quarto on the sculptures of Bamberg cathedral, which he had received only the day before. I brought it to him, and as I sat beside him with the open volume he whispered one by one the names of the most beautiful statues, and signed to me to hold the book up so that he could see them." [41] On October 12, Wharton wrote to Lapsley: "Walter had another stroke ten days ago, and died this morning. All my life goes with him. He knew me all through, and would see no one else but me." [42]

No experience of her adult life filled Edith Wharton with such oppressive misery. Four days after Berry's death, she wrote the starkest of notes to Lapsley. "No words can tell you of my desolation. He had been to me in turn, all that one being can be to another, in love, in friendship, in understanding, and I could give thanks, and warm my heart at the memory of it, but for the slow agony of the last year, and the terrible last days alone with him." [43] The message that she recorded in her own notebook is even more economical in its despair. "The Love of all my life died today, and I with him—." [44]

Walter Berry's sickness and death spanned the time during which Wharton was writing the first half of *The Children*. It is impossible to suppose that the novel was unaffected by them.

This is the saddest novel that Wharton ever wrote. Not tragic nor terrible like the great works of her earlier periods (it does not harbor such lofty aspirations), *The Children* is a simple tale of the chance encounter between age and youth. Only the boundaries of their lives touch, Boyne yearning to become part of Judith's hopeful exuberance and being thwarted—not by willful rejection, but by the obstinate fact of essential and ineradicable differences. Wharton's novel traces the meniscus, following the delicate outline of that momentary comradeship between the middle-aged bachelor and the girl just entering womanhood. And for much of the novel, time is held miraculously in suspension: Boyne,

Judith, the motley band of children, even the governess Scopy, all jumbled together in a never-never-land where generational differences seem not to matter. There is no central "place" in this fiction; the happy band seems constantly in motion, scheming to evade the wicked parents and behaving like some group of truants who play at being brigands and pirates. And then, suddenly, the games are over. Time asserts its claims again; youth returns to its appointed rounds. And Boyne is left to himself, a victim of time's casual, impartial cruelty, with nothing to sound in the long, empty corridors of his future but loneliness.

Both Martin Boyne and Rose Sellars are relics from the past; not merely middle-aged, they wear an anachronistic air of old-fashioned reticence that would be more appropriate to the generation of their parents or grandparents than to themselves.[45] In many ways—as we are clearly meant to infer—this defect is an exaggeration and perversion of something admirable. Thus when Boyne comes to know the Wheater children, he is moved to remember the security of his own childhood, "the warm cocoon of habit in which his own nursery and school years had been enveloped, giving time for a screen of familiar scenes and faces to form itself about him before he was thrust upon the world." [46] What had captivated him most about Rose Sellars was some answering quality in her own life—"stability . . . the way, each time he returned, she had simply added a little more to herself, like a rose unfurling another petal. A rose in full sun would have burst into quicker bloom; it was part of Mrs. Sellars's case that she had always, as Heine put it, been like a canary in a window facing north" (39). Yet in rejecting all of the excesses of modernity, these two fossils have confused stability and timidity; each year they hold themselves a little more aloof from the common lot, ever more fearful of grasping happiness or demanding fruition of life. And that is why they are now both so entirely alone.

An engineer by trade, Boyne supposes peevishly that romance might have sought him out (as an aspiring hostess seeks to cultivate acquaintance with the oldest and best of families). On such terms, "he would have loved adventure, but adventure worthy of the name perpetually eluded him; and when it has eluded a man till he is over forty it is not likely to seek him out later" (2). In that long interim of waiting, time has not dealt kindly with him. He has grown into a "critical cautious man" (3), fussy over small details (have they booked someone into the other half of his cabin?). Everything in his aspect is like his narrowed eyes of "a guarded twilight gray which gave . . . no encouragement whatever" (3).

When Boyne fell in love with Rose Sellars five years ago, she was another man's wife—"resigned, exemplary, and faithful in spite of his pleadings; now she was a widow. The word was full of disturbing implications, and Boyne had already begun to wonder how much of her attraction had been due to the fact that she was unattainable" (40). Rose is, perhaps, most in her element when she is waiting: like the heroine from some splendid novel of the eighties or nineties, she has a thousand fascinating and elusive turns of mind. And yet, this most Jamesian woman is quaintly out of place in a postwar world: her nature can be articulated only in the presence of impediments (like the cold light from the north that seems so oddly suited to her character); and since the impediments of Victorian America have been swept aside, she must create her own. Thus it is that she exudes an air of something "mincing, self-conscious—prepared. Yes; if Mrs. Sellars excelled in one special art it was undoubtedly that of preparation. She led up to things—the simplest things—with the skill of a clever rider putting a horse at a five-barred gate. All her life had been a series of adaptations, arrangements, shifting of lights, lowering of veils, pulling about of screens and curtains" (38).

If Boyne characterizes himself as "an old fogey out of the wilderness" (16), it is a terrain he shares with Rose Sellars—a wilderness of evasions and courtesies, where nothing is said directly and nothing is done and happiness is endlessly deferred. Yet there is another kind of wilderness in the novel: the Wheaters' world of yachts and Palace hotels. As Scopy cries desperately, " 'The wilderness? The real wilderness is the world *we* live in; packing up our tents every few weeks for another move. . . . And the marriages just like tents—folded up and thrown away when you've done with them' " (23). This other desolation is a world of boundless wealth and instant gratification: a grotesque inversion of those antique customs preserved by Boyne and Rose. And set against the two forms of wilderness—unconscious that she is already playing the role of "exploarer" (296) that she aspires to—is Judith.

The miniature league of nations over which Judith presides is a helter-skelter collection: the Wheaters' children and stepchildren, tossed together in an amiable chaos which is the result of careless coupling, careless divorce—elegant life in the new American-Continental manner. And surely, they *are* refugees from the wilderness, where their parents are terrible embodiments of that up-to-date life of "gaiety" and "style" which is the object of Wharton's satire. "Here it was, in all its mechanical terror—endless and meaningless as the repetitions of a nightmare. Every one of the women . . . seemed to be of the same age, to be dressed by the same dress-makers, loved by the same lovers, adorned by the same jewellers, and massaged and manipulated by the same Beauty doctors" (154–55). No one grows old in the Wheaters' world; and certainly no one is outmoded enough to be burdened with family. So only their offspring suffer, casualties to be left behind when their vagabond parents decide to go touring again. The present has been lost to the rustling of short skirts and the insouciant song of the jazz horn; but the future is still imponderable, for it lies in the hands of the children.

The puzzling group that tumbles into Boyne's life is not altogether reassuring on that score: Blanca's eyes are too evasively knowing, and the younger children are too volatile and intemperate. But they are captained by Judith; and a future with Judith would be sufficient to atone for the sins of the parents, even to compensate for a past as sterile as Boyne's. His first glimpse of the girl tells him that; and his very first involuntary reaction—" 'Jove—if a fellow was younger!' " (3)—suggests what he must learn. He has a part in the past, in the present; but as for the future, Martin Boyne is too late.[47]

The difference between Boyne and Judith cannot adequately be measured in years. Told to act her age, Judith starts to her feet, "quivering with anger. 'My age? My age? What do you know about my age? I'm as old as your grandmother. I'm as old as the hills' " (61). No warm cocoon of safe nursery memories has ever cushioned Judith's life. Scopy reflects sadly: " 'Judith's never been a child—there was no time' " (26). Like Nona Manford, Judith has taken the family's destiny upon herself. As she patiently explains to Boyne, " 'If children don't look after each other, who's going to do it for them? You can't expect parents to, when they don't know how to look after themselves' " (130).

Thus she has been left an uneven mixture of precocities and ignorance. On the one hand, she has not the faintest smattering of traditional education: " 'I suppose I'm much more ignorant than you could possibly have imagined' " (34), she ventures to Boyne. And she is, for at almost seventeen, she can't even spell properly. But then, there has been no opportunity for education in Boyne's sense of the term. " 'Go to school? Me?' " Judith cries out in amazement. " 'But when, I'd like to know?

. . . Why, I shall be too old for school before Chip is anywhere near Terry's age. And besides, I never mean to leave the children—*never!*' She brought the word out with the shrill emphasis he had already heard in her voice when her flock had to be protected or reproved. 'We've all sworn that,' she added" (60). No companion at all for Boyne's pedantic appreciations of Italian art, Judith is wise in things that Boyne will never fully know.

Lest she and the others be destroyed by the reckless impulsiveness of her parents' lives, Judith deploys her energy with the utmost efficiency. She dare not afford herself the pleasure of sentimentality over evil and suffering, and Boyne notices straightway that "her detached view of human weakness was perhaps the most striking thing about her" (15). It is coupled with enormous determination; and the oath sworn with innocent ferocity on Scopy's "Cyclopaedia of Nursery Remedies" fires her life with a kind of purpose that is entirely foreign to the likes of Martin Boyne and Rose Sellars (who spend their days fumbling among antique decorums and shaded reticences). Indeed, perhaps nothing else in Judith's nature shows Rose to such striking disadvantage: if Judith in her "exploarer" mood sweeps real and hypothetical obstacles aside with splendid courage, "it was not necessary for Rose Sellars to formulate objections; they were latent everywhere in her delicate person, in the movements of her slim apprehensive fingers, the guarded stir of her lashes" (169). One need hardly speculate whether Judith would have allowed herself to wane and dwindle in a miserable marriage until widowhood eventually freed her—five long years too late.

Judith's utter self-confidence genuinely isolates her from Boyne: he has never been young in that way—failing to see hazards, liberated from petty hesitations—and she has not yet acquired the cautions of age. There is no real world in which he could match her delighted optimisms, none in which she would consent to his gray mantle of cautions.

Even more important, they have developed entirely different sets of emotional habits. Judith has no evasions: she discusses her mother's flirtations and Doll Lullmer's suicide with the same youthful bluntness. When she requires Boyne's help, she flings herself and the other children upon him (a friend of her father's, after all) without so much as the flicker of an eye. When she is happy, she crows delightedly; when she is dejected, she weeps. When she discovers that he is to marry Rose Sellars, she unabashedly sends the gift they are most likely to need: a

cradle. Boyne is constantly being brought up short by Judith's directness, for he is completely unaccustomed to dealing in that way with
others. " 'Why Martin—I believe you're very unhappy!' " she exclaims
one day. " 'Unhappy? Unhappy?' He swung around on her, exasperated. 'Well, yes; I suppose I am unhappy. It's a way people have, you
know. But, for Lord's sake, can't you ever let things be? . . . I—oh,
damn it, Judy; look here, for God's sake don't cry! I didn't mean to say
anything to hurt you . . . I swear I didn't . . . Only sometimes . . .'
'Oh, I know, I know—you mean I have no tact!' she wailed" (268). It is
true: Judith has no tact. It is her most captivating quality. And it intimates what a passionate relationship might be—with a woman in
whom such fierce intensity has finally come to maturity.

In Judith it has not—not yet. And still, the promise of her nature casts
all of Boyne's earlier estimations of happiness into disarray. She sweeps
his imagination up with hers to soar briefly in some freer atmosphere
that he has never known before; and he begins to yearn to follow her in
all things as he follows her one laughing evening up the mountain, up
farther than he has gone before, bathed in the light of a transcendent
sunset. They stand, together and yet still inexorably separated, "facing
the sunset, and immersed, in their different ways, in the overwhelming
glory of the spectacle. Judith, Boyne knew, did not feel sunsets as Rose
Sellars did—they appealed to a different order of associations. . . . But
something of the celestial radiance seemed to reach her, remote yet en-
folding as a guardian wing. 'It's lovely here,' she breathed, her hand in
Boyne's" (184).

Judith, flushed and vibrant, has stolen into his life like some fairy
princess, wakening his dormant emotions with a kiss so light that it
brushes his cheek like petals. "His highest moments had always been solitary" (186); until now, he has not realized that they have been desolately
lonely as well. And marriage to Rose Sellars, once the vision that sustained him, assumes an omnious aspect now that Judith has begun to
throw open the windows of his soul. "He had schooled himself to think
that what he most wanted was to see Rose Sellars again. Deep within
him he knew it was not so; at least, not certainly so. Life had since given
him hints of other things he might want equally, want even more"
(81–82). The exultations and sudden ecstasies of Judith's nature are in-
fectious; "waves of buoyancy seemed to be springing beneath her feet"
(145), and as Martin casts his lot with the children's, they carry him

along. "Uninterrupted communion with the little Wheaters always gave Boyne the same feeling of liberation. It was like getting back from a constrained bodily position into a natural one" (245). Everything to do with youth begins to fill him with a suffocation of longing. Asked about a young man in his field, Boyne can only think: " 'God! I wish I was his age and just starting—for anywhere' " (240).

Surely, there is still time. Such is the hope that leads Boyne increasingly to recognize his passion for Judith—still time to fan the embers of his own youth. " 'She looks almost grown up—she looks kissable. Why should she, all of a sudden?' Boyne asked himself, suddenly disturbed, not by her increased prettiness (the nature of that varied from hour to hour) but by some new quality in it" (205). A boyish excitement invades his moments with her; her lips look "round and glowing, as they did in laughter or emotion; they drew his irresistibly" (269). And the sexual component that has been dormant in his feelings from the beginning slowly begins to dominate. Still time. "He was free, after all, if it came to that; free to chuck his life away on any madness" (307). Why not marry the girl? "Well, he'd had enough of reason for the rest of his days; and a man is only as old as he feels" (307).

Judith's reaction to Boyne's clumsy proposal might be construed as excessively naive; in one sense it is, for she is so totally immersed in her own concerns that she has failed to follow the modulations of Boyne's feelings. Yet Judith does have a clear understanding of the generational differences that divide them. For her, Boyne will always be the friend of her parents, the man who briefly courted her mother, the man who might become the children's guardian. If her dreams of keeping them together in some semblance of family are vaguely formulated—"a house which should be always full of pets and birds; [with her] leading there a life in which the amusements of the nursery were delightfully combined with grown up pursuits" (247)—at least they have one constant theme. Boyne is to be the parent that she has never known; stable, kind, thoughtful. Then, perhaps, she might have time for childhood. There is something infinitely wise in her unwavering certainty that with all her knowledge, she is still only a child, while Martin Boyne is an adult. Thus, when the moment of crisis comes and she turns delightedly to exclaim, " 'Oh, Martin, do you really mean you're going to adopt us all, and we're all going to stay with you forever?' " (309), her mistake betrays a sounder comprehension of life's possibilities than Boyne can muster.

The truth is that it *is* too late. Nothing captures that fact so painfully as the indirection of Boyne's declaration when it is compared with the spontaneity of Judith's reply. How quickly and unheroically the cautious middle-aged man seeks to repair the breach of tone. "There was nothing he would have dreaded as much as her detecting the least trace of what he was feeling. His first care must be to hide the break in their perfect communion—the fact that for a moment she had been for him the woman she would some day be for another man, in a future he could never share" (310).

We never see the workings of Judith's mind, save as they have been inferred and interpreted by Boyne; thus the reader of this novel cannot identify with the girl who flits so enchantingly out of Boyne's vision. The future is pulling away from us now, filled with expectation and promise; and the journey that we have shared with Boyne has been no more than a tantalizing interlude. Afterwards, "there echoed in his ears . . . a line or two from the chorus of Lemures, in 'Faust,' which Rose had read aloud one evening at Cortina.

> Who made the room so mean and bare—
> Where are the chairs, the tables where?
> It was lent for a moment only—

A moment only: not a bad title for the history of his last few months! A moment only; and he had always known it. 'An episode,' he thought, 'it's been only an episode' " (331–32).

What is left for Boyne? Not the saccharine accommodations of Rose Sellars; this brush with youth has dispelled that vision, at least. Another assignment, another journey. Growing old with no warm illusions.

One evening, three years later, Boyne finds himself in Biarritz, an unobtrusive man seated in the corner shadows, watching the young people dance. And in the midst of the jolly company is Judith. "Her eyes seemed to Boyne to have grown larger and more remote, but her mouth was round and red, as it always was when she was amused or happy. While he watched her one of the young men behind her bent over to say something. As she listened she lifted a big black fan to her lips, and her lids closed for a second, as they did when she wanted to hold something sweet between them. . . . Perhaps she was in love with the young man who had bent over her, and was going to marry him. Or perhaps she was still a child, pleased at her new dress, and half proud, half frightened in the waking consciousness of her beauty, and the power it exercised . . . Whichever it was, Boyne knew he would never know. . . . Two days afterward, the ship which had brought him to Europe started on her voyage back to Brazil. On her deck stood Boyne, a lonely man" (346–47).

The desolation of this ending allows us once again to appreciate the solidity of Newland Archer's achievements (for these last scenes offer an irresistible invitation to compare this novel with *The Age of Innocence*). How richly the "real" life of family and community commitment has rewarded Newland Archer, who can honor himself and honor the limited achievements of emotion well spent. For Newland, the future is an inevitable extension of what had been best in his relationship with May and the children; and old age can be a time of mellow fruition. And for Boyne, whose one experiment with youthful emotion came too late, there is nothing but emptiness. There are good days ahead, perhaps, but they will not be *his* days. The future belongs to others—to Judith and some young man, perhaps.

5

There is no doubt that Edith Wharton had begun to hear time at her back. Four days after her sixty-sixth birthday in January of 1928, she recorded a quotation from the Sermons of St. Bernard: "For my epitaph"—"Tranquillus Deus tranquillat omnia." [48] The weight of Berry's death was still with her, and her own health was far from robust. As early as 1918, she had begun to have disturbing evidence of heart trouble; by the mid-1920's, occasional episodes of "fatigue" forced her to rearrange her usually active life. [49] Finally, in early 1929, she suffered a genuinely severe crisis: an episode of flu reduced her to total exhaustion; her heart was affected; and "there was no questioning the fact that she had nearly died." [50] Any novel that she wrote now was liable to be her last novel, her last opportunity to make some statement through her fiction. Such conditions are not always conducive to great art. In Wharton's case, the results were deplorable.

Hudson River Bracketed (1929) and *The Gods Arrive* (1932) are her major *kunstlerromane*, her final attempts to sum up the artist's life; and they are both inferior even to the best work of this last period. Too long and loosely written, the novels are a tremendous disappointment. As Blake Nevius rightly observes, "The control which [Wharton] was able to exert over the separate and combined elements of *The Age of Innocence . . .* is missing in *Hudson River Bracketed;* there is no single view of the action that will satisfactorily explain all its parts. . . . [Furthermore], in style, there is little to differentiate *The Gods Arrive* from its predecessor except perhaps an increasing lack of precision and a deafness to prose rhythms." [51] It is appropriate to treat the novels together: both concern themselves with the continuing development of the young novelist, Vance Weston; evidently, Wharton herself thought of them as one extended enterprise—broken in half only by the exigencies of publication. [52]

Hudson River Bracketed begins with a tasteless attack upon the vulgarity and modernity of everything in Vance Weston's Midwestern background. Feeling the shallowness of his surroundings, Vance comes east to visit distant relations; and only then does he realize what his own origins lacked—refinement, a sense of the past, an accumulation of learning. All of these things come together in the old Lorburn house, "The Willows," on the Hudson River; and the keeper of this culture (eventually the owner of "The Willows") is Halo Spear, the daughter of a distinguished but impoverished old family. Vance and Halo become comrades the moment they meet: she is renewed by his untamed energy; he is desperate to share her sense of history. Eventually (many hundreds of pages later—at the conclusion of *The Gods Arrive*) they marry. In the meanwhile, however, Vance impetuously marries a pretty, shallow woman; and Halo marries Lewis Tarrant, whose money will make her parents' life easier. Most of *Hudson River Bracketed* deals with Vance's struggles, amidst great poverty, to care for his sick wife while making a slow and painful beginning as a novelist. Only at the end of this first novel (after Vance's wife has conveniently died) do Halo and Vance discover the depth of their feelings for each other.

When *The Gods Arrive* opens, Vance has published a successful novel; and he leaves for Europe with Halo still married to Lewis Tarrant, who will not permit her to obtain a divorce. Through most of the second novel, Vance drifts aimlessly about the continent, and Halo caters to his "artistic" whims, completely subordinating herself to him. Despite the relative ease of his life now, Vance cannot write. The relationship with Halo founders, and the couple separates. Halo returns to "The Willows," which she has inherited; Tarrant divorces her; and, unknown to Vance, she waits to bear his child. Vance continues to wander without resolution. Only slowly does he recognize that the pain of growing up and accepting limitation is a necessary condition for artistic productivity. The novel concludes as he returns to Halo, ready to undertake all the burdens of manhood.

These two novels display Wharton at her old-fashioned, lecturing worst. Over and over again they attempt to "explain" the creative process to the reader; and they become more like catechisms or primers than true fictions. Shrill in the defense of what she thinks to have been "her way," Edith Wharton has become, of all things, a bore.

Oddly, the works can be condemned by the very standards they assert. Repeatedly, Wharton returns to reflections like these: Vance "could not imagine putting down on paper anything that had not risen slowly to the verge of his consciousness, that had not to be fished for and hauled up with infinite precautions from some secret pool of being as to which he knew nothing as yet but the occasional leap, deep down in it, of something alive but invisible. . . . The artist has got to feed his offspring out of his own tissue." [53] Fiction flows from invisible inner resources, from the most potent distillation of the artist's life, of the artist's very being. It does not flourish in ease: that is Vance Weston's ultimate lesson. It grows out of pain. "By pouring his suffering into a story [Vance was] able to cleanse his soul of it." [54] Perhaps the principal lesson that Vance must learn as a writer is to confront the depths of his own pain; to use it; to make art of it. " 'Pain—perhaps we haven't made enough of it.' Those last words of his grandmother's might turn out to be the clue to his labyrinth. He didn't want to expiate—didn't as yet much believe in the possibility or the usefulness of it; he wanted first of all to measure himself with his pain, to wrestle alone with the dark angel and see how he came out of that conflict" (GA, 404).

All of Wharton's own best fiction is a testimony to the truth of this insight. She reached into the furthermost recesses of her own life, plumbed the final depth of pain, in order to make fictions. And with fictions, she cleansed her soul. She can tell us this fact; however, she cannot write a novel about it, not even now. Thus her novelist-hero is rendered in the most superficial way. His *real* life (that part of him that hovers at "the verge of his consciousness") must be postulated on some dark Midwestern plain at a time before the beginning of the novels in which we meet him. Wharton fails to explain why Vance Weston wants so desperately to write; she fails as well to demonstrate a convincing link between his life and work. Given the definitions of creativity that she asserts within the works themselves, *Hudson River Bracketed* and *The Gods Arrive* never do succeed in revealing that element of the writer's life from which his art originates.

There is an explanation for the enormity of Wharton's lapse here. Throughout both novels, Weston's work is praised for being "a trifle old-fashioned" (*HRB*, 234). The greatest danger to an author's work, as Weston's reliable friend Frenside puts it, is that it might be no more than " 'raw autobiography, or essays disguised as novels; but not real novels.' . . . It was [Frenside's] unalterable conviction that the 'me-book,' as he called it, however brilliant, was at best sporadic, with little reproductive power" (*HRB*, 231–32). Such was Edith Wharton's opinion as well. Indeed, she was almost phobic on the subject of the "me-book"—going out of her way, for example, to take a gratuitous swipe at *Ulysses* several times in the course of these two novels. Look back for a moment at the long uncoiling of her own work. It is not difficult to fathom the sources of her irrational truculence.

Long ago—it was now more than forty years—Edith Wharton had begun to write fictions. The early attempts failed because they came too explicitly out of her own life: written "at the top of her voice," they were primitive representations of self and little more. Visions, perhaps, but not fictions. It took Wharton many arduous years of apprenticeship before she felt confident of her ability to produce distinct fictional worlds. She knew, better than anyone else, how much of herself was bound into those worlds ("One good heart-break will furnish the poet with many songs, and the novelist with a considerable number of novels," she observed drily.[55]) But she also knew how important it had been in her case to make a clear separation between life and fiction. To be sure, she resurrected her own *problems* and put them into her works; but she used endless intricate disguises and displacements to reinforce the distance between her own experiences and the worlds of her novels. As we have seen, she had to labor at making this distinction; for her, it was the only pathway to good fiction.

A novel like *Ulysses*—especially *Ulysses*, because it was superb—threatened Edith Wharton. Not merely because it introduced innovations in the art of fiction; but because *its particular* innovations *seemed* to break down the barriers between life and fiction and so to lead insiduously back to the practices that had distorted her own first work. Thus were the limits of her growth as an artist finally measured by those very problems that had set her to writing in the first place.

Being unwilling or unable to write a novel that exhibited the *real* connections between an artist's life and work, Wharton filled up her two *kunstlerromane* with a host of subsidiary "subjects" that gave vent to her rage. The novels became a pulpit from which to attack bohemianism and the excesses of youth in general. They became a forum for the most petty grievances—against publishers who write contracts that are unfavorable to authors, against literary prizes (the "Pulsifer Prize" is excoriated with particular pleasure), against impertinent interviewers and people who send questionnaires to famous people. And, perhaps because she was weary at heart or perhaps because she was not possessed by her subject, they plagiarized her own earlier work shamelessly.[56] Working under the threat that this might be her last opportunity to speak, Wharton said a great deal too much; she said it poorly. And then, it turned out that she was given a substantial reprieve after the terrible illness of 1929. She published *The Gods Arrive* in 1932 when she was seventy, and she lived for five years after that, dying of heart failure only in the late summer of 1937. It is indeed fortunate that we have other relics of her last years to rectify the negative impression left by these two novels. Perhaps she *had* to vent her rage before achieving serenity.

Although ten years passed between the publication of *Xingu* (1916) and *Here and Beyond* (1926), the notebooks indicate that she was recording her ideas for short stories throughout this period and that in some cases she was writing them out.[57] *Here and Beyond* contains not one genuinely remarkable story. However, the next collection, *Certain People* (1930), exhibits distinct signs of improvement. At least one of its stories, "After Holbein," is quite compelling—a macabre little tale about two senile remnants of "high society" who hold a ghastly evening's entertainment at which each imagines that the old times have returned. *Human Nature* (1933) suggests an even more remarkable recovery, and several pieces in it are easily as good as her earlier short stories.

Human Nature is dominated by the opening selection, "Her Son," a work almost long enough to be classified as a novella. Wharton had come upon the premise of this story in June of 1925 when she was told the following true story: "Mansfield (the actor) and his wife lived together before they were married and had a child. The secret was kept, the child (son) smuggled away, looked after, but never seen by either of them. They then married and had another son, whom they adored. Mansfield died. The widow was left alone with her boy. He died at 22 of fever, in an American training camp, during the war. Utterly alone, she is now traveling in Europe, looking for a trace of the other, the repudiated son!—*What* a subject—." [58] It *was* a good subject, and it made up into a splendid tale.

More than anything else, "Her Son" suggests a resurgence of Wharton's capacity to control the fictional ramifications of a complex emotional situation with grace and economy. There are other signs of revival. "The Day of the Funeral"—a story about a man whose mistress deserts him once his wife is dead because she has come to sympathize with the wife's betrayed position and to pity her—begins with several of Wharton's funniest lines. "His wife had said: 'If you don't give her up I'll throw myself from the roof.' He had not given her up, and his wife had thrown herself from the roof." [59]

The briskness of this prose is encouraging: Edith Wharton had decided not to retire into permanent grumpiness; and she had not lost her ability to write effective fiction. The last collection of short stories, *The World Over* (1936), confirms the reclamation of her powers. Two pieces, "Pomegranate Seed" and "Roman Fever," can take their place among Wharton's best. The terrible shrillness of *Hudson River Bracketed* and *The Gods Arrive* has not prevailed, after all. Time continued, unappeasably, to make encroachments; but as she approached seventy, and then as she moved beyond, Edith Wharton began to take old age in stride.

Little by little, she could joke about her condition. After losing two cooks within the space of a month in 1930, she wrote to John Hugh-Smith: "We are a trio of old ladies, Mary B., Minnie and myself—. Fifty years ago we should have had no teeth, and could have been fed on gruel—but as it is, we need a cook." [60] After the disabling despair that followed Walter Berry's death, there followed a gradual sense of accommodation: Edith Wharton was prepared to make terms with life. "It's really more and more fun to be old," she confided to John Hugh-Smith, "and to see all the theories come full circle." [61]

It would be wrong to suppose that Wharton slipped into mere acceptance: she was too vigorous, still, for passivity; and she quickened to delights now as much as before. What the last letters and the final entries in her diary bespeak, instead, is a more and more acute awareness of the sense of completion that may be felt by those whose lives have been full. Old age was not a time to be wasted in remorse; it was a season with its own particular pleasures. On May 12, 1933, she muses: "Another year and the tired heart still beats as vehemently as ever. Ah, well—in summing it all up, let me say: Love and Beauty have poured such glowing cups for me that when the last drop of the last is drained I shall go away grateful—if not satisfied. Satisfied! What a beggarly state! Who would be satisfied with being satisfied?" [62]

In late May of 1933 Elise, Wharton's personal maid of many years, died; in October, Gross, her companion since adolescence, passed away. Always, now, there would be the death of dear friends (and these servants were as close as family to Edith Wharton); death would sadden her—fill her with occasional bouts of recurrent despair. But increasingly she could accept the grim eminence of death as no more than one more part of life: if the loss of those near to her brought sadness, it brought an upsurge in her own sense of aliveness, too. "Time's wingèd chariot is always with me since Elise's death," she wrote to Lapsley, "and there are so many places that I want to see and store up!" [63] Just a bit more than a month before her seventy-third birthday, Wharton's imagination could still go soaring with the lightness of insatiable expectation. "More than a year of silence," she muses in her irregularly attended diary, "but in the present roar of the world the still small Voice becomes almost inaudible.—I never cease to miss the comrade of my soul, and my two dear maids, and life without them is a hollow business. But here I am again, in a summer garden, and among my books, and still to wake in the morning is an adventure for me! Oh, incorrigible lover that I am . . ." [64]

Those who knew her during these last years sensed a difference in the moods that came over her. If there were episodes of sorrow—the death of her beloved dog Linky that left her feeling "for the very first time in my life, quite utterly alone and lonely"—such blows could be managed. Edith Wharton was more completely at peace than she had ever been before. No recollection of her captures this attitude more sensitively than the one recorded by Madame de Divonne for Percy Lubbock. She speaks of a quiet afternoon's visit with the elderly author in 1935 or 1936 at the Pavillon Colombe.

. . . For once I found her alone, without her usual encirclement, the barrier of duties and engagements, guests to be entertained, servants to be directed, by which she was commonly enclosed and defended. I had arrived early in the afternoon; it was a rainy day of autumn, one of those days when the year seems to stand still and time is endless. . . .

The hush of the hour could be seen in her face. The restless beat of the eyelids which I knew so well, as she looked about her for something amiss, requiring her touch, was slackened and stilled. . . .

Presently, while the glow of the firelight shone on the last roses of the year, the past was with us in the room, summoned by Edith to join us—in the form of an old scrap-book, in which, with a few photographs, a series of newspaper cuttings, notices and reviews of her first books, had been piously collected and pasted by her governess of early days, till there were too many of them to be kept. Edith turned the pages and showed me these relics with fond amusement. . . . I realised then, as never before, what Edith might have been for the children she never had. Most striking was the perfect simplicity with which she lingered over the record of the beginnings of her literary fame; she accepted her success without vanity and without false modesty, as a simple fact, as one accepts the heritage of one's race and blood. . . . She regarded the days dead and gone with a smile of kindness, while she affectionately drew me in to share them with her. . . .

I still see her pale hand as it turned the leaves of the album; it was like watching the dust of the past, dust with a glint of gold, stream between her fingers from page to page. Her work, her art, her fame, were the gold in it, and as the story grew the gleam absorbed it all. Sitting by her side, in the gracious and orderly room, with the rain beating and the leaves falling outside, I felt the presence of a power at rest.[65]

The power—it is still there—is at rest. The past filters into the present with harmonious accord; and one realizes "what Edith might have been for the children she never had." Wharton had made her final reconciliations; and nothing better captures the merry truce between youth and age than her last work—her very last, unfinished novel, *The Buccaneers*.

Gaillard Lapsley, who was Wharton's literary executor, decided to publish *The Buccaneers* because "the incomplete text contained some work too good to be kept back, so good indeed that she would herself probably have been satisfied with it . . . [and] because the unfinished passages have their interest and value too." [66] There are three scenes that Lapsley particularly admires: the confrontation between Lady Churt and the American girls, the scene depicting Laura Testvalley's arrival at Saratoga, and the episode of the virginia reel. There is no disputing Lapsley's judgment here: these are masterful literary achievements. Virtually everyone who has studied Wharton's work has found much to admire in *The Buccaneers:* Blake Nevius goes so far as to claim that it is "a novel which, had she finished it, would probably have taken its place among her half-dozen best and which even as it stands indicates that with a congenial subject she could still subdue her irritability and regain control of her style." [67] Given that the work *is* unfinished (and considering the superb quality of novels like *The Custom of the Country* or *The Age of Innocence* which reflect Wharton's abilities at the height of her powers), one might decide that Nevius has erred in the direction of enthusiasm. Nevertheless, his response is certainly understandable. One cannot judge the novel for unity or form; one cannot even claim that all of its passages rise to the level of those cited by Lapsley. Yet even after we have made these concessions, the novel compels our enthusiasm. It is a delicious romp— an ungrudging tribute to the high spirits of youth, to laughter and happiness and love. More than anything else, perhaps, it recalls the gentle, joyous shade of Jane Austen [68] This, and not those ponderous *kunstlerromane*, is Wharton's authentic last word; and with her last word, she cheerfully places the future where it ought to be—in the hands of the young.

The Buccaneers records a curious transformation. Wharton could never really understand the general run of young people after the war. Many of them became her great friends, many of them served almost in place of children for her; nevertheless, the jazz age and the age of the Great Depression were not eras that she felt herself to be an instinctive part of. The failures of social criticism in her late novels reveal as much. Nevertheless, in the last five years of her life, she came increasingly to accept the fact that her own time had passed, and she grew willing to relinquish all of life's glorious experiments to the generations that would follow her. In her very last days, she often mused quietly upon the transition. "She talked about Ronald Simmons and Walter Berry: 'Walter loved life so. . . . If he made friends of women much younger than himself, it was because youth and the joy of life go together.' " [69] Yet if Wharton wanted to make a fictional statement of her reconciliation, she could not set it in the present, for her sympathetic understanding of modern youth was insufficient to the task. Thus, for example, although the glowing presence of Judith suffuses the entire world of *The Children*, we never get into her mind at all; we see her entirely through Martin Boyne's eyes because Wharton could *feel* her way through the complexities of this middle-aged man while she could not quite negotiate herself into Judith's consciousness. (If we want confirmation of her difficulty, we need only examine the awkwardness of *Hudson River Bracketed* and *The Gods Arrive* when she tries to render Vance Weston's thoughts.)

How, then, might she draw up her legacy? The answer is dazzlingly apparent in *The Buccaneers*. If she cannot give the future to the young of the twentieth century, she will return to a time she knows; and she will bestow it not upon her own kind, not upon the "nice," well-bred young ladies of genteel old New York—but upon those "other" girls whose families will eventually vanquish Wharton's own. The invaders: girls who had seemed utterly unlike herself, then; girls who had smoked, and flirted, and known the mysteries of sex; carefree girls who dared to expose their tender complexions, without veiling, under the uncompromising glint of an American sun. The jubilant little band whom Wharton dubs "the Buccaneers."

The bulk of her novel belongs, then, to these girls—to Conchita Closson with her shocking red hair and dusky complexion, to Lizzy Elmsworth, and most of all, to Nan St. George—and it is their adventure that Wharton follows. But there is another character whose presence also commands our attention, and that is the small, dark governess, Laura Testvalley. Wharton has testified to the determined way in which this creature emerged from the shadow-realms of her creator's imagination and uncompromisingly asserted herself. "I may be strolling about casually in my mind, and suddenly a character will start up. coming seemingly from nowhere. . . . I watch; and presently the character draws nearer, and seems to become aware of me, and to feel the shy but desperate need to unfold his or her tale. . . . My characters always appear with their names. Sometimes these names seem to me affected, sometimes almost ridiculous. . . . Another such character haunts me today [1933–34]. . . . Laura Testvalley. How I should like to change that name! But it has been attached for some time now to a strongly outlined material form, the form of a character figuring largely in an adventure I know all about, and have long wanted to relate. Several times I have tried to give Miss Testvalley another name. . . . But she is strong-willed, and even obstinate . . . and I foresee that she will eventually force her way into my tale burdened with her impossible patronymic." [70]

The Buccaneers is Laura Testvalley's story, too. The story of her relationship with these girls is Wharton's last parable of age and youth: a tale of graceful generosity. Wharton claims not to know the sources of the decidedly peculiar name. Perhaps not. But we might hazard a guess. "Test Valley" is very like "Valley of Decision": what is more, Miss "Testavaglia" (for that was her name before it was Anglicized) has significant Italian roots. "Miss Testvalley's grandfather was the illustrious patriot, Gennaro Testavaglia of Modena, fomenter of insurrections, hero of the Risorgimento. . . . [His] fame lingered in England chiefly because he was the cousin of the old Gabriele Rossetti, father of the decried and illustrious Dante Gabriel" (40). We must cast our minds back almost forty years to understand the sly significance of this inheritance. *The Valley of Decision* had pivoted upon revolution and bitterly rebuked it; indeed, it had denounced the potential destructiveness of all man's passions. Now Miss Laura Testvalley has emerged to preside over Wharton's ultimate fiction, and she is the legatee of a glorious tradition of revolutions and passions. Her peculiar name bridges the gap between first novel and last; and her nature celebrates the change.

Change. The novel reverberates with it, begins by dropping us into its midst (like *Sanditon*, perhaps). We discover ourselves transported back to the 1860's, to the freewheeling world of Saratoga at the height of the racing season when "you could hardly tell a lady now from an actress, or—er—the other kind of woman; and society at Saratoga, now that all the best people were going to Newport, had grown as mixed and confusing as the fashions" (4). Newport, with its regimented round of calls and its tame festivities, had been Wharton's world, the world with which she had made peace in *The Age of Innocence;* and in Newport, the Mothers had reigned supreme. Saratoga is a different story entirely, for the Mothers here are timid and ignorant and sometimes downright vulgar; in no way malicious, they are simply incapable of rising to the style of life which their husbands' new wealth has conferred upon them. And so society has been left very much in the hands of their daughters. "Ah . . . the girls! . . . The fancy had taken them to come in late [to dinner] and to arrive all together; and now, arm-in-arm, a blushing bevy, they swayed across the threshold of the dining-room like a branch hung with blossoms, drawing the dull middle-aged eyes of the other guests from lobster salad and fried chicken . . . happy girls, with two new dancers for the week-end, they had celebrated the unwonted wind-fall by extra touches of adornment: a red rose in the fold of a fichu, a loose curl on a white shoulder, a pair of new satin slippers, a fresh *moiré* ribbon. . . . To those two foreigners [who had been added to the list of dancing partners], they embodied 'the American girl,' the world's highest achievement. . . . Could Newport show anything lovelier" (34–35).

Frequently throughout this novel, Wharton positions her narrator with Nan St. George, and in so doing she surrenders the fiction to a genuinely childlike sensibility for the first time since *Summer*. There is no doubt of the author's sympathy with Nan: it is reflected in the delightful quality of her innocent reveries and eager conversations. Like all girls, she prattles endlessly about boys. " 'Do you want to get married?' " Conchita Closson asks her. "Nan flushed and stared. Getting married was an inexhaustible theme of confidential talk between her sister and the Elmsworth girls; but she felt herself too young and inexperienced to take part in their discussions. . . . One of her quick blushes steept her in distress. Did she—didn't she—like 'love-making'? . . . The obvious answer was that she didn't know, having had no experience of such matters; but she had the reluctance of youth to confess to its youthfulness. . . . She gave a vague laugh and said loftily: 'I think it's silly' " (17–18). Occasionally, she actually ventures something "fast"—a cigarette, for example. "Nan swung up beside [Conchita], took a cigarette, and bent toward the match which her companion proffered. There was an awful silence while she put the forbidden object to her lips and drew a frightened breath; the acrid taste of the tobacco struck her palate sharply, but in another moment a pleasant fragrance filled her nose and throat. She puffed again, and knew she was going to like it. Instantly her mood passed from timidity to triumph, and she wrinkled her nose critically and threw back her head, as her father did when he was testing a new brand of cigar. 'These are all right—where do you get them?' she inquired with a careless air" (19). How exciting everything seems when it is reflected in the clear, sparkling eyes of such a youngster: so many things that are new, so many things to try—joys, tears, almost a whole lifetime still stretching before her like an endless world of inexhaustible wonders.

The American girls are all as charming as a nosegay of fresh spring flowers; but they have something more substantial than their artlessness to recommend them. They are innately generous (as the scene with Lady Churt demonstrates so nicely); and it is an amusement merely to be in their presence, for they are "fearless and talkative girls, who [say] new things in a new language" (159) with an unhesitating, American frankness. At the same time, they carry themselves with a "sort of moral modesty" (195) that relegates "flirting" to a clearly understood and harmless game. As Mable Elmsworth earnestly explains to a puzzled Englishman, " 'In America, when a girl has shown that she really cares, it puts a gentleman on his honour, and he understands that the game has gone on long enough' " (196). They have a quality of curiosity and energy that shows well against the somnolent English backdrop; and after they have been in London for only a little while, "the free and easy Americanism of this little band of invaders had taken the world of fashion by storm" (355). Above all, however, they have an instinctive sense of value: the best of them, like Nan St. George, resonate to tradition—not because it is a habit or obligation, but because so much that is worthwhile in human experience has been carried from past to present through pious reverences and remembrances. Thus when Nan visits Sir Helmsley's country home, her entire nature calls gently to the host of echoes that whisper through its corridors. "The stones of the house, the bricks of the walls, the very flags of the terrace, were so full of captured sunshine that in the darkest days they must keep an inner brightness. Nan, though too ignorant to single out the details of all this beauty, found herself suddenly at ease with the soft mellow place, as though some secret thread of destiny attached her to it" (136). It is the thread of life in all its infinite majesty that has entwined her nature.

These are good girls, not one of them selfish or mean. They are inexperienced, and they are foolish; sometimes, they are condemned to misery by their own impulsiveness. Yet they have fundamental quality. One can rest easy, knowing that they are the guardians of the future.

Certainly this is Miss Testvalley's evaluation. Laura Testvalley has never herself had the chance for girlhood. "She had never been invited to a ball, had never worn white tulle; and now, at nearly forty, and scarred by hardships and disappointments, she still felt that early pang" (79). At seventeen, she had already begun to work "to aid her own infirm mother in supporting an invalid brother and a married sister with six children, whose husband had disappeared in the wilds of Australia. Laura was sure that it was not her vocation to minister to others, but she had been forced into the task early, and continued in it from family pride" (41). Often, she recollects the deprivation: " 'If I'd been a man,' she sometimes thought . . .'' (41). Denied the opportunity for heroism and adventure, she must discover pleasures wherever she happens to find them. Romance has been no more for her than a brief encounter several years ago with the older brother of her English pupils. Long past now, not forgotten, but not regretted either. "She had paid its cost in some brief fears and joys, and one night of agonizing tears; but perhaps her Italian blood had saved her from ever, then or after, regarding it as a moral issue. In her busy life there was no room for dead love-affairs. . . . Fatalistically, she had registered the episode and pigeon-holed it" (75).[71] Thus it has fallen out that Laura Testvalley's chief delights must be vicarious. Instead of lapsing into jealousy because of her own lost youth, she identifies with the youth of her charges. And if *The Buccaneers* was to have recorded Nan St. George's quest for fulfillment, it was also to have captured Laura Testvalley's own odyssey as handmaiden to the future.[72]

Where *is* the future? Discovering it is Laura's first challenge. She begins in the shivering cold of an English nursery in the home of the Duchess of Tintagel where her days are spent bandaging the chilblains of the younger girls. She moves on to the New World, taking a position in the home of Mrs. Russell Parmore (a woman whose arrogant ignorance sweeps past us like the ghost of Lucretia Jones herself); but "life at the Parmores', on poor pay and a scanty diet, had been a weary business" (38). The future is not here, either, Miss Testvalley concludes; "after conscientiously 'finishing' Miss Parmore" (38) so that she can take her place among the Newport belles, once again Laura Testvalley follows the sun in its westward path, now to join Nan St. George. "She had suspected from the first that the real America was elsewhere, and had been tempted and amused by the idea that among the Wall Street *parvenus* she might discover it" (41). And when she alights from the train one bright afternoon at the height of the racing season in Saratoga, she knows that her first trial has been passed. She has found the *real* America, and with it, the future.

What intriguing, delightful vistas this future portends. "The dancing nymphs hailed her with joyful giggles, the poodle sprang on her with dusty paws, and then turned a somersault in her honour. . . . The enchanted circle broke, and the nymphs, still hand in hand, stretched a straight line of loveliness before her. 'Guess which!' chimed simultaneously from five pairs of lips, while five deep curtsies swept the platform; and Miss Testvalley drew back a step and scanned them thoughtfully. Her first thought was that she had never seen five prettier girls in a row; her second (tinged with joy) that Mrs. Russell Parmore would have been scandalized" (43).

There is a profound sense of rightness—of ultimate resolution—in this meeting, a sense of the world being set in order. The "motherless" girl and the childless woman have finally found each other.

As the novel unfolds and Nan's sensitive nature asserts itself, Laura becomes increasingly conscious of the spiritual kinship. Putting the restless child to sleep one evening with the melodious rhythms of Dante Gabriel Rossetti's poetry, the older woman recites softly, "sinking her voice as she saw Nan's lids gradually sink over her questioning eyes till at last the long lashes touched her cheeks. Miss Testvalley murmured on, ever more softly, to the end; then, blowing out the candle, she slid down to Nan's side so gently that the sleeper did not move. 'She might have been my own daughter,' the governess thought" (90).

At last, in this unfinished work, the envy of age for youth has vanished, and Wharton can show at length what she could only assert at the conclusion of *The Age of Innocence:* that the insufficiencies of one generation may be redeemed by the happiness of the next, that fulfillment in a child's life may bring joy to the parent whose own life has been impoverished. Alas, *The Buccaneers* takes us but partway along the journey that Wharton had planned. We see Miss Testvalley engineering a successful invasion of London by her girls; we see Nan's unhappiness in her marriage to the Duke of Tintagel; however, the beginnings of Nan's passion for young Guy Thwarte have only been hinted when the novel breaks off. For the rest, we have no more than Wharton's outline of the work's conclusion to suggest the extent to which age and youth will cooperate, now, to overturn repression.

> Sir Helmsley Thwarte, the widowed father of Guy, a clever, broken-down and bitter old worldling, is captivated by Miss Testvalley, and wants to marry her; but meanwhile the young Duchess of Tintagel has suddenly decided to leave her husband and go off with Guy, and it turns out that Laura Testvalley, moved by the youth and passion of the lovers, and disgusted by the mediocre Duke of Tintagel, has secretly lent a hand in the planning of the elopement, the scandal of which is to ring through England for years.
>
> Sir Helmsley Thwarte discovers what is going on, and is so furious at his only son's being involved in such an adventure that, suspecting Miss Testvalley's complicity, he breaks with her, and the great old adventuress, seeing

love, deep and abiding love, triumph for the first time in her career, helps
Nan to join her lover. (358)

This summary indicates the direction the novel would have taken, of
course, but it necessarily leaves us dissatisfied. We have seen how powerfully Wharton's fictions were influenced by imperatives that emerged
from the natures of her fictional beings as the novels unfolded. With no
more than these initial predictions, we can never be certain exactly how
The Buccaneers might have concluded.[73]

Nevertheless, Edith Wharton left more than enough to let us know
how far her personal journey took her. Long ago, three-quarters of a century in the past, she had begun as a frightened child, desolate and lonely;
and the lonely child had grown to timid womanhood, filled with confused longings, her character virtually obliterated by fear. And still, by
some feat of intellect and passion and will, that nearly extinguished
young woman had confronted life and become, if not its master, at least
its partner—so that with the end in sight, she could conclude her long
voyage exclaiming, "Oh, incorrigible lover that I am . . ." The buoyant
optimism of *The Buccaneers* suggests the jubilation with which the old
woman's intrepid spirit had succeeded in redressing the miseries of her
youth.

On December 10, 1934, after she had completed one hundred and
sixty-six pages of this novel, Edith Wharton wrote the last lines in her
last personal diary:

What is writing a novel like?

1. The beginning: A ride through a spring wood.
2. The middle: The Gobi Desert.
3. The End: A night with a lover.
          I am in the Gobi Desert.[74]

Who among us can fail to wish that she might have been spared just one
more—"night with a lover"?

Appendix
The Dating
of the "Beatrice Palmato" Fragment

Although Edith Wharton's letters may be found in a number of libraries, virtually all of the remnants of her fictions (both first copies of published material and all of the unpublished fragments and notebooks) are gathered together in the Beinecke Library at Yale University. The fictional archives are catalogued alphabetically, with no indication of date. Thus when I discovered the "Beatrice Palmato" fragment with story-outline (during a reading of the archives which had proceeded from no more sophisticated basis than beginning with the A's and concluding with the X's—there were no Z's), I needed to date the fragment if I wished to make any use of it in my estimation of Wharton's growth as a novelist. As I have indicated in the text, my deductions have led me to infer that the fragment was written in 1918 or 1919. It could have been written earlier (the sensuous tone of it leads me to suspect that it *may* have been written during the Moroccan adventure); however, it is highly unlikely that it was written later. Having asserted as much in the text, I offer here the evidence that led to my conclusion.

1. *The handwriting.* Not the most persuasive clue, perhaps, it is the first to come to eye. Wharton's handwriting changed dramatically during the 1920's. After the severe illness of 1929, it became unmistakably different from her earlier script; however, even before that date, it had begun to degenerate. The individual letters are larger, the strokes loopier and less precise, the lines less even. Although this quality is, perhaps, most apparent (especially in correspondence) during and after periodic bouts with the flu, an overall examination of longer pieces of writing (in plot-outlines and notebooks) reveals a rather steady decline that is markedly noticeable after about 1922. Several long handwritten pieces were left folded in the 1924–28 notebook—among them, an outline of *Twilight Sleep*, a list of stories (some with plot summaries) for a projected volume to be entitled "Silences," and an excerpt from *The Children*. These represent samples of writing from quite separate dates within that

period (1924–28), and every one of them reveals the qualities of Wharton's *later* handwriting. By the time of one of the last pieces she wrote, "A Little Girl's New York"—a first, handwritten, draft of which remains in the archives under the title "A Further Glance"—the writing has become virtually unreadable to one not familiar with Wharton's hand.

By contrast (and the contrast is quite marked), the "Beatrice Palmato" fragment is in an unmistakably earlier script. Not so early as the rather prim, almost schoolgirlish writing that we find in the pieces written at the beginning of the century, but certainly earlier than *any* of the material of the 1924–28 notebook. In fact, the "Beatrice" fragment resembles some things from the 1918–23 notebook rather closely: the various entries in the notebook itself, the incompleted fragment of "The Necklace," the preliminary note for *The Age of Innocence*, a three-page cover sheet for the plot summary of a projected sequel to *Glimpses of the Moon* that was tentatively entitled "Love Among the Ruins." With these preliminary clues in hand, an investigator is irresistibly impelled toward the 1918–23 notebook for further information; fortunately, that impulse is rewarded.

2. *The notebook evidence.* Fully to understand the significance of the notebooks, we must understand the use to which Wharton put them. And we must recall that she was almost always working on more than one fiction at a time.

A close examination of the notebooks reveals that Wharton had two regular uses for them. One was to jot down preliminary ideas for stories or novels—sometimes merely the name of a character, sometimes a clue as to plot. Almost never did she work out a lengthy plan for a fiction within the notebooks (two exceptions from this period are the notes for *A Son at the Front*, which occupy the first eight pages of the 1918–23 notebook, and the notes for *The Mother's Recompense*, which occupied pages 27–33 of the notebook and were later torn out and inserted into the next notebook). When she had decided to work out a donnée at some length, she always eventually moved beyond the notebook to the pad of blue writer's paper which she regularly used. One consequence of this use of the notebooks is that we cannot tell in what sequence Wharton worked on things—or even in what sequence ideas came to her—by noting their relative location in the notebooks. Wharton had the habit of jotting something down, perhaps making a few sketches from it, and moving on to something else. Knowing that she might come back to an idea and do further preliminary work on it, she left a substantial number of blank pages between one item and the next. After a while, however, when she knew that she had sketched an idea as fully as she wanted to in the notebook—or when she had begun to work an idea out on her writer's pad or when she thought an idea to be "dead" and of no further use to her—then she *would* come back to those blank pages to record yet another donnée. Given this habit of doubling back upon herself, she knew very well that the sequence of items in her notebook gave no reliable sign of the order in which she had actually thought of them or worked on them.

Yet she was orderly in her habits. She did wish to preserve a record indicating generally (and it would have to be generally) the period during which she worked on—or perhaps finished—the pieces in the notebook. This was the second use to which she put her notebooks, and for this purpose she kept a "Table of Contents" at the back. In the 1918–23 notebook, the table of contents reads:

Now this listing is neither in page sequence nor in alphabetical order, yet it bears the marks of care (indicating which stories were published, in some cases). Moreover, given what we know of Wharton's published work, the list does seem to be roughly chronological. Most important, it includes not one single example of anything other than a fiction (either projected or completed); it contains no names of characters, for example, unless they give their name to the fiction in which they are found. Virtually all of these items attach to significant remains—either published or unpublished. Sometimes the remains are difficult to find, but they are there. Take "The Cadum's Governess," for example. There is only this title and the briefest indication of plot in the 1918–23 notebook; but in the next notebook, the title undergoes a slow metamorphosis to "The Praslin's Governess" and then to "The Keys of Heaven" (of which there is a substantial fragment). Others are more elusive. For "Homo Sapiens," the projected sequel to *The Age of Innocence*, there is only a sentence or two in the notebook to indicate plot or subject. Yet we know from the correspondence that Wharton seriously contemplated a sequel to her great success; and it is plausible to suppose that whatever work she did on it was done outside the notebook (the blue writer's pad, again) and has been mislaid or lost.

So, Wharton's table of contents always lists données and completed works—roughly in the order that she worked on them. Given the "indelicate" nature of the "Beatrice Palmato" donnée, it is scarcely surprising that in this case Wharton moved immediately to her writer's pad to work on the plot summary and the "unpublishable fragment" (as she did later with "Cold Green-house," another explicit incest donnée—less shocking than "Beatrice Palmato"). Since she listed "Beatrice Palmato" in *this* table of contents, we are led inescapably to the conclusion that she conceived and executed it during this period.

In fact, Wharton has provided us with a clue of tantalizing precision. Aside from its inclusion in the table of contents, the work is referred to—once—in the body of the notebook. Page 25 has on it only the following notations:

~~(Begun 1919)~~

~~The Age of Innocence~~

Beatrice Palmato

That does lead one to suspect that our author *intended* future scholars to know that the provocative fragment (which she did not, after all, destroy) was written in 1919, give or take a year. Indeed, the year 1919 seems a compelling choice when we consider the placement of "Beatrice Palmato" in the table of contents: after *A Son at the Front* (begun in 1918 and "far advanced" in July of 1919) and before *The Age of Innocence* (begun in 1919, probably in mid-year). There are other clues that support this view and allow us to fix the date with *literary* confidence.

3. *Verbal echoes*. I have already dealt with some of these in the text, for "Beatrice Palmato" echoes passages in *Summer* rather clearly. Yet there are other echoes—less thematically significant, but more compelling with regard to date. We will recall that during 1919 and 1920 Wharton was dickering with Appleton about her next book: she wanted to write *A Son at the Front* for them; they wanted a "period piece" (eventually she did *The Age of Innocence*). The correspondence indicates that J. H. Sears had received four chapters of *A Son at the Front* by September 25, 1918. On July 25, 1919, Wharton wrote to Jewett that *A Son at the Front* was already *"far advanced"* and that she expected to be finished with it by August 1919. Allowing for exaggeration on Wharton's part (she tended to lie a bit to her publishers about her progress), we must assume that much of *A Son at the Front* had been written before July 1919. This fact is significant because twice in that novel, Wharton makes casual use of the adjective "Levantine" in a way that is explicitly derogatory and unmistakably sensual. "Ladislas Isador killed at the front! The words remained unmeaning; by no effort could Campton relate them to the fat middle-aged philanderer with his Jewish eyes, his Slav eloquence, his Levantine gift for getting on, and for getting out from under" (180). And, "the door [of the gypsy's apartment] opened again, and a young man with Levantine eyes and a showy necktie looked in" (243).

To my knowledge, these are the only times that Wharton ever employed this adjective in any of her published fictions. And Mr. Palmato is a Levantine.

In fact, the air of that Moroccan journey wafts through much of Wharton's fiction between 1918 and 1920. In July 1919, Wharton began serial publication of "The Seed of the Faith," a story about a missionary in North Africa. This tale was clearly related to the blood ritual that she had witnessed at Moulay Idriss. We might recall that in *A Son at the Front*, Campton and his son plan a holiday to North Africa that they never get to take. In the 1918–23 notebook, there is yet another echo of that adventure—a story entitled "Desert's Edge" that Wharton sketched, but never wrote.

Scene at coast town in Morocco. American missionary brings home second wife (young, tragic, mysterious). His daughter Netty is jealous. She
cannot bear to see her step-mother resigned to the life which she herself detests. At length, in a fit of rage, she goes off with a commercial traveller. He
abandons her at Marrakech after a few weeks, and she drifts into a maison
close. After a while she meets French officer and lives with him for a couple
of months—but he is a morphiaomane and a spendthrift, and she leaves him
and goes home. She finds her step-mother crushed and ill with the hard
dreary life, and tries to persuade her to go to Marrakech with her, representing the life there as glorious, free and happy. The step-mother believes her,
but resists to the end, though the husband is a narrow egotistical tyrant and
the life intolerable. She resists not from religious grounds, but from natural
pride and loyalty (18).

The incestuous overtones and the allusion to illicit sex and brothels—the
daughter's rivalry with the stepmother for the father's attention—all
these things suggest the themes of the more completely worked through
"Beatrice Palmato" fragment. That they were conceived during the same
period (and recorded on proximate pages of the same notebook) seems
entirely plausible.

I have already noted the literary kinship (through Beatrice Cenci) of
"Beatrice Palmato" and *The Mother's Recompense*. It might be worthwhile
to recall that the pages missing from the 1918–23 notebook, the pages on
which Wharton worked out the plot of *The Mother's Recompense*, are those
that immediately follow the one on which the title "Beatrice Palmato" is
noted. Probably the two works were not written at the same time; they
are recorded at widely different points in the Table of Contents, and
there is no evidence that *The Mother's Recompense* was reopened by Wharton as early as 1919. However, we might infer that they were associated
in Wharton's imagination. Indeed, if we imagine her paging through the
notebook, her eye falling upon the title "Beatrice Palmato," her mind
reverting to the donnée, we can easily suppose that she would fill the
next pages with another (later) variant upon the incest theme.

4. *The use of the incest motif.* As I have already noted with regard to the
published fictions, Wharton's *early* use of the incest motif focuses on the
child's feelings and on the process of sexual awakening. The "Beatrice
Palmato" fragment would accord with that pattern if we postulate it as
written in 1919. So, indeed (in a rather more tawdry way) would the
donnée for "Desert's Edge" quoted above.

In the later examples of incest in Wharton's published fiction, the dilemma is seen from the point of view of the older generation. Here, the sexual liaison represents not a sexual awakening, but explicit jealousy for the sexual opportunities of youth. The unpublished works corroborate this view as well. During the period 1924–28, Wharton kept a number of full-sized pages in her notebook by folding them and slipping them in between the leaves: we have already noted that among these items is a list of short stories for a proposed volume to be entitled "Silences"; and the second story named is "Cold Green-house."

There is a lengthy (but fragmented) donnée from about 1928 entitled "Cold Green-house" among Wharton's literary remains; it is in the un-mistakable late handwriting, and it centers on the theme of incest as a motif of envy in the aged for what they have missed. The fragment con-sists of three parts, no one of which is complete: the first, some five handwritten pages long, headed by a roman numeral I, is evidently the beginning of a short story; the second, of the same length as the first, is headed by roman numeral II (although it seems clearly an alternate beginning to the same story); the third, two pages in length, is headed "the end."

Both of the first two parts of the fragment introduce us to the same sit-uation: Mr. Legree was widowed when his third child, a son, was born; he has two additional children, daughters of about ten and twelve; shortly afterward, he was remarried to a much younger woman, Cath-erine, who was scarcely older than her stepdaughters. When the story opens, the daughters are middle-aged—prim, shriveled old maids. Their father has died, and their brother has been killed in the Civil War. In the first version, Cornelia, the older sister, recalls the stepmother bending over the bed of her stepson and murmuring, " 'Can you forgive me, Charles?' " The emphasis in this first fragment is on the dour spinsters' barren life. In the second fragment the focus is on the stepmother, a self-ish woman still relatively young—imperious, concerned with her own comforts and conveniences, tyrannizing over the two old-maid daugh-ters.

"The end" takes place after the stepmother's death; the "girls" are liberated—but too late. They sit together, timidly drinking port. Then Phoebe, the younger, ventures:

"Cornelia," . . .

"What is it, Phoebe?"

Phoebe's lips came close to her sister's ear. "Cornelia, I saw her once . . . I saw her kissing our brother Charles."

Cornelia felt the blood rush to her own pallid face. She drew her arm impatiently from Phoebe's hold. "Of course—when he was little . . . She used to kiss us all."

Phoebe's mouth and eyes became three staring circles. "I didn't mean when he was little, Neelie."

"Oh, well then—" Cornelia's voice sank. "On his death-bed. Of course. We both saw her kiss him on the forehead."

Phoebe shook her head. "Not on his death-bed. Not on the forehead. And he gave it back."

Cornelia's stare fastened itself on her insistent face. "What on earth do you mean?" She lowered her voice again. "What sort of a kiss?"

Phoebe burst into a long crowing laugh: her gaunt body rocked with it. At last she said: "The sort of a kiss you and I have never had, sister. She had it. It was in the cold green-house. And my brother Charles—"

Cornelia rose abruptly from the table. "Our brother Charles is dead," she said. . . .

The two sisters walked back in silence to the cold room where their stepmother lay, her body flat as an ironing-board, only her sharp nose raising the sheet.

Phoebe sat down again in the slipper chintz armchair, but Cornelia, kneeling at the foot of the bed, hid her face in her bloodless hands and wept.

THE END

It is too bad that Wharton never wrote this tale, for it is splendidly ghoulish. For our purposes, the chief interest lies in the obvious differences between "Cold Green-house" and "Beatrice Palmato."

In all of the late fiction, the vantage from which incest is seen is that of the disappointed older generation, while in the earlier fiction, we see incest from the point of view of the enraptured young person who was being initiated into sexuality. If anyone is undergoing initiation now, it is Charles, who figures as no more than a significant corpse. Within this story we get two vantages—the stepmother's and the two sisters'—and both are of essentially the same (older) generation.

Furthermore, the implications of incest are different in the later pieces. Incest is a "horror" in "Beatrice Palmato," that is true; but it is horrible principally because it is very attractive. In this little piece, as in other late pieces, the attraction of incest is lost in the envy that it reveals (here dexterously shifted to the sex-starved daughters, who are almost of an age with their stepmother). The *principal* implication is that something sinfully wrong has possessed the generation of parents; and the stepmother's culpability encompasses not only the fact that she satisfies her lascivious impulses in a union with her stepson, but also the fact that she tyrannizes her two stepdaughters, depriving them of their rightful chance for youth and happiness and sexual love.

Above all there is an immeasurable difference between the tone of these later fictional worlds and the breathless heat of *Summer* or the "Beatrice" fragment.

5. *Conclusion*. There is almost an excess of proof—the handwriting, the notebook evidence, the verbal echoes, and Wharton's consistent use of the incest motif in different ways at different times in her writing career. The proof is of many different varieties, and it combines to make it inescapably clear that the approximate date of the "Beatrice Palmato" fragment must be 1919.

Notes

I. A PORTRAIT OF THE ARTIST AS A YOUNG WOMAN

1. Edith Wharton, Quaderno dello Studente, Wharton Archives, Beinecke Library, Yale University, New Haven, Conn., 1. Wharton records this last sentiment in German: "Die einsame Zeit is allein was mir bleibt; wessen ich mich erinnere, das war in der Einsamkeit erlebt, u[nd] was ich erlebt habe, das hat mich einsam gemacht." The quotation is taken from "Buch der Liebe"—a section of a longer work by Bettine Brentano von Arnim entitled *Goethes Briefwechsel mit einem Kinde* [Goethe's correspondence with a child].

2. Ibid.

3. Edith Wharton, "Life and I," Wharton Archives, Beinecke Library, Yale University, New Haven, Conn., 22. "Life and I" is a long, autobiographical manuscript, probably written as early as 1920 or 1922 and almost certainly serving as a first draft of the published autobiography, *A Backward Glance* (1934). Some of the same material appears in both; however, "Life and I" is more candid, especially in its treatment of Wharton's childhood fears and the numerous difficulties with Lucretia. "Life and I" ends abruptly, before it has recounted that period during which the author was first engaged.

4. "Life and I," 6. In *Childhood and Society*, Erik Erikson speaks of the connection between the earliest sense of well-being or non-well-being and the child's sense of the cosmos. "The parental faith which supports the trust emerging in the newborn, has throughout history sought its institutional safe-guard (and, on occasion, found its greatest enemy) in organized religion. Trust born of care is, in fact, the touchstone of the *actuality* of a given religion. All religions have in common the periodical childlike surrender to a Provider or providers who dispense earthly fortune as well as spiritual health; some demonstration of man's smallness by way of reduced posture and humble gesture; the admission in prayer and song of misdeeds, of misthoughts, and of evil intentions; fervent appeal for inner unification by divine guidance; and finally, the insight that individual trust must become a common faith, individual mistrust a commonly formulated evil." See Erik Erikson, *Childhood and Society* (New York: W. W. Norton Co., 1963), 250.

5. "Life and I," 27, 40.

6. See the various remembrances in Percy Lubbock's memoir: *Portrait of Edith Wharton* (New York: D. Appleton Co., 1947).

7. Letter to Bernard Berenson, June 13, 1910, Berenson Archives, I Tatti, Florence, Italy.

8. Letter to Sara Norton, November 18, 1908, Wharton Archives, Beinecke Library.

9. Edith Wharton, *The Collected Short Stories*, ed. R. W. B. Lewis (New York: Charles Scribner's Sons, 1968), II, 676.

10. Erikson, *Childhood and Society*, 74.

11. For an account of these symptoms, see R. W. B. Lewis, *Edith Wharton: A Biography* (New York: Harper and Row, 1975), passim.
12. Edith Wharton, *A Backward Glance* (New York: D. Appleton Co., 1934), 78, 73.
13. "Life and I," 34.
14. *A Backward Glance*, 55.
15. Edith Wharton, "A Little Girl's New York," *Harper's Magazine*, CLXXVI (March 1938), 357.
16. *A Backward Glance*, 73–74.
17. "Life and I," 29.
18. *A Backward Glance*, 119.
19. "Life and I," 41.
20. *A Backward Glance*, 26.
21. Ibid., 1–2.
22. "Life and I," 13.
23. *A Backward Glance*, 57.
24. "Life and I," 25.
25. *A Backward Glance*, 39, 88.
26. Ibid., 27–28.
27. Animal phobias are very common in children of this age; indeed they are among the first evidences of mental illness that Freud commented upon. See, for instance, the case of "Little Hans" in Sigmund Freud, *Works*, trans. James Strachey in collaboration with Anna Freud (London: Hogarth Press, 1971), XVII—or "From the History of an Infantile Neurosis," *Works*, XVII. Perhaps the best concise discussion of animal phobias may be found in Anna Freud, *The Writings of Anna Freud* (New York: International Universities Press, 1966), II. As Anna Freud notes (p. 77), themes that bespeak fear of animals are by no means peculiar to severely neurotic children: "They are universal in fairy tales and other children's stories." And almost always, they emerge during the period of Oedipal conflict.

What function do these phobias serve? Primarily they allow children to conceptualize feelings and wishes that are too fearful to be thought directly, without disguise or displacement. In Wharton's case, we might break down the components of her fear of the "big bad wolf" in the following way.

1. I am in possession of powerful, irrational feelings (which she identifies with animals—that peculiar state of "usness" and "not-usness").
2. My feelings are bad or dangerous (hence they are embodied in a dangerous animal).
3. My feelings are so bad, in fact, that I am a bad girl for having them and should be punished (hence the animal threatens *her*; she has reversed her rage toward her mother and redirected it towards herself).
4. My feelings have to do with "hunger" (here Wharton is clearly conflating the sexual impulse with that earlier, unresolved *oral* need for love).
5. I must be prevented from acting upon my feelings (hence Wharton prohibits herself both from expressing rage toward her mother and from becoming too close to her father by postulating the wolf as an animal that chases her *until* she seeks refuge with Mother or Doyley).

It is the *degree* of Wharton's fear that suggests an abnormally severe problem; and even more, its persistence (in a variety of disguises).
28. "Life and I," 3–6.
29. Ibid., 7.
30. Ibid., 16–18.

31. Insofar as her letters are revealing, one of the most plaintively reiterated refrains is this one—in the letters to Berenson, to John Hugh-Smith, to all those who eventually were admitted into her small circle of confidence.

32. *A Backward Glance*, 4.

33. "As he is willing and able to suck on appropriate objects and to swallow whatever appropriate fluids they emit, he is soon also willing and able to 'take in' with his eyes whatever enters his visual field. His tactual senses, too, seem to 'take in' what feels good." Erik Erikson, *Psychological Issues: Identity and the Life Cycle* (New York: International Universities Press, 1959), 57.

34. Erikson, *Childhood and Society*, 77.

35. "Life and I," 10.

36. *A Backward Glance*, 54, 28, 128.

37. Louis Auchincloss, *Edith Wharton: A Woman in Her Time* (New York: Viking Press, 1971), 27.

38. *A Backward Glance*, 33.

39. "Life and I," 13–14.

40. *A Backward Glance*, 33.

41. Ibid., 33–35, 42–43.

42. "Life and I," 14–15.

43. *A Backward Glance*, 35.

44. Ibid., 35, 48, 68.

45. Ibid., 26.

46. Ibid., 26, 20.

47. Ibid., 17, 20.

48. Ibid., 24, 52, 49.

49. Erikson has a few words to say about the kind of mother who is most likely to inflict identity problems upon her child, and his description fits Lucretia very well. Such mothers often have "a pronounced status awareness, of the climbing and pretentious or of the 'hold-on' variety. [Lucretia, a member of that staid little clan of 'old New Yorkers' who were being displaced by new money, was obviously of the 'hold-on' variety.] They would at almost any time be willing to overrule matters of honest feeling and of intelligent judgment for the sake of a facade of wealth, propriety, and 'happiness.' . . . They also have the special quality of a penetrating omnipresence [and this last is most true of Lucretia]; their very voices and their softest sobs are sharp, plaintive, or fretful, and cannot be escaped within a considerable radius." See *Psychological Issues*, 136.

50. "Life and I," 20–21, 23.

51. Ibid., 31–33, 27.

52. Ibid., 33.

53. *A Backward Glance*, 18.

54. One expectable result of such a cultural situation would be the denying of feeling and the development of what D. W. Winnicott has called a "false self." That such a schizoid pattern was tempting to women like Wharton may be inferred from the characterizations of some of her early heroines: Lily Bart and Anna Leath, for example. However, Wharton's symptoms suggest that she managed to preserve her feelings to a large extent and that her physical ailments permitted her to obtain an indirect gratification of them. R. D. Laing's discussion of the difference between schizoid adaptions and hysterical adaptions is very illuminating. See *The Divided Self* (Harmondsworth, Eng.: Penguin Books, 1971), 94 ff.

55. "Life and I," 18.

56. Ibid., 33–34.
57. Ibid., 34–35.
58. *A Backward Glance*, 46.
59. Ibid., 3.
60. "Life and I," 1–2, 46–47.
61. *A Backward Glance*, 169.
62. Ibid., 172.
63. Ibid., 68.
64. "Life and I," 31–32.
65. Ibid., 23–24, 36.
66. *A Backward Glance*, 222–23.
67. "Life and I," 37.
68. Ibid.
69. I am indebted to R. W. B. Lewis for generously allowing me to use his copies of these juvenile pieces.
70. "Life and I," 38.
71. Ibid.
72. *A Backward Glance*, 75–76.
73. "Life and I," 43.
74. *A Backward Glance*, 87.
75. Auchincloss, *Edith Wharton: A Woman in Her Time*, 42.
76. Subjects and Notes, 1924–1928, Wharton Archives, Beinecke Library, 82.
77. Lewis, *Edith Wharton*, 49.
78. Ibid., 50–51.
79. Auchincloss, *Edith Wharton: A Woman in Her Time*, 48–49.
80. The Love Diary. I am indebted to R. W. B. Lewis for allowing me to use this document.
81. *A Backward Glance*, 92.
82. Letter to Sara Norton, Apr. 12, 1908, Wharton Archives, Beinecke Library.
83. Letter to Bernard Berenson, June 9, 1912, Berenson Archives.
84. *A Backward Glance*, 109.

II. LANDSCAPES OF DESOLATION

1. *A Backward Glance*, 209.
2. Letter to William Brownell, November 7, 1900, Scribner Archives, Firestone Library, Princeton University, Princeton, New Jersey.
3. Other problems of dating are of less critical interest. Wharton often did not publish her short stories immediately upon their completion; sometimes she did not even submit them for publication right away. Hence we often cannot ascertain when a given short story was written. For example, every item in *Xingu and Other Stories* (1916) was completed before World War I broke out. Thus when we talk about her short stories, we must often proffer approximate dates.
4. Letter to Edward Burlingame, July 10, 1898, Scribner Archives.
5. Lewis, *Edith Wharton*, 61.
6. Wharton, *The Collected Short Stories*, I, 14.
7. Ibid., 3.
8. Ibid., 5.

9. Ibid., 7.
10. Edith Wharton, *Xingu and Other Stories* (New York: Charles Scribner's Sons, 1916), 309, 311.
11. Ibid., 314.
12. Ibid., 314, 320.
13. Ibid., 333.
14. Ibid., 350, 358.
15. Ibid., 343.
16. Ibid., 378, 415, 421.
17. Wharton, *The Collected Short Stories*, I, 12–16.
18. Ibid., 19–20.
19. Millicent Bell, *Edith Wharton and Henry James* (New York: George Braziller, 1965), 55.
20. Wharton, *The Collected Short Stories*, I, 17.
21. Letter to Edward Burlingame, August 26, 1899, Scribner Archives.
22. *A Backward Glance*, 15.
23. Lewis, *Edith Wharton*, 67.
24. *A Backward Glance*, 106.
25. Lewis, *Edith Wharton*, 79.
26. Edith Wharton, *The Decoration of Houses* (New York: Charles Scribner's Sons, 1897), 20.
27. Lewis, *Edith Wharton*, 78.
28. Letter to Edward Burlingame, February 23, 1898, Scribner Archives.
29. Letter to Edward Burlingame, September 9, 1898, Scribner Archives.
30. Letter to Edward Burlingame, October 19, 1898, Scribner Archives.
31. Lewis, *Edith Wharton*, 101.
32. Letter to Sara Norton, August 18, 1901, Wharton Archives, Beinecke Library.
33. *A Backward Glance*, 112–13.
34. Letter to Edward Burlingame, March 26, 1894, Scribner Archives.
35. Letter to Edward Burlingame, December 14, 1895, Scribner Archives.
36. Wharton, *The Collected Short Stories*, I, 61.
37. Ibid., 58–59.
38. Lewis, *Edith Wharton*, 81, 76.
39. Ernst Kris, *Psychoanalytic Explorations in Art* (New York: International Universities Press, 1965), 253–54.
40. Ibid., 251.
41. Ibid., 59.
42. *A Backward Glance*, 199, 204–5.
43. Edith Wharton, The Commonplace Book, 32, 33. I am indebted to the Honorable William R. Tyler for allowing me to examine this document.
44. Marilyn Jones Lyde, *Edith Wharton: Convention and Morality in the Work of a Novelist* (Norman: University of Oklahoma Press, 1959), makes this point. "As a rule, critical studies of Edith Wharton begin with the *The House of Mirth;* and *The Valley of Decision*, if it is treated at all, is treated as an interesting but unimportant and uncharacteristic tour de force. . . . To so regard it is to make a basic mistake. Like most first novels, it is intellectually the most autobiographical work Edith Wharton ever wrote" (see 82).
45. Lubbock's short biography, *Portrait of Edith Wharton*, is launched from this site. Almost all of the critics who have taken an interest in her work have done so because she was deemed to have been a clever disciple of James. We might have conflicted feelings, for example, about Edmund Wilson's work in *The Wound and the Bow* (New York: Ox-

ford University Press, 1947), for although it kept her reputation as a novelist alive, it did so by pairing her with James (to Wharton's ultimate injury).

46. The original notebook in which Wharton sketched the outline and background for her first complete novel may be found in the Wharton Archives of the Beinecke Library. These notes to *The Valley of Decision* are revealing of her literary ambivalences, for they contain (in addition to the chronology—which one might expect for any novel) a long list of source readings, books like *The Memoires of Casanova* or Goldoni's plays. Preeminent among these is Stendhal's novel *The Charterhouse of Parma*, to which she alludes repeatedly in her own notes. This way of beginning a novel, almost as if it were a research paper, suggests the extent to which Wharton still felt doubts about her own ability. Yet, it suggests as well a species of presumption: for in choosing to *respond* to Stendhal (rather than to imitate him), Wharton was pretty clearly "taking on" one of the masters. If her novel succeeded, its success might partially be measured by the reputation of Stendhal.

47. Harry Levin, *The Gates of Horn: A Study of Five French Realists* (New York: Oxford University Press, 1966), 117.

48. Edith Wharton, *The Valley of Decision* (New York: Charles Scribner's Sons, 1902), I, 3. Hereafter, all references to this novel will be cited in text by volume and page number to this edition.

49. Blake Nevius, *Edith Wharton: A Study of Her Fiction* (Berkeley: University of California Press, 1953), 48–50.

50. Letter from Henry James to Edith Wharton, August 17, 1902, Wharton Archives, Beinecke Library.

51. Not to mince words, *Sanctuary* is a really bad little novel. Edith Wharton didn't like it—not even while she was writing it (it came to be known as "sank" around The Mount during its composition). It was not a great commercial failure and did not noticeably impair her reputation, but it was forgotten immediately by its author, and it will be mercifully forgotten here.

52. Letter to Sara Norton, May 19, 1902, Wharton Archives, Beinecke Library.

53. I have quoted from this August 17, 1902, letter to Edith Wharton from Henry James earlier; the story that accompanies it has become a famous literary anecdote. James had been given a copy of *The Valley of Decision;* he read it, liked it, and though he knew Edith Wharton only very slightly (they had met once or twice at largish parties), he sent her a long and lumberingly praising letter. Yet he concluded that letter (laudatory though it undubitably was) with an injunction:

> There is a thing or two I should like to say—some other time. You see what reasons I have for wishing a Godspeed to that talk. The particular thing is somehow mistimed while the air still flushes with the pink fire of The Valley; all the more that I can't do it any sort of justice save by expatiation. So, as, after all, to mention it in 2 words does it no sort of justice, let it suffer the wrong of being crudely hinted as my desire earnestly, tenderly, intelligently to admonish you, while you're in full command of the situation—admonish you, I say, in favour of the *American Subject*. There it is round you. Don't pass it by—the immediate, the real, the one's, the yours, the novelist's that it waits for. Take hold of it and keep hold, and let it pull you where it will. It will pull harder than things of mere tarabiscotage, which is a merit in itself. What I would say in a word is: Profit, be warned, by my awful example of exile and ignorance. You will say that *j'en parle à mon aise*—but I shall have paid for my ease, and I don't want you to pay (as much)

for yours. But these are impertinent importunities, from the moment they are not developed. All the same *Do New York!* The first-hand account is precious.

Wharton's next novel was *The House of Mirth* (in which she did New York most thoroughly). So—as the story goes—Henry James "took up" the fledgling novelist and put her on the track, beginning her "discipleship." The chronology is all there: Wharton did begin with an historical novel; James did write that roundabout letter enjoining her to "Do New York"; and she did do it. The only trouble is that the overt chronology lies. The letters reveal, the archival remnants of incompleted fictions by Wharton reveal, the notebooks and Donnée Books—all reveal that Wharton had seriously embarked on "Disintegration" well before she had heard a word from James. What is more, the merest glance at the short stories (pieces like "The Pelican" or "Souls Belated") will suggest to a perceptive critic that Edith Wharton knew very well her vocation to do New York. *The Valley of Decision* is a nervous and uncharacteristic beginning. Undoubtedly James's advice did serve to reinforce her own already strongly developed inclination (she did mention it in a letter to Burlingame); nevertheless, the relationship between James and Wharton was never—not even here, at its very beginning—one of masterful instructor and pliant student.

54. Wharton, *The Collected Short Stories*, I, 88.
55. Ibid., 67, 69, 73–77.
56. Sometime in 1899 or 1900 Edith Wharton began to keep systematic notebooks in which she recorded ideas for short stories, names or phrases that struck her, partial outlines for longer works, and so on. It is by no means the case that all of her unfinished fictions reside in these books—nor even that every fiction, published as well as unpublished, is recorded there. Nevertheless, these notebooks are a rich mine for those who are interested in dating the beginning of a work or in discovering the many steps by which Wharton reached one or another fiction. Wharton called the first two of these notebooks "Donnée Books." All may be found in the Wharton Archives at the Beinecke Library. The quotation cited in the text is taken from the first Donnée Book, page 118.
57. Ibid., 25, 115.
58. Ibid., 101.
59. Book review, *New York Times*, August 30, 1901.
60. Edith Wharton, *The Touchstone* (New York: Charles Scribner's Sons, 1900), 17.
61. Ibid., 4–5, 18.
62. Ibid., 67–68, 116–17.
63. Edith Wharton, "Leslie Stephen, *George Eliot*," *Bookman*, XXII (September 1905), 247, 248.
64. Ibid., 251.
65. It is, of course, not necessary to adopt these two extremes as the only possible alternatives for the feminine nature. It is certainly true that the society of Wharton's youth and adolescence had made the distinction between "doing" and "being" a rather sharp one—and that it had quite narrowly assigned only the second to nice women. Still, the almost grotesque way in which Wharton clings to the most exaggerated rendering of society's injunctions—her apparent helplessness to find, at this point in her life, some mediating position between them—is indicative of an admixture of personal problem to the already pernicious social customs.
66. Wharton, *The Collected Short Stories*, I, 381, 389.
67. Ibid., 393, 394.

68. See, for example, Anne Friman, "Determinism and Point of View in *The House of Mirth*," *Papers on Language and Literature*, II (1965), 175–78; James W. Tuttleton, "Leisure, Wealth and Luxury: Edith Wharton's Old New York," *Midwest Quarterly*, VII (1965), 337–52; Richard Poirier, "Edith Wharton, *The House of Mirth*," in *The American Novel*, ed. Wallace Stegner (New York: Basic Books, 1965); Irving Howe (ed.), *Edith Wharton: A Collection of Critical Essays* (Englewood Cliffs, N.J.: Prentice-Hall, 1962), passim; and Blake Nevius, *Edith Wharton*.

69. *A Backward Glance*, 207.

70. Letter to Sara Norton, October 26, 1906, Wharton Archives, Beinecke Library.

71. Edith Wharton, *The House of Mirth* (New York: Charles Scribner's Sons, 1895), 19. Hereafter, all references to this novel will be cited in text by page number to this edition.

72. Howard Mumford Jones, *The Age of Energy* (New York: Viking Press, 1970), 251.

73. Alice Meynell, *The Work of John S. Sargent* (New York: Charles Scribner's Sons, 1903), introduction.

74. Edith Wharton, Second Donnée Book (1910–18), Wharton Archives, Beinecke Library.

75. Edith Wharton, *The Custom of the Country* (New York: Charles Scribner's Sons, 1913), 195.

76. Jan Thompson, "The Role of Women in the Iconography of Art Nouveau," *Art Journal*, XXXI, no. 2 (Winter 1971–72), 158, 159.

77. See ibid., 163–64.

78. Edith Wharton insisted upon the importance of this first chapter. See "The Criticism of Fiction," in *Times Literary Supplement*, May 14, 1914, and *A Backward Glance*, 208.

79. The passage from Ecclesiastes is relevant (7:3–4):

> Sorrow is better than laughter
> for by sadness of countenance the
> heart is made better.
> The heart of the wise is in the house of
> mourning;
> but the heart of fools is in the house of
> mirth.

80. Nevius, *Edith Wharton*, 59.

81. Henry James, "John S. Sargent," in *The Painter's Eye*, ed. John L. Sweeney (Cambridge, Mass.: Harvard University Press, 1956), 226. James originally published this essay in *Harper's Magazine*, October 1887. It was reprinted with emendation in *Picture and Text* in 1893. Sweeney has reprinted the latter version.

82. Letter to Charles Scribner, November 22, 1905, Scribner Archives.

83. *A Backward Glance*, 190.

84. It is impossible to stress too strongly Wharton's genuine literary independence of James. In regarding her as his disciple, critic after critic has managed to overlook what was unique (and often best) in *her* work. As R. W. B. Lewis's recent biography shows, James was often dominated by Wharton in their personal relationship: her energy and sexual passion awed him, and her literary productivity (and financial success) sometimes made him envious. In the end, it is a gross injustice to James to bolster his reputation by a myth at which he would have laughed.

85. An excellent discussion of this psychological function of the form of fiction may be found in Simon O. Lesser's book, *Fiction and the Unconscious* (New York: Random

House, 1957). Chapter Five is central to this particular discussion, but the entire book is a valuable and pertinent work.

86. Edith Wharton, *The Writing of Fiction* (New York: Charles Scribner's Sons, 1925), 120.

87. *A Backward Glance*, 205.

88. Lewis, *Edith Wharton*, 181.

89. An interesting additional influence came in a tragic real-life event. Edith Wharton had become very friendly with one of her Lenox neighbors, a woman named Ethyl Cram. In July of 1905 Ethyl Cram was involved in a riding accident and sutained severe head injuries; she lingered unconscious until September, and then she mercifully died. Wharton was profoundly affected by this tragedy, and during the period of her friend's lingering coma, she more than once expressed herself in favor of euthanasia.

90. Lewis, *Edith Wharton*, 182.

91. Edith Wharton, Daily Appointment Book for 1905, Wharton Archives, Beinecke Library.

92. Wharton used this device of the double heroine (begun, we will recall, in "Bunner Sisters") in many of the major works up through this period. In *The Touchstone*, for example, the intellectual Margaret Aubyn is contrasted with the wifely Alexa Trent whom Glennard finally marries; in *The Valley of Decision* the contrast is again between intellect and—something else, worldliness perhaps, sensuality (Wharton's focus here is not entirely clear), and the contrast is made through the delineation of the two women who dominate Odo's life, Fulvia Vivaldi and the Duchess, Maria Clementina. Wharton often poses an emotional dilemma in terms of the strategy of a double heroine; probably it reveals many of her own persistent ambivalences.

93. Edith Wharton, *The Fruit of the Tree* (New York: Charles Scribner's Sons, 1907), 281. All further references to this novel will be cited in text by page number to this edition.

94. Letter to William Brownell, November 6, 1907, Wharton Archives, Amherst College, Massachusetts.

95. Letter to Sara Norton, January 24, 1902, Wharton Archives, Beinecke Library.

96. Millicent Bell, *Edith Wharton and Henry James*, 147.

97. Edith Wharton must have been radiating a sense of her newly discovered passionate depths. Several men announced their attraction to her: John Hugh-Smith (an English acquaintance whom she met through the circle of James's friends) was but one; his tone is by no means unique. The truth is that at last, in her mid-forties, Edith Wharton had become a very desirable woman. On December 19, 1908—just after meeting her—John Hugh-Smith wrote a letter expressing hesitant passion. "I need hardly say that I was right—you alarm poor Percy, but his admiration for you is that of all sane men. . . . As I anticipated I felt on Saturday very like a drunkard who is suddenly reduced to water, and I was depressed to think that so many weeks must pass before I can hold nine or even three hours continuous conversation with you. . . . The fact of such an obviously brilliant person such as you are being so exceptionally lucid to me has at times made me a little self-conscious—even when I was alone with you. . . . In Paris we shall be able to go ahead and eliminate this Jacobean element in our relations." Letter from John Hugh-Smith to Edith Wharton, December 19, 1908, Wharton Archives, Beinecke Library.

98. R. W. B. Lewis gives a splendidly complete account of Morton Fullerton, a most labyrinthine individual. See his biography of Edith Wharton, pp. 183 ff.

99. Edith Wharton, The Love Diary, 1–2. I am indebted for the use of this document to the kindness of R. W. B. Lewis. It is an atypically breathless form of prose for Edith Wharton. The reader should be aware that most of the dots in the text which might seem to indicate ellipses are Edith Wharton's own.

100. Lewis, *Edith Wharton*, 224.
101. Letter to Sara Norton, December 18, 1907, Wharton Archives, Beinecke Library.
102. The Love Diary, 3–4.
103. Ibid., 5, 7, 8.
104. Ibid., 10.
105. Ibid., 11–12, 19.
106. Ibid., 26.
107. Ibid., 33.
108. Ibid., 22.
109. Letter to Sara Norton, July 7, 1908, Wharton Archives, Beinecke Library.
110. Letter to Sara Norton, October 7, 1908, Wharton Archives, Beinecke Library.
111. *The Collected Short Stories*, II, 41–42.
112. Ibid., 46.
113. Ibid., 48–49.
114. There is a personal legend that gives ironic charm to this story. For many years a rumor had intermittently circulated that Edith Wharton was not Frederic Jones's daughter, but the product of a liaison between Lucretia and the tutor of Wharton's two older brothers. The story is absurd; as Louis Auchincloss remarks, one has only to look at a picture of the young Edith Wharton and one of her forbears on the father's side to see unmistakable resemblances. Edith Wharton thought the whole thing a silly joke and did not usually choose to dignify it with comment. However, "His Father's Son" may be her most direct statement on the matter: who could doubt her heritage—she is so unmistakably her father's daughter, just exactly in the way that Mr. Grew's son is unmistakably his father's son.
115. *The Collected Short Stories*, II, 102.
116. Nevius, *Edith Wharton*, 94–95.
117. *The Collected Short Stories*, II, 118, 119, 120.
118. Ibid., 126, 128.
119. Ibid., 130.
120. Edith Wharton, An Introduction to the dramatization of *Ethan Frome* by Owen and Donald Davis in 1936, Wharton Archives, Beinecke Library.
121. A copy of this letter to Mr. Scribner dated July 8, 1926, may be found among the letters to William Brownell in the Wharton Archives, Amherst College. Obviously Wharton sent a copy to Brownell when she sent the letter to Mr. Scribner.
122. *A Backward Glance*, 209.
123. Ibid., 295.
124. We can narrow this date in the following way. Charles Du Bos and Wharton first met each other on a November afternoon in 1905. Hence it is plausible to suppose that she was not sufficiently acquainted with him to ask his advice about a tutor much before early 1906. Edith Wharton met Morton Fullerton in October of 1907, and her Paris visit of 1907–8 was a heady, emotional period. It is unlikely that she was improving her French then. By October 1908, she apparently felt herself to be sufficiently proficient in written French to write and publish a short story in that language ("Les Metteurs en Scène," *Revue des Deux Mondes*, XLVII [October 1908], 692–708). From this evidence, a date in early 1907 seems most probable—that is, a date before she first met Morton Fullerton, a fact which might account for the flatness of the French sketch.
125. A transcription of this work has been published; see W. D. MacCallan, "The French Draft of *Ethan Frome*," *Yale University Library Gazette*, XXVII (July 1952).
126. Ibid., 40.

127. Edith Wharton, *Ethan Frome*, Modern Student's Library edition (New York: Charles Scribner's Sons, 1922), introduction, ix.
128. Edith Wharton, *Ethan Frome* (New York: Charles Scribner's Sons, 1911), 3. All further references to this work will be cited in text by page number to this edition.
129. In *A Backward Glance* (294), Wharton declares that the villages of western Massachusetts were, when she knew them, "still grim places, morally and physically: insanity, incest and slow mental and moral starvation were hidden away behind the paintless wooden house-fronts of the long village street, or in the isolated farm-houses on the neighbouring hills; and Emily Brontë would have found as savage tragedies in our remoter valleys as on her Yorkshire moors."
130. Critics of *Ethan Frome* have consistently missed the point of its structure, even though Wharton went to considerable lengths to call this feature of the novel to the public's attention. John Crowe Ransom's remarks are typical of the general dissatisfaction with Wharton's "clumsy" method. "We are allowed to anticipate the reporter who is gathering the story, and then we go back and see him make slight detective motions at gathering it; but we are forced to conclude that he did not gather it really; that, mostly, he made it up. Why a special reporter at all? And why such a peculiar chronological method? These are features which picture to me, if it is not impertinent, the perturbation of an author wrestling with an unaccustomed undertaking, uneasy of conscience, and resorting to measures. Forgetting the Preface, and the exterior or enveloping story, we attend strictly to Ethan's story. . . ," See "Characters and Character: A Note on Fiction," *American Review*, VI (January 1936), 273–74. Of course it is just the decision to *ignore* the "exterior or enveloping story" that has marred so many readings of *Ethan Frome*. Blake Nevius corrects those critics who misquote the narrator (reading "version" for "vision"); Nevius calls it to our attention, in fact, that the inner story is the narrator's "vision," but he makes no more than the linguistic correction. He does not see its significance.
131. Some critics have made much of Ethan's care-taking obligations. Lionel Trilling, "The Morality of Inertia," in *Great Moral Dilemmas*, ed. Robert M. MacIver (New York: Harper & Brothers, 1956), is one. Few, however, focus on the fact that care-taking obligations might have been discharged in any number of ways, that Ethan might have sold the farm and moved his parents to Florida (where he had a job once). That is, very few critics have noticed the *willed* quality of Ethan Frome's static hell.
132. Kenneth Bernard, "Imagery and Symbolism in *Ethan Frome*," *College English*, XXIII (December 1961), has remarked incisively on a number of metaphorical patterns in the novel. Bernard is the only critic to note that Frome wishes to die cradled in Mattie's arms—that, in effect, he regresses at the crucial moment.
133. *A Backward Glance*, 293. "For years I had wanted to draw life as it really was in the derelict mountain villages of New England, a life even in my time, and a thousandfold more a generation earlier, utterly unlike that seen through the rose-coloured spectacles of my predecessors, Mary Wilkins and Sarah Orne Jewett."
134. Ibid., 209, 197.

III. STUDIES OF SALAMANDERS

1. Lewis, *Edith Wharton*, 297.
2. *The Writing of Fiction*, 119–20.
3. Ibid., 32.
4. The Love Diary, 13–14.

5. Ibid., 17, 21.
6. The lines quoted here are from Wharton's poem "Terminus." The poem may be found in its entirety in R. W. B. Lewis's biography; these lines appear on p. 259.
7. Lewis, *Edith Wharton*, 259.
8. Ibid.
9. Letter from Katherine Fullerton to Morton Fullerton, Oct. 1899, Beinecke Library.
10. Letter from Katherine Fullerton to Morton Fullerton, Nov. 9, 1907, Beinecke Library.
11. Letter from Katherine Fullerton to Morton Fullerton, Nov. 22, 1907, Beinecke Library.
12. Letter from Katherine Fullerton to Morton Fullerton, Autumn, 1907, Beinecke Library.
13. Letter from Katherine Fullerton to Morton Fullerton, no date, 1908/1909 (?), Beinecke Library.
14. Letter from Katherine Fullerton to Morton Fullerton, Jan. 5, 1910, Beinecke Library.
15. Wharton, *The Collected Short Stories*, II, 185, 186, 186.
16. Ibid., 189.
17. Ibid., 195.
18. Ibid., 202.
19. Ibid., 203, 206. This story skims the superficies of Wharton's life, but scarcely plumbs the depths of her emotional past. Its conclusion, which must have resembled Wharton's own mixed final assessment of Fullerton and which did, of course, derive in part from the resolution of deep conflicts and more complex problems than the narrative embodies, is too strong for the story because it has grown out of Wharton's life experience (too mechanically transferred into the tale) and not organically out of the fiction itself.
20. Letter to William Brownell, Nov. 2, 1913, Wharton Archives, Amherst College, Amherst, Mass.
21. The Love Diary recapitulates the language of insatiable hunger in ways that suggest how blazingly intense Edith Wharton's adult passions were, how deeply they drew for that intensity upon the privations of her past (and how well she knew this fact). "Ah, how I see in all this the instinctive longing to pack every moment of my present with all the wasted driven-in feeling of the past! One should be happy in one's youth to be happy freely, carelessly, extravagantly! How I hoard and tremble over each incident and sign! I am like a hungry beggar who crumbles up the crust he has found in order to make it last longer!" (13).
22. In *Childhood and Society*, Erik Erikson speaks extensively about the rise of initiative as a component of the "Oedipal stage" of development (85–92, 255–58). Another and equally interesting discussion of this problem of initiative in the child at the stage of Oedipal crisis can be found in D. W. Winnicott, *The Family and Individual Development* (New York: Tavistock Publications, 1969), 34–40 ("The Five-Year-Old"). See also D. W. Winnicott, *The Maturational Processes and the Facilitating Evironment* (New York: International Universities Press, Inc., 1965), 15–29 ("Psycho-Analysis and the Sense of Guilt").
23. "The beauty of it is that it is, for all it is worth, a Drama, and almost, as it seems to me, of the psychologic Racinian unity, intensity and gracility. Anna is really of Racine and one presently begins to feel her throughout as an Eriphyle or a Bérénice: which, by the way, helps to account a little for something *qui me chiffonne* throughout: which is why the whole thing, unrelated and unreferred save in the most superficial way to its *milieu* and background, and to any determining or qualifying *entourage*, takes place

comme cela, and in a specified, localised way, in France—these non-French people 'electing,' as it were, to have their story out there." See *The Letters of Henry James*, ed. Percy Lubbock (New York: Charles Scribner's Sons, 1920), 281.

24. Needless to say, she might have met the challenge of her subject—even given the imperfect understanding of the two characters whose vantages she adopts—if *their* ignorance was a transparent vehicle for *our* understanding (as Maisie's is, for example, in *What Maisie Knew*). But she does not choose this route either; we are no more informed than Anna Leath or George Darrow about such intriguing mysteries as Sophy Viner.

25. Edith Wharton, *The Reef* (New York: D. Appleton and Co., 1912). Hereafter, all references to *The Reef* will be cited in the text, giving page number of this edition.

26. Nevius, *Edith Wharton*, 140.

27. Letter to Bernard Berenson, Nov. 23, 1912, Berenson Archives.

28. Letter to William Brownell, Aug. 29, 1918, Wharton Archives, Amherst College.

29. Lewis, *Edith Wharton*, 326.

30. Edith Wharton, Line a Day Diary, March 21, 1908, Wharton Archives, Beinecke Library.

31. Letter to John Hugh-Smith, February 12, 1909, Wharton Archives, Beinecke Library.

32. Letter from Nannie Wharton to Edith Wharton, Sept. 20, 1909, Wharton Archives, Beinecke Library.

33. Letter to Judge Robert Grant, April 4, 1910, Wharton Archives, Beinecke Library.

34. Ibid.

35. Letter from William Sturgis Bigelow to Edith Wharton, August 16, 1910, Wharton Archives, Beinecke Library.

36. Bell, *Edith Wharton and Henry James*, 315–16.

37. Eventually, as she grew more successful, she had agents, like any comparable male author. The point is that *she* dealt with the publishers and with her agents. No benevolent father-figure "took care" of her interests.

38. A nice example of her growing confidence can be seen in her negotiations concerning *The Reef*. Until the publication of this novel, all of her work had been brought out by Scribner's. However, Wharton had become increasingly aware of the fact that by limiting herself to this one house (where she had an extraordinarily cordial and personal relation with Burlingame and Brownell) she was limiting hserself in the matter of making money. Scribner's could not place the serial run of her fiction so advantageously as other houses, and they sometimes could not advertise her work as extensively as she wanted nor give her the kind of advance money that she was beginning to expect. Thus, in a calculated move toward independence, she published *The Reef* with Appleton. She continued to publish some of her work with Scribner's; but after 1912, she no longer felt tied to them and published (shrewdly) wherever she could obtain the best monetary arrangement.

39. Letter to Teddy Wharton, July 6, 1910 (continued on July 8), Wharton Archives, Beinecke Library. Edith Wharton kept a copy of this letter for her own files.

40. Letter from Teddy Wharton to Herman Edgar, May 8, 1911, Wharton Archives, Beinecke Library.

41. Letter to Teddy Wharton, May 30, 1911, Wharton Archives, Beinecke Library.

42. One reason that we know so many of the details of Teddy Wharton's illness and the slow, painful disintegration of the marriage is that Edith Wharton preserved them in this packet. It contained a series of doctors' reports documenting the severity and intractability of Teddy's illness; manuscript copies of five letters from Edith Wharton to her husband from July 6, 1910 to May 17, 1912; manuscript copies of two letters from

Edith Wharton to her brother-in-law, William Wharton, July 22 and 23, 1911; manuscript of a rough draft of a letter from Edith Wharton to William Wharton (written, probably, at The Mount in July or August of 1911); five letters from Nannie Wharton to Edith Wharton from Sept. 1909 to Oct. 1910; seven letters to Edith Wharton from her housekeeper, C. Gross, undated; nine letters to Edith Wharton from American friends and supporters reassuring her about the correctness of her divorce. (In addition, there were documents unrelated to the divorce: the letters sealing the agreement with Scribner's by which Edith Wharton circuitously passed a large advance to Henry James in 1913, and a letter about Wharton's work for the Children of Ypres.)

43. Letter to Edith Wharton from Thomas Newbold, April 9, 1913, Wharton Archives, Beinecke Library.

44. The year 1913 was a terrible one for Edith Wharton. In addition to her divorce, she entangled herself in a humiliatingly botched scheme to obtain a large gift of money for Henry James from his American admirers. In the notebook for that year, she records the following nightmare:

> My Dream (Queen's Acre Oct., 1913) *This was a real dream.* A pale demon with black hair came in, followed by four black gnome-like creatures carrying a great black trunk. They set it down and opened it, and the Demon crying out: "Here's your year—here are all the horrors that have happened to you and that are still going to happen!" dragged out a succession of limp black squirming things and threw them on the floor before me. They were not rags or creatures, not living or dead—they were Black Horrors, shapeless, and that seemed to writhe about as they fell at my feet, and yet were as inanimate as bits of stuff. But none of these comparisons occurred to me, for I *knew* what they were: the hideous, the incredible things that had happened to me in this dreadful year, or were to happen to me before its close; and I stared, horror-struck, as the Demon dragged them out, one by one, more and more, till finally, flinging down a blacker, hatefuller one, he said laughing: "There—that's the last of them!"
>
> The gnomes laughed too, but I, as I stared at the great black pile and at the empty trunk, said to the Demon:—*"Are you sure it hasn't a false bottom?"*

Another, more explicit reflection of Edith Wharton's guilt is manifest in a short story whose composition dates from this period—"Autres Temps." It is the tale of a woman who has divorced her husband almost twenty years ago and been doomed to a European exile because she was ostracized by everyone she knew. Now she is returning to New York to visit her daughter—a girl who has, herself, divorced her first husband and married another man and who has not suffered the slightest social inconvenience. The mother ponders the changing times. Her own rash action happened so long ago; she supposes that people have forgotten her—or that they no longer care about such things as her own divorce. She returns to discover that *for her,* the times have never changed, will never change. Everyone accepts the behavior of her daughter; the younger generation is allowed its freedoms. But the mother is still "cut" by her acquaintances; she is, and will forever remain, an "immoral" woman. The story concludes with her preparing to return to her European exile.

Eventually, we may assume, Edith Wharton accepted the *necessity* of her own divorce. She never was comfortable with the notion of divorce, however, and as late a novel as *Twilight Sleep* reflects her sustained ambivalence. In this respect she remained, forever, an old-fashioned woman.

45. See F. O. Matthiessen, *Dreiser* (United States: William Sloane Associates, 1951), 130.
46. She had begun "Literature" in Dresden during August of 1913; however, we may infer that the writing had been preceded by rather careful research into contemporary trends in fiction; for Wharton declined to continue it after the war because she felt herself to have become thoroughly out of touch with the literary world during the interim. (See letter to William Brownell, July 27, 1918, Wharton Archives, Amherst College.)
47. *A Backward Glance*, 207.
48. Edith Wharton, *The Custom of the Country* (New York: Charles Scribner's Sons, 1913), 254. Hereafter, all references to *The Custom of the Country* will be cited in the text, giving page number of this edition.
49. The "Oedipal" insistence of this novel is more obvious when we notice that at its core, it is a fiction wherein a younger new order supplants its predecessors. The explicitly sexual component is virtually nonexistent; nevertheless, the generational conflict is unmistakable.
50. Two different evaluations of Undine nicely illustrate the perversities of this novel. Blake Nevius maintains that Edith Wharton "clearly despises her protagonist. . . . So clearly is Mrs. Wharton at the mercy of her private feelings that Undine's father and Elmer Moffatt, simply because they are victims of Undine, are treated with proportionately more sympathy than as citizens of Apex they would otherwise have obtained" (see Nevius, *Edith Wharton*, 152–53). R. W. B. Lewis takes an altogether different view. "Each of the four main characters [in *The Custom of the Country*] bespeaks a portion of Edith Wharton herself and tells us a little more about that complex nature. . . . But the most of Edith Wharton is revealed, quite startlingly, in the charcterization of Undine Spragg. . . . There are smaller and larger telltale similarities. As a child Undine, like Edith, enjoyed dressing up in her mother's best finery and 'playing lady' before a mirror. Moffatt addresses her by Edith's youthful nickname, 'Puss.' Edith's long yearning for psychological freedom is queerly reflected in Undine's discovery that each of her marriages is no more than another mode of imprisonment; and Undine's creator allows more than a hint that the young woman is as much a victim as an aggressor amid the assorted snobberies, tedium, and fossilized rules of conduct of American and, even more, French high society" (see Lewis, *Edith Wharton*, 349–50).
51. This is just one instance of Wharton's ambivalence toward divorce. Clearly we are meant to judge Clare harshly for failing to employ divorce as a means out of her degrading marriage to Van Degen and as a way of giving genuine substance to her relationship with Ralph. At the same time, Undine's multiple and casual divorces are meant to be seen as disgusting.
52. Again, the threshold here is the dividing line between passivity (and regression) and activity (and maturity). Ralph's tendency to lurk back in his secret cave is a sign not only of weakness but of infantile passivity.
53. The satirical attack on old New York's inertia occupies a more prominent place in this novel than the attack on provincial French aristocracy that is mounted in the portrait of Chelles (possibly because it was more bitterly and immediately a part of Wharton's own life). Nevertheless, the distortion of energy is seen in the French portions of the novel as well as in the American scenes.

Here the target is a world where energy has been channeled into grotesquely perverted remnants of a once-vital culture. Raymond de Chelles is not weak as Ralph Marvell is: Moffatt rightly observes that he has a genuine vocation. " 'His ancestors are his business' " (574). Yet the informing values of his world have ceased to have genuine content. "Family" might be a valid concern; "ancestors" reeks with the stench of decay, and all of the members of Chelles's family carry the odor of contamination about them. The Princess Estradina, for instance, speaks lengthily and eloquently about the virtues of motherhood; she seems genuinely attached to her little girls, yet she avows a preference for the younger that she frankly ascribes "to the interesting accident of its parentage" (389). Raymond holds "old-fashioned" views of his wife's duties; at the same time, he is casually unfaithful to her and would allow her to be unfaithful to him so long as she maintained appearances. In the management of his estate, his attention is absorbed entirely in the minutiae, since he has lost sight of the grand original design of seigneurship, and he has the mincing mind of a small shopkeeper or a petty bookkeeper. His strength has hardened into rigidity, and he is capable of a kind of frozen, ruthless indifference that puts him beyond the reach of any human appeal.

Later, after World War I, Wharton was to grow in her admiration of the French people (*French Ways and Their Meaning* is an almost adulatory book). Yet, on balance, she was always aware of the essential silliness of many of the important distinctions that made up the French notion of decorum. This novel of 1913 captures her early and harsher estimation of this culture. An account in *A Backward Glance* gives hilarious insight into her own first encounter with the rigidities of the French system as she is forced to ponder the weighty problem of a "correct" placement of guests at a dinner pary (see pp. 259–61).

54. This description, so full of movement, is the culmination of descriptions that we have already noted: of Justine in *The Fruit of the Tree* and of Sophy in *The Reef*. In those earlier novels the language was effective—but its implications were not entirely clear. Here, finally, the meaning and the impact of description coincide in the brilliant presentation of Undine.

55. One cannot avoid noticing the extent to which this portrait of Undine—indeed, the entire world of this novel—anticipates Fitzgerald's *The Great Gatsby*. Almost certainly Fitzgerald's postulation of postwar frenzy was consciously indebted to Wharton's language of the precipice. For example, Daisy Buchanan is undeniably an Undine. We discover her in her element: "a bright rosy-colored space, fragilely bound into the house by French windows at either end. . . . A breeze blew through the room, blew curtains in at one end . . . and then rippled over the wine-colored rug, making a shadow on it as wind does on the sea." The nervous, unfocused energy that had infused Wharton's novel is here, too—in Tom Buchanan's restless eyes, in the agitation of Daisy's body—but most of all in the dream-visions that float like loosely anchored balloons on a windswept summer day. Here, too, is the mocking heroic echo (but not the epic itself), immortal longings and wine-dark seas all bound together in the colossal vitality of Gatsby's illusion.

Fitzgerald admired Wharton's work. See the hilarious accounts in Mizener's (revised) biography: Arthur Mizener, *The Far Side of Paradise* (Boston: Houghton Mifflin Co., 1965), 168, 202–3.

56. Wharton often changed the title of a novel as she worked on it; it is significant that although she worked on this novel for many years the title was never changed. The allusion to the play is surely intended: her library contained not only the Jacobean dramatists' works, but also a book by Lytton Strachey on Beaumont and Fletcher.

57. Beaumont and Fletcher, *Works*, ed. by Arnold Glover, Vol. I (New York: Octagon Books, 1969), 303, 377.

58. "Life and I," 5.

59. "Life and I," 32–33.

60. Lewis, *Edith Wharton*, 353–54.
61. Ibid., 350.
62. Lubbock, *A Portrait of Edith Wharton*, 54.
63. There is no doubt of this. The affair with Fullerton served a purpose (perhaps, even Fullerton himself did little more than serve a purpose): given Edith Wharton's problems with trust, it seems likely that she would find it easier to abandon herself passionately in a relationship where she felt no real, binding emotional tie and where she unconsciously sensed herself to be superior to her partner in the nonsexual areas of their lives; in such a situation, only a part of herself would be vulnerable. Certainly she retained a fondness for Fullerton even into old age. But she *loved* Walter Berry.
64. Edith Wharton, *Fighting France* (New York: Charles Scribner's Sons, 1915), 4. Hereafter, all references to *Fighting France* will be cited in the text, giving page number of this edition.
65. The war was scarcely a surprise to Edith Wharton, and *The Custom of the Country* quite consciously anticipates such an upheaval. Fullerton was a political journalist and Walter Berry was active in international law; both men were fully apprised of the European situation and had talked with Edith Wharton about it.
66. Lewis, *Edith Wharton*, 371.
67. Lubbock, *A Portrait of Edith Wharton*, 126.
68. *A Backward Glance*, 355.
69. Letter to William Brownell, July 27, 1918, Wharton Archives, Amherst College.
70. *A Backward Glance*, 356.
71. Jean Cocteau, quoted in *Stravinsky in the Theatre*, ed. with an introduction by Minna Lederman (New York: Pellegrini and Cudahy, 1949), 14.
72. See Edith Wharton, Second Donnée Book, 8, 9. The meditation might well have been influenced by the Stravinsky piece, for it renders the music as an emanation of natural creativity: "Suddenly a single note dropped from a violin like a seed from a split calyx." The language here distinctly anticipates that in *Summer*.
73. Igor Stravinsky, *Igor Stravinsky: An Autobiography* (New York: W. W. Norton Co., 1962), 31. The only important solo in the ballet is the dance of the sacrificial maiden. Again, the suggestion of a relationship between this work and Wharton's novel is strong.
74. Lewis, *Edith Wharton*, 361.
75. Second Donnee Book, 28.
76. Edith Wharton, *Summer* (New York: D. Appleton and Co., 1917), 7–8. Hereafter all references to *Summer* will be cited in the text, giving page numbers to this edition.
77. We might note that Charity's defense echoes Edith Wharton's own adolescent maneuver: both manage the threatening sexual passions of their own natures by interposing an older woman between themselves and the proximate male who is the most immediate object of these feelings. Charity demands a "hired woman"; Edith Wharton developed a morbid dependency upon her own mother.
78. Lubbock, *A Portrait of Edith Wharton*, 103.
79. Edith Wharton, Subjects and Notes (1918–1923), Wharton Archives, Beinecke Library, 1.
80. *A Backward Glance*, 369.
81. Edith Wharton, *In Morocco* (New York: Charles Scribner's Sons, 1920), 3. Hereafter, all references to *In Morocco* will be cited in the text, giving page numbers to this edition.

82. See the Appendix for an explanation of the dating of this manuscript fragment.
83. Edith Wharton, Beatrice Palmato: plot summary of story with "unpublishable" fragment, Wharton Archives, Beinecke Library.
84. Among such stories may be counted: "The Eyes," "The Triumph of Night," "Miss Mary Pask," and "All Souls'." In half of these stories, the forbidden impulse is clearly of sexual origin.
85. These stories of adulterous love include: "The Duchess at Prayer" (often not included among Wharton's ghost stories, but clearly of the genre), "The Lady's Maid's Bell," "Kerfol" (possibly her best ghost story), "Bewitched," and "The Pomegranate Seed." Not surprisingly, the sympathy of the tale is often with the illicit liaison—even though the author often chose to "punish" the illegal love in one or another manner. Though it is rendered through a series of disguises and displacements, the Oedipal situation seems quite clear in most of these stories.
86. "Life and I," 17, 19.
87. Wharton, *The Collected Short Stories*, II, 875, 878.
88. One literary source for the incest motif in this story was undoubtedly the tale of Beatrice Cenci. There is excellent reason to suppose that Wharton had this literary precedent explicitly in mind when she wrote "Beatrice Palmato." The association may be traced deviously. *The Mother's Recompense* was not published until 1925; however, the notebooks show definitively that it was elaborately outlined (probably with sketches of some of the chapters) in 1919. In *The Mother's Recompense*, when Kate Clephane returns to her husband's home in New York, she discovers a portrait of "the same red-eyed Beatrice Cenci above the double bed." The picture is appropriate to Kate's dilemma; nevertheless, we may assume that it appears more or less as a carry-over from the "Beatrice Palmato" fragment.

   There is, of course, a personal source for the name Beatrice. It wa Morton Fullerton's name for his "sister," Katherine, when he found himself entangled in that "incestuous" relationship. Moreover, chances are (given Wharton's own devotion to Dante during the spring of 1908 and given that she and Fullerton read *Paradiso* together) that it was a name used in Wharton's own passionate encounters with M. F.
89. We must remark that the sexual encounter as Wharton envisions it here has an unmistakably powerful oral component. If we recollect the extent to which the child's, the adolescent's, and the woman's sexual longings had been intensified by the even more consuming need of that earlier unsatisfied oral stage, then it is not in the least surprising that when genital sexuality does emerge, it should contain a substantial oral component. The longing for oral satisfaction can never be eliminated; it can only be immersed in this other, more adult longing for genital sexuality.
90. *In Morocco*, 200–201.
91. Wharton, *Fighting France*, 230. The contrast between France and Morocco at this time must have been very strong in Wharton's mind, must have colored her retrospective reevaluation of old New York. For her it was the contrast between order (even, perhaps, to the point of rigidity) and absolute indulgence, and between these two extremes, there could be no doubt that order was preferable to license; this was the most insistent lesson of the war.
92. *A Backward Glance*, 369.
93. Letter to Gaillard Lapsley, December 17, 1915, Wharton Archives, Beinecke Library.
94. Letter to Gaillard Lapsley, Sept. 24, 1920, Wharton Archives, Beinecke Library.
95. *A Backward Glance*, 175, 179.
96. See the introduction by R. W. B. Lewis to *The Age of Innocence* (New York: Charles

Scribner's Sons, 1968). See also R. B. Dooley, "A Footnote to Edith Wharton," *American Literature*, XXVI (Mar. 1954–Jan. 1955), 78–85.

97. Edith Wharton, *The Age of Innocence* (New York: D. Appleton Co., 1920), 124. Hereafter, all references to *The Age of Innocence* will be cited in the text, giving page number of this edition.

98. Erik Erikson, *Identity, Youth and Crisis* (New York: W. W. Norton Co., 1968), 22.

99. Erik Erikson, *Young Man Luther* (New York: W. W. Norton Co., 1958), 253–54.

100. Erikson, *Childhood and Society*, 268.

101. Note Edmund Wilson's remark in *The Wound and the Bow* that Edith Wharton was "the poet of interior decoration" (New York: Oxford University Press, 1947), 163.

102. Interestingly enough, when Newland does "get into the drama," he does so by imitating the sentimental renunciation scene of *The Shaughraun*.

103. The word "mysterious" occurs repeatedly in Newland's musings about Ellen. It perfectly captures her almost incorporeal quality in his life. He does not *explore* the mysteries of Ellen's world; he prefers her to remain a mystery—conveniently blurred and obscured in his perception.

104. There are many implications of this improbable cooperation between Ellen and May. For one thing, it suggests that the values that had been polarized in the depiction of the two heroines of *The Reef* have now been conjoined in some coherent and meaningful estimation of life. In terms of Wharton's personal development, the cooperation is even more significant.

   In order to come back "for good" to the days of her childhood, Edith Wharton had to accept that part of herself that represented an internalization of Lucretia and Lucretia's values. She had to come to final terms with "Mother"—yes—but even more important, she had to accept that part of herself that imitated Mother and reflected Mother's ways.

   We have said that in *The Reef* Wharton made a fiction out of the disparate parts of herself—and in that fiction, these parts never come together. In *The Age of Innocence*, she pursues much the same tactic: Newland Archer, Ellen Olenska, and May all represent variations of Edith Wharton's "self"; however, now they are in harmony, and now they can be made to cooperate with each other.

105. Erikson, *Childhood and Society*, 267.

106. Ibid., 268–69.

107. Edmund Gosse, "The Lamp at the Window," in *The Legend of the Master*, ed. Simon Nowell-Smith (New York: Charles Scribner's Sons, 1948), 119–20.

IV. DIPTYCH: YOUTH AND AGE

1. Edith Wharton, *Twilight Sleep* (New York: D. Appleton Co., 1927), 14.

2. Quaderno dello Studente, 5.

3. *A Backward Glance*, 363.

4. Quoted by Lewis, *Edith Wharton*, 421. The correspondence with the Tylers is not available to general scholars.

5. Lubbock, *A Portrait of Edith Wharton*, 210.

6. Letter to Gaillard Lapsley, July 5, 1921, Wharton Archives, Beinecke Library.

7. See Mark Schorer, *Sinclair Lewis* (New York: McGraw-Hill Co., 1961), 347.

8. Letter to Sinclair Lewis, Aug. 6, 1921, Lewis Archives, Beinecke Library, Yale University, New Haven, Conn.

9. Edith Wharton, *The Glimpses of the Moon* (New York: D. Appleton Co., 1922), 319. All further references to this novel will be cited in text by page number to this edition.

10. There is a charming correspondence between Edith Wharton and this little boy who became her godson; unfortunately, these letters are not available to general scholars. R. W. B. Lewis quotes from them in his biography: see pp. 373, 385–86, 414, 493, 518, 529–30.

11. *A Backward Glance*, 369.

12. The novel is full of places where the prose degenerates into propagandistic slogans. "Paris went on. She had had her great hour of resistance, when, alone, exposed and defenceless, she had held back the enemy and broken his strength" (111). "The German menace must be met: chance willed that theirs should be the generation to meet it; on that point speculation was vain and discussion useless" (193). "And every night, when one laid one's old bones on one's bed, there were those others, the young in their thousands, lying down, perhaps never to rise again, in the mud and blood of the trenches" (367). There is no doubting Wharton's sincerity in these passages; she felt the war very deeply, lost many that she loved, and witnessed a nation rising to greatness in defense of traditions that she had come increasingly to honor. Nevertheless, the emotions did not translate into good fiction, not even into good prose. When she manages to reduce the war to a personal level (as in her treatment of Campton), she can be authentic; however, when she reaches for blazing, dramatic generalization (as she too often does in this fiction), her effectiveness fails. The quotations above are taken from: Edith Wharton, *A Son at the Front* (New York: Charles Scribner's Sons, 1923). All further references to this novel will be cited in text by page number to this edition.

13. Whatever her relationship with Walter Berry (and she seems to hint after his death that they had, indeed, been lovers—see note 43 below), they led independent lives and maintained separate establishments. Much as she evidently loved her own company, there is little doubt that Edith Wharton sometimes missed the daily contact with intimates that a family would have given her. This fact becomes especially evident in the later letters because she spends so much time and energy arranging to be with people (have them visit, visit them, take a trip together). Her disappointment when a projected plan falls through is poignant testimony to her bouts of loneliness.

14. It was, we must remember, Wharton's novel: she could have chosen to let the son live. But that would have required her to confront Campton's quandary head-on. Probably the fictional decision to have George die is a sign of her desire to finesse the problem.

15. Given Wharton's habit of working simultaneously on several pieces of fiction, it is sometimes virtually impossible to impose strict chronological ordering. The correspondence with Appleton suggests that she wrote "The Old Maid" in early 1921; her journal lists "New Year's Day" as having been written in January and February of 1922; "False Dawn" was accepted for publication in *The Ladies' Home Journal* in August 1922; and she finished "The Spark" under some pressure from Appleton in September 1923. Viewed simply in terms of these dates, *Old New York* would appear to antedate both *The Glimpses of the Moon* and *A Son at the Front*. However, an elaborate chapter-by-chapter summary of *A Son at the Front* begins on the reverse of the first page of her notebook for the years 1918–23. The novel was almost certainly at least half finished in 1920 when she published *The Age of Innocence*. Probably *The Glimpses of the Moon* was well along at this point, too. In the chronological listing at the end of the 1918–23 notebook, all of the novellas in *Old New York* (save "The Old Maid," which is not recorded in any of the notebooks) follow both *The Age of Innocence* and *A Son at the Front*. (*The Glimpses of the Moon* is not listed in the notebooks.) Undoubtedly she was still

working on *A Son at the Front* and *The Glimpses of the Moon* at the time that she began to draft the novellas; however, probably the novels had reached a stage close to completion—at least in her conception of them—before she began even "The Old Maid."

16. Blake Nevius prefers "False Dawn" to the others in this collection and condemns "The Old Maid" for its "Victorian emphasis on seduction and Mother love" (*Edith Wharton*, 192). However, others clearly do not concur. The play based upon it, starring Helen Menkin and Judith Anderson, won the Pulitzer Prize for drama in 1935; and there was an affecting film version starring Bette Davis and Miriam Hopkins.

17. Edith Wharton, "The Old Maid," in *Old New York* (D. Appleton Co., 1924), 14–15. Hereafter, all references to "The Old Maid" will be cited in text by page number to this edition.

   If we are to understand the tale correctly, it is important to realize that it is not primarily a satire of the insufficiencies of old New York; and this warm passage about old-fashioned marriage (so explicitly different from the particularly unpleasant experiences of Wharton's own life) makes that fact clear. What is central to Wharton's vision is a notion of individual life as inevitably limited; aging requires everyone to come to terms with the particular ways in which his life has been circumscribed. The remarks about Clement Spender's middle age seem deliberately injected to assure the reader that Delia's life would have been far from perfect if she had "waited for him." In fact, her discovery of Jim's unspoken acquiescence in the plot to save Chatty's baby is (like Newland's belated discovery of the depths of May's knowledge) a suggestion that she has, perhaps, chosen the best of the options life had to offer—and that *even so*, advancing age brings inevitable regret for what might have been.

18. First Donnée Book, 70. See also pp. 69 and 71.

19. In lieu of dedication, Wharton inscribed the following notation at the beginning of this novel: "My excuses are due to the decorous shade of Grace Aguilar, loved of our grandmothers, for deliberately appropriating, and applying to uses so different, the title of one of the most admired of her tales." Since this novel, like *The Custom of the Country*, carried the same title unchanged over the many years that elapsed between its conception and final birth, the allusion must be taken seriously. The connection with Aguilar's novel would undoubtedly have been clearer to an audience in 1901 (when Aguilar's work was still read occasionally) than in 1925; thus it is even more significant that Wharton still insisted upon the relationship.

   Aguilar's novel *The Mother's Recompense* was published in 1850. It was designed as a sequel to *Home Influence: A Tale for Mothers and Daughters;* the first work borders on being a Puritan conduct book—an illustration of domestic education—while the second, so the introduction to it tells us, is intended to demonstrate the *effect* of conscientious maternal devotion. At its conclusion (after the many and stormy trials that afflict the family during the children's adolescence), the Mother turns to her married daughter and explains the nature of the reward she has finally reaped. " 'There are many sorrows and many cares inseparable from maternal love, but they are forgotten, utterly forgotten, or only remembered to enhance the sweetness of the recompense that ever follows. Do you not think to see my children, as I do now around me, walking in that path which alone can lead to eternal life, and leading their offspring with them, bringing up so tenderly, so fondly, their children as heirs of immortality, and yet lavishing on me, as on their father, the love and duty of former years? Is not this a precious recompense for all which for them I may have done or borne?' " (498).

   Wharton wished to juxtapose the effects of modern "freedom" and the consequences (and recompenses) of "old-fashioned virtue"; and she deliberately employed a novel whose popularity had vanished to make her ironic point. See: Grace Aguilar, *The Mother's Recompense* (New York: D. Appleton & Co., 1859).

20. Edith Wharton, *The Mother's Recompense* (New York: D. Appleton Co., 1925), 3. All further references to this novel will be cited in text by page number to this edition.

21. Under the title of this novel Wharton inscribed, "Desolation is a delicate thing"—from Shelley's *Prometheus Unbound*. The quotation gives unmistakable indication of Kate's inevitable plight. However, the contrast between the sentiment of this particular line and the romantic, visionary postulations of Shelley's play as Wharton would have seen them suggests an ironic touch very much like that of the title. Kate wants—in a host of ways—to be "unbound"; it is precisely that obsession which has "killed" her.

22. Letter to John Hugh-Smith, May 25, 1925, Wharton Archives, Beinecke Library.

23. Letter to Bernard Berenson, Jan. 6, 1923, Berenson Archives.

24. Letter to Gaillard Lapsley, Feb. 14, 1925, Wharton Archives, Beinecke Library.

25. Letter to Gaillard Lapsley, April 17, 1923, Wharton Archives, Beinecke Library.

26. *A Backward Glance*, vii.

27. Letter to Gaillard Lapsley, April 13, 1927, Wharton Archives, Beinecke Library.

28. Edith Wharton, *Twilight Sleep* (New York: D. Appleton Co., 1927), 324. All further references to this novel will be cited in text by page number to this edition.

29. *A Backward Glance*, 379.

30. No image of Edith Wharton has done more to confirm the illusion of her stately majesty and aloofness than the curiously mixed one in Percy Lubbock's book. On the one hand there are any number of uncensored recollections by friends like Charles Du Bos and Gaillard Lapsley that display Wharton to sympathetic advantage; nevertheless, the tone of the book is disquieting, and it has been set by Lubbock himself. For the last ten years of her life, Edith Wharton cast him out of her charmed circle of friends, relegated him to the humbling position of hanger-on. The cut deeply wounded Lubbock's sense of self-esteem. Indeed, even in the "good" days of their friendship, Wharton may have regarded Lubbock as little more than an interesting young person of minor talent. His aggrieved recollection suggests as much, and he gives us the image of a rather snobbish lady (only incidentally a novelist) whose principal attribute is her inaccessibility.

"Now was the time when she might turn her attention to the unobtrusive young man, believed literary in his aspirations, who was still there in the background; but she wasn't in the habit of delving into shyness, she was accustomed to see gifts laid before her, and this poor creature's gifts, if he had any, were seldom to hand at the right moment. And then the way of approach to her, the only apparent way, seemed still distressingly public—up a red carpet, so to speak, in a strong light, to a spot where you might, but after all might not, be pressed to take a seat beside her. The young man was interesting when you knew him—but would she see it? Yet she was a writer of books—books that I had finely read and acutely admired, books that I had even criticised in print; there was common ground between us if she chose to take it. But I had never seen a writer in our old world who kept such state as she did, and I couldn't go faltering up the royal carpet by myself, with my awkward step. It *was* a little disappointing—a little aggrieving too. But there it was; my place was in the shade" (*A Portrait of Edith Wharton*, 9).

For many years, Lubbock's was the *only* complete memoir we had of her.

31. Mizener, *The Far Side of Paradise*, 202.

32. Lubbock, *A Portrait of Edith Wharton*, 77–78, 79.

33. Quaderno dello Studente, 5, 5, 6.

34. Kenneth Clark, "A Full-Length Portrait," in *Times Literary Supplement*, December 19, 1975.

35. It is true that Morton Fullerton was a few years younger than Edith Wharton (to be precise: she was forty-five when they met, and he was forty-two). However, in the light of his vast and varied amatory experience—and her incredible ignorance, even then—it is scarcely to be believed that her three-year seniority entered either of their minds. They were at an age, after all, when such differences matter very little. In fact, insofar as lovemaking was concerned, M. F. was just the sort of man to make Edith Wharton feel very much the "amorous child." Old as she was, this experience was clearly one of initiation. Her own associations foster such a view. In the "Love Diary," for instance, the actual age difference simply never comes up; there is no evidence whatsoever that she thought of herself as a "baby-snatcher" in the Fullerton affair. Quite the contrary. What she *does* express is wonderment and a sense of complete inexperience.

36. I must also mention that the initial failure of trust clearly made this last life crisis very difficult for her. To anyone who is (still) to some degree "starving" for affection, the unavoidable fact that life is ending and recompense can never, ever come, is a bleak and harsh reality to accept. The language of hunger turns up once again, then, in the portraits of Kate Clephane, the elder Manfords, and Martin Boyne.

37. One of the ways that Edith Wharton managed her unhappiness over the aging process was by establishing relationships with young men that had a "flirting" element: the friendship with Ronald Simmons during the war is a clear case in point. Surely it was gratifying when young men found her company vivacious and delightful. To infer anything more "serious" seems merely salacious. Indeed, this characteristic in Wharton would probably not even be remarkable had she been a man (for we are accustomed to accept the fact that young girls will flirt harmlessly with older men).

38. The one exception is the episode in *Hudson River Bracketed* when Vance catches sight of his leering grandfather scuttling into the bushes with the town tramp (whom Vance himself has earlier bedded). Yet this "incest" is still used as a thematic indication that there is something awry in the elder generation's relation to the younger.

39. Summary of *The Children*, inserted into the 1924–28 notebook, Wharton Archives, Beinecke Library.

40. We can ascertain these dates in the following way. There is a notation at the top of the outline of *The Children* indicating that the original (of which the carbon remains in Wharton's notebook) had been sent to Appleton on Feb. 1, 1927—along with Chapter I of the manuscript. In a letter to Gaillard Lapsley dated Jan. 17, 1928, Wharton announces that she has finished *The Children* on that day.

41. *A Backward Glance*, 115–16, 117–18.

42. Letter to Gaillard Lapsley, Oct. 12, 1927, Wharton Archives, Beinecke Library.

43. Letter to Gaillard Lapsley, Oct. 16, 1927, Wharton Archives, Beinecke Library. One is very much inclined to infer from this letter that Wharton intended Lapsley to understand that she and Berry had been sexually intimate. The distinction between "in love" and "in friendship" is one that Wharton would not make casually.

44. Quaderno dello Studente, 8.

45. It is important to keep in mind, yet once more, that although Boyne's *problem* may have borne an intimate resemblance to those that Wharton faced herself, he is in no particular way to be identified with her.

46. Edith Wharton, *The Children* (New York: D. Appleton Co., 1927), 44. All further references to this novel will be cited in the text by page number to this edition.

47. Wharton is again plagiarizing herself; this beginning is unmistakably similar to that of *The Reef*. Here the reuse of her own material is successful (as it is not in some of the other late novels).
48. Quaderno dello Studente, 10: "The tranquility of God makes all things tranquil."
49. As early as Aug. 31, 1925, Wharton wrote a cautionary message to Lapsley concerning a projected trip. "All this is conditional, however, for great are the mysteries of heart and arteries, and Kresser [her doctor] may say he doesn't want me to go on any long 'randangs' yet." Letter to Gaillard Lapsley, Wharton Archives, Beinecke Library.
50. Lewis, *Edith Wharton*, 488.
51. Nevius, *Edith Wharton*, 226, 235.
52. See Lewis, *Edith Wharton*, 490.
53. Edith Wharton, *Hudson River Bracketed* (New York: D. Appleton Co., 1929), 176–77, 394. All further references to this novel will be cited in text (preceded by *HRB*) by page number to this edition.
54. Edith Wharton, *The Gods Arrive* (New York: D. Appleton Co., 1932), 323. All further references to this novel will be cited in text (preceded by *GA*) by page number to this edition.
55. *The Writing of Fiction*, 21.
56. There are any number of places in these works where Wharton quite blatantly (and unsuccessfully) draws upon earlier work. A few obvious instances: the scenes that depict the deteriorating state of Laura Lou recall Ethan Frome's situation with his sick wife; Bunty Hayes is a rewrite of Elmer Moffatt; Floss Delaney is a rewrite of Undine; the fireworks display that Vance watches with Floss literally recapitulates the language of the fireworks scene in *Summer*.
57. "The Young Gentlemen," "Miss Mary Pask," "Velvet Earpads," and "The Temperate Zone" were all written before 1924—according to Wharton's notebook records.
58. Edith Wharton, Notebook for 1924–28, Wharton Archives, Beinecke Library, 91.
59. *The Collected Short Stories*, II, 669.
60. Letter to John Hugh-Smith, Aug. 5, 1930, Wharton Archives, Beinecke Library.
61. Letter to John Hugh-Smith, Aug. 20, 1930, Wharton Archives, Beinecke Library.
62. Quaderno dello Studente, 12.
63. Letter to Gaillard Lapsley, Sept. 13, 1933, Wharton Archives, Beinecke Library.
64. Quaderno dello Studente, 13–14.
65. Lubbock, *A Portrait of Edith Wharton*, 225, 213–14.
66. Edith Wharton, *The Buccaneers*, with a concluding "note" by Gaillard Lapsley (D. Appleton Co., 1938), 361. All further references to this novel will be cited in text by page number to this edition.
67. Nevius, *Edith Wharton*, 237.
68. Wharton reread Jane Austen's work in the early 1930's, and in letters to Lapsley declared herself interested in writing an article on Austen and Trollope, whose work she was also reading.
69. Lewis, *Edith Wharton*, 531.
70. *A Backward Glance*, 200–203.
71. In the casual mention of Laura Testvalley's brief affair with Richard, we might infer a substantial resolution even of the theme of cross-generational sex. Laura enters into the liaison because there are no men for her to become romantically involved with—save her employer (who is much her senior) and her employer's son (somewhat her junior). In spirit, she is closer to the younger generation, and so she becomes briefly involved with the young man. This relationship really does not smack of "incest" in the way

that the relationships in the earlier novels of this period did: in fact, this sort of "incest" seems to have become almost entirely without ominous overtones by the time Wharton was writing *The Buccaneers*.

72. Perhaps the most serious flaw in the incompleted manuscript is the fact that one cannot tell whether Laura Testvalley's story or Nan's romance will dominate the finished novel. Wharton passed the novel among several of her friends while she was writing it, and all—most notably Lapsley in his appended note—comment upon the growing importance that the governess seemed to acquire as the book progressed.

73. At the very end of Wharton's summary, she dismisses Laura Testvalley. After the old adventurer sees her favorite pupil through these romantic perils and into a successful marriage with Guy Thwarte, she goes "back alone to old age and poverty" (359). Given the development of Laura Testvalley's character, this ending—formulated when Wharton was just beginning the novel—is hardly credible. Indeed, given the direction in which Nan's character is developing, it is impossible to believe that the girl would allow her beloved friend to sink into such indignities.

74. Quaderno dello Studente, 14.

Published Works of Edith Wharton

I am heavily indebted to the bibliography of Wharton's work that may be found in Blake Nevius' excellent book *Edith Wharton: A Study of Her Fiction*. California: University of California Press, 1953.

I have not included here the many poems that Wharton published singly.

Novels and Novellas

The Touchstone. New York: Scribner's 1900. Published in England as *A Gift from the Grave* (London: John Murray, 1900).
The Valley of Decision. New York: Scribner's, 1902. 2 vols.
Sanctuary. New York: Scribner's, 1903.
The House of Mirth. New York: Scribner's, 1905.
Madame de Treymes. New York: Scribner's, 1907.
The Fruit of the Tree. New York: Scribner's, 1907.
Ethan Frome. New York: Scribner's, 1911.
The Reef. New York: Appleton, 1912.
The Custom of the Country. New York: Scribner's, 1913.
Summer. New York: Appleton, 1917.
The Marne. New York: Appleton, 1918.
The Age of Innocence. New York: Appleton, 1920.
The Glimpses of the Moon. New York: Appleton, 1922.
A Son at the Front. New York: Scribner's, 1923.
Old New York: False Dawn (The 'Forties); *The Old Maid* (The 'Fifties); *The Spark* (The 'Sixties); *New Year's Day* (The 'Seventies). New York: Appleton, 1924. 4 vols.
The Mother's Recompense. New York: Appleton, 1925.
Twilight Sleep. New York: Appleton, 1927.
The Children. New York: Appleton, 1928.
Hudson River Bracketed. New York: Appleton, 1929.
The Gods Arrive. New York: Appleton, 1932.
The Buccaneers. New York: Appleton-Century, 1938.

Collected Short Stories

The Greater Inclination. New York: Scribner's, 1899.
Crucial Instances. New York: Scribner's, 1901.
The Descent of Man, and Other Stories. New York: Scribner's, 1904. Published in
England under the same title (London: Macmillan, 1904) but with the
addition of one story, "The Letter."
The Hermit and the Wild Woman and Other Stories. New York: Scribner's, 1908.
Tales of Men and Ghosts. New York: Scribner's, 1910.
Xingu and Other Stories. New York: Scribner's, 1916.
Here and Beyond. New York: Appleton, 1926.
Certain People. New York: Appleton, 1930.
Human Nature. New York: Appleton, 1933.
The World Over. New York: Appleton-Century, 1936.
Ghosts. New York: Appleton-Century, 1937.
The Collected Short Stories of Edith Wharton, ed. R. W. B. Lewis. New York: Scrib-
ner's, 1968, 2 vols. These two volumes contain all of the short stories
(both collected and previously uncollected) with the exception of "Bunner
Sisters," which may be found in *Xingu and Other Stories*.

Non-Fiction (Books)

The Decoration of Houses (with Ogden Codman, Jr.). New York: Scribner's, 1897.
Italian Villas and Their Gardens. New York: Century, 1904.
Italian Backgrounds. New York: Scribner's, 1905.
A Motor-Flight through France. New York: Scribner's, 1908.
Fighting France from Dunkerque to Belfort. New York: Scribner's, 1915.
French Ways and Their Meaning. New York: Appleton, 1919.
In Morocco. New York: Scribner's, 1920.
The Writing of Fiction. New York: Scribner's, 1925.
A Backward Glance. New York: Appleton-Century, 1934.

Poetry (Books)

Verses. Newport. C. E. Hammett, Jr., 1878.
Artemis to Actaeon and Other Verse. New York: Scribner's, 1909.
Twelve Poems. London: The Medici Society, 1926.

Articles, Translations, Editions, and Reviews

"More Love Letters of an Englishwoman." *Bookman*, XLI (February, 1901), 562.
Review of Edwin H. and Evangeline W. Blashfield, *Italian Cities*. *Bookman*, XIII
(August, 1901), 563–64.
Review of Stephen Phillips, *Ulysses*. *Bookman*, XV (April, 1902), 168–70.

Review of Mrs. Fiske's performance in Lorimer Stoddard's dramatization of Hardy's *Tess of the D'Urbervilles*. New York *Commercial Advertiser* (May 7, 1902), 9.

Review of Leslie Stephen, *George Eliot*. *Bookman*, XV (May, 1902), 247–51.

The Joy of Living. By Hermann Sudermann. Translated from the German by Edith Wharton. New York: Scribner's, 1902.

"The Three Francescas." *North American Review*, CLXXV (July, 1902), 17–30.

"The Vice of Reading." *North American Review*, CLXXVII (October, 1903), 513–21.

Review of Howard Sturgis, *Belchamber*. *Bookman*, XXI (May, 1905), 307–10.

Review of Maurice Hewlett, *The Fool Errant*. *Bookman*, XXII (September, 1905), 64–67.

Review of Eugene Lee-Hamilton, *The Sonnets of the Wingless Hours*. *Bookman*, XXVI (November, 1907), 251–53.

"George Cabot Lodge." *Scribner's Magazine*, XLVII (February, 1910), 236–39.

"The Criticism of Fiction." *Times Literary Supplement* (May 14, 1914), 229–30.

"Jean du Breuil de Saint-Germain." *Revue Hebdomadaire*, XXIV (May 15, 1915), 351–61.

The Book of the Homeless. Edited by Edith Wharton. New York: Scribner's, 1916.

"Les Français vus par une Américaine." *Revue Hebdomadaire*, XXVII (January 5, 1918), 5–21.

"L'Amérique en guerre." *Revue Hebdomadaire*, XXVII (March 2, 1918), 5–28.

"How Paris Welcomed the King." *Reveille*, no. 3 (February, 1919), 367–69.

"Henry James in His Letters." *Quarterly Review*, CCXXXIV (July, 1920), 188–202.

"Christmas Tinsel." *Delineator*, CIII (December, 1923), 11.

"The Great American Novel." *Yale Review*, n.s. XVI (July, 1927), 646–56.

"William C. Brownell." *Scribner's Magazine*, LXXXIV (November, 1928), 596–602.

"A Cycle of Reviewing." *Spectator* (London), CXLI (November 23, 1928), supplement, 44.

"Visibility in Fiction." *Yale Review*, n.s. XVIII (March, 1929), 480–88.

"Confessions of a Novelist." *Atlantic Monthly*, CLI (April, 1933), 385–92.

"Tendencies in Modern Fiction." *Saturday Review of Literature*, X (January 27, 1934), 433–44.

"Permanent Values in Fiction." *Saturday Review of Literature*, X (April 7, 1934), 603–4.

"A Reconsideration of Proust." *Saturday Review of Literature*, XI (October 27, 1934), 233–34.

"Souvenirs du Bourget d'Outremer." *Revue Hebdomadaire*, XLV (June 21, 1936), 266–86.

"A Little Girl's New York," *Harper's Magazine*, CLXXVI (March, 1938), 356–64.

Eternal Passion in English Poetry. Selected by Edith Wharton and Robert Norton, with the collaboration of Gaillard Lapsley. New York: Appleton-Century, 1939.

Introductions

A Village Romeo and Juliet. By Gottfried Keller. Translated by Anna C. Bahlmann. Introduction by Edith Wharton. New York: Scribner's, 1914.

Futility. By William Gerhardi. Introduction by Edith Wharton. New York: Duffield, 1922.

Ethan Frome. Introduction by Edith Wharton. New York: Scribner's, 1922.

The House of Mirth. Introduction by Edith Wharton. London: Oxford University Press (World Classics edition), 1936.

Benediction. By Comtesse Philomène de Laforest-Divonne [pseud. Claude Silve]. Translated by Robert Norton. Foreword by Edith Wharton. New York: Appleton-Century, 1936.

Index